Effective Healthcare Information Systems

Adi Armoni, Ph.D.
Tel Aviv University, Israel

D1406717

IRM Press
Publisher of innovative scholarly and professional
information technology titles in the cyberage

Hershey • London • Melbourne • Singapore • Beijing

Acquisitions Editor: Mehdi Khosrowpour
Managing Editor: Jan Travers
Assistant Managing Editor: Amanda Appicello
Copy Editor: Amanda Appicello
Cover Design: Tedi Wingard
Printed at: Integrated Book Technology

Published in the United States of America by
    IRM Press
    701 E. Chocolate Avenue, Suite 200
    Hershey PA 17033-1240
    Tel: 717-533-8845
    Fax: 717-533-8661
    E-mail: cust@idea-group.com
    Web site: http://www.irm-press.com

and in the United Kingdom by
    IRM Press
    3 Henrietta Street
    Covent Garden
    London WC2E 8LU
    Tel: 44 20 7240 0856
    Fax: 44 20 7379 3313
    Web site: http://www.eurospan.co.uk

Library of Congress Cataloging-in-Publication Data

Armoni, Adi, 1959-
    Effective healthcare information systems / Adi Armoni.
        p. cm.
    Includes bibliographical references and index.
    ISBN 1-931777-01-2 (paper)
        1. Health services administration--Computer networks. 2. Medical care--
Computer networks. 3. Medicine--Computer networks. 4. World Wide Web. I. Title.

RA971.23 .A75 2002
362.1'0285--dc21   2001059441

eISBN: 1-931777-20-9

British Cataloguing in Publication Data
A Cataloguing in Publication record for this book is available from the British Library.

Other New Releases from IRM Press

- **Human Computer Interaction Development and Management,** Tonya Barrier (Ed.)
  ISBN: 1-931777-13-6 / eISBN: 1-931777-35-7 / approx. 336 pages / US$59.95 / © 2002
- **Data Warehousing and Web Engineering,** Shirley Becker (Ed.)
  ISBN: 1-931777-02-0 / eISBN: 1-931777-21-7 / approx. 334 pages / US$59.95 / © 2002
- **Information Technology Education in the New Millennium,** Mohammad Dadashzadeh, Al Saber and Sherry Saber (Eds.) /
  ISBN: 1-931777-05-5 / eISBN: 1-931777-24-1 / approx. 308 pages / US$59.95 / © 2002
- **Information Technology Management in Developing Countries,** Mohammad Dadashzadeh (Ed.) / ISBN: 1-931-777-03-9 / eISBN: 1-931777-23-3 / approx. 348 pages / US$59.95 / © 2002
- **Strategies for eCommerce Success,** Bijan Fazlollahi (Ed.)
  ISBN: 1-931777-08-7 / eISBN: 1-931777-29-2 / approx. 352 pages / US$59.95 / © 2002
- **Collaborative Information Technologies,** Mehdi Khosrow-Pour (Ed.)
  ISBN: 1-931777-14-4 / eISBN: 1-931777-25-X / approx. 308 pages / US$59.95 / © 2002
- **Web-Based Instructional Learning,** Mehdi Khosrow-Pour (Ed.)
  ISBN: 1-931777-04-7 / eISBN: 1-931777-22-5 / approx. 322 pages / US$59.95 / © 2002
- **Modern Organizations in Virtual Communities,** Jerzy Kisielnicki (Ed.)
  ISBN: 1-931777-16-0 / eISBN: 1-931777-36-5 / approx. 316 pages / US$59.95 / © 2002
- **Enterprise Resource Planning Solutions and Management,** Fiona Fui-Hoon Nah (Ed.)
  ISBN: 1-931777-06-3 / eISBN: 1-931777-26-8 / approx. 308 pages / US$59.95 / © 2002
- **Interactive Multimedia Systems,** Syed M. Rahman (Ed.)
  ISBN: 1-931777-07-1 / eISBN: 1-931777-28-4 / approx. 314 pages / US$59.95 / © 2002
- **Ethical Issues of Information Systems,** Ali Salehnia (Ed.)
  ISBN: 1-931777-15-2 / eISBN: 1-931777-27-6 / approx. 314 pages / US$59.95 / © 2002
- **Intelligent Support Systems: Knowledge Management,** Vijay Sugumaran (Ed.)
  ISBN: 1-931777-00-4 / eISBN: 1-931777-19-5 / approx. 318 pages / US$59.95 / © 2002
- **Human Factors in Information Systems,** Edward Szewczak and Coral Snodgrass (Eds.)
  ISBN: 1-931777-10-1 / eISBN: 1-931777-31-4 / approx. 342 pages / US$59.95 / © 2002
- **Global Perspective of Information Technology Management,** Felix B. Tan (Ed.)
  ISBN: 1-931777-11-4 / eISBN: 1-931777-32-2 / approx. 334 pages / US$59.95 / © 2002
- **Successful Software Reengineering,** Sal Valenti (Ed.)
  ISBN: 1-931777-12-8 / eISBN: 1-931777-33-0 / approx. 330 pages / US$59.95 / © 2002
- **Information Systems Evaluation Management,** Wim van Grembergen (Ed.)
  ISBN: 1-931777-18-7 / eISBN: 1-931777-37-3 / approx. 336 pages / US$59.95 / © 2002
- **Optimal Information Modeling Techniques,** Kees van Slooten (Ed.)
  ISBN: 1-931777-09-8 / eISBN: 1-931777-30-6 / approx. 306 pages / US$59.95 / © 2002
- **Knowledge Mapping and Management,** Don White (Ed.)
  ISBN: 1-931777-17-9 / eISBN: 1-931777-34-9 / approx. 340 pages / US$59.95 / © 2002

Excellent additions to your institution's library!
Recommend these titles to your Librarian!

To receive a copy of the IRM Press catalog, please contact
(toll free) 1/800-345-4332, fax 1/717-533-8661,
or visit the IRM Press Online Bookstore at: [http://www.irm-press.com]!

Note: All IRM Press books are also available as ebooks on netlibrary.com as well as
other ebook sources. Contact Ms. Carrie Stull at [cstull@idea-group.com] to receive
a complete list of sources where you can obtain ebook information or
IRM Press titles.

Effective Healthcare Information Systems

Table of Contents

Other New Releases from IRM Press

Effective Healthcare Information Systems

Table of Contents

Foreword

Health and medical informatics encompass a very broad field, which is rapidly developing in both its research and operational aspects. The discipline has many dimensions, including social, legal, ethical and economic.

In the following overview, I would like to share with the readers my thoughts, beliefs and experiences (both academic and practical) regarding the most important and promising fields of the medical information systems domain.

The combination of the two revolutions, that of information and that of telecommunication, is altering medical practice. Telemedicine is changing the shape of medical practice – both in relation to the patient and to interaction between physicians and medical institutions.

Information technology application in healthcare has a long history, triggered from two separate areas of interest. On the one hand, the development of medical instruments has incorporated information technology in a vast number of instances, varying from monitor equipment to CT and MRI scanners. On the other hand, requirements on the registration and processing of medical services and hospital bills, often imposed by government or insurance companies, have led to extensive Electronic Data Processing facilities (EDP), Hospital Information Systems (HIS) and ancillary registration systems.

There are two major objectives implementing healthcare information systems. One is the clinical and research point of view, and the other deals with all the administrative and healthcare economic related issues. Performance Improvement through Information Management compiles a variety of perspectives on the critical role of information technology in health care. A unifying theme is that health information systems differ according to each provider's unique needs. That is why we have to begin with a comprehensive survey of the market forces affecting health care, because the ability to plan and design appropriate information systems depends on understanding the effects of managed care on their utilization, cost, and quality and the associated information requirements. Then we have to deal with a strategic analysis and its implications for healthcare information systems and to realize how market structures affect the formulation of information system strategy, noting that there is no cookie-cutter approach for investing in healthcare information technology.

The next stage in our efforts to define an effective healthcare information system is to focus on transformation processes, including planning, information architecture, process design, care delivery and management, and the emerging role of the network manager. I strongly believe that as we do on other market and industry fields such as finance, insurance, industrial MIS etc, we have to continue our process with a strategic information management planning. This approach considers the provider's strategic direction and uses benchmark data regarding ambulatory systems, clinical data repositories, and Internet applications to formulate an organization-specific plan for investment in healthcare information technology.

On the other hand, from the clinical point of view one may notice a huge progress, in the implementation of the computerized systems into the clinical process. For example, in radiation oncology specialization, medical information has changed the manner of practice. Soon, all procedures will be fully computerized, from the planning stages to the administration, documentation and quality assurance. "*Onco-Link*", furthermore, provides, oncologists with up to date trials and treatment information, in addition to serving as an educational resource for the patients and their families.

In general, patients will now be much more exposed to medical data, sometimes insuppressible and uncorroborated data, via the Internet, thus challenging their physicians and impacting on the physician-patient relationship.

Health systems take on new meaning in the midst of the international communication revolution. Health services are a natural candidate to join and even become an integral part of the *"Information Highway"*. Terms such as *Telemedicine, Telehealth, Teleradiology, Teledermatology,* etc., have been integrated into technical and academic jargon and have become the object of research and organization.

One of the main objectives of Healthcare information systems is to provide the user with the ability of transforming the data into information. Data warehouses are a relatively new approach in healthcare. Although basically just another database, what sets it apart is that the information it contains is not used for operational purposes, but rather for analytical and decision making tasks. After an episode in which a patient's medical care has been concluded, the data collected has historical importance only. Functionally, the data warehouse integrates operational and historical data from multiple, disparate data sources and preserves it by collecting these scattered data fragments. Users can employ the stored data for decision making, both clinical and administrative, and ultimately, for the future well being of patients and for their institutions.

The nature of the data involved with Healthcare Information Systems raises dilemmas concerning privacy and medico legal aspects. Collaborative work would need to be done involves the Ministry of Health, Department of Justice, Medical Quality assurance personnel, Healthcare information systems analyzers and developers, and finally the Congress. All of these in relation to the legislation of electronic information such as data compression in radiology, the legal value of electronic documentation, as well as securing the patients privacy. There are also ethical issues related to medical data. Access to medical information compiled on a person might lead interested parties to draw conclusions about that person's likeliness to develop a certain disease. Such information could jeopardize one's chances of employment, or influence a decision on receiving health coverage or other insurance.

Among the most fascinating healthcare information systems research and practice areas we may find:

Applications and Products to Support Care - quality management, knowledge-based systems, decision support and expert systems, electronic patient record, image processing, HIS management, patient monitoring, minimum data sets, telemedicine, computer-supported interventions, diagnosis related systems, operations/resource management, management of the supply chain etc.

Human and Organizational Issues such as: managing change, human factors, communication management, organization, legal issues (privacy, confidentiality, security), ethics, assessment-evaluation, process, user-computer interface, compliance, cognitive tasks, collaboration, implementation-deployment, diffusion, needs assessment etc.

Data-Infrastructure related aspects such as: linguistics, terminology-vocabulary, data acquisition-data capture, data entry, data protection, data analysis-extraction tools, data policies, syntax, database design, classification, coding systems, standards, concept representation-preservation (clinical disciplines), indexing, language representation, lexicons, thesaurus tools, nomenclatures, modeling etc.

Information Technology Infrastructure contains subjects as: health professional workstation, networks, chip cards in healthcare, archival-repository systems for medical records, security, interfaces, distributed systems, pen-based technologies, speech recognition, user interfaces, neural networks etc.

The wide variety of computer based platforms and the sophistication of the technology together with a huge volume of data and information needs to support the medical decision-making processes makes the field of Healthcare information systems both magnificent and fascinating. In the near future, we will witness huge research and implementation efforts in the fields related to the Internet and Information highway. Online medical data retrieval systems, as well as consultant services, will establish using the web, instead of the traditional services.

Man Machine Interface will certainly move toward the voice recognition systems, allowing the physicians to dictate their diagnosis and instructions directly to the computer. More integration between "computerized islands" such as MRI, Labs, electronic medical record (EMR), demographically based information systems, Cath labs Information etc, will allow gathering all the medical data regarding the patient, into ONE comprehensive database. That is why, the field of data bases, especially those gathering text, images, motion and sounds, will be the favorites areas for research and development. Together with ethical and legal aspects, various kinds of application and users pose an enormous challenge to the field of Healthcare Information Technology, and promises to keep it at the edge of the information innovation revolution.

Adi Armoni
Tel Aviv University, Israel
October 2001

Preface

Healthcare has long been dependant upon emerging technologies to improve the quality and efficiency of care received. Newer technologies aid in diagnosis and emerging technologies can also simplify the administration aspect of the healthcare industry. As emerging technologies offer newer and innovative methods of managing healthcare related services, healthcare researchers and managers must be able to keep up with these technological innovations and challenges. This book provides insights into some of the latest research finding related to the trends, issues and challenges of information technology utilization and management in the healthcare industry. The following chapters outline the trends in healthcare information systems and communications technologies and provide practical guidance, the latest research and useful case studies describing the successes and pitfalls of technology use in the healthcare industry. From data processing systems to telemedicine, the latest trends are discussed and the most up-to-date research and developments are described.

Chapter 1 entitled, "Strategies for Healthcare Information Systems" by Ton Spil and Robert Stegwee of the University of Twente (Netherlands) addresses the issues of why many large-scale implementations of healthcare information systems has not come to fruition yet. The authors provide broad coverage of the field from strategic analysis to real-life project implementation. This chapter demonstrates that the healthcare organization is a realistic laboratory for information and communication technology students to do research.

Chapter 2 entitled, "Experiences in SIS Implementation in UK Healthcare" by Stuart Barnes of the University of Bath (United Kingdom) stems from a research project focusing longitudinally on the implementation of Case Mix, a program aimed at financial audit processes in four UK hospitals. The chapter reports general findings and details a framework for strategic IS implementation as generated from the cases and supported by current literature.

Chapter 3 entitled, "Technology-Based Marketing in the Healthcare Industry: Implications for Relationships Between Players in the Industry" by Grace Johnson, Anand Kumar, Arkalgud Ramaprasad and Madhusudhan Reddy of

Southern Illinois University at Carbondale (USA) examines how Web technology is affecting the patient-physician relationships through its impact on players and processes both inside and outside a clinic or hospital setting.

Chapter 4 entitled, "The Use of Artificial Intelligence Techniques and Applications in the Medical Domain" by Adi Armoni of Tel Aviv University (Israel) presents a general review of the main areas artificial intelligence and its applications to the medical domain. The review focuses on artificial intelligence applications to radiology, robotically-operated surgical procedures and different kinds of expert systems.

Chapter 5 entitled, "An Intelligent Data Mining System to Detect Healthcare Fraud" by Guisseppi Forgionne, Aryya Gangopadhyay and Monica Adya of the University of Maryland-Baltimore County (USA) begins with an overview of the types of healthcare fraud and a discussion of the current fraud detection. The chapter develops information technology based approaches and illustrates how these technologies can improve current practice. Finally, there is a summary of the major findings and implications for healthcare practice.

Chapter 6 entitled, "Experiences from Health Information Systems Implementation Projects Reported in Canada Between 1991 and 1997" by Francis Lau of the University of Alberta and Marilynne Hebert of the University of British Columbia (Canada) describes the authors' findings on the outcome of information systems implementation projects reported at the Canada's Health Informatics Association conference. The authors review fifty implementation projects published in the conference proceedings and interviewed 24 of the authors or designates of these projects. This chapter is a summary of their findings.

Chapter 7 entitled, "The Role of User Ownership and Positive User Attitudes in the Successful Adoption of Information Systems within NHS Community Trusts" by Crispin Coombs, Neil Doherty and John Loan-Clarke of Loughborough University (United Kingdom) proposes that two factors in the role of success or failure of systems development projects: user ownership and positive user attitudes as issues that warrant further investigation. The authors use the results of a multiple case study of five Community Healthcare Trusts. These results indicate that user ownership and positive user attitudes were mediating variables that were crucial to the success of a community information system.

Chapter 8 entitled, "Introducing Computer-Based Telemedicine in Three Rural Missouri Counties" by Kimberly Harris of Dusquesne University and Joseph Donaldson and James Campbell of the University of Missouri Columbia (USA) investigates the predictors of utilization of the computer-based telemedicine in three rural Missouri counties. The results of a survey given to employees enrolled in the Rural Telemedicine Evaluation Project were analyzed to see how percepts and demographic variables predicted utilization. The authors conclude that strategies need to be developed to encourage the use of these technologies and suggest possibilities.

Chapter 9 entitled, "VDT Health Hazards: A Guide for End Users and Managers" by Carol Clark of Middle Tennessee State University (USA) outlines major health issues like vision problems, musculoskeletal disorders and radiation effects on pregnancy as evidenced by the literature and medical research associated with VDT. The chapter provides practical suggestions for both end users and managers to help eliminate or reduce the potential negative health effects of VDT use.

Chapter 10 entitled, "The User Interface for a Computerized Patient Record System for Primary Health Care in a Third World Environment" by P.J. Blignaut and T. McDonald of the University of Orange Free State (South Africa) reports on the transition from a manual, paper-based system to a computerized system to keep track of patient history in a black, urban, third world area. The results of the investigation indicate that special attention should be paid to the design of the user interface for systems primarily used by those in the third world who do not want the computer to interfere with or hinder them in their daily tasks.

Chapter 11 entitled, "The Knowledge Medium—A Conceptual Framework for the Design and Implementation of a Platform Supporting the Community of AIDS Researchers and Practitioners" by Rolf Grutter and Katarina Stanoevska-Slabeva of the University of St. Gallen and Walter Fierz of the Institute for Clinical Microbiology and Immunology (Switzerland) uses the Swiss HIV Cohort Study (SHCS) as the core community and starting point of its analysis. Currently, the technical infrastructure supporting the SCHCS includes various legacy laboratory systems at the cohort centers and a relational database system at the coordination Data Center. All data (including data electronically available) are manually processed on a paper study form including various media breaks. As a result, the creation and dissemination of new knowledge based on study data is considerably delayed. This chapter examines a Web-based platform that was designed and implemented based on the concept of knowledge medium.

Chapter 12 entitled, "Mobile Computing at the Department of Defense" by James Rodger of Indiana University of Pennsylvania and Parag Pendharkar and Mehdi Khosrow-Pour of Pennsylvania State University (USA) relates the rationale of the Department of Defense to utilize telemedicine to meet increasing global crises and for the U.S. military to find ways to more effectively manage manpower and time. The chapter discusses a mobile telemedicine package that has been developed by the DOD to collect and transmit near-real-time, far-forward medial data and to assess how this improved capability enhances medical management of the battle space.

Chapter 13 entitled, "Physician Use of Web-Based Technology: Hype vs. Reality" by Linda Roberge of Syracuse University (USA) reports on a survey of 511 physician practice Web sites to assess how the promise of the technology compares to reality. The chapter reports that 94-95% of sites were using one or more site design elements, and providing educational content that would be attractive to potential patients. However, only 73% of the sites provided the professional credentials of the health care providers. It further reports that few sites incorporated legal disclaimers or provided a secure connection for patients.

Chapter 14 entitled, "The Quality of Medical Information on the Internet: Some Current Evaluation Frameworks" by Carmine Sellitto of Victoria University of Technology (Australia) provides an overview of some of the criteria that are currently being used to assess medical information found on the World Wide Web. Drawing from the evaluation frameworks discussed, a simple set of easy-to-apply criteria is proposed for evaluating on-line medical information. The suggested criterion covers the categories of information accuracy, objectivity, privacy, currency and authority. The author also provides a checklist for Web page assessment and scoring.

Chapter 15 entitled, "Information System Failures in Healthcare Organizations: Case Study of a Root Cause Analysis" by Pamela Paustian, Donna Slovensky and Jacqueline Kennedy of the University of Alabama at Birmingham (USA) reports a root cause analysis following an information system failure that compromised the organization's ability to capture clinical documentation for a 33 hour period. The chapter indicates that frequent testing and improvement of the recovery plan is more desirable than a successful recovery in a disaster situation. The authors note that it is essential to maintain effective plans because businesses change so rapidly that constant updating is necessary.

Chapter 16 entitled, "Intermediation Structures in Electronic Healthcare Portals" by Jonathan Wareham and Richard Klein of Georgia State University (USA) focuses upon the healthcare industry, sector of the economy that has witnessed a surge in electronic intermediation. The chapter is founded on a survey of leading healthcare portals and documents and analyzes four predominant patterns of functional intermediation in this new form of an IT-enabled commercial institution. Based upon a historical analysis of healthcare portals, the authors posit functional, generalizable patterns of intermediation.

Chapter 17 entitled, "CORBAMed and DHE Middleware Service Approach in Healthcare Information Systems" by Dongsong Zhang and Ralph Martinez of the University of Arizona (USA) analyzes the status of today's healthcare information systems and the challenges that they have. The chapter further introduces two middleware service frameworks for information systems, namely CORBAMed and DHE in detail. The middleware service can address heterogeneous problems and significantly assist interoperability of function and the integrity of information systems by providing common services and a set of standard interfaces that enable different applications to interact with each other.

Chapter 18 entitled, "Scanning and Image Processing System (SIPS) for Medication Ordering" by Stephan Chan of Hong Kong Baptist University (Hong Kong) presents a physician order entry system in the ward for medication prescriptions by using scanning and image processing. The chapter presents important design and operational requirements. The chapter describes how SIPS integrates different information technologies including scanning, bar code and other marks recognition. SIPS uses specially designed order forms for doctors to write orders that are then scanned into the computer that performs recognition and image processing. The resulting orders, including the doctor's handwritten images and other order information are transmitted to the destinations electronically. The chapter reports that SIPS reduces human effort and errors and that SIPS is an innovative use of information technology to meet the needs of a hospital that requires paper-and-pen operations. The authors speculate that SIPS can be extended to meet other operational needs as an alternative input method.

Chapter 19 entitled, "Organizational Implementation ad Issues of Patient Data Management Systems in an Intensive Care Unit" by Nathalie Mitev of the London School of Economics and Sharon Kerkham of Salford University (UK) is a case study which details the events surrounding the introduction of a patient data management system into an intensive care unit in a UK hospital. The chapter shows that the implementation was complex and involved organizational issues related to the cost of healthcare, legal and purchasing requirements, systems integration and staff expertise as well as relationships with suppliers.

Chapter 20 entitled, "Studying the Translations of NHSnet" by Edgar Whitley of the London School of Economics and Political Science and Athanasia Pouloudi of Brunel University (UK) explores the ways in which innovative information systems projects take on a life of their own. The chapter begins by reviewing some of the more traditional ways of making sense of this phenomenon: resistance to change, escalation and unintended results, before introducing the sociology of translation. The introduction provides a theoretical framework for viewing the transformations that an information system project undergoes. The framework is then applied to the case of NHSnet project in the United Kingdom. Using the language of sociology translation, the authors consider the underlying stakeholder relations in the case study and draw more general conclusions for the responsibilities of stakeholders involved in an information systems lifecycle.

Telemedicine, healthcare information systems, business process reengineering, the information highway, and disaster recovery planning are just a few of the important topics addressed in this timely new book. The healthcare industry has always been cutting edge in its use and application of technologies. The chapters in this book represent the best research and practice of information systems, telecommunications, management and information technology as it is applied in healthcare. Leading experts in these fields share their years of expertise and outline the road to successful technology implementation and share practical tips on how to avoid some of the pitfalls that may lie ahead in the implementation of these technologies. This book provides practical guidelines for researchers and practitioners alike. Additionally, the research contained herein is an excellent resource for academicians and students.

IRM Press
October 2001

Chapter 1

Strategies for Healthcare Information Systems

Ton A.M. Spil and Robert A. Stegwee
University of Twente, The Netherlands

It is widely recognized that the healthcare industry does not use information technology to its full potential. This book uncovers many of the reasons why large-scale implementation of healthcare information systems has not come to fruition yet. The authors provide a broad coverage of the field, ranging from strategic analysis to real-life project implementation. Moreover the book provides strategies to avoid pitfalls and direct your healthcare organization to strategic use of healthcare information systems. This section of the book will introduce the five main themes of the book and will show that the healthcare organizations are realistic laboratories for the information and communication technology scientists to do research. The five main themes are: Strategy, Network Healthcare Chain, Process Management, Knowledge Management, Standardization.

INTRODUCTION

The environment of the professional healthcare organizations handled in this chapter is changing. Where it should be complex and stable, according to reference models (Mintzberg, 1983;, Heijnsdijk, 1990), the environment is becoming more and more unstable. The size of most healthcare organizations in the Netherlands is growing by mergers and natural growth. This means that these professional organizations have to use strategic variables that they have never used before with a new technical system. There is need for structural

Figure 1: Strategies of Healthcare Information Systems Themes

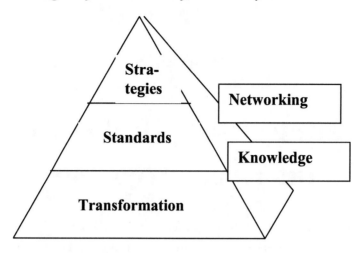

changes to strengthen middle management but even more need for cultural changes to balance the autonomous and heteronomous powers in the organization (Scott, 1982). This book argues that information management can contribute in these changes for the good and the bad.

Information Strategy in healthcare organizations is an ad hoc static planning process (Spil, 1998) which does not fit the dynamic environment the healthcare organizations are facing. In this research, a more dynamic approach is developed to adapt to the specific organization and the specific environment. The environment (government, suppliers, patients, professional groups) determines for a great deal which planning possibilities are available. That is why in four cycles--agreeing, aligning, analyzing and authorizing--a yearly planning approach is built in which the information projects can be chosen and monitored and changed when necessary (Spil & Salmela, 1999). An action study plan is built to put this approach into healthcare practice in both Finland and the Netherlands.

Information Structure is well developed in healthcare organizations where we regard information structure as heterogeneous socio-technical networks (Hanseth & Lundberg, 1999), in which both social and technical actors take part. Agreements and standards, like healthlevel seven, can support a wide range of applications and create a common language both internal and external. Still, healthcare organizations are struggling with all kinds of new developments on a structural level. The developments focus on management information, Internet, intranet and archiving. Management information is implemented in various ways as networks (Lines, 1999), as clinical management systems (Spil, 1998) and as information warehouses (Zviran & Armoni, 1999). Our e-health group wants to make a comparative study on management information systems and wants to study standardization and specifically HL7 in depth.

Many Internet possibilities in healthcare organizations are not implemented because of privacy problems concerned with opening up the internal network. In cooperation with the National Insurance Netherlands, our healthcare research group wants to support new implementations, especially between hospital physicians, home physicians and pharmacies. This study has started with a thorough description of a hospital information system with system components (Sikkel et al., 1999) that both fit the HIS and the structure of the hospital. The second phase is to investigate the workflow and relate this workflow to the (electronic) information flows. The functional integration of all system components (in a hospital admission, out-patients agenda, medical services communication) is an objective that might be utopia, but HIS and EMR combined with the strong communication facilities create many possibilities to put a step into the right direction.

Communication is a strong weapon for the strategic use of information systems. E-health will open possibilities that were only for imagination three years ago. We think healthcare information systems can be the enablers of transformation in the healthcare chain, and to become an enabler there is need for strategies for healthcare information systems. The next five sections introduce the five sections of this chapter.

STRATEGIES

The editors of this book have assisted in many information strategy studies in healthcare organizations and have never seen such an external view on information systems like it is today. The subjects of the book support this external thinking by showing that you should not look at one organization but have to look at healthcare organizations as a chain. The interactions between the actors in this chain are the main subjects of research in our research group.

Strategy is the definition of the overall end goals and the means of action to meet these goals. To measure these strategies we look at seven dimensions (Burton & Obel, 1995):
- Product and process innovation,
- Product and market breadth,
- Concern for quality,
- Price level,

- Control level,
- Technology and
- Capital requirement.

In this introduction we will not handle every dimension but some highlights will introduce other sections in this book.

In the third section, *process innovation* is preferred above *product innovation* because we expect a longer lasting effect. This does not mean that ICT is not apparent in product innovation, because the medical technology is highly dependent on ICT. The implementation of healthcare information systems can be seen as a process innovation . Stuart Barnes argues in the next chapter that without a framework for strategic IS implementation, many healthcare information systems are doomed for failure.

The cooperation of many healthcare organizations shows the changes that are taking place on the dimension *product and market breadth*. Healthcare organizations have to rethink their strategy and start strategic alliances. In the fourth chapter the role of ICT in forming these networks is described.

Concerns of quality is always a dimension that is seen as important in healthcare organization. It is not a coincidence that the first three dimensions mentioned are the main objectives of a hospital in one of our case studies (Spil, 1996). Three changes are taken from the corporate strategy-plan. The hospital wants to:

- grow to be a top hospital with many educational facilities and with clinical and technical research of high quality;
- derive economy of scale reached by the merger of several smaller institutions;
- deliver high quality healthcare to the patients.

These three objectives do not always go together because economic factors, like the *price level*, often collide with quality factors. In our recent research we explicitly study the cost reduction of medicine prescription as described in the third chapter. One of the conclusions of that section is that time seems to be far more important to the professional than price levels.

The *control level* is a completely different issue. Management of healthcare organizations complain that they do not have enough management information to control the organization. Although many systems exist to deliver this information, the problem seems to have a more organizational nature. On one hand the professionals do not want to be controlled, on the other hand management does not have much variety of alternatives. New information and communication technology like datawarehouses and intranet solutions explore a new kind of control systems. This book does not specifically address these problems, but in literature there are some examples that look promising but are not yet established (Berndt, 2000; Zviran & Armoni, 1999).

Technology requirements therefore are high both on product and process of the healthcare organizations. Reima Suomi and his research group try to find explanations why ICT adoption in healthcare seems to be gaining momentum as described further on in this section.

Finally, when discussing strategy, the budget determines what can be implemented. The dimension *capital requirements* is often questioned in the following way: "How much money should we invest in ICT?" In general terms the ICT budgets vary from 1% to 15% of the revenue when the role of ICT is respectively support and strategic. In most healthcare organizations ICT is seen as the latter. Experience learns that although the budget is rather high, there is not that much strategic variety because many ICT projects are determined by contingency. One big example of the last year is the millennium bug which absorbed a huge pie of the ICT budget in healthcare, but also the government and the suppliers determine ICT actions.

STANDARDIZATION

In the previous paragraph we described the strategic wish of healthcare organizations to gain more control on the operational core. Professionals will see monitoring systems as a reduction of their autonomy. The scale of hospitals urges managers to implement management information systems but up till now these systems are mainly used financially. Managers try to standardize medical processes and the control is mainly on the procedures. The professionals are responsible for the quality of the products and processes.

In light of external collaboration, we want to broaden the scope of the use of standards. Lundberg and Hanseth show the difference between local standards and global standards, and we like to grasp which global standards have to be developed at this moment and in the future. To this end Stegwee and Lagendijk have developed a framework which helps in specifing the need for standardized information exchange by specific applications. Using this framework to categorize available standards enables us to select appropriate standards for our application and to assess possible blind spots and overlaps when using a combination of standards. This assessment can also guide the future development of standards.

The need for standards becomes more clear when looking at the Electronic Patient Record in terms of a constellation of independent yet integrated information systems. Toussaint and Berg elaborate the topic of the Electronic

Patient Record and show us new ways to look at it, both from a technical and from an organizational point of view. In the long run many EPR systems will consist of specialized modules, tailored to the needs of specific user groups, and standardized to communicate efficiently and effectively with other such components in a global network.

TRANSFORMATION

The professionals who work in the operating core want to be free to do what they think is best. They will not allow managers to decide on professional matters. An occupational group that regulates the access to the profession establishes the power of the professionals. There are healthcare organizations that are very autonomous, meaning that the professional or his representatives determine the strategy, structure and operational activities of the organization. Other healthcare organizations are heteronomies by nature in which the management regulates the activities and also feels responsible for the content of the primary process.

Business transformation is now the central management challenge and the primary, if not the sole, task of business leaders (Gouillart & Kelly, 1995). According to these authors the business management should change from a mechanical to a biological model. This transformation should go in four stages:

- Reframe (mind)
- Restructure (body within)
- Revitalize (body and environment)
- Renew (spirit)

The institutional mind of healthcare organizations should change from intramural to extramural. In chapter four these thoughts are put to paper, but before the healthcare organizations can change their vision to the environment, they have to restructure internally. Process management can help with the restructuring.

Process management tries to identify the most important processes of the organization and integrate them by means of information interaction. Instead of suboptimalization of functions in the organization, there is a chance of optimizing the overall process. The process management literature has grown from the business process reengineering thoughts but also stems from process-oriented development methods. The first group described radical change of the processes of organization, but this is nowadays seen more evolutionary. The second group thoroughly described the processes of the organization but only made small changes. Process management can be the best of both worlds and can be used to transform the healthcare chain.

We think the internet will be the medium to link the institutional healthcare bodies to the environment. In five chapters in this book, the Internet technologies take an enabling role to revitalize the healthcare community. To reach this revitalization it is necessary that on a standardization level, global agreements have to be made to accelerate the developments.

Last but not least we are back in this chapter where the spirit of healthcare organizations has to be renewed by building strategies for healthcare information systems. Renewal deals with the people side of transformation and therefore information systems should be seen as sociological interactive systems in stead of computer systems. With the renewal we also arrive at the last section of the book, knowledge management, because it involves the rapid dissemination of knowledge inside the firm.

An important new development is that process management is not only internally oriented any more but focuses on the processes and information flows in between organizations. The two chapters, network organizations and process management, therefore are rather strongly connected to each other. Especially the chapter of Klein and Schadt combines both worlds. Another clear connection is to the standardization because there is no interorganizational process management possible if there are no standards to communicate between the different stakeholders.

This book shows that the transformation can take place on different levels and in different places in the healthcare organizations. Klein and Schadt focus on the transformation of the hospital–supplier relation. Lagendijk, Schuring and Spil evaluate the first processes in the healthcare chain, and More and McGrath look at the same problem from a macro perspective for the whole of Australia--again global and local initiatives that have to get together in the future.

NETWORK ORGANIZATIONS

Healthcare organizations have to rethink their borders and have to make strategic alliances to be able to cope with the changes in the environment. This does not only mean a changing relation with the supplier, as described in the process management chapter by Klein and Schadt, but also a changing relationship with other kinds of healthcare organizations. Spanjers, Hasselbring, Peterson and Smits suggest an evolution from intradepartmental to interdepartmental to interorganizational healthcare chains. In their case a relation is sought with specialistic healthcare organizations but alliances can take form in many different constellations. Chan and Ramsden studied the electronic networks in Canada where the client is directly involved in the external interaction from and to the healthcare organizations. Many changes will occur in this area in the near future, and therefore more research in this direction is needed.

A network of organizations can be defined as a decentralized organism without steady borders and without a specific center. There is no top or bottom, just relationships (Kelly, 1996). Healthcare organizations have made their first step into this insecure, relative virtual world as we can see in the cases in Germany, The Netherlands, Australia, the United States and Canada.

KNOWLEDGE MANAGEMENT

The main focus of information management in organizations went through an evolution from costs via functionality and integration towards knowledge as described in Table 1 (Spil, 1996).

Many healthcare organizations are still concerned with integration but start to recognize the possibilities of knowledge management in healthcare. Professionals learn by doing and therefore can make use of knowledge systems, expert systems and decision support systems. The last group can have a large influence on the specialist's job (Boonstra, 1994) but is not yet common in the operational kernel.

Davenport et al., (1998) identify four broad types of objectives for knowledge management:
- Create knowledge repositories
- Improve knowledge access
- Enhance knowledge environment
- Manage knowledge as an asset

If we look at these objectives, we must observe that healthcare organizations still have some work to do to start reaching them.

Table 1. The information system evolution (Spil, 1996)

Period	Performance	Market	IS
1950-1975	Efficiency	Price	Costs
1975-1985	Quality	Quality	Functionality
1985-1995	Flexibility	Choice	Integration
1995-200?	Innovation	Uniqueness	Knowledge

Professionals have a high educational level and can pick up new developments in communication relatively easy if they are supported in the right way. A distinction can be made in external and internal communication. External possibilities for scientists are evident. External access to Internet, electronic mail, electronic journal (Boonstra, 1994), but also video conferencing for consultancy of colleagues and other links with outside professionals (Jordan, 1994), are essential for the professional of the future. Yet there are not that many movements in healthcare organizations. They are still focused on the patient flow and the internal databases and basic hospital information systems.

The last two chapters in this book explore this future direction, one in the administrative function with a thorough knowledge management base (Larsen & Pedersen) and one trying to enable medical working groups (Wickramasinghe & Silvers). We think part of the medical future lies in the knowledge area, but we have to notice that the promise of decision support and expert systems in healthcare has not shown many results in the past decade. It might be that the Internet possibilities speed up these developments because knowledge gets more and more available, as is happening in the world of the academic library.

CONCLUSIONS

Although it is impossible to show all developments that take place around the world on healthcare information systems, we think this book shows the main streams in which these information systems are moving on strategic level:

- Standardization and integration of the healthcare chain;
- Transformation of the healthcare processes (from push to demand);
- Externalization of healthcare organizations.

Global standards and clear local definitions must pave the way to integrated care pathways in the future. In an optimal situation all healthcare information interactions will have an international standard with enough freedom to apply local systems for specific situations.

The changing environment forces the healthcare organization to transform their processes from a client push to a client demand situation. The patient will change in the near future from a will-less victim to a knowing client.

There is a need for innovation in the healthcare organizations, and the main way of bringing innovation is using knowledge as a driver. An important support for knowledge in the organization will be the information and communication technology.

REFERENCES

Arrow, K.J. (1974). *The Limits of Organizations,* New York:Norton.

Berndt, D., Hevner, A. R. & Studnicki, J. (2000). Community Health Assessments: A datawarehousing approach, *Proceedings of the European Conference on IS*, Vienna.

Boonstra, A. (1994). Strategieen voor informatiemanagement bij professionele organisaties, *Informatie*, 36(5), 333-342.

Broadbent, M., Weill, P. & O'Brien, T. (1996). Firm context and patterns of IT infrastructure capability, *ICIS 96,* Cleveland.

Brown, A D (1995). *Organizational Culture*, Pitman, London.

Burton, R. & Obel, B. (1995). *Strategic Oorganizational Diagnosis and Design, Developing Theory for Application,* Kluwer Academic Publishers, Boston.

Cash, J. I., Mc Farlan F. W., Mc Kenney, J. L. & Applegate, L. M. (1992). *Corporate I S Management* Irwin, Boston.

Chandler, A. D. (1962). *Strategy and Structure: Chapters in the History of the Industrial Enterprise*, MIT press, Cambridge.

Child, J. (1973). Predicting and understanding organization structure, *Administrative Science Quarterly,* 18, 168-185.

Daft, R. L. (1997). *Organization Theory and Design,* South-Western College Publishing, Cincinnati, Ohio.

Davenport, T. H., De Long, D. W. & Beers, M. C. (1998). Successful knowledge management projects, *Sloan Management Review,* Winter 1998, 43-57.

Duncan, R B.(1979),What is the right organization structure, *Organizational Dynamics*, winter, 59-79.

Earl, M. J. (1989). *Management Strategies for Information Technology.* Prentice Hall, London.

Gouillart, F. J. & Kelly, J. N. (1995). *Transforming the Organization,* Mc Graw Hill, New York.

Handy, C. (1978). *Gods of Management,* Penguin, London.

Handy, C. (1996). Find meaning in uncertainty In: Gibson, R, *Rethinking the Future,* Nicholas Brealey publishing Ltd, London.

Hanseth, O. & Monteiro, E. (1998). Changing irreversible networks: Institutionalisation and infrastructures, *Proceedings of the Sixth ECIS,* June, Aix en Provence, France.

Harrison, R. (1972). Understanding your organization's character, *Harvard Business Review,* 50(2), 119-128.

Heijnsdijk, J. (1990). *Vitale Organisaties (in Dutch),* Wolters Noordhof, Groningen.

Jans, E. J. (1996). *Grondslagen Administratieve Organisatie(in Dutch),* Samson, Alphen a/d Rijn.

Jordan, E. (1994). Information strategy and organization structure, *Information Systems Journal,* 4, 253-270.

Kelly, K. (1996). The company as a living organism, In: Gibson, R, *Rethinking the Future,* Nicholas Brealey publishing Ltd, London.

Lederer, A. & Sethi, V. (1988). The implementation of Strategic IS Planning methodologies *MIS Quarterly* 12,3, September.

Leifer, R. (1988). Matching computer-based IS with organizational structures, *MIS Quarterly,* 12, March,   63-73.

Lines, K. (1999). MIS in local government health care organizations, *Proceedings of the 22th IRIS Conference,* August, Keuruu, Finland, volume 2, 337-348.

Mantz, E. A. & Kleijne, D. & Zijden, F. A. P van der (1991). Planning en realisatie informatie-voorziening nog ver uit elkaar (in Dutch), *Informatie* 33,12, pp. 847-856.

Markus, L. (1984). *Systems in Organizations,* Pitman, London.

McDonald, P. & Gandz, J. (1992). "Getting value from shared values," *Organizational Dynamics,* Winter, 64-77.

Miller, D. (1987). Strategy making and structure: analysis and implications for performance, *Academy of Management Journal,* 30(1), 7-32.

Mintzberg, H. (1979). *The Structuring of Organizations,* Prentice Hall, Englewood Cliffs.

Mintzberg, H (1983).*Structures in fives:Designing effective organizations,* Prentice Hall, Englewood Cliffs, New York.

Nicholson, N., Rees, A. & Brooks-Rooney, A. (1990). "Strategy, innovation and performance," *Journal of Management Studies,* 27(5), 511-534.

Perrow, C (1967). A framework for the comparative analysis of an organization, *American Sociological Review,* 32(2).

Porter, M & Millar, V (1985). How information gives you competitive advantage. *Harvard Business Review,* July/August, 149-160.

Quinn, R G & McGrath, M R (1985). The transformation of organizational cultures: a competing values perspective, in Frost, Moore, Louis, Lundberg & Martin (eds),*Organizational Culture,* Newbury Park, California Sage, 315-334.

Raelin, J A (1991). *The clash of cultures; Managers managing professionals,* Harvard Business School Press, Boston.

Robbins, S P (1990). *Organization Theory:Structure, Design and Application*,Prentice Hall,Englewood cliffs

Sääksjarvi, M (1988). Information Systems Planning: What makes it uccessful? *Australian Computer Conference proceedings*, 523-542.

Scott, W R (1982)'Managing professional work: Three models of control for health organizations. Healthservices research,17(3), 213-240.

Scott Morton, M S (1991). *The Corporation of the 1990s: Information Technology and Organizational Transformation,* Oxford Press, New York.

Sikkel, K, Spil, T A M, Weg, R L W van de (1999). A real world case in information technology for undergraduate students, *Journal of systems and software,* 49, 2-3, 30 December.

Spil, T A M (1996). *The effectiveness of strategic information systems planning in professional organizations*, PhD thesis University of Twente, Enschede, ISBN 90 90009588-8.

Spil, T A M (1998). From professional healthcare to where? A healthcare information management reference model. *Proceedings 1998 IRMA conference,* Boston, USA, 285-294.

Stolz, C (1987). Corporate culture and strategy – the problem of strategic fit. *Long Range Planning*, 20(4), 78-87.

Wassenaar, D A (1995). *Informatieplanning in transactioneel perspectief (in Dutch),* PhD Thesis, Free University, A'dam Weggeman, M, Wijne, G & Kor, R (1994)*Ondernemen binnen de onderneming:* essenties van organisaties (in Dutch), Deventer, 1994, ISBN 90 267 1660 5.

Woodward, J (1965). *Industrial Organization Theory and Practice,*Oxford University Press, Oxford.

Zuurbier, J J (1993). *Financial control in hospitals,*PhD thesis University of Twente.

Zviran, M & Armoni, A (1999). Integrating hospital information systems, *International journal of Healthcare Technology and Management*,1(1), 168-179.

Chapter 2

Experiences in SIS Implementation in UK Healthcare

Stuart J. Barnes
University of Bath, UK

Implementing large strategic IS in the UK health sector has recently become the subject of much debate, as hospitals have undergone wide-reaching government-led institutional reforms involving the introduction of IT. Many of the developments have followed the patterns in the U.S. One such example is that of Case Mix, introduced strategically as part of the Resource Management Initiative and aimed at the facilitation of both clinical and financial audit. Moreover, Case Mix was implemented alongside significant changes in hospital structure and culture, requiring clinicians to get involved in management tasks and decision making within the structure of the hospital, supported by a new information infrastructure.

Case Mix was implemented blanket-fashion throughout many UK hospitals, and the success of such systems has varied significantly. A number of lessons can be learned from the way that the implementation was approached. This chapter stems from a research project focusing longitudinally on the implementation of Case Mix in four UK hospitals. It draws a number of findings from the cases, and importantly, explicates a framework for strategic IS implementation, as generated from the cases and supported by the extant literature. Such a framework has implications for both theory and practice, and assists in the understanding of what is often a dynamic and poorly understood situation.

Previously Published in *Strategies for Healthcare Information Systems* edited by Robert Stegwee and Ton Spil, Copyright © 2001, Idea Group Publishing.

INTRODUCTION

The implementation of information systems (IS) is an important theme in the literature (Cooper and Zmud, 1990; Keen, 1981; McFarlan, 1981; Swanson, 1988). Much of it appears to suggest a gloomy outlook, with many systems doomed to failure. Indeed, there are many case examples to support this (e.g., Computing, 1993; Beynon-Davies, 1995a; Oz, 1994; Tate, Hunter, McPartlin and Duffy, 1993), and numerous statistics of IS failure (e.g. Lyytinen and Hirschheim, 1987; Willcocks and Lester, 1993). Hockstrasser and Griffiths (1991), for example, suggest that around two-thirds of all large IS implementations are not successful.

The overwhelming focus for most studies of IS has, until recently, been the private sector. However, in the last decade, the public sector in the UK has been the subject of wide-ranging reforms involving the introduction of competitive practices, and significantly, the introduction of IS and information technology (IT) to aid in this task (Brown, 1992; 1995; Beynon-Davies, 1995a). Among these has been the health care sector, which previously had very little in the way of IT infrastructure. Included within this new area of IS implementation, we find systems associated with the National Health Service (NHS) Resource Management Initiative (RMI). The Initiative revolves around cultural and structural change, and the provision of relevant information for clinical and management audit. At the heart of the Initiative are Case Mix systems, which are patient-centered databases for all aspects of hospital operations.

Although it is a large-scale and expensive development and the UK NHS is the largest employer in Europe, Case Mix has received very little attention in the IS literature. The study presented here investigates the organizational changes that influence the successful implementation of Case Mix. It presents some of the results from the study, and in particular, draws a number of important lessons for those attempting to implement IS in healthcare. To this end, it provides a framework for considering IS implementation at a strategic level.

BACKGROUND TO THE RESEARCH

Despite the notable increasing sophistication of information technologies, systems continue to fail either during development, or at the points of implementation and use (Holmes & Poulymenakou, 1995). In the words of Lyytinen (1987):

The information systems community faces a paradox: despite impressive advances in technology, problems are more abundant than solutions; organizations experience rising costs instead of cost reductions, and information systems misuse and rejection are more frequent than acceptance and use.

Until very recently in the UK, these problems have largely focused upon organizations in the private sector. However, during the last decade, the public sector has been the subject of wide-ranging reforms involving the introduction of IS and IT. A major objective of such change has been to push public sector units into becoming more competitive. The external pressures, in the form of legislation and direct Government control, have sought to elicit changes in organizational culture, often in the face of significant resistance. Change has been sought in the ways that services are managed and delivered, the evaluation of the quality of aforesaid services, and in accountability and costing. One of the most predominant of such changes has been the introduction of competition for services, the motivation of which has been to invite efficiency, effectiveness and related benefits ensuing from the accrual of economies. These reforms, pursued over the last 15 years or so, have been introduced by a series of mechanisms. For example, in the NHS, competition has been catalyzed by the imposition of an internal market; while in local authorities, a major component of reforms has involved the extension of compulsory competitive tendering for their services (Hackney and McBride, 1993).

Pivotal to such change has been an explosion in the introduction of a variety of information systems to meet such challenges. Focusing on healthcare, a large part of the work of the NHS involves collecting and handling information, from lists of people in the population to medical records (including images such as X-ray pictures), to prescriptions, letters, staffing rosters and huge numbers of administrative forms. Yet until recently, the health service has been woefully backward in its use of the technology to handle information by the standards of private industry.

This has been quickly changing in recent years, and the UK public sector now typically spends an estimated £2 billion per annum on IT, equating to around 1% of the public purse (Holmes & Poulymenakou, 1995), while the NHS spends around £220 million annually on IT in hospitals (Audit Commission, 1995). This investment is still small by the standards of the private sector, at less than 1% of operating costs compared to around 2-15% for a forward-looking business (dependent on industry sector). However, it is all the more significant when we consider that healthcare is an industry which has been slow to adopt IT, and one which presents some of the biggest IT opportunities (Cross, 1992).

Subsequently, and increasingly as a result of this investment, the public sector is beginning to experience problems with the implementation of IT. In fact, estimates suggest that problems with projects in the public sector in the last 12 years have cost over £5 billion (Collins, 1994). Associated with the technological change, there are an increasing number of examples of IS failure in the NHS, including that of Wessex Regional Health Authority's Regional Information Systems Plan (RISP; at a cost £63 million) (Health Economics Research Group, 1991), the London Ambulance Service's Computer Aided Dispatch (LASCAD) system (£1.1 to £1.5 million) (Beynon-Davies, 1995a), and more recently various Resource Management Initiative (RMI) Case Mix failures (£1 to £3 million) (Brown, 1995).

The Resource Management Initiative was a driving force in the move towards information systems and cultural change in the NHS (DHSS, 1986). First announced in 1986, the functions of RMI were twofold: (1) to provide clinicians and other hospital managers with the information they required to use the resources they controlled to maximum effect, generally by the introduction of new IT; and, (2) to encourage clinicians to take more interest and involvement in the management of the hospital and community units in which they worked, by making them responsible for the operational and strategic decisions taken in their place of work.

Figure 1: The role of case ix in NHS hospitals (after Brown, 1995)

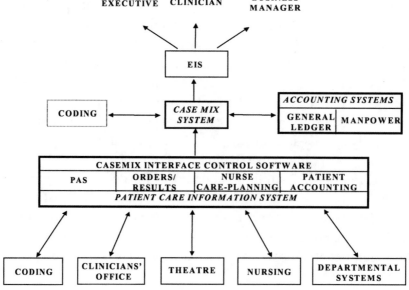

Put bluntly, the RMI was going to help clinicians and other hospital managers to make better-informed judgments surrounding how the resources they control can be used most effectively. The Initiative was not only aimed at persuading clinicians to own the management process, but to provide them with accurate, up-to-date and relevant information which could be used to cost medical activities and improve patient care. The response to this need for improved information services available to hospital units was the development and implementation of a sophisticated and extensive package of IT referred to as the 'Case Mix' information system (CMIS) with the purpose of clinical and management audit (Black and Moore, 1994; Kramer and Ellertson, 1993; Rea, 1994; Richards, 1986).

Prior to RMI, the introduction of IT in the NHS was patchy and limited (Cross, 1992; Hackney and McBride, 1993). Where systems existed, the technology was very varied, incompatible, archaic, and dependent upon Regional computer departments to deliver necessary operational systems. The development of Case Mix, with its dependence on data fed from other systems such as the Patient Administration System (PAS), radiology, pathology, theatre and nursing systems, provided a catalyst for the adoption of operational systems throughout the hospital (Naude, Proudlove and Bellingham, 1994).

Case Mix takes a central position in the hospitals' IT infrastructure, as shown in Figure 1 (an illustrative example, specifications may vary depending upon the hospital), providing a tool for collecting and analysing data from all areas of hospital operations. As we can see from Figure 1, there are two main types of data feed: financial and medical. The financial feed consists of pulling data from the general ledger and manpower systems, particularly standard costs and budgets. This contrasts with the other main feed to Case Mix, that of the 'patient care information system' which is a label given to the array of feeder sub-systems providing information on all aspects of patient treatment and care (Brown, 1995).

Each of the feeder systems is interfaced with Case Mix, so as to provide appropriate data in an acceptable format. Such data is accumulated by Case Mix within the care profile sub-system: this stores the actual tests, treatments, costs, number of cases and so on to be compared with expected 'ideal' profiles or projected activity levels as drawn from the financial data, enabling financial audit.

Regarding clinical audit, Case Mix provides the tool for assessment of the professional clinical practices of each clinician. The kinds of general information that is routinely provided in Case Mix includes lengths of stay (LOS), deaths, re-admissions and so on, whilst more specific information such as drugs administered and operative procedures performed is available via the appropriate feeder systems. The data allows aspects of Case Mix, clinical management, diagnostic accuracy and patient outcomes to be compared. For these purposes, at the apex of the architecture is an executive information system (EIS). This system takes summary data from the Case Mix (and therefore its feeders) and enables, for example, graphical and tabular analysis of the aggregated data by clinicians, executives and business managers.

On reflection, the Case Mix experiment may have turned sour. Evidence suggests that success has been difficult to achieve, and that hospitals have found it difficult to achieve any tangible benefits (e.g., see Brown, 1992, 1995; Cross, 1992; Hackney and McBride, 1993; Health Economics Research Group, 1991; Jones and Worsdale, 1993; Rea, 1994; Robinson, 1992). Evaluating investments is made all the more difficult by the fact that published evidence is scarce. Lock (1996a, 1996b) found that only 5% (by value) of all investments were the subject of published assessment, which may be an indicator of the poor value of such investments. Even published studies are far from conclusive: the 'official' Resource Management evaluation conducted by Brunel University found "no measurable patient benefits" in its review of the six pilot sites, while costs were more than double those expected (Health Economics Research Group, 1991). Thus, the situation can be characterised as one of uncertainty.

The research examined here was part of a larger study aimed at giving a detailed insight into the context, process and outcomes of the CMIS development. It is one of very few IS-oriented academic studies into this recent area of IS implementation. The purpose was to find determinants of the outcomes (success or otherwise) of such developments to assist in understanding the phenomena. Moreover, it sought to develop explanatory and normative frameworks to meet such ends. The following section briefly examines the methodology used for the research.

METHODOLOGY

The research design involves intensive grounded theory research (Strauss and Corbin, 1990). The units of data within this methodology are four quasi-longitudinal case studies of CMIS introduction in NHS hospitals, and as a consequence, aspects of the case study method (Eisenhardt, 1989; Yin, 1984, 1994) and some of those of longitudinal research (Pettigrew, 1990, 1992) are integrated in a complementary manner. The longitudinal case research provides an in-depth and time-integrated view, enabling the identification of

causal processes between events over a period of time. In this study, data was collected in three key phases of IS introduction: planning and evaluation, mid-implementation and post-implementation.

Most of the study data was gathered by means of semi-structured interview schedule using a cross-section of stakeholder groups: senior management, IT staff, users and heads of user departments. In total, 96 interviews were conducted on 32 respondents in each of three time periods. The main focus for the discussion were 'anchor' themes/concepts drawn from preliminary interview sessions, supported by a synthesis of themes in the literature (e.g., King and Grover, 1991; Roberts and Barrar, 1992; Schultz, Slevin and Pinto, 1987). In each case, the respondents were asked about each theme/concept, its causes or antecedents and its effects or outcomes as they see them. Further emerging concepts were similarly treated.

THE DEVELOPMENT OF AN IMPLEMENTATION FRAMEWORK

While all the hospitals studied implemented Case Mix as part of RMI, their experiences differ significantly. Comparative analysis implied that differences can be attributed to disparity in the process of change, the contextual environment within which the implementation is situated, plus the behaviour of key agents around the implementation of Case Mix.

A very brief summary of the cases, as structured around the core conceptual grounded theory categories, is given in Table 1. Moreover, it is possible to attempt to generalise the patterns distinguished. By approaching the possible association of the grounded theory with elements of present formal theory, a more general substantive theory can be produced (Glaser and Strauss, 1967, p. 34). Eisenhardt (1989, p. 545) also advocates this method, suggesting:

> Overall, tying the emergent theory to existing literature enhances
> the internal validity, generalizability and theoretical level of theory
> building from case study research.

In approaching this issue, it is important to be selective. There are a great many frameworks that could be used to tell us about the studies. Here we attempt to confine ourselves to one major framework stemming from the literature, drawing some comparisons and making some developments to fit the frame of the results.

Table 1: Case summaries

GROUNDED THEORY CATEGORY	CASE 1: ALPHA	CASE 2: BETA	CASE 3: GAMMA	CASE 4: DELTA
EXTERNAL CONTEXT	Central directives exercised locally by Region, including RM. Regional data requirements and project milestones. News of NHS IS failure prevalent in the media. Competitive pressures from purchaser/provider split. Immature systems and stretched resources of vendors.	IS failure in the Media. Internal competition. Local Political agenda as 'flagship.' Pressure and requirements from Region, and tenuous relations. Kept local not Regional IS focus. Procurement effort to find mature system and resourced company. Unclear coding signals, kept to central ICD.	Regional and Government policies. Unclear central messages regarding clinical coding. Regional control, funding, and criticism of coding and third party information, fading after Trust status. Hospital cynical of poorly developed and supported systems from well-known companies.	Regional and Government influences of policy, and control of the RMI. Issues regarding the choice of vendor and Regional influence, falling away after Trust status. Failure of CMIS in the media forced the hospital to look beyond standard solution towards underdeveloped OC/CMIS market.
ORGANIZATIONAL CONTEXT	Non-RM initiatives including contracting. Centralised, fragmented structure and cultures, difficult to devolve. Traditional NHS culture, inert, alien to IT. Autonomous clinical culture. Clinicians into management. Isolated status of RM. Politics over clinical coding. Top management had some changes, resistance to devolvement, and lacked understanding of IT.	Central to devolved organization. Progressive, fragmented subcultures, two sites. Improved management-clinician relations. Issues of IT vs. patient care, clinical vs. financial use, data confidentiality. Lacked IT awareness/skills, culturally inert. Integrated project via clinical RMI manager. Top management. support new structure and IT. Other NHS initiatives and priorities.	Devolved, fragmented structure on two sites. Political friction between subcultures, e.g. RM/CS, coding clerks/medical secretaries, and clinicians/managers. Lacked awareness of IT value: traditional culture, inert and devoid of IT. Positive, enlightened management appreciated IT in new structure. Issue of clinical priority of CMIS via clinicians.	Other changes, inc. quality initiatives, directorates, and DHA split into two Trusts. New senior management, opposed to devolvement, forced RMI re-evaluation. Traditional cultural and structural divisions, inertia, and general lack of IT awareness. RM in difficult political situation between supportive clinicians and unsupportive top management.
RMI & IS CONTEXT	Limited existing IT. PAS data mistrusted. Formal RM structure, some individuals from outside NHS, inexperienced in IT. First manager had finance role, left/replaced. No IS/IT strategy. Funds tight - required extra resources for completion.	Few areas of IT. No IS/IT strategy. Structured project. Respected RMI manager, a clinician, facilitator and communicator. Technically able team which 'gelled'. Delays diminished resources.	Little IT and strategy. Project structured, headed by a respected nurse, organizational rather than IT oriented. Experienced, able team, worked together. Resources restrained by delay, and required extension for completion.	Limited existing IT. Defined structure with strong, ambitious but insensitive manager and cohesive, competent RM team. Clear path and IT strategy mapped during re-evaluation. Uncertainty about long-term funds.
CONDITIONS FOR	Central evaluation and objectives. Benefits realisation. Direction af-	Central justification. Localised objectives and procurement, user sen-	Evaluation of CMIS centrally. Tailored objectives to meet needs,	Re-evaluation for a locally-specific solution. Resultant objectives

MENTING CASE MIX	ment inexperience, poor OR/MOS, limited user involvement. Underdeveloped CMIS market. Vendors oversold systems.	contracting. Strong documentation and negotiation. Vendors professional, aimed for mutual benefit.	thy procurement, tightly controlled and documented, influenced by political relationships.	Procurement influenced by existing vendor relationships and appeared to be cost-effective, although system not fully developed.
IMPLE-MENTING CASE MIX	Good initial hospital communication, later limited to within project structure. No user groups. System not user-friendly, underdeveloped, problems with feeders. Limited user involvement. Inadequate training resource. Informal project management/control. Weak vendor management, poor vendor support. Debate - ICD vs. Read	Organization-wide communication. Discussion with other hospitals. Tight contract. Slow to develop clinical card, feeder interfacing difficult. Selective user involvement. Limited training and priority. Formal project man-agement/con-trol vendor mgt. Vendor supportive. Single ICD coding and HRGs.	Communication limited to key stake-holders. Project management "loose". Binding contract. Network, interfacing and software issues. User involvement conservative. Sufficient quality of training, and much still outstanding. Problematic vendor support and flexibility. Coding problems - political and practical.	Limited communication outside of RM. Poor contract: difficult to control supplier, slow to develop CMIS and give support. High clinical involvement and training for pilot clinicians in OC. Poor senior management control. Difficult to formalise project management. Clinical coding remained central in ICD.
ACTIONS AND REACTIONS TO IMPLE-MENTATION AND USE	Positive, committed, motivated team, some friction. Morale fell with progress. Dual role for RMI manager in finance, not accountable, high commitment/motivation fell with delays. Manager left/replaced. top mgt. apathetic, no ownership. Clinical users sceptical, inert, apathetic. Business users more supportive. Difficulties with medical secretaries' clinical coding. 'Cut and run' vendor	Positive, committed team and manager with common goals. Morale fell with poor progress. Ownership and accountability from RMI manager. Users positive and responsive to clinical RM manager. Top management interest, commitment, support. Vendor aimed for mutual benefit.	Team committed and enthusiastic. Manager motivated, influential, technically limited. Clinical user ownership, support, diminishing with poor progress. Other users less supportive. Secretaries' difficulties with Read. Top management interested, supportive. Vendors GHI committed and supportive, but not JKL.	RM team and manager motivated and committed, strong leadership. Morale affected by politics and uncertainty about project. Clinicians supportive and committed to 'their' system. Other users felt distanced or sceptical. Top management unsupportive. Vendors slow, lacked commitment and resources.
OUTCOMES	Exceeded budget and time-scale, required extra funds. Objectives not fulfilled. Incomplete system and information. Financial benefits. Lack of clinical benefits. Introduced IT infrastructure, strategy, facilitated cultural/structural change, IT awareness.	Ran over time and budget. Long-term benefits required. Financial and planning benefits. No clinical card/audit. IT infrastructure, feeders interfaced. Catalyst for change, IT awareness. Experience to help other hospitals.	IT awareness and infrastructure. Project delays. Require funds to complete. System/ information incomplete, but some clinical pilot use. Few benefits and objectives met, but some potential.	Delayed. Required resources for completion. System incomplete. Operational OC benefit. Infrastructural and cultural benefits. Overall, both clinical and financial benefits, & the main objectives, were not met.

Notes/Key: Region = Regional Health Authority (RHA), one of 14 regional administrative zones; DHA = District Health Authority, a subdivision of each RHA; Trust = semiautonomous hospitals which manage their own budgets; OR = operational requirements; MOS = memorandum of specifications; CS = computer services department; Read = an alternative coding standard to the International classification of diseases (ICD); HRG = health-related grouping, a clustering of ICD codes.

Sauer's Framework

A useful framework for analysing organizational interactions surrounding IS implementation and its resultant outcomes is that deriving from Sauer's case analysis of IS failure (Sauer, 1993). He refers to the complex intertwining of relationships in the context of IS as a *web model* of explanation (see Figure 2), pointing out that web explanations are necessarily complex and do not offer simple linear explanations of phenomena.

Sauer's focus for the model he develops is on exchange relations. He suggests that there are three components which play a part in IS development (ISD), which he portrays as an innovation process: the project's organization, the IS itself and the supporters of the IS. These elements are linked together in a triangle of dependencies, as given in Figure 2. The information system depends on the project organization, requiring the efforts and expertise of the project organization to sustain it. The project organization in turn depends on its supporters, support coming in the form of material resources to help cope with contingencies. Finally, the supporters depend on the information system. Thus, we have a cyclical pattern of dependencies.

Figure 2: The dependencies model of IS failure (after Sauer, 1993)

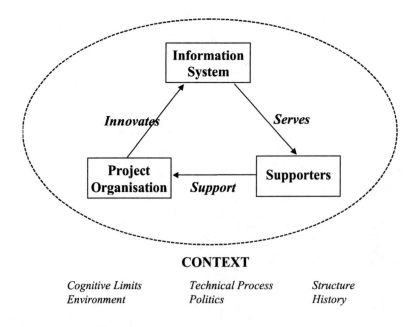

CONTEXT

| *Cognitive Limits* | *Technical Process* | *Structure* |
| *Environment* | *Politics* | *History* |

However, this is by no means a closed system. Contextual factors can control the ways in which each of the dependencies are instigated. Sauer suggests that context is made up of six dimensions:
- cognitive limits, such as the limits of communication;
- technical process constraints, arising from the nature of the IS (e.g., developing and fixing an abstract specification for organizational processes), or the development process (e.g., the constraints of the ISD methodology);
- environment, referring to the constraints and contingencies instigated by customers, suppliers, competitors and so on;
- politics, the exercise of power in the organization;
- structure, particularly internal project structure; and
- history, that is antecedents in the form of prior constraints and contingencies (e.g., those set up by previous information systems projects).

Sauer suggests that IS is the product of a process which is, by nature, open to flaws. By a flaw, we mean that stakeholders perceive that they are confronted with undesired situations, posing problems to be solved. In fact, every IS is likely to be flawed in some way. However, flaws do not necessitate failure: flaws may be corrected within an innovation process at a cost, or accepted at a cost. Examples of such flaws are organizational changes, and technical issues about hardware and software.

The idea of a flawed IS is one of the key ways that Sauer distinguishes his conception of termination failure to that of Lyytinen and Hirschheim's expectation failure (Lyytinen & Hirschheim, 1987). Expectation failure is defined as the inability of an IS to meet a specific stakeholder group's expectations: there is a gap between some existing and desired situation for members of such a group. Stakeholders are defined as any group of people who hold a set of values that define what desired IS features are, and how one should go about implementing them. Termination failure occurs only when development or operation of an IS actually ceases, leaving a vacuum where stakeholders are dissatisfied with the extent to which the system has served their interests. In this latter definition then, a system cannot therefore be considered a failure until all interest in progressing an IS project has ceased.

Beynon-Davies (1995b), building upon the work of Land (1976), makes some changes to Sauer's framework. Beynon-Davies points out the ambiguous and misleading nature of the term supporter as used in Sauer's framework, suggesting that not all interest groups with a stake in an IS may necessarily support it. Indeed, Beynon-Davies points out examples where stakeholder groups may have a negative interest in the success of a project. Thus, the term supporter is substituted by the term stakeholder.

The Implementation Cube

Sauer's model has some parallels to the grounded theory drawn from the case studies. In particular, the cases emulate the importance and interrelationships of the IS, the project and stakeholders, all within a specific context.

However, in order to provide a more useful framework by which to generalise and provide explanation of CMIS implementation, consider a number of developments to the model. Firstly, we break up the model into its separate components: IS, project organization and stakeholders. Next, we reassemble the elements into a quite different, but familiar mode, whereby each of the components provides an axis in a three-dimensional cube (Figure 3). In doing so, we establish some differences in the reconfiguration of axes. Thus, the axes become three important influences on the implementation of CMIS: IS localisation, project integration and stakeholder support. A final element, context, is not shown, but, like in Sauer's model, provides an overarching influence on implementation.

In order to establish the importance of the new framework, let us consider its design. In doing so, we demonstrate how it fits the frame of our results. First, the x-axis, IS localisation, refers to CMIS, the extent to which it fits and serves the organization, and whether the central solution has been tailored to local needs. As such, this is subtly different to Sauer's original model (where

Figure 3: The Implementation Cube

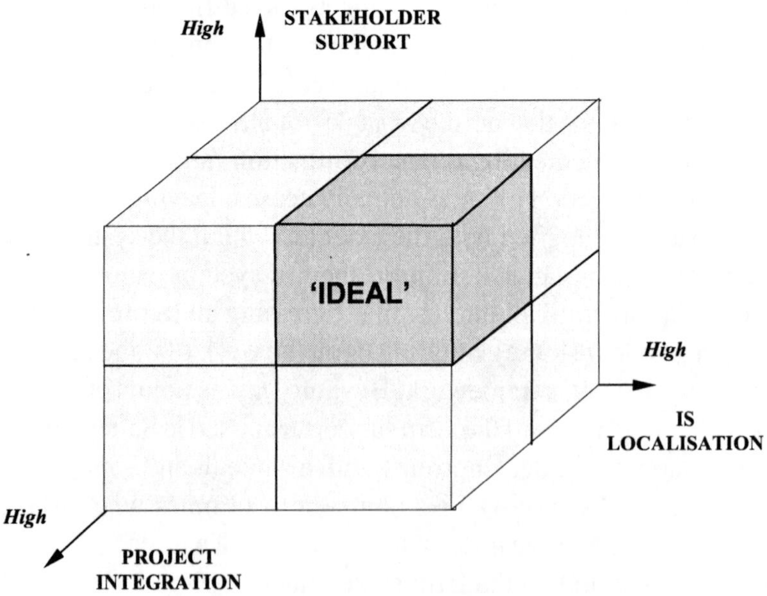

Sauer concentrates on IS features rather than evaluation or objectives), pivoting on the finding that *local* evaluation is an important influence on projects. Prior research has underlined the importance of evaluation in successful implementation, here we suggest that local evaluation is important in terms of, for example, ownership. This axis approximates to the category Conditions for Implementing Case Mix, as given by the grounded theory. The y-axis refers to the project organization, and the extent to which efforts are directed to integrate the IS into the hospital, e.g., technical integration, communication, user involvement, training and so on. This relates largely to the Implementing Case Mix category in the grounded theory. Finally, the z-axis is associated with the Actions and Reactions to Implementation and Use of Stakeholders, particularly as they exercise their support or otherwise of the IS project. Important stakeholder groups were users (particularly clinical and managerial), top management, the RMI manager, the RMI team and vendors. As in the Sauer framework, these processes operate within the organizational environment. These are indicated by the grounded theory in terms of External Context, Organizational Context and RMI & IS Context.

The 'ideal' box, refers to a situation where a system has been planned and designed to fit the requirements of the organization, with clear and pertinent objectives. This is important for large-scale, cross-functional systems like CMIS (although for projects that differ from CMIS, other boxes may provide suitable alternatives, e.g., small, highly structured projects may not need significant user involvement – see McFarlan, 1981). In the 'ideal' box the IS has also been absorbed into the organization by way of strong project management, including attention to planning, vendor management, sensitive clinical coding solutions, technical integration and interfacing, control, communication, consultation and involvement of stakeholders, and education and training. As a result, stakeholders are supportive of the resultant system, and the system should be used productively as intended.

However, this utopian situation is difficult to achieve, at least in its entirety (the furthest most point from the origin in the ideal box). One or more flaws are likely to push a system from the origin to an adjacent box, and it may move several times before a project reaches an equilibrium (by project we refer to a phase of development such as a CMIS).

To illustrate the relevance of the framework, consider comments made by the RMI manager at Alpha Hospital in the last phase of the research, describing the environment for IS implementation:

> ...we are in an impossible situation. The [central] Case Mix idea is
> not a good one for Alpha. It doesn't meet the call of the medics, who
> fancy that it is a financial toy...this is made all the worse by the

increasing importance of contracting and the changes that this has had on things. Medics find it hard to get enthusiastic about Case Mix, since it doesn't yet do anything that they want...it is restricted to the business side.

I suppose the way that we have gone about things could be better...maybe medics could have been more involved in the process of defining the project. Teaching them about computers was not easy...older medics were simply not interested...it was difficult to get the time to teach them individually.

...those at the top don't want Case Mix and do not give the control and support we need. The system [as part of RMI] poses a threat to their control by the reins. Medics think Case Mix is a tool of management and sit on the other side. We sit somewhere in the middle.

The implications of such discourse surfaces clearly through the framework. Thus, using the Implementation Cube, we should be able to analyse the hospitals' experiences with Case Mix.

Analysing the Cases with the Implementation Cube

All of the hospitals studied had quite distinctive experiences with the implementation of the Case Mix strategic IS. In this section, we analyse and explore these experiences, drawing on pertinent aspects of the Implementation Cube to provide explanations and conclusions. Note that the names of the hospitals have been changed to provide confidentiality.

Alpha Hospital

Alpha Case Mix is perhaps the least successful of all hospitals studied. In this sense, it is perhaps a good case to begin with: Alpha demonstrates that there are a number of causes that may combine to restrict progress. At a fundamental level, the strategic IS project did not come from within the hospital and fit localised IS needs: the objectives and finance were delivered centrally, and were affected by the shifting priorities of the NHS. A more solid, localised justification and set of objectives would have been more likely to withstand the tides of organizational change.

The issue of aims created problems for stakeholder support, as many had difficulties coming to terms with the value and relevance of Case Mix. Neither was the issue helped by the poor integration of the Case Mix project within the hospital environment. The project lacked resources: although it seemed like a lot of money to stakeholders at the time, the relative IT content was high. The vendor, ABC, knew little about the problem and oversold an expensive, poorly developed and ill-supported system, which did not really provide a full and viable solution. Furthermore, the integration strategy lacked project management experience and rigour, the involvement of and communication to all stakeholders, and education and training were curtailed. Numerous technical and operational difficulties were also an obstacle to technical integration and use. The future clinical use of the strategic IS was uncertain, dependent upon whether technical and operational difficulties (coding, data issues) could be overcome. However, financial and business aspects were useful, and it was likely that such areas would be rolled out before those of clinicians.

Overall for the Alpha case, there were shortfalls in each of the implementation axes, and it struggled to provide a locally relevant solution and implement the strategic IS in a situationally sensitive manner without marginalizing key players. The hospital found it difficult to break out of the origin box. However, obviously some inroads were made in providing a solution, particularly in finance and planning. Hence, we place the hospital near the adjoining *low localisation, high integration, low support* box.

The other three hospitals found themselves in a variety of different positions. All of them attempted to provide locally relevant solutions, largely by increasing the clinical components of CMIS. Thus, in attempting to place them, we confine ourselves to the rightmost four boxes of Figure 3, which include the 'ideal' box. Let us consider each of them in turn.

Beta Hospital

Beta appears a more successful case than that of Alpha. The hospital attempted to create a system that met local objectives and requirements, assisting in organizational integration and in gaining support. Furthermore, the choice of a respected and able clinician as project manager was an extremely effective measure in gaining stakeholder (user, top management, team) support, and in providing a catalyst for CMIS integration within the hospital. Project and vendor management was efficient and formalised, and communication channels were clearly established. Where problems occurred these were largely via the centrally imposed organizational changes (which caused some confusion in the direction of the project), in technical integration and development (e.g., interfacing, and the inclusion of a clinical card) and through the lack of resources for training. Support and integrative activity began to fall with poor progress during the last phase of the research. Notwithstanding, Beta had the feel of a potentially successful case. Much of the ground had been laid for the future success of the system. Business and clinical use was growing, and with the development of additional clinical features and further training, the system would be likely to flourish.

Overall, Beta took an involved and clinically oriented approach, headed by a respected senior pharmacist. The work in achieving integration via user involvement and communication, and the positive responses of stakeholders pushes it just into a low position on the *'ideal'* quadrant. Clearly much work was still required in completing CMIS to further this position.

Gamma Hospital

The Gamma project appeared to approach many aspects in a positive manner. The project aimed to adjust objectives to the new hospital environment, and get clinical users involved in defining the project and breaking the standard CMIS binds, thereby presenting a locally relevant solution. Unfortunately, this period of procurement was so prolonged that it had serious implications on the availability of time and resources for the remaining tasks.

Embarking upon integrative activities, RM personnel were positive and communicative, and stakeholder perceptions were positively influenced by the respect and influence commanded by the project manager. Training for pilots was of a sufficient quality. However, the project was affected by technical development and integration difficulties, partly due to difficulties with vendors, and problems regarding the implementation of Read codes. In a sense, Gamma fell into the trap that it had most tried to avoid, that of an underdeveloped and unfit system. User involvement was also selective, and whilst there was support from clinicians and some senior management, this was less so with more distant stakeholders. Cultural barriers to IT were apparent, although being eroded, and structural and sub-cultural fragmentation caused political friction between some key stakeholder groups (i.e., Resource Management/Computer Services, coding clerks/medical secretaries and clinicians/managers). In the last phase of the research, the system was limited to clinical pilot use, but given funds and time, many potential benefits could be unleashed: there was a core of support which would be valuable to the project.

Gamma took a more conservative approach to integration, led by a respected senior nurse and focusing on a few key stakeholders. The responses of clinicians were positive for 'their' system, but this was less so for other users. Poor progress was likely to diminish support, much work was still outstanding in completing and integrating the system. The hospital can be placed in the *high support-low integration* box.

Delta Hospital

Delta attempted to provide a locally relevant system and objectives, tailored specifically to clinicians. Alongside, there was a high level of clinical involvement. Combined, these had a powerful effect on clinical support and ownership. However, support was not widespread. Senior management were opposed to the machinations of devolution, but forced into submission by the changing structure and politics at Delta. Similarly, business and finance users were more distanced and sceptical of CMIS.

In terms of integration, Delta had the benefit of strong project management from the manager, team, IS strategy and project plan, although vendor management and contractual arrangements were not strong. Integration suffered as a result of the externally imposed changes on the hospital environment, including the Trust split and the unpredicted slow system development. Thus, although progress had been made in Order Communications, other areas were less successful: the system needed more time and money to continue, whilst support began to fall with poor progress. Notwithstanding, the clinical focus of the project held significant promise for the potential success and benefits of the system in the future.

Overall, the Delta project was led from the front by clinicians who were highly involved and supportive, although at the expense of other users. Senior management were opposed to the project, "a tool of devolution," and the system sat uncomfortably between this group and clinicians. Progress was slow, and a great deal of work was required to complete CMIS and train users (although Order Communications was working successfully). Within Figure 3, like Gamma, Delta should be placed just inside the *high support-low integration* box, but fairly close to the high integration border.

In summary, we have seen that the Implementation Cube classification can be used, either ex ante or ex post, to explain, envision or appraise the organizational changes allied to Case Mix. For example, a centrally driven Case Mix development is likely to ill-fit a hospital, engendering poor support and difficulties in integration. Such integration requires acute attention to project management if it is to be successful, with education, communication and stakeholder involvement being particularly important. On the other hand, a hospital that pays attention to gaining support and providing for the local community is likely to integrate more easily and provide productive solutions. The next section considers these and other issues, exploring the implications of the framework.

IMPLICATIONS OF THE IMPLEMENTATION CUBE

The implications of the aforementioned framework may be divided into two areas: theoretical and practical.

Theoretical Implications

At a theoretical level, empirical validation and elaboration of concepts and the framework in additional environments is certainly required. The theoretical framework was produced by examination of four cases, albeit in depth. Further empirical grounding and comparisons will hone and enrich the concepts and framework generated here, and render a more involved understanding of the phenomenon. Three initial strategies for future research are suggested.

Firstly, it is necessary to investigate different contexts where Case Mix has been introduced. The four hospitals studied here had a number of common contextual characteristics, such as size, clinical specialisms and the area of study (i.e., Manchester in the UK). Similarity was also shared to some degree in hospital structure and NHS culture, although there were some differences. They still only represent a few organizational types. More organizations need to be examined to ascertain whether the proposed concepts and framework are relevant in other situations. In this way, the analytic generalisation posited here, that other hospitals' experiences with Case Mix will resemble the patterns detailed above, will be tested and elaborated.

Furthermore, in terms of wider generalisation, research into similar organizational IS developments in the health sector (e.g., hospital information systems or HIS) will give an indication of the broader applicability of the research. This is an important alternative to further CMIS research, particularly in consideration of the fact that, at the time of writing, very few CMIS projects were beginning. Thus, the opportunities for further longitudinal CMIS research are limited.

Second, some of the dimensions in the Implementation Cube may need to be elaborated or refined. While a tripartite categorisation was adequate for this study, it is possible that future empirical work will require extending the dimensions, or providing a different configuration. For example, we may consider incorporating a greater variety of concepts, or making more explicit use of context (e.g., Orlikowski, 1993).

Third, we note that the implementation cube results are limited to three boxes. In order to broaden our knowledge and understanding, other positions on the implementation cube should also be studied to find out the organizational consequences of such combinations. Empirical research into such experiences will help to establish the particular content, context and process associated with these alternatives.

Practical Implications

Moving on from theoretical issues, it is useful to consider whether the research has ramifications for IS implementation practice. In particular, we draw attention to three areas:

- *Understanding IS implementation.* The framework provides a useful resource for enhancing the understanding of a complex and dynamic situation.
- *A blueprint for planning.* The framework draws attention to a number of important areas of concern for IS implementation planning. Failure to address these can lead to later problems.
- *A tool for diagnosis.* The framework could be used to trace problems and pinpoint areas of deficiency in IS implementation.

The theoretical framework generated matches the qualifications of practical applicability posited by Glaser and Strauss (1967). First, it fits a substantive area of study. The concepts and relations posited as central are intimately related to (because they are derived from) the arena of Case Mix implementation. Second, the resultant theoretical framework is sufficiently general to be applicable to a range of situations around the implementation of Case Mix and other similar IS applications. Third, it is readily understandable by practitioners, and should accordingly serve as a useful direction in the change management designs of hospitals introducing Case Mix. By providing practitioners with some insight into the context, structure and process of CMIS implementations, the framework serves as a basis from which the IS practitioner can appraise and manage what is characteristically a poorly understood, complex and dynamic situation.

The framework developed and presented here has important implications for IS practitioners. It suggests that before the implementation of CMIS, or a similar technology, the project manager should pay explicit attention to: providing a system which fits *local* aims and objectives, ultimately with the involvement of stakeholders; clearly articulating such objectives and gaining the support of further stakeholders, particularly users; and assessing the full context of IS implementation. These items will significantly influence the change process and resultant organizational consequences. Having examined and articulated these issues, key players can more effectively plan the implementation of Case Mix, and facilitate the action required to enact the intended changes. Moreover, a clearly defined and supported project is more likely to "weather the storm" of the kind of externally imposed organizational changes experienced in the hospitals.

Managing integrative activity properly is a critical issue in achieving a fully implemented and supported IS, and will mediate its success and benefits. Here we need to consider social integration via education, training, communication and involvement, as well as other formal project management activity, such as procurement, planning, vendor management and technical integration and development, particularly in terms of clinical coding and IT standards (e.g., platforms, networks and so on). The ensuing process will further shape reactions, appropriations and consequences of the system. All of this occurs within context.

Critically then, in managing such projects, the implementers need to consider IS localisation, project integration and stakeholder support *together* and within *context*: the implementation cube provides a blueprint for planning the implementation of an IS. Inadequacy in any of these areas is likely to mean a loss of benefits or success of some kind, whether, for example, it is an inappropriate project or system, a poorly managed project which runs over time or budget or a loss of support and an unused system.

In addition to planning, the framework can easily be used as a means of assessment or diagnosis for implementation. If CMIS is unsuccessful, we can trace the antecedents of such problems using the framework, and come to some conclusions about the influences on such outcomes. On a more pragmatic level, reference against the framework during implementation can pinpoint areas of deficiency that may require attention in order to avoid significant shortcomings.

While these findings have been generated by only four organizational sites and require further investigation, they do have considerable face validity, and a number of documented instances of CMIS implementation have hinted at one or other such influence (e.g., Brown, 1995; Hackney and McBride, 1993).

SUMMARY AND CONCLUSIONS

This chapter has argued that the implementation of strategic IS within hospitals is a complex phenomenon, and that much can be gained by researching and managing it accordingly. The research has been useful in generating a set of insights, concepts and processes that address the critical organizational elements involved in implementing and using Case Mix. Generally, such elements have been largely overlooked in the IS literature, and have certainly not been examined in detail for RMI CMIS. The theoretical framework generated from the empirical findings suggests that the content of implementation, the change process, as well as the social context, critically influence what changes are associated with Case Mix. The framework also provides valuable insights for practitioners, detailing the important facets of organizational implementation that are associated with CMIS and how these might be assessed and managed. Thinking more broadly, such issues have considerable implications for achieving other strategic objectives for IS in healthcare, such as networking and standardization, both of which are explored in detail in later chapters.

REFERENCES

Anonymous (1993). MPs throw book at health chiefs over Wessex fiasco. *Computing*, vol. 13, 7.

Audit Commission. (1995) *For Your Information: A Study of Information Management and Systems in the Acute Hospital.* London: HMSO.

Beynon-Davies, P. (1995) Information Systems 'Failure': The Case of the London Ambulance Service's Computer-Aided Dispatch Project. *European Journal of Information Systems,* Vol. 4, pp. 171-184.

Beynon-Davies, P. (1995) "Information systems 'failure' and risk assessment: The case of the london ambulance service computer-aided dispatch system. *Proceedings of the Third European Conference on Information Systems*, Athens, June, pp. 1153-1170.

Black, N.A. and Moore, L. (1994). Comparative Audit Between Hospitals: The Example of Appendectomy. *International Journal of Health Care Quality Assurance.* 7(3), 11-15.

Brown, A. D. (1992) "Managing Change in the NHS: The Resource Management Initiative", *Leadership and Organizational Development Journal*, Vol.13, No. 6, pp. 13-17.

Brown, A.D. *(1995) Organizational Culture*, Pitman, London.

Collins, L. W. (1994) "CIOs Must Look Beyond the IS Horizon", *Computers in Healthcare*, Vol. 12, No. 5, pp. 39-40.

Cooper, R. B. and Zmud, R. W. (1990) "Information Technology Implementation Research: A Technological Diffusion Approach", *Management Science*, Vol. 36, No. 2, pp. 123-139.

Cross, M. (1992) "Computing the Cost of Health Care", *New Scientist*, Vol. 130, pp. 22-23.

DHSS (Department of Health and Social Security), *Health Services Management: Resource Management (Management Budgeting) in Health Authorities.* Health Notice (86) 34, HMSO, London, 1986.

Eisenhardt, K. M. (1989) "Building Theories from Case Study Research", *Academy of Management Review*, Vol. 14, No. 4, pp. 532-550.

Glaser, B.G. and Strauss, A..L. (1967) *The Discovery of Grounded Theory*, Aldine, Chicago.

Hackney, R. and McBride, N. (1993) "Interpreting Information Systems Strategy in the Public Sector", *Proceedings of the Third Annual National BIT Conference*, Manchester Metropolitan University, Manchester, May, 1993.

Health Economics Research Group. *(1991) Final Report of the Brunel University Evaluation of Resource Management*, Brunel University, Uxbridge.

HMSO (Her Majesty's Stationery Office), *(1993) Wessex Regional Health Authority Regional Information Systems Plan*, 63rd Report of the Committee of Public Accounts, HMSO, London.

Hockstrasser, B. and Griffiths, C. (1991) *Controlling IT Investments: Strategy and Management*, Chapman and Hall, London.

Holmes, A. and Poulymenakou, A. (1995) "Towards a Conceptual Framework for Investigating Information Systems Failure", *Proceedings of the Third European Conference on Information Systems*, Athens, June, pp. 805-823.

Jones, B. and Worsdale, G. (1993) "Can IT Help in Working for Patients?", *Health Services Management*, Vol. 89, No. 2, pp. 3-16.

Keen, P. G. W. (1981) "Information Systems and Organizational Change", *Communications of the ACM*, Vol. 26, No. 6, pp. 24-33.

King, W. R. and Grover, V. (1991) "The Strategic Use of Information Resources: An Exploratory Study", *IEEE Transactions on Engineering Management*, Vol. 38, pp. 293-305.

Kramer, A. K. and Ellertson, R. J. (1993) "Using PCs for Effective Case-Mix Based Budgeting", *Healthcare Financial Management*, Vol. 47, No. 6, pp. 52-58.

Land, F. (1976) "Evaluation of Systems Goals in Determining a Design Strategy for a Computer-Based Information System", *The Computer Journal*, Vol. 19, No. 4, pp. 290-294.

Lock, C. (1996) "What Value do Computers Provide to NHS Hospitals?", *British Medical Journal*, Vol. 312, pp. 1407-1410.

Lock, C. (1996) "The Assessment of IT in Healthcare and the Relevance of the Private Finance Initiative", *Proceedings of the Third European*

Conference on the Evaluation of Information Technology, Bath, November, pp. 63-72.

Lyytinen, K. (1987) A taxonomic perspective of information systems development: Theoretical constructs and recommendations. in Boland, R.J. and Hirschheim, R.A. (Eds.), *Critical Issues in Information Systems Research*. Chichester: Wiley, pp. 3-42.

Lyytinen, K. and Hirschheim, R.A. (1987) "Information Systems Failures, A Survey and Classification of the Empirical Literature", *Oxford Surveys in Information Technology*, Vol. 4, pp. 257-309.

McFarlan, F. W. (1981) "Portfolio Approach to Information Systems", *Harvard Business Review*, Vol. 59, No.5, pp. 142-150.

Naude, P., Proudlove, N. and Bellingham, R. (1994) "Group Decision Support for IT Procurement", *OR Insight*, Vol. 7, No. 3, pp. 6-11.

Orlikowski, W. J. (1993) "CASE Tools as Organizational Change: Investigating Incremental and Radical Changes in Systems Development", *MIS Quarterly*, Vol. 17, No. 3, pp. 309-340.

Oz, E. (1994) "When Professional Standards are Lax: The CONFIRM Failure and Its Lessons", *Communications of the ACM*, Vol. 37, No. 10.

Pettigrew, A. M. (1990) "Longitudinal Field Research on Change: Theory and Practice", *Organization Science*, Vol. 1, No. 3, pp. 267-292.

Pettigrew, A.M., Ferlie, E. and McKee L. (1994) *Shaping Strategic Change*, Sage, London.

Rea, D.M. (1994) "Better Informed Judgements: Resource Management in the NHS", *Accounting Auditing and Accountability Journal,* Vol. 7, No. 1, pp. 86-110.

Richards, B. (1986) "Computers in Clinical Medicine", *Data Processing*, Vol. 28, No. 10, pp. 543-546.

Roberts, H. J. and Barrar, P.R.N. (1992) "MRP II Implementation: Key Factors for Success", *Computer-Integrated Manufacturing Systems*, Vol. 5, pp. 31 -38.

Robinson, R. (1992) "Roll-call after Roll-out", *The Health Service Journal*, Vol. 102, pp. 18-19.

Sauer, C. (1993) *Why Information Systems Fail: A Case Study Approach*, Alfred Waller, London.

Schultz,R.L., Slevin, D.P. and Pinto, J.K. (1987) "Strategy and Tactics in a Process Model of Project Implementation", *Interfaces*, Vol. 17, pp. 34-46.

Strauss, A. and Corbin, J. (1990) *Basics of Qualitative Research: Grounded Theory Procedures and Techniques*, Sage, London.

Swanson, E.B. (1993) *Information Systems Implementation*, Irwin, Homewood, 1988.

Tate, P. Hunter, P., McPartlin, J.P., and Duffy, M. "London's Embarrassing Mistake", *Wall Street and Technology*, May.

Willcocks, L. and Lester, S. (1993) *Evaluating the Feasibility of Information Technology*, Research and Discussion Paper RDP93/1, Oxford Institute of Information Management, Oxford.

Yin, R. (1984) *Case Study Research*, Sage, Beverly Hills.

Yin, R. (1994) *Case Study Research: Design and Methods*, Sage, London.

Chapter 3

Technology-Based Marketing in the Healthcare Industry: Implications for Relationships Between Players in the Industry

Grace Johnson, Anand Kumar, Arkalgud Ramaprasad
and Madhusudhan Reddy
Southern Illinois University at Carbondale

The past few years have seen Web-based technology diffusing into a wide cross-section of industries, cutting across various barriers, and changing the way many companies do business. The healthcare industry, though relatively slow to adopt information technology (Eder and Darter, 1998), is no exception. Information technology is transforming the healthcare environment in ways that go beyond simple consumer health information Web sites (Hagland, 1997). Increasingly, the industry is leveraging information technology effectively to manage its business and address issues affecting patient care (Lankford, 1999).

At the heart of the healthcare industry lies the patient-physician relationship. The interaction between these two players usually occurs in a clinic/ hospital setting. It is generally believed that the relationship between the patient and the physician is influenced not only by this interaction, but also by other interactions that a patient may have *inside* a clinic/hospital setting, such as interactions with nurses, staff, the registration desk, etc. However, changes brought about by information technology (a) allow players outside the clinic/ hospital setting to influence the patient-physician relationship and (b) affect the way in which players and processes inside a clinic/hospital setting influence the patient-physician relationship. This chapter examines how Web

Previously Published in *Managing Healthcare Information Systems with Web-Enabled Technologies* edited by Lauren Eder, Copyright © 2000, Idea Group Publishing.

technology affects the patient-physician relationship through its impact on players and processes both *outside* and *inside* a clinic/hospital setting.

The healthcare industry is complex and comprises many relationships between different players in the industry, for example, physicians, patients, pharmaceutical firms, and insurance firms. These relationships are often developed as separate dyads that are independent of each other. This has led to the healthcare industry being described as diverse and disconnected (*Business Wire*, 1999). However, information technology is changing the industry by introducing technology applications that increase and strengthen *connectivity* between the different players in the industry. The increased on-line connectivity is influencing marketing practices within the industry, which in turn are affecting the dynamics of the relationships between the different players in the industry.

In this chapter, we focus on the impact of Web-based technology on marketing practices within the healthcare industry and its impact on the relationships between the major players in the industry. In particular, we focus on the relationship between the patient and his/her physician. The first part of the chapter examines the dynamics of this relationship in the context of exchanges and interactions that patients and physicians have with the pharmaceutical and insurance companies, i.e., players outside the clinic/hospital setting. We present a simple conceptual model that shows how relationships in the industry have evolved as a result of technologically driven marketing practices. In the second part of the chapter, we examine how Web technology affects the way in which players and processes inside the clinic/hospital setting influence the patient-physician relationship. Specifically, we explore how Web technology streamlines administration within a clinic/hospital, increases patient education about their illness, enhances communication between patients and physicians and leads to an overall improvement in the quality of patient care. We balance our discussion of the virtues of Web technology by briefly discussing thorny legal and public policy issues that have been raised by the use of this technology in the healthcare industry.

CONCEPTUAL MODEL DEPICTING INFORMATION FLOW

The traditional flow of information between three important players in the healthcare industry has been *sequential* as shown in Figure 1.

The exchange that typically takes place between the pharmaceutical company, physician, and the patient can be depicted as sets of *informational exchanges* or *transactions*. Pharmaceutical companies communicate directly

Figure 1: Model of Traditional Communication Flow between Primary Players in the Healthcare Industry.

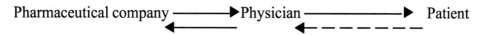

with physicians to promote their products to them while physicians interact with the company representatives to learn more about their products. The information flow is two-way: from the company to the physician, and from the physician to the company.

The physician and the patient also form a dyad where exchange of information takes place. Interestingly, in this dyad, it is very likely that the amount of relevant information that is exchanged between the two parties is asymmetric. This asymmetry arises from differences in motivation and knowledge structure between the two parties. The patient comes to the doctor because he/she needs information on his/her condition or ailment and describes his/ her symptoms. The physician combines this *external* information from the patient with an *internal* source of information, his/her prior knowledge and experience, to make a diagnosis. Once a diagnosis is made, a decision for the best possible treatment for the patient has to be made. The physician does not have the time or the motivation to engage in a detailed discussion of suitable alternatives with the patient. Instead, the physician decides which drug would be the most suitable for the patient and conveys only what he/she thinks is "relevant" information to the patient. The result of this decision process results in a prescription that the patient will use to obtain the specified product from the pharmacy.

It is interesting to note that the patient, the actual *consumer* of the product, who also pays for it, is more or less a recipient of the one-way flow of information (Mechanic, 1998) calls such a physician-patient relationship a *paternalistic* relationship). Patients usually do not and cannot participate in the communication process as equal partners as they have limited knowledge abou medicines and treatments. However, pharmaceutical firms, the sellers of the prescribed drugs, need to promote their products, but under the model shown in Figure 1, these firms did not directly interact with the end consumer, the patient. Instead, they relied completely on a *push* strategy to increase sales of their products. That is, they would try to convince physicians to prescribe their products and then hope that a large enough number of prescriptions would be generated by patients purchasing their prescribed drugs.

As depicted in Figure 1, there was no direct interaction between all three parties; the three parties performed as two separate sets of *dyads* or pairwise relationships (Hall, 1996). Also, as shown in Figure 1, flow of information from the patient to the physician was tentative and minimal. It was confined to a recounting of the signs or symptoms he/she was experiencing. The flow from the physician to the patient would account for the major portion of this interaction, because of the knowledge, expertise, experience, and perceived power imbalance between the two parties.

It would be quite natural to expect this perceived "power" imbalance because patients only visit a physician when they have a problem and insufficient information to solve it by themselves. ("Power" is defined as the capacity of one party to influence the behavior of another). The marketing and social psychology literature have identified various sources of power (Eyuboglu and Atac, 1991; French and Raven, 1959). According to this literature, the physician's medical expertise gives him/her *expert* power, which is based on medical knowledge. Another kind of power is *information* power (the physician has information that is relevant to the patient but the patient does not have that information). The different power bases in Figure 1 all favor the physician.

With the advent of the relatively new phenomenon known as direct-to-consumer advertising (DTCA) of prescription drugs, the flow of information changed quite dramatically, as shown in Figure 2.

Figure 2 shows a new link connecting the three parties; it shows an arrow from the pharmaceutical company to the patient, representing information flow between the two for the first time. This has had some impact on the physician-patient relationship; a solid line has replaced the dotted arrow of Figure 1. The reason for this is explained below.

DTCA came about partly due to relaxation in regulations relating to prescription drug advertising, and partly because of increasing competitive

Figure 2: Model of Current Communication Flows Between Selected Members of the Healthcare Industry

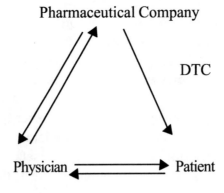

pressures within the pharmaceutical industry. As more and more brands and categories of drugs proliferated in the market, companies found it increasingly difficult to communicate messages about their products to the physician, the important influencer in the purchase. Since the 1980s, this factor, together with concern about losing market share particularly to generic drugs, led to a new direction of promotional activity, this time targeted at the consumer. Advances in information technology also made it possible for marketers to think in terms of targeted marketing where firms would send marketing communications directly to an individual through direct mail campaigns. Beginning in the Eighties, but much more prominently in the early Nineties, several companies began to utilize various forms of direct-to-consumer advertising. In 1983, the FDA imposed a moratorium on this strategy, and then lifted it in 1985 (Food and Drug Administration, 1985). In August 1997, the FDA further relaxed regulations governing DTC marketing of prescription drugs on television and radio by issuing exploratory guidelines that permitted marketers to run commercials naming the prescription product, the condition it is used to treat, and some side effects. This resulted in a virtual explosion of spending on such advertisements. Figures rose from $55 million in 1991 to $516 million in 1996 to over $1.3 billion in 1998, and are projected to reach $6 billion by 2005 (*Business Wire*, Nov 19, 1998).

The introduction of DTCA coincided with the explosion of information availability via electronic media such as the Internet. The hitherto passive patient became an active *consumer* of information. It is estimated that there are at least 10,000 World Wide Web sites devoted to healthcare, with information on everything from innumerable medical conditions, to individual advice, second opinions, support groups, and actual diagnoses ("Practicing Medicine on the Net," 1997). Consumers obtain information from these Web sites and initiate dialogues with their physicians on the basis of this newly obtained knowledge (Kaplan, 1998). DTCA prompts patients to initiate dialogues with their physicians, asking questions about specific brands of drugs. By adopting DTCA, pharmaceutical firms were explicitly incorporating a *pull* strategy in their marketing plans. Firms tried to push their products to the physicians so that physicians would prescribe these products *and at the same time*, tried to get patients to ask their physicians for these products, thus creating a demand (pull) for these products.

The net effect of patients getting additional information from various sources including direct-to-consumer advertising has been that many patients are now motivated to learn more about medical conditions and treatment options, and to consult their physicians more (Holmer, 1999). These patients may be called "empowered patients," as they are empowered with greater levels of information relevant to their situation. Such patients can and often will query the physician about the prescribed treatment and also about alternatives that may not have been mentioned by the physician initially. Figure 2 captures this change in the physician-patient relationship by having a solid line showing the exchange between the patient and the physician. Many physicians might perceive the empowered patient to be a threat to their authority. But, as has been pointed out by some commentators, the patient has been empowered with *information*, not prescribing authority (Holmer, 1999). The physician's information power base is weakened in the Figure 2 scenario compared to that in Figure 1. However, his/her expert power base remains the same, because the power to write prescriptions still rests with the physician. Once the dialogue has been started, the physician's role always takes precedence. With adequate cooperation from the physician, communication flows can be continuous, sustained, and enhancing to the relationship.

The separate *dyads* of Figure 1 have merged to some extent to form a single *triad*, but it must be noted that the information flow is not perfectly symmetric and balanced in the triad. A greater balance and symmetry of information exchange is seen in what we call the third phase of our conceptual model.

The third phase is (and will be) characterized by extensive diffusion and use of on-line technology in the healthcare industry. This phase is currently in its infancy. What is described here is our envisioning of the very near future. Web technology can enable hitherto disperse players in the industry to forge stronger communication links, enabling a high degree of *connectivity*. Instead of separate pairs of dyads or triads, we can increasingly observe the formation of *networks* of relationships characterized by increased levels of collaboration. The improved collaboration efforts are focused on the patient, now perceived as a *consumer* of healthcare.

Figure 3 shows our conceptualization of the communication flows between four key players in the health care industry enabled by on-line connectivity. Under the new model, the patient-physician relationship is an ongoing one supported by online communication such as e-mail whereas previously, the relationship was a series of discrete interactions. There is also a greater perceived equality in the exchange of information between physician and patient, enabled by continuous patient education with Web resources. Our model also suggests relationships between other players in the healthcare industry and thus allows us to explore the impact of technology on the healthcare industry as a whole.

Figure 3: Diamond Model of Technology-Enabled On-line Interconnectivity

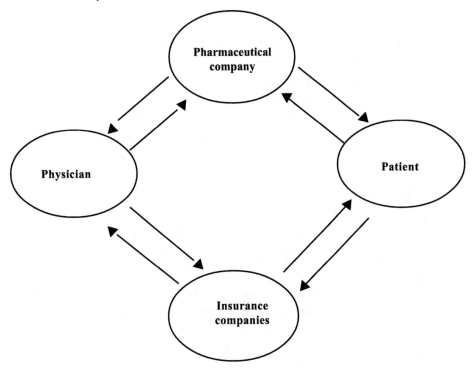

Insurance Companies and Connectivity

Insurance companies can be connected online to both patients and physicians. Insurance companies can be connected electronically to physicians' offices for rapid, efficient claims processing that could potentially cut down costs, time, and paperwork. Actual transfer of money can also be done electronically (*Star Tribune,* Oct. 1998). In addition to expediting payments, the claims process can be entirely transparent to the patient over the Web so that he/she can observe whether the company has processed a particular bill. Patients can correspond with the companies by e-mail, so that communications such as filing a complaint can be responded to very quickly.

Currently, most insurers have Web sites and use them for some or all of the following services: descriptions of the plans they offer, but not the prices for each plan; lists of doctors affiliated with their plan; and basic preventive health information, such as timetables of children's immunizations.

Spurred by the new connectivity, some insurance companies have progressed much more than others have. For example, Aetna has included a health encyclopedia that it has jointly developed with Johns Hopkins University (http://www.aetnaushc.com). Kaiser also offers an online encyclopedia at its members-only site (http://www.kponline.com). Other innovative services include:

- On-line health assessments that identify patients' biggest health risk and provide links to follow-up information;
- On-line advice from nurses and pharmacists, who will respond by e-mail within 24 hours;
- On-line discussion groups on topics ranging from HIV to parenting, some moderated by doctors.
- Appointment making online.

Kaiser officials envision a "virtual medical center" that will cater to a wide range of patient needs. All these developments show how technology can be used in the healthcare industry to improve the patient-insurance company relationship. Given the present debate in the United States over Patients' Bill of Rights, insurance companies should welcome the opportunity provided by technology to enhance their relationship with their clients, the patients.

The implications of technological advances for insurance companies are that they are going to be much more closely involved with their customers. In terms of business practices, this will mean that patients will come to expect a lot more information and many more services from them. As patients get more informed about various illnesses, they will have more questions for the insurance and pharmaceutical firms. To ensure that insurance companies provide accurate responses that are likely to satisfy their customers, they may have to be in closer contact with physicians and pharmaceutical firms, not just in terms of being connected electronically, but also in terms of exchange of information. For example, if information provided by an insurance company is contradicted by a patient's physician or a pharmaceutical firm, it is likely to erode the credibility of the insurance firm.

The Diamond model in Figure 3 also suggests implications for marketers in the healthcare industry that are a result of the patient-insurance company-physician-pharmaceutical company relationships. We illustrate the marketing implications of the aforementioned relationships by considering the following scenario. A patient may see an advertisement for a particular drug on the television or in a magazine. While this may prompt the patient to ask his/her physician about this drug (which is the goal of current DTC advertising by pharmaceutical firms), it may also prompt the patient to ask his/her insurance company whether that particular drug was covered by their policy. Many patients will not want to ask their physician about a drug that is not covered by their policy. These patients will first contact their insurance company and if they find that the drug is covered by their policy, then they are likely to ask their physician about this drug. If the advertised drug is cheaper than the drug presently being prescribed by the physician, the insurance companies are likely to put some pressure on the physician to change his/her prescribing habits. Any such action on the part of an insurance provider represents a threat for a pharmaceutical firm whose drug is presently being prescribed and an opportunity for another firm whose drug is not being prescribed. The physician may also be forced to seek more information from a pharmaceutical firm about a drug, especially if he/she has limited knowledge about it. Though the above scenario was based on the patient – insurance company – physician – pharmaceutical firm relationship, it serves as an illustration of how any relationship shown in the Diamond model in Figure 3 can either directly or indirectly influence marketing practices in the healthcare industry.

Pharmaceutical Firms and Connectivity

Pharmaceutical companies can continue to communicate with consumers directly through advertisements (and also through on-line communications using e-mail and relevant discussion groups). However, instead of the burden of responding to patients' queries being placed fully on physicians, companies can support queries interactively through their Web sites. Doctors and other qualified company personnel can be available online to help assess individuals' suitability for the advertised drugs. Patients can also have access to all the research related to the drugs through links. In order not to alienate physicians in this process, the companies can be available online to talk to doctors also. They can respond to their questions and requests for samples, and can support physicians with updates on the latest research findings and progression of clinical trials.

In fact, in many instances, pharmaceutical firms may find that the increased levels of connectivity can enable them to offset and complement their sales representatives' efforts at detailing the physician. For example, a physician may not give much time to the sales representative of a pharmaceutical firm selling drug A. The physician may regularly be prescribing drug B and ignoring the efforts of the drug A salesperson. However, inquiries from the patient and/or the insurance company may lead the physician to seek information about the drug. At this point, the pharmaceutical company gets an opportunity to persuade the physician about the merits of its drug and can possibly persuade the physician to give its sales representative a few minutes of his/her time. Thus, increased connectivity can be a useful tool for pharmaceutical firms if it is used in a strategic manner to complement their existing marketing practices.

The greatest help that pharmaceutical companies can offer patients and physicians through the enhanced connectivity brought about by technology is in the area of *patient compliance*. Poor patient compliance is one of the biggest problems encountered by physicians, as it directly affects the successful outcomes of the prescribed treatment. Pharmaceutical companies can directly tackle this problem through on-line connectivity and database technology. They can do this by establishing connections with patients and supporting them through the duration of the therapy, something that physicians just do not have the time or resources to do. For example, AllerDays is a new comprehensive wellness program for patients on Hoechst Marion Roussel's Allegra. It is operated by McKesson Corporation through its database-driven Patient Care Enhancing Program. The program enables manufacturers such as Hoechst, in cooperation with retail pharmacies, to enhance patient understanding of their conditions and adhere to their prescribed drug regimen. The program has seen excellent response and significantly increased compliance rates (*Business Wire,* Sept. 1998). It can easily be envisioned how these compliance rates can be further enhanced with on-line support.

IMPLICATIONS FOR DYADIC AND NETWORK RELATIONSHIPS

It is relevant and important for the different players in the industry to understand the impact of the enhanced relationship between members of any one dyad on other dyads in the health care industry. We believe that proactive firms will attempt to understand the implications of these changes being brought about by information technology and be prepared to not only deal with the consequences, but also plan on ways to leverage these changes to their advantage.

Clearly, patients who have a high level of connectivity with the pharmaceutical and insurance companies, and who make use of the above listed services being offered by these firms, will have a very different knowledge structure about their health than patients who do not make use of these services. It is important for physicians to anticipate and be aware of the changes in their patients' knowledge structures, because such changes will lead to changes in the patients' expectations of information to be received from the physician. Physicians who are unprepared for these changes are likely to respond to all patients in the way they have dealt with them in the past. This may lead to many patients feeling dissatisfied with the amount of information they receive or the level of detail provided to them by the physicians. Prior research in marketing has shown that satisfaction with information has a major effect on overall satisfaction with a product or service (Spreng et al., 1997). Thus, physicians who do not understand the implications of increased connectivity in the different dyads in the health care industry are likely to be faced with problems related to patient satisfaction. Though we have used physicians as an example in the scenario described above, the necessity of understanding the impact of technology and increased connectivity between players in the healthcare industry is equally critical for every player in the industry.

The rest of this chapter examines how information technology influences the patient-physician relationship in a hospital setting and discusses other important issues that are raised by the new connectivity.

WEB TECHNOLOGY IN THE CLINIC/ HOSPITAL SETTING

Streamlining Administration and Enhancing Communication

Marketers know the importance of overall customer experience with a firm in influencing a customer's loyalty to that firm and his/ her desire to talk favorably about that firm to others. In the literature on marketing orientation, it is pointed out that in market oriented firms, marketing is not viewed as the sole responsibility of the marketing department. There is a company-wide focus on marketing as every department realizes that it can influence customers directly or indirectly. Highly market-oriented firms are typically characterized by better levels of inter-departmental coordination than firms that are less market oriented (Kohli and Jaworski, 1990). These findings from the marketing literature are equally applicable in a hospital/clinic setting where patients' overall experience is determined not only by the interaction with the physician but also by their interactions with various other employees such as the nurses. Information technology can now make it possible for hospitals/ clinics to coordinate their various activities much better than before and enhance the overall patient care experience provided by these institutions.

A recent survey conducted by editors of *Hospitals and Health Networks* and Deloitte Consulting queried 277 health organizations nationwide on their use of online technology and classified respondents into "most wired" organizations and "less wired" depending on the extent of usage of this technology (Solovy and Serb, 1999). In this survey, the hundred most wired health organizations offered a variety of patient services online. These included (in decreasing order of availability) preregistration (73%), physician referral, support groups, nurse advice, reviewing test results, reporting self-tests, appointment scheduling, claims query, and prescription renewal (4%).

Similarly, services offered to doctors and nurses using the Internet were access to patient data (29%), viewing radiology results, viewing lab results, viewing pathology results, decision support, lab order entry, pathology order entry (12%), pharmacy order entry (12%), and radiology order entry (12%). The following types of patient data were available online, for access by authorized medical personnel — clinical results, current medical record, medical history, nurses' notes, and patient demographics. Sixty-one to eighty percent of the most wired organizations had this type of information available online compared to 21 to 40 percent of less wired organizations.

The above functions are primarily those that use technology to streamline clinical and administrative operations, and are the very basic improvements to organizational efficiency and effectiveness that online technology can bring about. We look beyond these, and explore the possible greater contributions that Internet and intranet technology can make, to improving the *quality of care* that the consumer, the patient, receives.

At their core, Intranet and Internet technologies are a mechanism for improving communication and connectivity. Improving formal and informal communication channels has been one of the most appreciated contributions made by this technology. For example, many physicians are increasingly using e-mail to communicate with their patients. Kansas University Medical Center has found that patients find the convenience and comfort of e-mailing their physicians far outweigh their confidentiality concerns (Hagland, 1997). E-mail interactions can enable a physician to make a more considered response to patient inquiries than on the phone, at his/her own leisure. This can also be time efficient for physicians constantly under time pressure.

E-mail and related services are also used by physicians to enhance their communication and connectivity with other physicians. This might not affect the patient directly, but in the long run, is likely to enable higher quality of care rendered to the patient. These higher levels of patient care would be a result of sharing of information, knowledge, and experience. Physicians are also joining on-line news groups and listservs to obtain clinical consultations with large groups of colleagues or specialists (Pinkowish, 1999).

Patient and Provider Education in Disease Management

Patient education has been an issue widely discussed as exemplifying the impact of the Information Age on health care. Forty percent of people surfing the Web use it to get health care information (Solovy and Serb, 1999). A number of health care organizations give their patients online access to information about their chronic conditions, ranging from AIDS to diabetes to substance abuse (Solovy and Serb, 1999).

Many physicians have had the experience of a patient bringing a printout from a medical Web site to their office. If the information obtained is from a reputable source such as the Mayo Clinic Web site, the only negative aspect might be that the patient does not understand the material. If the information is incorrect or misleading, there is potential for plenty of damage to the patient personally, and also to the patient-physician relationship. There is evidence of numerous unscrupulous sellers wanting to sell medications, devices, and services on the Internet (Pinkowish, 1999). Apart from Web sites, patients may also obtain virtually unlimited information from the thousands of discussion groups that supply medical advice, information and support. These on-line groups have been described as being "double-edged swords," as the potential for *misinformation* is as high as that for education.

In discussing patient education, it is important to differentiate between the *informed* patient and the *knowledgeable* patient. The difference between the two is the mere possession of information on the part of the informed patient and the possession of knowledge by the latter. The patient possessing information is largely unequipped to put that information to any use because of his/her lack of technical knowledge or expertise. Ideally, the physician can help the patient process the information he/she brings into the interaction, place the processed information in the context that is most relevant for the patient, and point out ways in which the knowledge so generated can be applied to best benefit him/her. Doctors have the medical judgment to filter and explain information from the Internet and help patients interpret it with appropriate skepticism (Sandrick, 1998). Researchers have pointed out that a dialogue between patient and physician that is open, nontechnical, compassionate, and receptive to questions can, in most cases, bring about meaningful patient comprehension and can serve a valuable therapeutic purpose at the same time (Greenfield et al., 1985).

Some physicians have pointed out that as long as potential misinformation is an issue, it would be in the patients' and the physicians' best interest for the doctor to point out suitable Web sites where the patient can be assured of reliable information. This would suggest that doctors and/or clinics would be expected to be aware of relevant medical Web sites and patients may expect the doctors to give their evaluation of the content at different sites. This would be a new role for many physicians who are unprepared for the rapid changes affecting the industry. On the other hand, physicians who anticipate such patient expectations may promptly guide the patient to sites such as Healthfinder (http://www.healthfinder.org), which was developed by the U.S. Department of Health and Human Services, and is designed to contain links only to high-quality health information (Pinkowish, 1999).

Many organizations have exploited Web resources to benefit physicians in their education and continuing education. This education can have two purposes: to update their professional employees on technology, and encourage them to use the Web as an online library. Physicians, as a group, lag behind other scientific and technical professionals in their facility with computers (Pinkowish, 1997). Though all information available online is also available in print, the advantage with using on-line resources is the ease of access and substantial savings in time.

Group Health Cooperative, a Seattle-based HMO, has made this technology part of the core of its operations, and has received national recognition for its success with disease management. Its Clinical Roadmaps disease management program is entirely supported by an extensive on-line library. Doctors have access to a wealth of practice knowledge on some of the most common chronic diseases they work with every day (Hagland, 1997). The advantage is that doctors can stay up-to-date in their knowledge and thus contribute directly to the quality of service offered to their patients. To support physician education, an increasing number of medical textbooks are available online. MD Consult is a very comprehensive source for on-line textbook access, with links to nearly 40 full texts online. These electronic textbooks have the tremendous advantage of being updated on a regular basis. In addition, nearly all the major, peer-reviewed medical and scientific journals have an on-line presence (Pinkowish, 1997).

In addition to influencing the quality of care provided, shared knowledge can facilitate collaborative patient/physician decision making (also called participative decision making). When patients are more *involved* in their own care and *understand* the treatment being offered them, their *compliance* with the treatment is likely to improve significantly. This will directly impact the effectiveness of the outcome of the interaction, both for the physician, whose performance is being implicitly evaluated by this measure, and for the patient who needs to comply in order to see progress.

Physicians work under dynamic and difficult conditions in trying to provide the best care for their patients (*Business Wire*, 1999). Web technology can make easily available all the information they need for quick and effective decision making, allowing them to focus on what is really important—patient care.

Legal and Public Policy Issues

There are some prickly legal and public policy issues that accompany the tremendous opportunities presented to the healthcare industry by information technology. We discuss some issues that are a consequence of the industry's attempt to leverage information technology to manage its business.

The first legal issue that arises from the use of communications over the Internet pertains to the security of documents transmitted in this manner. E-mail may not be secure and breaches of patient confidentiality are possible. Attorneys particularly warn that forwarding, printing, and copying e-mail messages from or to patients be done with a great deal of caution. Some go so far as to recommend obtaining informed consent before using e-mail (Pinkowish, 1999). The legal issues are far from clear or resolved. A recent editorial in *JAMA* discussed how lawyers have yet to reach a consensus on whether encryption of e-mail messages is needed to preserve attorney-client privilege (Spielberg, 1998). Some organizations have preempted any potential problems by incorporating e-mail messages into the formal patient medical records maintained. In such cases, doctors routinely copy all communications to the medical records section, where they are printed out. When a patient comes in, the doctor requests that he/she go through the printed message and sign it in order to validate it (Hagland, 1997).

A second legal and public policy issue that is raised by the industry adopting technological applications pertains to licensing physicians to practice medicine (Keltner, 1998). Under the present laws, anybody who practices medicine has to be licensed by the state in which he/she intends to practice. However, the Web makes it possible for a person sitting in one state to advise patients sitting in another state, another country, or even another continent. It is unclear how we as a society should deal with this development. Should we have laws that govern physicians practicing over the Internet? If we do need laws, should the states make these laws (just as states give licenses) or should it be national-level legislation, or should it be an international standard?

Public policy efforts are aimed at protecting the public from individuals who might be unqualified to render medical diagnoses and opinions. While that argument would suggest that there is a need to have some kind of licensing requirement for those who practice medicine (or give medical advice) over the Internet, the same argument would then raise some more questions about some common practices seen on the Internet today. The questions that are raised pertain to the accuracy of medical information provided on the Web. Patients can get information by clicking through hyperlinks from one site to another, i.e., an insurance company's Web site may have information about coverage for diabetes treatments and then one can click on a hyperlink to go to a site giving medical information about diabetes. If the patient comes across and uses inaccurate information which harms him/her, then who should be held responsible for the damage caused — the insurance company or the site that put up the information as a free service and has no contractual relationship with the patient? If public policy aims to protect individuals from getting advice from unqualified sources, should it matter whether the source is a live person or a Web site that has the aura of medical authority. How far can public policy go with legislation on these issues? At present, most companies that provide hyperlinks to sites containing medical information tend to provide prominent disclaimers that clearly state they are not responsible for any damages that may result from the use of information contained at these sites (Keltner, 1998). Should public policymakers intervene or is it appropriate for insurance or pharmaceutical firms to put a disclaimer and not worry about the accuracy of the information that can be accessed from their site? These are indeed thorny issues that have the potential to slow down the rate of adoption of information technology in certain areas of the healthcare industry.

FUTURE RESEARCH

Though patient care, in general, seems to be the beneficiary of the changes being brought about by information technology, one of the most promising areas for future research is the impact of this technology on rural health care. Our discussions with information technology specialists and healthcare professionals, including physicians and managed care providers, suggest that rural healthcare is likely to be the area where information technology can make its biggest impact by radically improving the quality of patient care. For example, rural areas tend to have far fewer physicians servicing large areas. Often, physicians in rural areas travel to a different town on different days of the week to look after their patients. Information technology is now making it possible for patients in rural areas to have much better access to their physicians. The physicians, in turn, are able to better serve their patients. It is possible for them to stay in one place and coordinate activities in others. They could have their patients' test reports sent to them electronically from different places, communicate with their patients electronically, and in some cases, (as with the elderly) even monitor patient compliance. These are fascinating developments made possible by information technology and future research should address the best ways for us to harness the technology and improve the quality of patient care.

CONCLUSIONS

The impact of information technology is being felt by the healthcare industry in many different ways. At the core of the industry lies the physician-patient relationship. The average number of physician contacts per person per year has ranged between 5.3 and 6.0 during the period 1987 to 1995 in the USA. In 1987 it was 5.4 and in 1995 it was 5.8. It peaked in 1993 and 1994 at 6.0 and was the lowest in 1988 and 1989 at 5.3 (Pamuk et al, 1998). Given the above trend, or more correctly the absence of one, it is unlikely that the *number* of physician contacts per person per year will be significantly affected by the increased connectivity and interactions fostered by the emerging information technology in the healthcare industry.

However, in contrast to the constancy of the number of physician contacts, the *nature* of physician contacts has already changed significantly and is likely to change even more dramatically. As depicted in the Diamond Model of Figure 3, every physician contact involves two physically present participants—the physician and the patient—and two virtually present participants — the pharmaceutical companies and insurance companies. Although the latter two have always been "present" during a physician-patient interaction, they have lurked in the shadows. The pharmaceutical companies have acted through the physicians; the insurance companies have acted after the contact. Now, due to greater connectivity and interactions, the pharmaceutical companies are acting through the physician and the patient; the insurance companies are acting prior to, during, and after the contact.

Naturally, the new relationships among the four key players in the healthcare industry have changed and will continue to change the balance of power, especially informational power. These changes, when harnessed properly, can dramatically improve the *quality* of the physician contact. One of the major constraints in healthcare is the physician's time. It is not surprising therefore that about two-thirds of physician office visits last less than 15 minutes (Woodward, 1997). The new technologies make it possible to focus the few available minutes on the core issues concerning the physician and the patient, rather than on peripheral issues that can be addressed without the need for physical contact between the physician and the patient. The emerging connectivity makes it possible for both physicians and patients to obtain and assimilate information asynchronously online rather than synchronously on-site — in the presence of the other party. An informed patient can be an asset to a physician in diagnosing and treating his or her own disease. Such a patient is also more likely to comply with a course of treatment than an uninformed patient. The new technologies can help inform the patient prior to and following the physician contact and thereby reserve the contact time for processing the information.

In concluding, one must acknowledge the possibility of adverse effects as well. An uninformed patient may be benign and an informed patient an asset, but a misinformed patient may be a liability. Such a patient can diminish the quality of the physician contact. The very technology that makes it possible to inform a patient also makes it possible to misinform him/ her. There are many Web sites that provide information of questionable credibility. Either out of ignorance or out of desperation many patients may be drawn to these sites. The physician is then compelled to correct the misinformation during his or her contact with the patient. One can minimize such dysfunction if the pharmaceutical companies, insurance companies, and hospitals ensure the availability of certified, credible information and the physicians point their patient to such information.

REFERENCES

Business Wire (1998), "Boston Area Doctors Use the Internet to Share Medical Data for Faster Diagnosis," (June 15), New York.

Business Wire (1998), "McKesson's Patient-Direct Program Generates 9.2% Response Rate for "AllerDays" Wellness Program; Informed Patients Adhere to Drug Regimens for Better Outcomes," (Sep. 1), New York.

Business Wire (1998), "Physicians' Online to Help Doctors Create Web Presence, Obtain Prescription Samples Via Internet," (Sep. 18), New York.

Business Wire (1999), "CyBear to Partner with Sun Microsystems to Develop Healthcare Internet," (Feb. 1), New York.

Business Wire (1999), "Data General and HealthGate Alliance Brings Critical Information to Patients," (Feb. 22), New York.

Business Wire (Nov 18, 1998), "$5 Million Online marketing program landed by Mediconsult.com: One of the largest Direct-to-Consumer Web Marketing Programs," New York: Business Wire.

Ditto, Steve and Briggs Pile (1998), "Marketing on the Internet," *Healthcare Executive*, Sep/Oct., 54-55.

Eder, Lauren and Marvin E. Darter (1998), "Physicians in Cyberspace," *Communications of the ACM*, 41(3), 52-54.

Eyuboglu, Nermin, and Osman A. Atac (1991), Informational Power: A Means for Increased Control in Channels of Distribution, *Psychology and Marketing*, Fall, 197-213.

Food and Drug Administration (1985), "Direct-to-consumer advertising of prescription drugs: withdrawal of moratorium," *Federal Register*, (September 9), 50:36677-36678.

French, John R.P., and Bertram Raven (1959), *The Bases of Social Power in Studies in Social Power*, ed. Dorwin Cartwright, Ann Arbor, MI: University of Michigan, 612-613.

Greenfield, S., S. Kaplan, & J.E. Ware, Jr. (1985), "Expanding patient involvement in care: Effects on patient outcomes," *Annals of Internal Medicine*, 102(4), 520-528.

Hagland, Mark (1997), "How "WebCare" is Changing Health Care Delivery, Hit by Hit," *Health Management Technology*, (March), 22-26.

Hall, Richard H. (1996), *Organizations- Structures, Processes, and Outcomes*, (6th ed.), Englewood Cliffs, NJ: Prentice-Hall.

Holmer, Alan F. (1999), "Direct-to-consumer prescription drug advertising builds bridges between patients and physicians," *Journal of the American Medical Association*, 281, 4 (Jan 27), 380-382.

Kaplan, Debbie (1998), "Working with the Internet—and your Patients," *Patient Care*, 32(4), 4.

Keltner, Kristin B. (1998), "Networked Health Information: Assuring Quality Control on the Internet," *Federal Communications Law Journal*, 50(2), 417-439.

Kohli, Ajay K. and Bernard J. Jaworski (1990), "Market Orientation: The Construct, Research Propositions, and Managerial Implications," *Journal of Marketing*, 54 (April), 1-18.

Lankford, Dawn (1997), "Health Care Moves into Cyberspace," *Wichita Business Journal*, (Jan. 3), 1.

Mechanic, David (1998), "Public Trust and Initiatives for New Health Care Partnerships," *The Milbank Quarterly*, 76(2), 281-302.

Medical Economics (1997), "Practicing Medicine on the Net," 74, 23, 64(3).

Pamuk E, Makuc D, Heck K, Reuben C, Lochner K (1998), "Socioeconomic Status and Health Chartbook," Health, United States 1998, Hyattsville, Maryland: National Center for Health Statistics.

Pinkowish, Mary Desmond (1997), "The Physician's Guide to the Internet," *Patient Care*, 31, 3, 26-53.

Pinkowish, Mary Desmond (1999), "The Internet in Medicine: An Update," *Patient Care*, 33, 1, 30-54.

Prelter, Robert (1998), "Vendors expand Web sites from Marketing to Transactions, Data Management, Communications," *Employee Benefit Plan Review*, 52(12), 30-34.

Solovy, Alden and Chris Serb (1999), "Health Care's Most Wired," *Hospitals and Health Networks*, 73, 2, 43-51.

Spielberg, A.R. (1998), "On Call and Online: Sociohistorical, Legal, and Ethical Implications of Email for the Patient-Physician Relationship," *Journal of the American Medical Association*, 280, 1353-1359.

Spreng, Richard A., Scott B. MacKenzie, and Richard W. Olshavsky (1996), "A Reexamination of the Determinants of Consumer Satisfaction," *Journal of Marketing*, 60 (July), 3, 15-34.

Star Tribune (1998), "How Internet Could Change Patient Care," (Oct. 1), Minneapolis, Minnesota.

Woodwell, David A. (1997) *National Ambulatory Medical Care Survey: 1995 Summary*, U.S. Department of Health and Human Services, Centers for Disease Control and Prevention, National Center for Health Statistics.

Chapter 4

The Use of Artificial Intelligence Techniques and Applications in the Medical Domain

Adi Armoni
Tel-Aviv College of Management, Israel

In recent years we have witnessed sweeping developments in information technology. Currently, the most promising and interesting domain seemed to be the artificial intelligence. Within this field we see now a growing interest in the medical applications. The purpose of this article is to present a general review of the main areas of artificial intelligence and its applications to the medical domain. The review will focus on artificial intelligence applications to radiology, robotically-operated surgical procedures and different kinds of expert systems.

INTRODUCTION

The true challenge of artificial intelligence lies in the duplication of the mental capacities of ordinary people, such as vision and natural language (the language of speech as opposed to computer language). These actions may seem simple and natural to most of us, but in order to express them on the computer we will require the most complicated algorithms. "The fact that we are able to carry out the complicated act of vision at minimal effort, compared to complicated acts of multiplication, is almost an error of evolution ...." (Nilsen, 1990).

Indeed, research and development in the field of artificial intelligence mainly focus on the attempt to imitate "basic" human actions such as: speech recognition, vision, and various mechanical actions (assembly, analysis,

Previously Published in *Healthcare Information Systems: Challenges of the New Millennium* edited by Adi Armoni, Copyright © 2000, Idea Group Publishing.

dividing samples into petri dishes, storing professional knowledge and producing it when required expertise).

There are different definitions of artificial intelligence, Charniak's definition (Charniak, McDermott, 1989) : "Artificial intelligence is studying mental capacities through the use of computerized models." It is easier to understand the potential value of artificial intelligence when we confront it with human intelligence. According to Kaplan (1994), artificial intelligence has a number of clear commercial advantages over natural intelligence:

- Artificial intelligence is more "steady," as it does not depend on workers' rotation, nor is it based on their memory. It ensures that as long as the software and hardware are in good shape the use we create will not change.
- Artificial intelligence ensures easy distribution and duplication. The process of transferring knowledge from one person to another is long and complicated, and it is almost impossible to duplicate human experts, unlike the duplication of computerized systems.
- As artificial intelligence is computerized technology, it is consequential and accurate (of course to the extent that the information fed into the database is consequential and accurate), compared to natural intelligence which is founded on the lack of stability of the human expert.
- The actions and decisions received from computerized systems are easy to document by following the stages of their receipt and therefore it is possible to study and examine them. On the other hand, the human expert is capable of drawing a conclusion, while at a later stage he will be unable to explain the sequence of deductions leading to this conclusion.

Compared to the advantages of artificial intelligence mentioned above, natural intelligence also has a few striking advantages:

- Natural intelligence is creative, compared to the rigidity characterizing artificial intelligence. Human beings possess the ability to acquire knowledge and draw conclusions, whereas artificial intelligence adapted to the requirements of the system, is generally fixed and well planned.
- Human beings are able to make immediate use of information received through the senses, whereas the computerized system requires symbolic signal processing.
- The most important advantage is the ability of human beings to integrate relevant knowledge from a number of fields and expertise and coordinate this in order to find the solution to a certain problem. Compared to this ability, the computerized systems are merely based on narrow, central-ized information.

THE CONCEPT OF KNOWLEDGE IN ARTIFICIAL INTELLIGENCE

In the field of information systems, a distinction is usually made between data, information and knowledge. In data terms it is common to refer to strings of numeric or alpha-numeric values which in themselves are of no importance.

These strings may include numeric values or facts that must be processed.

On the other hand, information is a group of facts which is organized and processed in a manner that is significant to the person who receives it.

Information has many definitions, one of the best is by Turban (1995) "information includes all the clear and the concealed limits connected with a certain object, for the activities and the interactions of this object. The information also includes specific heuristic rules and procedures of drawing conclusions, all of them connected with the situation one wishes to model and which pertain to the object in question.

The facts, information and knowledge may be classified in accordance with the extent to which they are abstract and according to their quantity (Figure 1) when the information is abstract to the highest degree and exists in the smallest quantity.

Figure 1: Mesuring the Quantity and Abstruction of Knowledge, Information and Facts

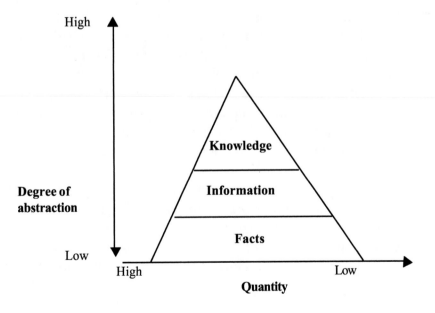

MAIN FIELDS OF RESEARCH AND APPLICATION

During recent years we witness a great interest and progress in implementing artificial intelligence techniques dealing with processing and retrieving medical knowledge, diagnostic tolls, decision support and expert systems, and computerized supplies to perform an invasive procedures.

We will discuss and demonstrate the up-to-date research topics and application of artificial intelligence. Among those topics we can find techniques of robotics, computerized vision, expert systems, speech recognition, neural networks, etc.

ROBOTICS

We must remember that it is very difficult to define and execute actions that are not founded on explicit algorithm. For example, although it seems as if housework is a simple act, and not as complicated as powerful precision welding, from the robot's point of view, the latter is much easier, for the part arrives exactly at the right time at the right place, and all that remains is to carry out the welding.

On the other hand, housework requires the robot to see and understand everything around him. He must distinguish between the piano and the bed, know where the sheets are (they are placed differently each time), etc.

The main problem still remains the ability to transfer the "human feeling and perception" to the robot. If we recall that the human hand is capable of holding a piece of paper in various ways without creasing it, a wet glass without letting it slide, or crack a hard nut, we will understand how hard it is to impart these natural talents to an artificial limb which has no feeling and understanding of the meaning of the action (Amato, 1992). The main medical applications of robotics focus on three fields:

Surgery – including laparoscopic cholecystectomy (Ganger, 1996). Introducing miniature robots via the blood vessels in microsurgery (Wickham, 1994) accurate and swift prostatectomy, whereby the robot carrying out the section is placed via an image obtained from the ultrasound device (Ng et al, 1993).

Surgery to replace the hip bone, when the robot assists in the entire process of planning, locating, directing and carrying out the surgery. A three-dimensional form of the area of the operation, together with the geometric basis of knowledge, allow the robot to direct the surgeon and automatically carry out the required drilling and cutting at the optimal location (Matesen, 1993).

Laboratories — Analysis of genetic sequences and dividing blood samples into serological tests, when the robot uses the division of the material into samples in a systematically, accurate and efficient manner, prevents human errors and drastically (up to 50%) reduces the time of work (Caillat, et al., 1995; Wilson, 1995).

Locating and conveying of medical equipment —After a number of years in which the artificial intelligence technology has been implemented at various levels of sophistication at industrial warehouses, these applications have also arrived at medical locations. The system that was developed enables the computerized locating of drugs at pharmacies and conveying them to the party ordering them (Landis, 1993). Automatic conveying of medical equipment from warehouses to hospital wards and departments (Tadano, 1995).

COMPUTERIZED VISION

This is defined as an addition to artificial intelligence, capable of monitoring and analyzing visual information received from various sensors (video cameras, electronic scanners, etc.) and adding it to the information existing in the system. The recognition technique is based on the analysis of the received input and verifying it against the data stored in the computer's database. Computerized vision uses complicated techniques and mathematical algorithms, most of which are based on the techniques of pattern recognition (Turban, 1995). The information analyzed by the system may, for example, be used for controlling a robot's movement, monitoring the speed of a conveyor belt, and automatic quality control of items under production.

There is a wide range of applications of computerized vision in the medical field. We will divide these applications into three main groups:

Pathological diagnosis — Through automatic input of data from the mammography machine (Vyborny and Giger, 1996) or oral lesions according to direct input from the computerized tomography instrument (Brooks, 1995). The application of computerized vision is also presented for automatic follow-up and classification of the size of the pituitary microadenoma (Cannavo, et al., 1992), and on-line cytological diagnosis according to the data supplied by a needle introduced into the suspected tumor (Wolberg, et. al., 1995).

Recognition of the structure of materials —Comparing the molecular structure with the computerized database to the molecular structure seen by the computerized system makes it possible to recognize the chemical and physical structure of the material (Heiden, et. al., 1995), or changes in the mineral bone composition (Robertson, 1996), or automatic location of materials through the identification of the amino-acid structure (Ficher, et al., 1995).

Graph analysis—Mostly through techniques of pattern recognition for the purpose of comparing graphs from the computerized data base with the input values received from the system/the medical instrument. There are leading applications in the field of retina lesions through the analysis of the results of fields of vision tests (Martin, 1995), diagnosis and recognition of phases in the course of sleep through the analysis of output received from the EEG instrument (Hasan et. al., 1995), or studying the cortical vision mechanisms (Miyashita et. al., 1995).

EXPERT SYSTEMS
General

This is the artificial intelligence field with the largest number of applications. The expert systems are very important because of their inherent potential to replace experts in fields in which it is expensive to find people who possess the knowledge.

In these systems we endeavor to learn the expertise of the person (or in professional language: to extract the expert's knowledge) and integrate this knowledge in the computerized system's database. Unlike the computerized systems familiar to all of us, which include a database and a models base, in the expert systems we find an additional module called "knowledge base." In this module the information extracted from the human expert will be stored.

Striking expert systems are to be found in the medical diagnostic field, electronics and computers (for example: for examination and automatic location of failures in electronic components).

The most frequently mentioned and described system is no doubt the **Mycin** (Buchanan and Shortliffe, 1984) system, developed at Stanford University in the early seventies.

The purpose of the project was described as the development and application of a system that would point out the best way of treating a patient suspected of suffering from an infectious disease. This system identifies the virus (the most likely one) causing the infection, and in accordance with what is found, as mentioned above, it recommends the best method of treatment.

In the early eighties an expert system was developed at Pittsburgh University in the field of internal medicine. This system, called **Internist -1** enables the physician to carry out an accurate differentiated diagnostic process (Miller, et. al., 1992).

For the diagnosis and treatment of the group of glaucoma diseases, an expert system was developed in the early eighties at Rutgers University, called **Casnet** (Kulikowski and Weiss, 1992).

This expert system, like the Mycin system, contributed significantly to the development of expert systems, basing themselves on the expert systems generator called **Expert** (Weiss et. al. 1992).

With the use and the contribution to the development of this generator which is independent in the field of application, the systems created a very powerful tool for the definition of additional medical expert systems.

Neomycin (Clancey and Letsinger, 1991) and **Caduceus** (Pople, 1985) belong to the second generation of expert systems. In this generation of expert systems, stronger emphasis is placed on the presentation of the cause and effects of the disease, the control procedures have become more complicated, and much work was invested in the addition of information and its reorganization in the data base of the systems. Indeed, the **Neomycin** system is an improved version of the **Mycin** system and the **Caduceus** system is an improved version of the **Internist -1** system.

There are still reasons, some of them objective (such as the problem to include huge quantities of information, accurate and consistent extraction of the expert's knowledge), and others subjective (the physician's fear of basing himself on computerized systems), which prevent the large-scale use of these systems.

However, we are quite certain that the progress of medical science and the huge quantities of information to which the physician is exposed will oblige those occupied in medicine to use the computerized systems in the diagnostic process. It is quite clear that a physician who uses an expert system in his field will be more consistent and methodical in the process of diagnosis than a physician who operates without such a system.

Because the expert systems are so important in the application of artificial intelligence in medicine, I shall provide a more detailed description of four of the most famous systems surveyed above.

The MYCIN System for Diagnosis and Treatment
of Infectious Diseases

This is the best known and most often described expert system among medical systems. This project was already started at Stanford University in 1972 and was based on the cooperation between a team composed of computer scientists and people treating infectious diseases at this university's school of medicine.

The target of the research was defined as the development and application of a system that would provide a guideline for the best way to treat a patient suspected of suffering from an infectious disease. The development of this project was considered very important, as the decisions regarding treatment must often be carried out under conditions of partial lack of certainty regarding the identification of the virus causing the infection. It is possible to make a perfect diagnosis of a large part of the infectious diseases, but only very rarely can the treating physician "allow himself" to wait a few days to receive the results of the lab tests (Buchanan BG & Shortliffe EH, 1997).

The information available to the physician at the stage in which the recommended treatment must be determined is mainly based on the patient's medical history, present symptoms and initial results of the lab tests. On the basis of these facts and the knowledge of experts of infectious diseases extracted from the experts which is presented in the database of the system, we expect MYCIN to carry out the following two stages:

- To identify the virus (the most likely one) causing the infection.
- To recommend, on the basis of the finding mentioned in section A above, the best manner of treatment.

As we mentioned above, one of the aims of the system is to discuss the subject of missing information and lack of certainty. In order to deal with the problem of lack of certainty, the term "certainty factor" was developed. At each and every stage of the process of diagnosis, we encounter a number of assumptions vying with each other as to the explanation of the phenomenon (attention : there is not only one single assumption, for in that case there is no lack of certainty at all).

The system attaches a numeric value to each of the assumptions describing the amount of certainty (strength) with which this assumption supports the explanation of the phenomenon.

This number value fluctuates between 1, i.e., absolute certainty regarding the quality of the assumption, through 0, indicating total lack of information or, alternatively, an identical amount of proof in favor of and against the assumption, and including 1, which indicates the assumption in no way supports the explanation of the phenomenon (absolute certainty that the assumption is not correct).

That is why this system is so important as a landmark in the development of expert systems in the medical field.

The INTERNIST 1 System for the Diagnosis of Diseases in Internal Medicine

This system was developed at Pittsburgh University in the early eighties (Miller, et. al., 1992). From the beginning the emphasis in this system as placed on the correct application of the differentiated diagnostic process, based on a process of creating a set of diagnoses supporting at different levels of clarity findings that came to light in the clinical tests or the lab tests. At a later stage the tests whose clarity is at a lower level than the others will be eliminated from this set of tests.

We will distinguish between two kinds of entity in the database of the system: the diseases on the one hand, and the findings on the other hand. This database includes 500 diseases and about 3550 findings. For each disease a list of findings was defined that are known to be connected with this disease (this list was called "the profile of the disease" by the developers). The internist-1 system was developed in order to provide the physician with a tool to carry out an analysis in the field of internal medicine.

The diagnosis in this system is founded on two processes. One of them examines what findings are present or absent, and on the strength of these two facts creates a group of possible diseases. The other develops the heuristics that create the questions for the person using it for the purpose of obtaining additional information (clinical or lab tests) to enable support of the chosen diagnosis. At this stage a numeric value is attached to each diagnosis, stating the extent to which the findings support the diagnosis. In general, findings that are in the "profile of the disease" and were found with the patient add a positive value in support of the diagnosis; on the other hand, findings that are found in the "profile of the disease," but were not found with the patient, derogate from the credibility of the diagnosis.

Once the iterative process of the diagnosis is completed, the diagnosis which obtained the highest number of points from among the set of initial diagnoses is chosen.

CASNET System for the Diagnosis and Treatment of the Glaucoma Diseases Group

This system was developed in the early eighties at Rutgers University. It supplies methodology for expressing the interaction between the pathophysiological situations and the development of the disease.

The best known application of this methodology deals with the group of glaucoma diseases (Kulikowski and Weiss, 1992).

The system deals both with the process of diagnosis and the process of curing the diseases. Three kinds of objects are defined in Casnet findings (called observations), pathophysiological situations and categories of diseases. Each of these objects may be in one of the following situations: correct/confirmed, wrong/unconfirmed or unknown/undefined. It is possible to refer to the three kinds of objects as if they are on three separate levels, inter-linked and linked to the other levels through the situations described above.

The findings are the direct evidence pertaining to the patient (pain, lab test results). The pathophysiological situations are the summary of events that are different from ordinary behavior. These situations describe internal developments which may be presumed to take place in the patient's body, but cannot be observed externally. The pathophysiological situations are linked to each other through "response creating" relations. There may, of course, be more than one reason for a certain situation and this situation may create more than one response.

CASNET, like other expert systems in the medical field, fluctuates between examination of the patient's present problem on the strength of existing facts, and the need to ask additional clarifying questions (which are indeed asked in the course of the process).

The examination of the CASNET system's validity was carried out in various ways (Kulikowski and Weiss, 1992). However, the most comprehensive empirical test of the system's validity was carried out by linking the system to the Onet computer system used jointly by a number of eye clinics in the USA. In this test the system was examined on a large number of patients, and a 75% success rate was reported in the diagnosis of serious and complicated cases of glaucoma.

PIP System for the Diagnosis of Kidney Diseases

The PIP (Present Illness Program) system was developed by a group of scientists from MIT, together with colleagues from Tufts University's School of Medicine. The true purpose of the development of this system was the attempt to carry out a computerized simulation of the decision-making process in the medical field.

The researchers estimated on the strength of Elstein's work (Elstein, et. al., 1992) that human experts are very pressed in the process of creating hypotheses pertaining to the patient's situation, and do not have enough patience to examine a broad spectrum of facts, deduct the hypotheses with the highest probability and continue to raise additional questions on the strength of these hypotheses.

The medical field in which the PIP system was developed deals with the diagnosis of various kinds of kidney disease

The system includes sets of diseases and findings. There are characteristics for the various findings, and values were attached to these characteristics. For example, edema is a finding whose characteristics may be: presence (yes/no), location (legs, hands, etc.) rate of seriousness (accompanied by pain, not accompanied by pain), etc.

The information pertaining to each disease is organized in a frame which includes a number of cells. For each disease a status is defined that may be active, semi-active or not active. The group of diseases with the active status of course constitutes the group on which discussion must focus. Work in the system starts by feeding a group of general findings pertaining to the patient into the computer: age, sex, main symptoms. For each disease a group of "stimulant findings" is defined. In the event such a finding is received, the disease becomes active.

However, in addition to the list of "stimulant findings," there is an additional list of findings that may be related to the various diseases (not with absolute certainty and therefore they are not "stimulant findings"). Each time additional findings are received, a calculation is made of scores and rating of all the stimulant and semi-stimulant diseases. The score process is very complicated and actually consists of two parts :

- **Matching score**: assesses the extent to which the new findings match those that were anticipated, in accordance with the pattern characterizing the disease. This   score actually assesses the extent to which our expectations from the new findings were realized.
- **The binding score**: assesses the extent to which the disease constitutes an accurate explanation of the findings received, i.e., what proportion of the findings received is explained by the disease. After evaluation of the active and semi-active hypotheses the discussion naturally focuses on hypotheses that have the highest score. At this stage the system (in accordance with the value of the score) decides whether to ask for additional evidence or point to the hypotheses that have the highest probability (Pauker, et al., 1996).

SPEECH RECOGNITION

This application includes the recognition of vocal input by the computer, i.e., the computer recognizes and decodes the vocal input and acts in accordance with what is said on it. The main applications that exist in medicine at present are in the field of assisting the disabled suffering from serious problems of movement (Taylor, et al., 1993), by issuing instructions to the robot with their voice; actions such as steering the wheelchair, operating electrical appliances and phone-dialing are carried out (Bach, 1995). There are also reports about experiments aimed at assisting and guiding reading for those suffering from serious eye problems. This guidance is carried out by comparing the written text with the text read by the patient and extending vocal feedback to the patient (Buning and Hanzlik, 1995). Medical applications are also found whose purpose it is to reduce the time of activity and the errors in printing diagnoses. For example, diagnosis of x-ray results by the physician and reading them out to the computer (La Fianza, et al., 1995; Mrosek, et al., 1995). This is based on a vocabulary of 20,000-30,000 words the physician will use. In a test (Buning and Hanzlik, 1995) carried out on the subject of the diagnosis of oral x-rays, it was reported that the time of treatment in the diagnosis according to voice recognition was 671 seconds, compared to merely 182 seconds in ordinary dictation to the typist.

This huge time gap is one of the reasons for the present failure of technology, which still requires adjusting the system to each user (through studying his voice) and is based on a closed vocabulary.

NEURAL NETWORKS

The name "neural networks" refers to two directions of research that are linked to each other: one deals with building models for components and functions of the nervous system in animals attempting to obtain maximum adjustment of anatomical and physiological facts. The other focuses on examining theoretical-mathematical computational systems with a structure that recalls a group of neurons.

The models in the first field refer to different levels in the nervous system:
- Single nerve cell—properties of the electric transmission in it, ionic ducts activity and the action organism of synopsis (Agmon and Segev, 1995, Powers, 1995).
- Group of nerve cells with emphasis on collective phenomena of their action (42, 43).
- Areas of the brain and mental functions such as memory (Zipser et al., 1993; Ruppin, et al., 1995).

There are also various functional emphases, for example in the ability of a model to show pathological situations or adaptation (Hinton, 1992). Moreover, in the past years an effort was made to develop and build network hardware, i.e., electronic chips whose activity is based on a large number of simple processing units, a kind of neuron, instead of a powerful and fast central processor, existing in the present computers. Together with the ripening of the neural networks theory, the applications increase (Armoni, 1998).

The potential for use is vast and includes almost any kind of information processing: statistical classification and regression, signal processing, image processing, etc. (Regia, 1993).

In this respect the computational nerve networks must be considered part of the entire range of statistical methods and modern information processing tools.

From the physician's point of view, neural networks may assist in day-to-day work and even in medical management at the department level.

Unlike expert systems based on rules drafted by professionals, neural networks can process unprocessed information: numeric results of tests, EEG, ECG (Edenbrandt et. al., 1995), imaging (Miller, et al., 1992; Cappini, et al., 1992). They are capable of finding complicated statistical correlation hidden even from the expert's eyes, and thus improve the standard of diagnosis (Boon and Kok, 1995; Cohen, et al., 1995).

Furthermore, the networks are capable of recognizing the relevant facts for diagnosis and prognosis from among tens and sometimes hundreds of possible variables (Baxt,1992). This makes it possible to shorten the diagnostic process, save on tests and efficiently manage the limited resources available to the medical field.

We would like to mention, as an example, improvement in the prediction of the natural history of disease and treatment of the mentally ill (Modai, 1993), cancer patients (Burke, 1996, Kappen and Neijt, 1995), and prediction of the period of time in which the patients will have to remain in intensive care (Tu and Guerriere, 1995).

Increasing attention is already being paid at present to computational neural networks, by intelligent use they will be able to improve activity in the field of medicine.

DISCUSSION

During the last years we witnessed a growing trend of utilizing a variety of artificial intelligence techniques in the medical domain. Those applications cover all branches of medicine, from diagnosis to the performance and interpretation of computerized tomography and end in numerous invasive procedures. The article supplies a comprehensive and up-to-date overview of artificial intelligence use in medicine, and points out the most promising trends and directions of evolution.

Since the greatest advance was in the field of retrieving, encoding, and using the expert's knowledge in knowledge-based systems, we found it proper to emphasize and examine more precisely part of our review on the expert systems domain.

It is clear to distinguish the two main advantages of the artificial intelligence over the human intelligence. The first is stemming from the consistent and accurate way of handling huge amount of data concerning symptoms, and disease and the continuous update, storage and accurate retrieve of this information (for example, expert systems, and all kinds of knowledge bases attached to diagnostic instruments).

The second advantage is related to the opportunity of focused and accurate performance of surgical and invasive procedures, while minimizing the dependence in the expert's skills.

The author has no doubt that in the next two to three years, the use of artificial intelligence will dramatically increase since the human brain and skills are not able to handle competitively the enormous quantity of data, information and knowledge, and to gain the full advantage of the high performance diagnostic appliances, but using the mentioned above artificial skills and techniques.

REFERENCES

Agmon-Shir H & Segev I. (1995). Signal delay and input synchronization in passive dendritic structures. *J Neurophysiol*, 70, 2066-2085.

Amato, I. (1992). In search of the human touch. *Science*, 258, 1436- 1437.

Armoni, A.(1998). Utilization of Neural Networks in Medical Diagnosis, M.D. *Computing*, Vol. 15, 100-104

Bach J.R. (1995). Comprehensive rehabilitation of the severely disabled ventilator-assisted individual. *Monaldi Arch Chest Dis*, 48, 331-345.

Baxt W.G.(1992). Analysis of the clinical variables driving decision in anartificial neural network trained to identify the presence of myocardial infarction. *Ann Emerg* Med, 21, 1439-1444.

Boon M.E. & Kok L.P. (1995). Neural network processing can provide means to catch errors that slip through human screening of pap smears. *Diagn Cytopathol*, 9, 411-416.

Brooks SL.(1995). Computed tomography, *Dent Clin North Am*, 37, 575-590.

Buchanan B.G. & Shortliffe E.H. (1997. Rule Based expert systems *: The MYCIN experiments of the stanford Heuristic Progarmming Project.* Reading, Mass : Addison-Wesley.

Buning M.E .& Hanzlik J.R. (1995). Adaptive computer use for a person with visual impairment. *Am J Occup Ther*, 47, 998-1008.

Burke H.B. (1996). Artificial neural networks for cancer research : outcome prediction. *Semin Surg Oncol*, 10, 73-79.

Caillat S., Garchon H.J., Costantino F. & al. (1995). Automation of large scale HLA oligotyping using a robotic workstation. *Biotechniques*, 15, 526-528.

Cannavo S, De Natale R, Curto L & al. (1992). Effectiveness of computer assisted perimetry in the follow-up of patients with pituitary microadenoma responsive to medical treatment, *Clin Endocrinol*, 37, 157-161.

Cappini G, Poli R, Rucci M, & al. (1992), A neural network architecture for understanding discrete three dimensional scenes in medical imaging. *Comput Biomed Res*, 25; 569-585.

Cendrowska J. & Bramer M.A. (1984). A rational reconstruction of the MYCIN consultation system. *Int J Man-Machine Studies*, 20, 229-317.

Charniak E & McDermott D. (1989). *Introduction to artificial intelligence.*, Addison Wesley Publishing .

Chawanya T, Aoyagi T, Nishikawa I & Okuda K. (1995). A model for feature linking via collective oscillations in the primary visual cortex. *Biol Cybern*, 68, 483-490.

Clancey W.J. & Letsinger R. (1991) . NEOMYCIN : reconfiguring a rule based expert system for applications to teaching. In : *Proc IJCAI-81*, 2, 829-836.

Cohen IL, Sudhalter V, London D & al. (1995). A neural network approach to the classification of autism. *J Autism Dev Disord*, 23, 443-466.

Edenbrandt L., Devine B.& Macfarlane P.W. (1995). Classification of electrocardiographic ST-T segments - human expert vs artificial neural network. *Eur Heart J*, 14, 464-468.

Elstein A.S., Shulman L.A. & Sprafka S.A. (1992). *Medical problem solving : an anlysis of clinical reasoning.* Cambridge, Mass : Harvard Univ Press.

Fischer D, Wolfson, H & Nussinov R, (1995). Spatial sequences-ordering dependent structural comparison of alpha/beta proteins : evolutionary implications. *J Biomol Struc Dyn*, 11, 367-380.

Ganger M., Begin E. & Hurteau R. (1996). Robotic interactive laparoscopic cholecystectomy, *Lancet*, 596-597.

Hasan J., Hirvonen K., Varri A. et al. (1995). Validation of computer analysed polygraphic patterns during drowsiness and sleep onset. *Electroencephalogr Clin Neurophysiol*, 87, 117-127.

Heiden W., Moeckel G. & Brickmann J. (1995). A new approach to analysis and display of local lipophilicity / hydrophilicity mapped on molecular surfaces. *J Comput Aided Mol Des*, 7, 503-514.

Hinton G.E. (1992). How neural networks learn from experience. *Sci Am*, 267, 144-151.

Kaplan SJ. (1994), The industrialization of artificial intelligence: from by line to bottom-line. *AI magazine*; 34 : 345-351.

Kappen H.J. & Neijt J.P. (1995). Advanced ovarian cancer. Neural network analysis to predict treatment outcome. *Ann Oncol*, 4, 31-34.

Kulikowski C.A. & Weiss S.M. (1992). Representation of expert knowledge for consultation : the CASNET and EXPERT projects. In : Szolovits P, ed. *Artificial intelligence in medicine*. Boulder, Colorado : Westview Press, 21-56.

La Fianza, A., Giorgetti S., Marelli P. & Campani R. (1995). Vocal recognition and oral radiology, *Radil Med*, 86, 432-435

Landi,s N.T. (1993). Pharmacies gain staff time as new "employee" lends a hand. Am *J Hosp Pharm*, 50 : 2236-2242.

Martin, LM. (1995). Computer assisted interpretation of resolution visual fields from patients with chiasmal and retrochiasmal lesions. *Ophtalmologica*, 207 : 148-154

Matesen, F.A, Garbini J.L. (1993). Robotic assistance inorthopaedic surgery. A proof of principle using distal femoral arthroplasty. *Clin Orthop*, 296 : 178-186.

Miller, A.S., Blott B.H., & Hames T.K. (1992). Review of neural network applications in medical imaging and signal processing, *Med Biol Eng Comput*, 30,449-464.

Miller, R.A., Pople H.E. & Myers J.D. (1992). INTERNIST-1, an experimental compute based diagnostic consultant for general internal medicine, *N Engl J Med*, 307, 468-476.

Miyashita Y, Date A & Okuno H. (1995), Configurational encoding of complex visual forms by single neurons of monkey temporal cortex, *Neuropsychologia*, 31, 1119-1131.

Modai I. (1993), Clinical decisions for psychiatric inpatients and their evaluation by a trained neural network, *Methods Inf Med* , 32; 396-399.

Mrosek B., Grunupp A., Keppel E. et al. (1995). Computer assisted speech recognition and display of x-ray findings, *Rofo Fortschr Geb Rontgenstr Neuen Bildgeb Verfahr*, 5 : 481-483.

Ng W.S., Davies B.L., Timoney A.G., et al. *(*1993). The use of ultrasound inautomated prostatectomy. *Med Biol Eng Comput*, 31, 349-354.

Nilsson J. (1990). *Principles of artificial intelligence*, Morgan Kaufmann Publishers Inc.

Pauker, S.G., Gorry G.A. & Kassirer J.P. (1996). Towards the simulation of clinical cognition : taking a present illness by computer. *Am J Med*, 60; 981-986.

Pauker, S.G. & Szolovits P. (1997). Analysing and simulating taking the history of the present illness : concept formation. In : Schneider W, Hein A-LS, eds. *Computational linguistics in medicine*. Amsterdam: North Holland.

Pople, H.E. (1985). Evolution of an expert system : from internist to caduceus. In : De Lotto I, Stefanelli M, eds. *Artificial Intelligence in medicine;* Survey lectures, 1-30.

Powers, R.K. (1995). A variable threshold motoneuron that incorporates time and voltage-dependent potassium and calcium conductances, *J Neurophysiol*; 70; 246-262.

Regia, J.A. (1993). Neural computation in medicine. *Artif Intell Med*, 5, 143-157.

Robertson, D.D. (1996). Distal loss of femoral bone following total knee arthroplasty. Measurement with visual and computer processing of roentgenograms and dual-energy x-ray absorptiometry. *J Bone Joint Surg Am*, 76, 66-76.

Ruppin E., Hermann M. & Usher M. (1995). A neural model of the dynamic activation of memory, *Biol Cyber*, 68,455-463.

Sompolinsky, H. & Seung H.S. (1993). Simple models for reading neuronal population codes, *Proc Natl Acad Sci USA*, 90,10749-10753.

Tadano, J. (1995). Robot handling system and conveying system of hospital laboratory, *Rinsho Byori*, 95 : 23-31.

Taylor, B., Cupo M.E. & Sheredos S.J. (1993).Workstation robotics : a pilot study of a Desktop Vocational Assistant Robot, *Am J Occup ther*, 47, 1009-1013.

Tu, J.V. & Guerriere M.R. (1995). Use of neural network as a predictive instrument for length of stay in the intensive care unit following cardiac surgery. *Comput Biomed Res*, 26, 220-229.

Turban E. (1994), *Expert systems and applied artificial intelligence*, Macmillan Publishing Comp.

Turban, E. (1995). *Decision support and expert systems*, Macmillan Publishing Comp.

Vyborny C.J. & Giger M.L. (1996). Computer vision and artificial intelligence in mammography, *Am J Roentgenol*, 162, 699-708.

Weiss S.M., Kern, K.B. & Kulikowski, C. (1992). *A guide to the use of the EXPERT consultation system*, Brunswick, New Jersey : Rutgers Univ, Report CBM-TR-94.

Wickham, J.E. (1994). Minimally invasive surgery. Future developments, *BMJ*, 308, 193-196.

Wilson, R.K. (1995). High throughput purification of M13 templates for DNA sequencing. *Biotechniques*, 15, 414-416.

Wolberg W.H., Street W.N. & Mangasarian O.L. (1995). Breast cytology with digital image analysis. *Anal Quant Cytol Histol*, 15, 396-404.

Zipser D., Kehoe B., Littlewort G., et al. (1993). A spiking network model of short term active memory, *J Neurosci*, 13, 3406-3420.

Chapter 5

An Intelligent Data Mining System to Detect Healthcare Fraud

Guisseppi A. Forgionne, Aryya Gangopadhyay and Monica Adya
University of Maryland Baltimore County, USA

INTRODUCTION

There are various forms of fraud in the health care industry. This fraud has a substantial financial impact on the cost of providing healthcare. Money wasted on fraud will be unavailable for the diagnosis and treatment of legitimate illnesses. The rising costs of and the potential adverse affects on quality healthcare have encouraged organizations to institute measures for detecting fraud and intercepting erroneous payments.

Current fraud detection approaches are largely reactive in nature. Fraud occurs, and various schemes are used to detect this fraud afterwards. Corrective action then is instituted to alleviate the consequences. This chapter presents a proactive approach to detection based on artificial intelligence methodology. In particular, we propose the use of data mining and classification rules to determine the existence or non-existence of fraud patterns in the available data.

The chapter begins with an overview of the types of healthcare fraud. Next, there is a brief discussion of issues with the current fraud detection approaches. The chapter then develops information technology based approaches and illustrates how these technologies can improve current practice. Finally, there is a summary of the major findings and the implications for healthcare practice.

Previously Published in *Healthcare Information Systems: Challenges of the New Millennium* edited by Adi Armoni, Copyright © 2000, Idea Group Publishing.

BACKGROUND

Fraud in healthcare transactions refers to knowingly and willfully offering, paying, soliciting, or receiving remuneration to induce business that healthcare programs will reimburse. Healthcare fraud can result from internal corruption, bogus claims, unnecessary health care treatments, and unwarranted solicitation. As in any commercial enterprise, unscrupulous provider or payer employees can misappropriate healthcare payments for personal purposes. Providers can also issue claims for treatments that were never, or only partially, rendered. Corrupt healthcare providers also can induce patients to undergo unnecessary, or even unwanted, treatments so as to inflate charges to the payers. In addition, unethical providers can willfully solicit business from unprincipled, or unsuspecting, patients for the sole purpose of generating billable procedures and treatments.

According to a 1993 survey by the Health Insurance Association of America of private insurers' healthcare fraud investigations, the majority of healthcare fraud activity is associated with diagnosis (43%) and billing services (34%). In Medicare, the most common forms of fraud include billing for services not furnished, misrepresenting the diagnosis to justify payment, falsifying certificates of medical necessity, plans of treatment and medical records to justify payment, and soliciting, offering, or receiving a kickback (Health Care Financing Administration, 1999).

Early cases of healthcare fraud have applied to gross issues such as kickbacks, bribes, and other fairly transparent schemes. Increasingly, however, the Office of the Inspector General has demonstrated a willingness to pursue cases that are in the gray area and courts have tended to interpret antifraud statues more broadly so as to make criminal prosecution more likely (Steiner, 1993). For instance, waiving a patient's co-payment when billing third-party payers and not disclosing the practice to the insurance carrier has been deemed as fraud and resulted in prosecution (Tomes, 1993).

Fraud has a substantial financial impact on the cost of providing healthcare. Medicaid fraud, alone, costs over $30 billion each year in the United States (Korcok, 1997). According to CIGNA HealthCare and Insurance groups, the healthcare industry is losing an estimated $80 to $100 billion to fraudulent claims and false billing practices (CIGNA, 1999). Investigators have shown that fraud is found in all segments of the healthcare system, including medical practice, drugs, X-rays, and pathology tests, among others.

The timely detection and prevention of fraud will not only provide significant cost savings to insurance companies but will also reduce the rising cost of healthcare. Money wasted on fraud will be unavailable for the diagnosis and treatment of legitimate illnesses. In the process, research monies may be reduced and critical research may be delayed. Ineffective and cost inefficient treatments may continue. Administrative effort may be diverted to fraud detection instead of being concentrated on the effective management of healthcare practice. As a consequence, patient care may suffer and healthcare costs may continue to soar.

MAIN THRUST OF THE CHAPTER

There are several issues, controversies, and problems associated with fraud detection. An analysis of these issues recommends a solution based on artificial intelligence techniques.

Issues, Controversies, and Problems

In the past, claim fraud has been identified through complaints made, among others, by disgruntled healthcare competitors, beneficiaries and recipients, and present or former employees of providers. A significant volume of false claims, however, still go undetected. Consequently, fraud is still rampant in the healthcare system. The rising costs of, and the potential adverse effects on quality health care, have encouraged organizations to institute measures for detecting fraud and intercepting erroneous payments, especially through electronic means.

Due to the documentation typically required by payers, all forms of healthcare fraud will leave a paper, or electronic, trail that can serve as the basis for detection. However, the transactions useful for fraud detection will generally be buried in the documentation. Furthermore, these transactions may be from disparate sources and in diversified formats. Often, the needed transactions are also discarded as a normal part of transmitting claims from providers to payers.

Another major barrier to fraud detection is the reactive nature of the current approaches. For the most part, detection relies on: (a) complaints made by disgruntled interested parties, (b) random examinations by payers of provider submitted records, and (c) occasional detailed studies by public and private oversight agencies (Tomes 1993). Since such methods tend to be relatively narrow in scope, few fraud cases will be detected in this manner. Even in the identified cases, detection will be time consuming, costly, and difficult to correct.

Solutions and Recommendations

With the increasing number of healthcare transactions and persecution of situations with such uncertainty, it is possible to increase the chances of detecting fraud through the use of information technology. Such technology can be utilized to develop a proactive and effective healthcare fraud detection strategy based on data warehousing, data mining, artificial intelligence, and decision support systems.

Data needed to support the identification of fraud routinely flow, often electronically, between healthcare providers and payers as medical transactions. By filtering and focusing the transactions, warehousing the focused data, and creating tailor-made data marts for the appropriate recipients, requisite information can be made available for significant data mining analyses (Abraham and Roddick, 1998; Davidson, Henrickson, Johnson, Myers, and Wylie, 1999). Artificial intelligence then can be used to help providers and payers detect the underlying fraudulent patterns in the data and, with the aid of additional information technology, form effective proactive correction strategies (Burn-Thornton and Edenbrandt, 1998; Hornung, Deddens, and Roscoe, 1998; Makino, Suda, Ono, and Ibaraki, 1999).

Data Warehousing

Data warehousing involves the physical separation of day-to-day operational healthcare data from decision support systems. Benefits of data warehousing include clean and consistent organization-wide data, protection of transactional and operational systems from user's query and report requirements, and effective updating and maintenance of applications. The more significant purpose of the data warehouse is to support multidimensional analyses of both historical and current data.

A multidimensional model is developed using the MOLAP (multidimensional on-line analytical processing) design. Several data cubes are populated with historical and current data. An example of a three-dimensional data cube consists of patient demographics, time, and procedure code as the dimensions, and the payment as the measure. The actual analysis could require dimensionality reduction, such as a time-series analysis of payment records for patients that underwent a given treatment. In this case only two dimensions of the data cube are investigated. Such an analysis could be required to establish a historical pattern of the amount of payments made for a given medical procedure, sudden changes of which may cause an alarm for further investigations. Average values of payment amounts for medical procedures over a given data set can be used as a normative value to trigger any significant variations in current payment amounts. Other examples of multidimensional analyses include pivoting or cross tabulating measures against dimensions, dicing the cube to study a subpopulation of the data collected over a period of time, and rollup or drill down along dimensions to study any changes that might have taken place along individual dimensions.

Data Mining and Classification Rules

Data mining is an emerging technique that combines artificial intelligence (AI) algorithms and relational databases to discover patterns with or without the use of traditional statistical methods (Borok, 1997). It typically employs complex software algorithms to identify patterns in large databases and data warehouses. Data mining can facilitate information analysis using either a top-down or a bottom-up approach (Limb and Meggs, 1995). While the bottom-up approach analyzes the raw data in an attempt to discover the hidden trends and groups, top-down data mining tests a specific hypothesis.

Effective data mining relies on an effective and representative data warehouse. By definition, data mining is a pattern discovery process that relies on large volumes of data to infer meaningful patterns and relationships between data items. Once the data is "mined" from the warehouse and patterns are cataloged, the patterns themselves can be converted into a set of rules (Borok, 1997). These rules that explain healthcare behavior will be coded into a rule-base and be used for analyzing individual instances.

Classification rules deal with identifying a class of regularities in data (Adam, Dogramaci, Gangopadhyay and Yesha,1998; Ramakrishnan 1997). A classification rule is an expression $(l_1 \leq X_1 \leq U_1) \wedge (l_2 \leq X_2 \leq U_2) \wedge \ldots (l_k \leq X_k \leq U_k) \rightarrow (l_y \leq X \leq U_y)$, where $X_1 \ldots X_k$ are attributes used to predict the value of Y, and $l_1 \ldots l_k$, $U_1 \ldots U_k$ are the lower and upper bounds of the corresponding attribute values, respectively. As an example, in detecting healthcare fraud, a classification rule would be $X \rightarrow (Y \leq l_y)$ or $(U_y \leq Y)$, where X is a surgical procedure and (l_y, U_y) is the prescriptive range of values for the payments made (Y).

A classification rule is said to have a support s if the percentage of all cases satisfying the conditions specified in the rule equals or exceeds the support. In other words, s is the ratio to the total number of cases where both X and Y values are within the specified ranges. The confidence c of a classification rule is defined as the probability that, for all cases where the value of X falls within its specified range, the value of Y will also be within the range specified for Y. In other words, c is the ratio of cases where the values of X and Y are within their respective specified ranges, to the total number of cases where only the X values are within the specified range.

Both support and confidence can be user or system specified as percentages or ratios.

If the support for a certain rule is low, it indicates that the number of cases is not large enough to make any conclusive inference. In that case, no further analysis is done with the current data set. If the support is large but the confidence is low, the rule is rejected. If both the support and confidence exceed the values specified by the user (or system) then the rule is accepted. Such a case would trigger a flag for a potential fraud and recommend further investigation, which is done by isolating the cases that triggered the flag.

Illustrative Example

Take the instance of determining physician charges for a surgical procedure. Charges for this procedure may vary somewhat by, among other things, physician, location of the practicing facility, and the regulations of the insurance provider. It is challenging, therefore, to identify an acceptable and representative range of charges using traditional statistical techniques. This requires understanding the physicians' practice procedures, determining the practice patterns implicit in the data, and possibly identifying practice patterns over the past few weeks.

Data mining can discover such patterns in the historical data. More importantly, it can uncover atypical patterns of practice within a group. For instance, mining on a large sample of nationwide data may identify that for a simple dental procedure, physicians charge a fee of $45.00 to $60.00 in the state of Maryland. If there is a sufficient number of cases in the data warehouse that support the correlation between the procedure and the range of charges, then the support and confidence in this rule will be high. Otherwise the rule will be rejected and will not be included in the rule-base. If the rule is accepted, a new case regarding this procedure can now be compared against the rule and can trigger a fraud alert if the charges deviate significantly from those specified in the rule.

In another instance, data mining may support the analysis and understanding of temporary conditions which may be incorrectly triggered as a fraud alert. Suppose the classification rules above indicate an increase in the incidence of emergency hospitalizations than in other regions around the area. This deviation can set up a trigger whereby further analysis may reveal the presence of a high-risk construction facility for the next two years. This factor will allow the healthcare providers to prepare for the situation both during and after the construction activity and possibly aid in the prevention of emergency situations at this facility. Similar analysis can be used for chronic conditions such as breast or lung cancer in specific regions.

FRAUD DETECTION SYSTEM

In the next few sections, we suggest the development of a decision support system to support the identification of fraud in healthcare transactions. The architecture for this system is proposed in Figure 1. As this figure shows, the system interactively processes inputs into the outputs desired by healthcare users.

Inputs

The fraud detection system has a data base that captures and stores historical, and industry standard, data on healthcare providers, claims, and payments. These data are extracted from the data warehouse that captures the relevant transactions from the providers to the payers, and vice versa.

Provider information includes the name, address, ID, and other demographics. Claims information includes the patient ID, procedure code, charge, billing dates, and other financial statistics. Payment information includes the patient and provider IDs, deductibles, co-payments, covered remuneration, and relevant payment dates.

There is also a model base that contains classification rules and artificial intelligence algorithms. The classification rules would establish lower and upper limits, supports, and confidence levels for each covered procedure from historical data and industry standards. These rules would be derived through the data mining tool, and the classification algorithm would determine the support and confidence of the classification rules.

Processing

The health official (health plan administrator, auditor, or other staff assistant) uses computer technology to perform the fraud detection analyses and evaluations. Computer hardware includes an IBM-compatible Pentium-based microcomputer with 16MB of RAM, a color graphics display, and a printer compatible with the microcomputer. Software includes the SAS information delivery system running through the Microsoft Windows operating system. This configuration was selected because it offered a more consistent, less time-consuming, less costly, and more flexible development and implementation environment than the available alternatives.

Users initiate the processing by pointing and clicking with the computer's mouse on screen-displayed objects. The system responds by automatically organizing the collected data, structuring (estimating and operationalizing) the classification rules, and simulating fraud performance. Results are displayed on the preprogrammed forms desired by health officials. Execution is realized in a completely interactive manner that makes the processing relatively transparent to the user.

As indicated by the top feedback loop in Figure 1, organized data, structured classification rules, and fraud performance reports created during the system's analyses and evaluations can be captured and stored as inputs for future processing. These captured inputs are stored as additional or revised fields and records, thereby updating the data and model bases dynamically.

The user executes the functions with mouse-controlled point-and-click operations on attractive visual displays that make the computer processing virtually invisible (transparent) to the user.

Outputs

The above procedures generate visual displays of the outputs desired by health officials. Outputs include fraud forecasts and reports. These reports are in the form of tables and graphs. Each table displays the forecasted payment value relative to its lower and upper limits for a specified medical procedure. The corresponding graph highlights deviations outside the limits and allows the user to drill down to the supporting detail (which includes the provider, any extenuating circumstances, and other relevant information). The user has the option of printing or saving the reports.

As indicated by the bottom feedback loop in Figure 1, the user can utilize the outputs to guide further processing before exiting the system. Typically, the feedback will involve sensitivity analyses in which the user modifies support and confidence levels, upper and lower limits, or other pertinent factors and observes the effects on fraud performance.

System Session

There is a graphic icon on the Windows desktop. By double clicking this icon, the user accesses the fraud detection system. Once in the system, the user performs the fraud detection analyses and evaluations by navigating with point-and-click operations through the displays overviewed in Figure 2.

The Welcome display (shown in Figure 3) enables the user to access an embedded executive information system (EIS) shown in Figure 4. Once in the EIS, the user can interactively access the data warehouse, by selecting the database management system (DBMS) button, or go directly to DSS reports by selecting the REPORTS button. Selecting the DBMS button will enable the user to

Figure 1: Fraud Detection Conceptual System Architecture

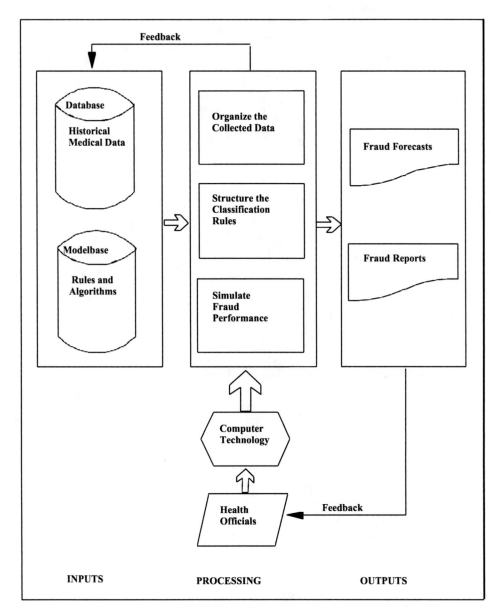

Figure 2: Display Relationships

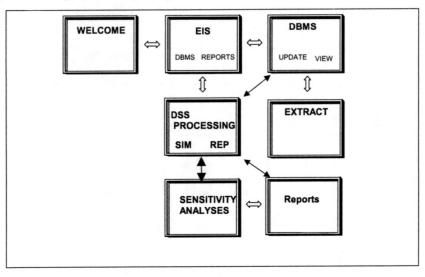

Figure 3: Welcome Screen

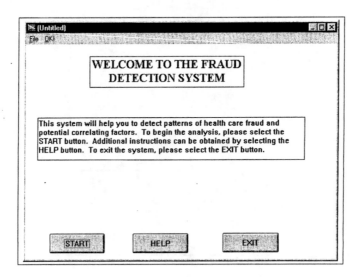

Figure 4: EIS Screen

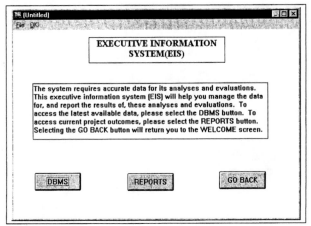

Figure 5: Database Management System Screen

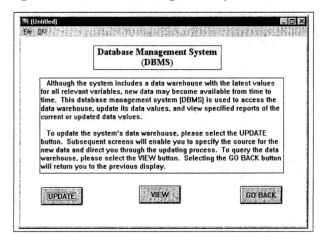

UPDATE the data warehouse and VIEW the contents of the existing or updated warehouse.

In the DBMS, the user can UPDATE the data warehouse and VIEW the contents of the existing or updated warehouse, as shown in Figure 5. Selecting the UPDATE button will place the user in the EXTRACT screen shown in Figure 6. Once there, the user will interactively select the data source for the updating operation from the predefined list. The selection reads data from the specified source, reformats the data (if necessary), and updates the data warehouse values.

Selecting the VIEW button from the DBMS will access a display that prompts users for the desired information (shown in Figure 7). These selections will form the

Figure 6: Extract Screen

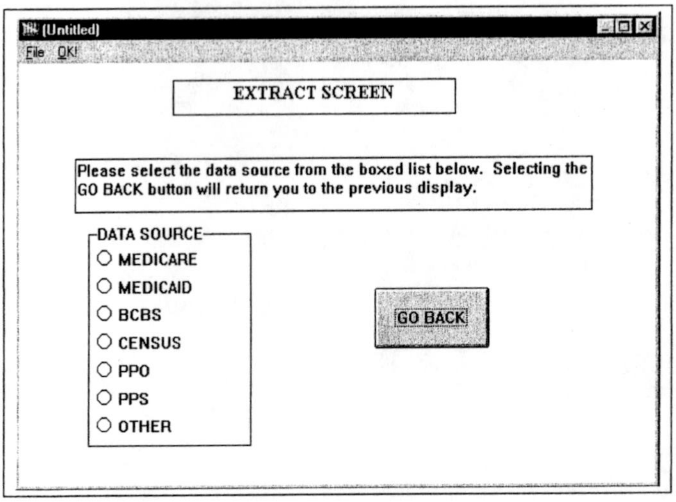

Figure 7: View Screen

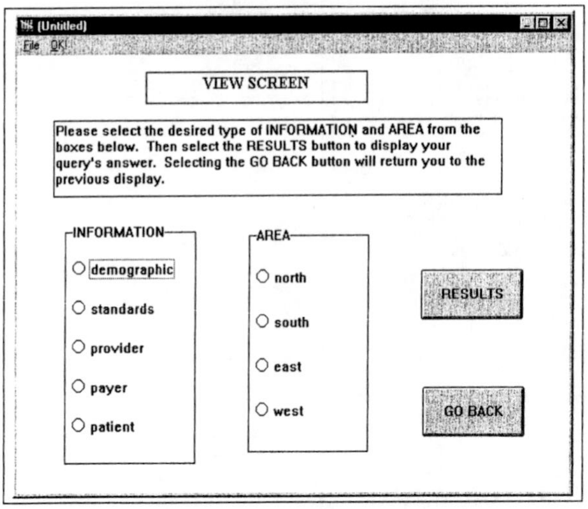

pertinent Structured Query Language (SQL) call to the data warehouse and generate the desired custom report.

Selecting the REPORTS button from the EIS display will run the fraud detection analysis with the updated or existing data and bring the user to the DSS PROCESSING screen shown in Figure 8. Once there, the user can simulate fraud performance by selecting the simulate (SIM) button. The decision support system will generate the required DSS database from the data warehouse, operationalize the appropriate models, and perform the needed analyses and evaluations. It is here that data mining techniques will be used to identify new patterns in the updated databases. In deeper level screens,

Figure 8: DSS Processing Screen

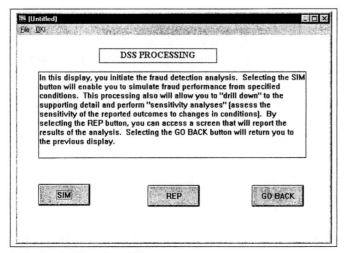

Figure 9: Reports Screen

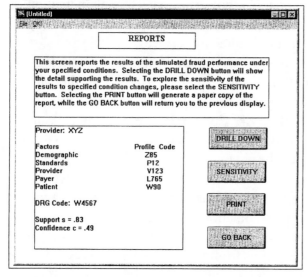

the user will be supported with features that allow the development of classification rules from patterns that hold consistently on data samples. These rules can then be used on incoming transactions to proactively identify fraudulent activities. A report (REP) button selection will display the results in the desired predefined format on the Reports screen (shown in Figure 9).

From the output screen, the user can perform sensitivity analyses on the results. By making the desired selection from the predefined "What If" list, the user can experiment with changes in: (a) provider characteristics, (b) key local factors, (c) patient demographics, and (d) financing alternatives. Results from the what-if analyses are displayed on the SENSITIVITY ANALYSES screen. Such experimentation can continue in sequence, or the user can generate an entirely new experiment.

Acting as an electronic counselor, the decision support system sequentially guides the user through an effective fraud detection analysis and evaluation. System operations, which are performed in an intuitive, timely (typical five-minute-session) and error-free fashion, liberate the user to focus on the creative aspects of fraud detection and correction.

FUTURE TRENDS

Web-based electronic commerce is an emerging trend that can benefit the healthcare community and the nation in a variety of ways. Such commerce enables the health care organization to be proactive rather than reactive. Transactions can be captured as they are generated, thereby allowing healthcare organizations to compare actual and expected patient outcomes. Such comparisons can help predict, among other things: (1) patient problems, (2) required healthcare interventions, (3) time required for implementation of healthcare services, (4) accessibility of healthcare services, (5) quality of healthcare services, and (6) cost of healthcare services.

The fraud detection system is conceived as a Web-based technology. A Web site will be established to collect the pertinent data from the various sources. Geographic data would be obtained from state and local government base map files, U.S. Postal Service ZIP Code files, U.S. Geological Survey hydrology data files, and U. S. Bureau of the Census TIGER files. General population characteristics would be obtained by census blocks from the U.S. Bureau of the Census, while health-related demographic data would be acquired from the U.S. Health Care Financing Administration and the National Health and Nutrition Examination Surveys. Health outcome and care data would be obtained from state-specific public health data files. Environmental data would be acquired from state and federal survey data files on water quality, pollutant, toxic waste, ambient air and source emission, air quality, radiation, powerline, and chemical usage and waste generation.

Utilizing the electronic commerce concept, data suppliers will access the system's Web site and select appropriate screen icons (Gerull and Wientzen, 1997). These selections will automatically obtain the data from the supply source and transfer the elements to a data warehouse (Tsvetovatyy, Gini, and Wiecckowski, 1997).

The system's EIS will extract the pertinent data, capture the extractions in user-oriented data marts, and make the marted data available for ad hoc queries by users. Ad hoc queries can be made at the users' sites in an easy-to-use, convenient, and interactive manner, utilizing the Web-based fraud detection system. Results will be displayed in formats anticipated by the requesting parties.

In effect, then, the proposed system provides a vehicle to utilize the emerging Web-based electronic commerce for proactive fraud detection and correction. Without the system, fraud detection involves a very complex process that requires extensive training for provider and payer analysts. By decreasing the volume of documentation, by simplifying the educational process, and by simplifying and automating much of the detection process, the proposed system can be expected to save the medical community millions of dollars per year in fraud detection and correction costs.

With the embedded EIS, an analyst can interactively conduct the initial phase of fraud detection at a computer terminal in a matter of minutes at a nominal expense. Next, the EIS can be used to access pertinent data, mine patterns from the accessed data, and relate the pattern variables with other correlates. The DSS then can be used to develop an explanatory model and use the model to simulate fraud performance under selected conditions. The fraud detection system can be developed and implemented for a small fraction of the potential cost savings.

From a diagnosis perspective, the manual search for fraud detection patterns is a tedious process that often results in inaccurate, incomplete, and redundant data. Such data problems can leave fraud inadequately detected and corrected. With the proposed system, the user identifies all data relevant to the fraud detection process, and the system provides a mechanism that facilitates data entry while reducing errors and eliminating redundant inputs. Reports from the system also offer focused guidance that can be used to help the user perform fraud searches, detections, and corrections.

Challenges

Realizing the strategic potential will present significant challenges to the traditional healthcare organization. Tasks, events, and processes must be redesigned and reengineered to accommodate the concurrent electronic commerce. Clinicians and administrators must be convinced that the electronic commerce will be personally as well as organizationally beneficial, and they must agree to participate in the effort. Finally, the organizational changes will compel substantial informational technology support.

The organization can have several stand-alone systems to provide the decision analyses and evaluations (Tan, 1995; Tan and Sheps, 1998). Integrating the stand-alone functions, however, can enhance the quality and efficiency of the segmented support, create synergistic effects, and augment decision-making performance and value (Forgionne and Kohli, 1996).

When implemented fully, the innovation will alter the work design for, and supervision of, fraud detection and correction. Requisite operations and computations will be simplified, automated, and made error-free. Training requirements will be reduced to a minimum. Processing efficiency will be dramatically increased. User-inspired creative fraud detection experimentation will be facilitated and nurtured. Management learning will be promoted. Knowledge capture will be expedited.

In short, the fraud detection system's usage would substantially reshape the organizational culture. Faced with significant time pressures and limited staff, healthcare leadership may be reluctant to take on this burden at the present time. In addition, public health officials have developed and cultivated strong and enduring relationships with practitioners and vendors. These practitioners and vendors also have important contacts and allies within the government agencies that oversee healthcare programs. For these reasons, it may be politically wise for public health officials to preserve these practitioner and vendor relationships.

Future Research Opportunities

There are a number of future research opportunities presented by the fraud detection system. To ensure that the information system accurately replicates the inputs, the final version of the system should be tested against Web-collected data from existing institutions. In the testing, warehoused data should be compared against actual values. Statistical tests should be conducted on the estimated models. There should be evaluations of user satisfaction with: (a) the speed, relevance, and quality of ad hoc query results; (b) the system interface; (c) model appropriateness; and (d) the quality of the system explanation. Simulations should be statistically tested for accuracy, and confidence intervals should be established for the results. Tests should also be conducted on the system's ability to improve the decision-making maturity of the user.

Enhancements can be made to the fraud detection architecture. Machine learning techniques can be developed to improve the intelligent modeling, database management, and user interface operations of the system. Communication links can be created to more effectively disseminate system results to affected parties.

The fraud detection system concept can also be adapted for a variety of adjunct healthcare applications. Similar systems can be applied to the diagnosis and treatment of cancer, mental disorders, infectious diseases, and additional illnesses. Effectiveness studies can be done to measure the economic, management, and health impacts of the additional applications.

CONCLUSIONS

The fraud detection system presented in this paper is a combination of data warehousing, data mining, artificial intelligence, and decision support system technology. This system offers the healthcare official a tool that will support a proactive strategy of health care fraud detection. The system's use can reduce the time and cost needed to detect healthcare fraud, and the system can substantially lower the public and private expenses associated with such fraud.

The fraud detection system delivers the information and knowledge needed to support fraud detection in a comprehensive, integrated, and continuous fashion. The comprehensive, integrated, and continuous support from the system should yield more decision value than the non-synthesized and partial support offered by any single autonomous system. Improvements should be observed in both the outcomes from, and the process of, strategic claims and other electronic commerce decision making (Lederer, Merchandani, and Sims, 1997). Outcome improvements can include advancements in the level of the users' decision-making maturity and gains in organization performance (Whinston, Stahl, and Choi, 1997). Process improvements can involve enhancements in the users' ability to perform the phases and steps of decision making.

To achieve the potential benefits, healthcare officials will have to meet significant challenges. First, a data warehouse must be established to capture the relevant transactions. In particular, there must be continuous user-involvement including careful upfront examination of business requirements and identification of quality and standards. The warehouse must be iteratively developed to deliver increasing value to the organization. Second, to support effective data mining, data marts must be formed to filter and focus the data for fraud detection. A strategy must be formulated for developing the tool. Once again, because of their domain knowledge, users must play a central role in such development. Thirdly, appropriate data mining techniques should be made available to the user and more importantly, validation routines will need to be built into the system to support effective validation of data mining outcomes. Finally, users must be convinced about the efficacy of the fraud detection system and trained in the use of the proactive technology.

Regardless of the proposed system's legacy, the application offers useful lessons for Web-based healthcare decision technology systems' development and management. The system is effectively delivering to the user, in a virtual manner, embedded statistical, medical, and information systems expertise specifically focused on the health care problem. Any single human technical specialist typically will not: (a) be proficient with, or even aware of, all pertinent tools, or (b) possess sufficient domain knowledge to fully understand the medical situation, propose trials, or interpret outcomes. While practitioners will have the domain knowledge, they usually will not have the technical expertise to effectively develop and implement relevant technology.

The proposed effort suggests that system design, development, and implementation should be a team effort. In addition, the team should be composed of the affected practitioners, information system personnel, and technological specialists proficient with the tools needed to address the healthcare problem.

Fraud detection is inherently a semi-structured (or even ill structured) problem. When initially confronted with such situations, analysts have a partial understanding of the problem elements and relationships. Typically, their understanding evolves as they acquire more information, knowledge, and wisdom about the problem. The fraud detection system is designed to support such decision making.

Relying on the information center, or other traditional information system organization, to design and develop a Web-based fraud detection system will likely be ineffective. These types of organizations typically are staffed by personnel with general skills, limited technological expertise, and restricted problem-specific knowledge. Development and implementation will follow a prescribed pattern designed to provide standard solutions to relatively well-understood and well-structured problems.

A hybrid project-technology organization may work well for Web-based fraud detection system design, development, and implementation in a healthcare environment. The organization would be virtual rather than physical. A project team would be established and administered by the practicing healthcare professional. Team technology specialists would be drawn from within and outside the organization to match the expertise needed for the specific project. Telecommuting and distributed collaborative work would be allowed and possibly encouraged.

REFERENCES

Abraham, T., & Roddick, J. F. (1998). Opportunities for knowledge discovery in spatio-temporal information systems. *Australian Journal of Information Systems*, 5(2), 3-12.

Adam, N. R., Dogramaci, O., Gangopadhyay, A., & Yesha Y. (1998). *Electronic Commerce: Technical, Business and Legal Issues*. New Jersey: Prentice-

Hall.

Adam, N. R. & Gangopadhyay, A. (1997). *Database Issues in Geographic Information Systems.* Boston/Dordrecht/London, Kluwer Academic Publishers.

Borok, L. S. (1997). Data mining: Sophisticated forms of managed care modeling through artificial intelligence. *Journal of Health Care Finance.* 23(3), 20-36.

Burn-Thornton, K. E., & Edenbrandt, L. (1998). Myrocardial infarction—Pinpointing the key indicators in the 12-lead ECG using data mining. *Computers and Biomedical Research.* 31(4), 293-303.

Chen, R. (1996). Exploratory analysis as a sequel to suspected increased rate of cancer in a small residential or workplace community. *Statistics in Medicine,* 15, 807-816.

CIGNA (1999). CIGNA HealthCare and Insurance Groups Web-site at http://www.insurance.ibm.com/insur/cigna.htm.

Davidson, G. S., Hendickson, B., Johnson, D. K., Meyers, C. E., & Wylie, B. N. (1999). Knowledge mining with VxInsight: Discovery through interaction. *Journal of Intelligent Information Systems: Integrating Artificial Intelligence and Database Technologies.* 11(3), 259-285.

Fischer, M. M. and Nijkamp, P (eds.) (1993). *Geographic Information Systems, Spatial Modeling, and Policy Evaluation.* New York: Springer-Verlag.

Forgionne, G. A. and Kohli, R. (1996). HMSS: A management support system for concurrent hospital decision making. *Decision Support Systems.* 16, 209-223.

Grimson, R. C. and Oden, N. (1996). Disease clusters in structured environments. *Statistics in Medicine* 15, 851-871.

Geographic Information System for the Long Island Breast Cancer Study Project (LIBCSP). National Cancer Institute's Electronic RFP Number NO2-PC-85074-39. Bethesda: National Cancer Institute, 1998.

Gerull, D. B. and Wientzen, R. (1997). Electronic commerce: The future of image delivery. *International Journal of Geographical Information Systems.* 7(7) 38-51.

Heath Care Financing Administration. (1999). Medicare fraud Web-site at http://www.hcfa.gov/medicare/fraud.

Hornung, R. W., Deddens, J. A., & Roscoe, R. J. (1998). Modifiers of lung cancer risk in uranium miners from the Colorado Plateau. *Health Physics.* 74(1), 12-21.

Huxhold, W. E. (1991). *An Introduction to Urban Geographic Information Systems.* Oxford: Oxford University Press.

Kalakota, R. and Whinston, A. B. (1997). *Electronic Commerce: A Manager's Guide.* Reading, Massachusetts: Addison-Wesley.

Keegan, A. J. and Baldwin, B. (1992). EIS: A better way to view hospital trends. *Healthcare Financial Management,* 46(11), 58-64.

Korcok, M. (1997). Medicare, Medicaid fraud: A billion-dollar art form in the US. *Canadian Medical Association Journal.* 156 (8), 1195-1197.

Laden, F., Spiegelman, D., and Neas, L. M. (1997). Geographic variation in breast cancer incidence rates in a cohort of U. S. women. *Journal of the National Cancer Institute* 89, 1373-1378.

Lederer, A. L., Merchandani, D. F., and Sims, K. (1997). The link between information strategy and electronic commerce. *Journal of Organizational Computing and Electronic Commerce.* 7(1), 17-25.

Limb, P.R., and Meggs, G. J. (1995). Data mining -tools and techniques. *British Telecom Technology Journal.* 12(4), 32-41.

Makino, K., Suda, T., Ono, H., & Ibaraki, T. (1999). Data analysis by positive decision trees. *IEICE Transactions on Information and Systems.* E82-D(1), 76-88.

Oden, N., Jacquez, G., and Grimson, R. (1996). Realistic power simulations compare point- and area-based disease cluster tests. *Statistics in Medicine* 15, 783-806.

Ramakrishnan, R. (1997). *Database Management Systems.* Boston: McGraw-Hill.

Regional Variation in Breast Cancer Rates in the U. S. – NIH. National Cancer Institute's Electronic RFA Number CA-98-017. Bethesda: National Cancer Institute, 1998.

Robbins, A. S., Brescianini, S., and Kelsey, J. L. (1997). Regional differences in known risk factors and the higher incidence of breast cancer in San Francisco. *Journal of the National Cancer Institute* 89, 960-965.

Steiner, J. E. (1993). Update: Fraud and abuse Stark laws. *Journal of Health and Hospitals.* 26, 274-275.

Sturgeon, S. R., Schairer, C., and Gail, M. (1995). Geographic variation in mortality rates from breast cancer among white women in the United States. *Journal of the National Cancer Institute* 87, 1846-1853.

Tan, J. K. H. (1995). *Health Management Information Systems.* Gaithersburg, Maryland: Aspen.

Tan, J. K.H., and Sheps, S (eds.)(1998). *Health Decision Support Systems.* Gaithersburg, Maryland: Aspen.

Tomes, J.P. (1993). *Healthcare Fraud, Waste, Abuse, and Safe Harbors: The Complete Legal Guide.* Chicago, Illinois: Probus Publishing Company.

Tsvetovatyy, N., Gini, M., and Wieckowski, Z. (1997). Magma: An agent-based virtual market for electronic commerce. *Applied Artificial Intelligence.* 11(6), 501-509.

Whinston, A. B., Stahl, D. O., and Choi, S. (1997). *The Economics of Electronic Commerce.* Indianapolis, Indiana: Macmillan Technical Publishing.

Workshop on Hormones, Hormone Metabolism, Environment, and Breast Cancer, New Orleans, Louisiana, September 28-29, 1995. *Monographs in Environmental Health Perspectives* supplement 1997, 105(3), 557-688.

Chapter 6

Experiences from Health Information System Implementation Projects Reported in Canada Between 1991 and 1997

Francis Lau
University of Alberta, Canada

Marilynne Hebert
University of British Columbia, Canada

Canada's Health Informatics Association has been hosting annual conferences since the 1970's as a way of bringing information systems professionals, health practitioners, policy makers, researchers and industry together to share their ideas and experiences in the use of information systems in the health sector. This paper describes our findings on the outcome of information systems implementation projects reported at these conferences in the 1990s. Fifty implementation projects published in the conference proceedings were reviewed and the authors or designates of 24 of these projects were interviewed. The overall experiences, which are consistent with existing implementation literature, suggest the need for organizational commitment; resource support and training; managing project, change process and communication; organizational/user involvement and teams approach; system capability;

Previously Published in the *Journal of End User Computing, vol.13, no.4*, Copyright © 2001, Idea Group Publishing.

information quality; and demonstrable positive consequences from computerization.

INTRODUCTION

Canada's Health Informatics Association, known historically as COACH (Canadian Organization for the Advancement of Computers in Health), has been hosting annual conferences since the 1970's as a way of bringing information systems (IS) professionals, health practitioners, policy makers, researchers and industry together to share their ideas and experiences in the use of information systems in the health sector. These conferences usually consist of keynote speakers describing the latest IS trends; presentations of new ideas, key issues and implementation projects; special interest group meetings; and IS vendor exhibits.

One area of ongoing interest for conference participants is the implementation projects reported at the COACH conferences. Considering the high cost involved in planning, implementing, managing and evaluating health information systems, any successes, failures and lessons learned from these projects can provide valuable information for future projects. While one can certainly gain insights from the individual implementation projects reported, there has been no systematic effort to examine the cumulative experiences from these projects such as common issues, enablers and barriers that influenced the implementation process and success.

Over the years, numerous articles have also appeared in health informatics literature on systems implementation. Thus far, it is recognized that people and organizational issues are equally if not more important than technology itself when implementing IS (Lorenzi et al. 1997). Reasons cited for failures include ineffective communication, hostile culture, underestimation of complexity, scope creep, inadequate technology, lack of training and failed leadership (Lorenzi and Riley 2000). Anderson (1997) has stressed that IS affect distribution of resources and power as well as interdepartmental relations. As such, successful implementation requires active user involvement, attention to workflow and professional relations, and anticipating/managing behavioral and organizational changes. To date there has been little research done on Canadian experience in health information systems implementation.

This paper reports the findings of our study on outcome of IS implementation projects reported at the COACH conferences in the 1990's. First, we outline the study approach used. We then describe the results in terms of expectations being met, key implementation issues, system usage and changes over time, and lessons learned. Based on our findings we conclude with a summary of the experiences from these implementation projects, and how they compare with health informatics literature on implementation.

APPROACH

Study Scope

The scope of this study included only articles published in the annual COACH Conference proceedings from 1991, 1992, 1993, 1994 and 1997. Proceedings from 1995 and 1996 were not available. An article was included in the study only if it described the past, present or future implementation of a particular health information system.

Research Question

The overall research question in this study was *"What is the outcome of IS implementation projects reported at the COACH conferences from 1991 to 1997?"*

More specific questions included:
- Have these systems met the expectations?
- What were the key implementation issues and how were they addressed?
- Are these systems still being used? Why or why not?
- Have these systems been changed since they were first reported? If so, why and how?
- What are the lessons learned from these projects?

Also included after our initial study was the question of how these findings compared with what's reported in the health informatics literature.

Study Phases

The four phases in this study, which took place from January to July 98, consisted of: (a) selecting articles describing system implementation from the COACH proceedings and summarizing them according to predefined criteria; (b) establishing a contact list of original authors and conducting telephone interviews with these authors or their designates; (c) analyzing article summaries and interview results; (d) writing the findings as a final report for the COACH organization. The interviews allowed us to determine if the authors' views had changed over time since publishing their articles.

Data Collection and Analysis

The two researchers reviewed the proceedings independently to select articles that were considered implementation projects. The two lists were then compared and merged into a common list of 50 articles. The research assistants summarized each article according to technology used; implementation experiences reported; and project evaluation conducted. For reliability, 10 of the articles were reviewed by at least two of the assistants. Discrepancies noted were discussed and resolved before proceeding with the remaining articles.

The assistants located the original authors (or, if not available, individuals who were familiar with the system), prepared the contact list, arranged interviews with these authors or designates, conducted the interviews, and transcribed the interview responses. The interviews addressed all five specific research questions. The researchers analyzed the results independently, compared the findings for consistency and produced a summary report for the COACH organization.

There are several limitations to this study: (a) only the authors/designates were contacted regarding the projects, but the organization or users involved were not. It is recognized that their views may differ from the original author's. (b) not all authors took part in the study, which further reduced the sample size and validity of the findings; (c) many implementation projects that took place in Canada during the study time period were not reported through COACH, so the findings may not be representative of all IS implementation projects in the Canadian health setting.

RESULTS

This section summarizes findings from the articles reviewed and interviews conducted. It includes a profile of the articles and contacts, the technology described in the articles, whether the expectations were met, key implementation issues identified, continued system use and changes reported, and the lessons learned.

Profile of Articles and Contacts

The number of articles related to IS implementation projects that were published between 1991 and 1997 ranged from 8 to 13 each year (Table 1a). The articles averaged from two and a half to three pages between 1991 and 1994, but increased to close to eight pages in 1997. The overall proceedings averaged 100 pages, although the total number of articles dropped from a previous average of 30 per year to 13 in 1997. Twenty-four interviews were conducted. Almost half the authors and their designates were unavailable or chose not to participate in an interview (Table 1b).

The Technology Used

The technology described in the articles included the types of computer systems, software applications, databases and technical support that were planned or implemented. Over half of the 50 articles mentioned the type of computer systems used in the project, which included four main types:

Table 1a: Number of articles and interviews by year

Year	Number of implementation articles/total articles	Length of articles/length of proceedings	Average length of articles	Number of interviews/number of articles (%)
1991	11/26 (42%)	30/97 pages	2.7 pages	2/11 (18%)
1992	13/27 (48%)	31/104 pages	2.4 pages	7/13 (54%)
1993	9/31 (29%)	29/106 pages	3.2 pages	5/9 (55%)
1994	8/31 (26%)	20/108 pages	2.5 pages	3/8 (38%)
1997	9/13 (70%)	70/94 pages	7.8 pages	7/9 (78%)

Table 1b: Summary of numbers of articles and contacts

	Contacted	Interviewed	Declined/No contact
Original author	33	19*	13
Designates	13	6	7
Total contacts made	46	25*	20
No contact made	4	n/a	4
Total	50	24**	24
*1 interview conducted for two articles; **1 interview incomplete and excluded			

- mixed platforms such as mainframes with Unix and/or PC based workstations;
- standalone or networked PC systems;
- high-end Unix workstations and/or minicomputers; and
- special devices such as smart cards and pen-based computers.

No one type of system listed above was found to be predominant. Most of the articles also mentioned the type of software application used in the project. These were categorized using an adaptation of the 1996 Resource Guide from Healthcare Computing & Communications Canada (COACH 1996). The five most common types of applications included:

- core patient information systems;
- comprehensive Hospital Information Systems (we added this term as some projects included applications across several categories);
- departmental systems (we added this term to represent several categories in the Guide that relate to specific departments);
- patient care systems; and
- decision support systems.

In some articles, the actual type of application used was not clear and had to be inferred by the researchers. Only some of the articles mentioned the type of database used in the project. Of these articles, relational databases such as Informix and Oracle were the most common. The other database types were flat files, spreadsheets, hypertext and proprietary databases. The types of support resources needed to plan or carry out the implementation project were described in only some of the articles. While most of these articles recognized the need for support from different parts of the organization, many emphasized strong and ongoing support from the IS staff. A few projects were collaborative in nature, involving multiple partners such as vendors, government and national health organizations.

Were Expectations Met?

The implementation experiences described in the 50 articles were examined for their objectives and/or expectations, strengths and weaknesses (or costs and benefits). These are summarized in Table 2. Ten of the 24 interviewees confirmed their expectations had been met; 10 were partly met; 2 not met; and 2 exceeded expectations. The most common expectations from interviewees were similar to the objectives, strengths and benefits from the articles and summarized in Table 2. These are:

- improved information availability, data collection or standards;
- increased efficiency or service provision;
- user acceptance, involvement or stress reduction; and
- cost reduction, funding availability and affordability.

Table 2: Implementation expectations, benefits and costs

Objectives / expectations (most articles)	Strengths and benefits (majority of articles)	Weaknesses and costs (less than half the articles)
• provide accessible, accurate, useful information • improve service, efficiency, utilization and productivity • provide cost-effective, high quality care • interface/integrate different information systems • have user-friendly systems • standardize care and methods, evaluate outcome • achieve cost-savings from automation	• improved accuracy and accessibility of information • better planning, control and decision making • improved efficiency and utilization of services • reduced cost or increased cost-effectiveness • integrated, accessible systems	• protection of individual's privacy • limitations in high quality information • implementation process lengthy, delayed and frustrating • limitations in functionality, storage capacity, performance • user interface inefficient, no time savings • difficulty in getting user acceptance • long period required to monitor for trends • variation in terms and definitions • comparison of systems difficult • costly to implement and maintain • Cost less than expected or cost figures provided

Four categories of reasons were given for why expectations were not met by the interviewees, which are similar to the weaknesses and costs listed in Table 2:

- user apprehension, staff turnover, lack of buy-in or involvement;
- systems lacking functionality, high maintenance or technology limitations;
- loss in efficiency; and
- insufficient information from the system.

Key Implementation Issues

Six categories of key implementation issues were also identified in the interviews. These issues related to:

- training;
- systems capability or information accuracy;
- process changes or information flow;
- user involvement and expectations;
- support resources or champions; and
- management support or project planning.

The interviews also identified four of the most common methods of addressing these issues, which consisted of:

- process management, planning or communication;
- support resources;
- training resources; and
- management support.

The key implementation issues identified from the 24 interviews were also sorted by year to determine if they differed over the years. As seen in Table 3, training had been among the top two issues over the years except in 1994. Change in process and information flow was the second top issue in 1992 and 1994, and tied for second in 1991 and 1997. User involvement and expectations was the top issue in 1997. System capability and information accuracy was also among the top two issues in 1993 and 1994, and tied for second in 1991 and 1997.

Table 3: Top two implementation issues from interviews (8 tied for second)

1991	1992	1993	1994	1997
Training	Training	Training	System capability, information accuracy	User involvement, expectations
Change in process information flow*	Change in process, information flow	System capability, information accuracy	Change in process, information flow	Training*
System capability, information accuracy*				System capability, information accuracy*
Management support, project planning*				Change in process, information flow *

It would appear that, one of the top implementation issues consistently identified over the years was training, with the other top issues being change in process and information flow, system capability and information accuracy, and more recently user involvement and expectations. These findings make sense in that the implementation issues were mostly concerned with deploying systems, reorganizing work practices, ensuring system function as required, and providing information needed.

Continued System Use and Change

Many of the systems described in the 24 projects were still being used at the time of the interview; five were partly used and two not used at all. The interviewees identified reasons for continued use, systems not being used, and changes in systems, as well as types of changes made, and effects of change (summarized in Table 4).

Information on evaluation includes whether evaluation was part of implementation, evaluation method used and its results, and project status at the time of conference publication. Over half of the 50 projects were already implemented when the articles were published; some were being implemented in varying stages; and for a few others implementation was being planned at the time. Only 20% reported some form of evaluation conducted as part of implementation. In a few articles, the authors noted that evaluation was being planned. Five evaluation methods were reported in 10 projects:
- pilot study or field test;
- pre/post implementation surveys or interviews;

Table 4: Summary of continued system use and change

Reasons for continued use	Reasons for systems not used	Reasons for change (almost all systems)	Types of change	Effects of change
• system features, integration over time • adequate resources • user commitment or satisfaction • cost savings or too expensive to replace • improved efficiency, care or work practices	• technology not available, lack of integration • users not satisfied • cost • regionalization • pilot project only	• system changes or refinement • improved services or practices • user initiated changes • improved information accuracy, availability	• new functionality or expansion to other users and departments • technology upgrade • application refinement	• improved performance, service, efficiency or functionality • user resistance, unrealistic expectations to no effect • organizational or user satisfaction • improved information accuracy, accessibility or decision making

- cross-sectional interviews or focus groups;
- trend analysis or comparison with the stated objectives;
- literature review as part of the evaluation.

Evaluation results were reported in the following categories:
- increased knowledge, efficiency or functionality;
- needs met, but no further elaboration;
- improved information, documentation or decision making;
- differences noted between planned and actual events, with further work needed;
- no difference in staff attitude and level of computer knowledge; and
- results to be reported later.

Lessons Learned

A total of 74 types of lessons were mentioned in 26 of 50 articles reviewed. Similarly, 64 lessons were identified in the 24 interviews. There were no substantial differences between lessons noted in the articles and interviews. These lessons were merged according to similarities and categorized under six themes in Table 5. The key themes for lessons learned are the need for:
- organizational commitment, training, and resource support;
- managing the project, communication and change process;
- organization and user involvement using a teams approach;
- system capability including flexibility, functionality, user-friendliness, integration;
- information quality;
- demonstrated positive consequences of computerization.

The lessons learned from interviews were sorted by year to determine if they differed over the years. Table 6 shows organizational commitment and training/ resource support were the two most frequently mentioned lessons learned. On the other hand, managing projects, including communication and change process was the other most frequently mentioned lesson in 1991, 1992, 1994 and 1997. For 1993 and 1994, the other lesson mentioned was organization, user involvement and teams approach. System capability tied for second place in 1991 and 1992 but dropped below the top two lessons thereafter.

DISCUSSION

Summary of Experiences

The implementation outcomes from the articles and interviews are summarized in Table 7 according to the original research questions: (a) whether expectations

Table 5: Summary of lessons learned

Themes from lessons	74 lessons learned from articles	64 lessons learned from interviews
Organizational commitment, training, resource support	• training, dedicated resources, ongoing support • commitment, management support, policy changes	• dedicated, ongoing resource with expertise, transferable skills • organizational commitment, steering committee, influential sponsors • different types and frequency of training needed • adequate funding
Managing project, communication and change process	• accommodate change, adapt systems, review practices/systems • communication, cooperation • project management, infrastructure • fit with practice, difficult to formalize, agreeing on requirements • knowledge of organization, services • different implementation methods	• project planning, communication, staged implementation, management • managing/understanding change in process, organization, culture
Organization and user involvement, teams approach	• involve stakeholders at all stages, esp. physicians, champions, users • partnership, teamwork	• user participation, IS input, addressing user concerns • teamwork
System capability	• flexibility, functionality of system, user-friendliness • need for complete order entry	• system flexibility, ease of use, integration, performance • understanding technical need, avoid customization, ensure affordability
Information quality	• data collection is a substantive task, ensure quality of data • access to information, security, confidentiality • patient access/control of information as empowerment	• understanding information need, collecting only information needed • information management and sharing are complex, difficult to do
Consequences of computerization	• costing framework, link to premiums, realizing benefits • impacts of lengthy process	• realizing benefits, cost savings, improvement in services, efficiency

Table 6: Top two lessons from interviews sorted by year (8 tied for second)

1991	1992	1993	1994	1997
Managing projects, communication, change process	Organizational commitment, training, resource support	Organizational commitment, training, resource support	Organizational commitment, training, resource support	Organizational commitment, training, resource support
Organizational commitment, training, resource support*	Managing projects, communication, change process*	Organization, user involvement, teams approach	Managing projects, communication, change process*	Managing projects, communication, change process
System capability*	System capability*		Organization, user involvement, teams approach*	

were met; (b) key implementation issues encountered; (c) reasons for continued system use; (d) system changes over time; and (e) lessons learned.

The authors and interviewees noted a number of lessons learned over the years from these implementation projects: need for organizational commitment, resource support and training; managing the project, change process and communication; organizational and user involvement, and teams approach; system capability; information quality; and demonstrable positive consequences from computerization. These findings are consistent with recent literature on the organizational, people and technology aspects of medical informatics - system implementation is as much a process of social change as it is a technology deployment endeavor within the organization (e.g. Detmer and Friedman 1994; Lorenzi et al. 1997; Massoleni et al. 1996; Weir et al. 1995).

Specifically, organizational commitment is needed to provide the leadership, resources and support necessary to implement the systems. Equally important is the ability to manage the project, change process, communication and expectations, which can bring about apprehension, stress and anxiety from the staff if not addressed effectively. To be successful the stakeholders, especially the users, must be involved at all stages of the process, and be provided with appropriate training based on individual ability, task requirement, and project timing (e.g. do not train

Table 7: Summary of implementation outcomes

Expectations	Implementation issues	Continued system use	System changes	Lessons learned
• expectations met or partly met in 22 out of 24 interviews	issues addressed by: • planning, process management, communication • training, support resources • management support	• 22/24 interviews mentioned systems still used	• all 24 interviews mentioned systems changed since first reported	• 74 lessons from 26 articles • 64 lessons from 24 interviews • 6 themes for lessons
• improved service, savings, efficiency • accessible, accurate information • cost-effective, quality care • interface and/or integrate systems • user-friendly • standardized care, methods, outcome evaluation	• system capability, information accuracy, quality • change in process, information flow • user involvement, expectations • resource support, champions • management support, project planning • training	• system functionality, integration evolved over time • user commitment, satisfaction • cost savings, too expensive to replace • improved efficiency, care, work practices • adequate resources	• new functionality, expansion to other users and departments • improved services, work practices • user initiated changes • improved information accuracy, availability	• managing project, change process, communication • organizational support, commitment, training resources • organization and user involvement • system capability • information quality • consequences of computerization

too far in advance of the actual implementation, as users will forget what they have learned).

Having champions or the "right" persons on the project team who can persuade, promote and influence their colleagues is important, since there is always a tendency for individuals to cling to existing work practices out of familiarity and comfort. Also paramount are the capability of the system and the quality of the information being automated, which should lead to some demonstrable benefits for the users and the organization as a whole. Nothing is more frustrating for the users than working with a computer system that crashes, produces incomplete or inaccurate information, and requires more effort to complete the tasks with questionable benefits.

The project team also needs to promptly identify and resolve implementation issues that emerge when deploying the system. The key issues identified from our interview findings are the same as the lessons learned. To be successful, the team must be willing to devote time, effort, resources and compassion to resolve these issues in a time responsive manner. As can be seen from the findings, many of the systems continued to evolve over time after they were implemented. In some cases, the work practices were also adapted to take advantage of the functionality of these systems. These findings are consistent with implementation literature in suggesting that systems can be implemented and adapted over time, along with work practice changes, to emerge as unique systems in distinct settings (Anderson 1997; Kaplan 1994). As such, the project team and its organization must be prepared to dedicate adequate resources to manage the project, system, change, training and support on an ongoing basis to ensure the system can continue to meet the evolving needs of the organization and its users.

The two most frequent lessons learned were cited almost every year: the need to have organizational commitment, training and resource support, as well as to manage the project, change process and communication well. Similarly, the top implementation issues mentioned year after year were consistently around training, change process, user involvement and managing expectations. These should be areas of attention for organizations and project teams about to embark on new implementation projects. It is also interesting to note that, while the level of technology sophistication may have improved over the years, the implementation issues and lessons learned were still essentially the same.

Need for Evaluation

A major shortcoming noted in this study is the lack of evaluation of the implementation projects described. Such evaluation is important in justifying the IT investment made by the organization, as well as being a valuable resource for others wishing to implement similar systems. Even conducting a simple review of relevant literature, which was only mentioned once in the 50 projects we examined, might have provided some insight prior to system implementation. The adoption of some type evaluation framework such as the IS success model by DeLone and McLean (1992) can provide a consistent approach to assessing these systems. Such a framework typically covers a wide range of measures including effectiveness of the implementation process, quality of the system, quality of the information, usefulness and use of the system and its information, as well as overall impacts on the individual, group and the organization.

CONCLUDING REMARKS

This study was conducted to determine the outcome of implementation projects presented at the COACH conferences between 1991 and 1997. Our intent was to identify key implementation issues involved and lessons learned to gain a better understanding of systems that have been implemented over the years in the field setting. Also of interest was how such experiences relate to health informatics literature on implementation. We believe sharing such cumulative experiences and providing suggestions for improvement are important ways to advance the practice of health informatics in Canada.

ACKNOWLEDGEMENTS

We acknowledge the help of our research assistants Janny Shum, Les Wold and Tina Strack in collecting and organizing the data for this project. We thank the individuals who participated in the interviews to share their insights. Most importantly, we extend our gratitude to COACH for their funding and support to make this study a reality.

REFERENCES

Anderson, J. (1997). Clearing the way for physicians' use of clinical information systems. *Communications of ACM*. 40(8):83-90.

COACH. (1996). Resource Guide. *Healthcare Computing & Communications Canada* 10(3).

DeLone, W.H. and McLean, E.R. (1992). Information systems success: the quest for the dependent variable. *Information Systems Research*. 3(1): 60-95.

Detmer, W.M. and Friedman, C.P. (1994). Academic physicians' assessment of the effects of computers on health care. *Proceedings of AMIA*. 558-62.

Kaplan, B. (1994). Reducing barriers to physician data entry for computer-based patient records. *Topics in Health Information Management*. 15(1):24-34.

Lorenzi, H.M. and Riley, R.T. (2000). Managing change: An overview. *Journal of American Medical Informatics Association.* 7(2):116-124.

Lorenzi, N.M., Riley, R.T., Blyth, A.J.C., Southon, G. and Dixon, B.J. (1997). Antecedents of the people and organizational aspects of medical informatics: review of the literature. *Journal of American Medical Informatics Association.* 4(2):79-93.

Mazzoleni, M.C., Baiardi, P., Giorgi, I., Franchi, G., Marconi, R. and Cortesi, M. (1996). Assessing users' satisfaction through perception of usefulness and ease of use in the daily interaction with a hospital information system. Cimino J (ed). *Proceedings 20th AMIA.* 752-6. Hanley & Belfus, Inc. Philadelphia.

Weir, C., Lincoln, M., Roscoe, D. and Moreshead, G. (1995). Successful implementation of an integrated physician order entry application: a systems perspective. Gardner RM (ed). *Proceedings 19th SCAMC.* 790-4. Hanley & Belfus, Inc. Philadelphia.

APPENDIX

Table 1: The articles from the 1991 proceedings that were implementation projects. *denotes articles that were included in the interviews.

Author	Title
Bardeau-Milner D, Homer L, Copping A	Computer support for food production at Rockyview General Hospital
Choat N	Computers and quality assurance: the experience of a 300 bed community hospital
Dornan J, Garling A, Powell DG	Benefits of clinician's HIS utilization: expectations and potentials
Gatchell S, Waisman MS, Gadd D	Workload measurement for clinical nutrition
Genge P, Wojdylo S*	Strategies towards a successful implementation of a totally computerized nursing system
Germain D	Executive information systems, executive patient costing systems
Greenburg M, Manninen Richmond, Osolen H	Design of a medical information system to support research in paediatric haematology/oncology
Merrifield K*	Implementing a dietary computer system
Persaud D, Dawe U	A winning combination: hospital risk management and the personal computer
Strudwick W, Terry J	Working with an on-line human resource system - or life in the fast lane
Carnvale F, Gottesman RD, Malowany, Roger K, Yien C, Lam A	Development of an automated bedside nursing workstation

Table 2: The articles from the 1992 proceedings that were implementation projects.
*denotes articles that were included in the interviews.

Author	Title
Adaskin E, et al.*	The impact of computerization on nursing
Assang W, Clement H, Goodman J*	Implementation of a clinical support system
Depalme MJ, Shewchuk M*	Operating suite automation for the 21st century
Evans J, Parboosingh J*	Apple and IBM - they can exist together!
Goldbloom AL	Selection and implementation of a medical information system in a major teaching hospital: process over product
Jefferson S	Victoria hospital's "tower of Babel": supporting a multi-vendor systems environment
Lake P*	Implementing a connectivity strategy in a health care facility
Laporte J	Presentation of the Sidoci project
Malanowich N, Volk T	The B.C. Cardiovascular Surgery System: Clinical & Management Support System
Powell G, Douglas N, Westlake P.*	Physician participation in the hospital corporation information system "why bother?"
Ross S, Semel M, Fitzpatrick C	Nursing management data set: maximum utility, maximum benefit
Thrasher P	Network systems in the Ottawa Civic Hospital
Zilm D, Harms R*	Forms overlay laser printers - a unique opportunity for cost savings

Table 3: The articles from the 1993 proceedings that were implementation projects.
*denotes articles that were included in the interviews.

Author	Title
Blunt DW, Nichols DK*	Ambulatory patient cases: DC+PC+MC=RM
Glazebrook J	Case study: successful implementation of open systems in a community hospital
Hurley D, Lawson B*	Automated medication system - benefits for nursing
Laukkanen E	Evaluation of pen based computing in an out-patient cancer centre
Nusbaum MH*	Extending LAN boundaries to the enterprise and beyond
Percy J, Fan D*	Data for the user
Simpson J, Simpson J, Blair-Clare B	Post-implementation of an order entry/results reporting system: curing "performance dip" and interdepartmental stress
Slusar G, Enright C	Northwestern health services: the integrated client record
Tracy S, Parsons D, Wesson P, Lane P*	The Ontario Trauma Registry

Table 4: The articles from the 1994 proceedings that were implementation projects. *denotes articles that were included in the interviews.

Author	Title
DeBeyer T*	The long term care client information system: a tool for the management and administration of client placement information
Geiger G, Gordon D, Vachon B, Mitra A, Kunov H	A Disability Resource Information System
Genge P*	Recognizing the full benefits of computerization
Magnusson C*	The hand-held computer: more than a game boy
McMaster G, Allison A	Using technology to improve client care and inter-agency communications
Podolak I	Database development in long term care, chronic care and rehabilitation
Simpson J	The effects of a computerized care planning module on nurses' planning activities
Smith D	Optical disk technology - community hospital applications, a case presentation

Table 5: The articles from the 1997 proceedings that were implementation projects. *denotes articles that were included in the interviews.

Author	Title
Andru PJ*	Hospital-community linkages: community information needs, data warehousing, and pilot projects
Eagar EA, Eagar F*	The University Park Medical Clinic success story: a case study in continuous computerization towards 2000
Gordon D, Marafioti S, Chapman R*	Management decision support and data warehousing
Johnstone R, Wattling D, Buckley J, Ho D, Bestilny S*	Alberta mental health information system (AMHIS): a provincial strategy and implementation
Monaghan BJ, Vimr MA, Jefferson S	Data driven decision making: the cardiac care network of Ontario experience
Niebergal D*	Benefit realization of computer-based patient records in medical group practices
Rivera K	The Ontario smart health initiative
Sisson JH, Park GS, Pike L*	Integrating critical care patient data into an enterprise-wide information system
Warnock-Matheron A, Sorge M, Depalme M*	New opportunities and challenges during restructuring

Chapter 7

The Role of User Ownership and Positive User Attitudes in the Successful Adoption of Information Systems within NHS Community Trusts

Crispin R. Coombs, Neil F. Doherty and John Loan-Clarke
Loughborough University, UK

The factors that influence the ultimate level of success or failure of systems development projects have received considerable attention in the academic literature. However, despite the existence of a 'best practice' literature many projects still fail. The record of the National Health Service has been particularly poor in this respect. The research reported in this paper proposes that two additional factors; user ownership and positive user attitudes warrant further development and investigation. The current study investigated these two factors in a homogenous organizational sector, Community NHS Trusts, using a common type of information system, in order to eliminate the potentially confounding influences of sector and system. A multiple case-study design incorporating five Community Healthcare Trusts was utilized. The key results from the analysis indicated that both user ownership and positive user attitudes were important mediating variables that were crucial to the success of a CIS. In addition, it was also identified that the adoption of best practice variables had a dual role, directly influencing the level of

Previously Published in the *Journal of End User Computing, vol.13, no.4*, Copyright © 2001, Idea Group Publishing.

perceived success but also facilitating the development of user ownership and positive user attitudes. These results will be of particular interest to practising IM&T managers in the NHS and also to the wider academic research community.

INTRODUCTION

The challenge for the NHS is to harness the information revolution and use it to benefit patients (Rt. Hon Tony Blair, 1998)[1]

Over the past twenty years the level of penetration and sophistication of information technology has grown dramatically, with computer-based information systems actively supporting all key business processes and significantly enhancing both the operational effectiveness and the strategic direction of organizations of all types. The UK's National Health Service (NHS) is one, particularly large and complex, organization that has been keen to harness the potential of IT to enhance its administrative, managerial and clinical performance. Unfortunately, in both the public and private sectors, the successful acquisition and introduction of information technology is still dogged by high failure rates (Lyytinen & Hirschheim, 1987; Kearney, 1990; Hochstrasser & Griffiths, 1991; Clegg et al., 1997). More specifically, there is much evidence to suggest that the NHS's record has been particularly poor, with respect to the successful deployment of computer-based information systems (for example: National Audit Office, 1991; Keen, 1994; National Audit Office, 1996).

There is, therefore, still a pressing need for well-focussed research to provide insights into how levels of failure can be reduced from both a general perspective and with regard to the NHS in particular. To help investigate these issues a research project was initiated to explore the factors that affect the success of Community Information Systems (CIS) within the NHS. It was envisaged that the application of CIS within the community healthcare sector would provide a particularly fertile research domain for the following two reasons:

1. Community Trusts form a reasonably homogeneous organizational sector, distinct from the acute sector and community information systems provide different instances of a common type of application; consequently the number of confounding factors in the study are greatly reduced;

2. Two recent official reports (Audit Commission, 1997; Burns, 1998) have identified a high degree of variability in the quality of CIS with many existing systems failing to deliver the anticipated benefits. Consequently, it would be possible to compare and contrast the experiences of Trusts, which had experienced a range of different outcomes.

The initial phases of this project entailed a detailed case study, based upon interviews with a wide variety of staff at Central Nottinghamshire Healthcare (NHS) Trust (CNHT)[2] and a survey of IT managers within Community Trusts (Coombs et al., 1998; Coombs et al., 1999). These studies provided important insights into the role and impact of CIS and helped to focus the research objectives, for the later stages of the project. More specifically, in addition to confirming the importance of factors such as training; senior management commitment and participation; testing and user involvement, the results from these preliminary studies, also indicated the critical roles of user ownership and positive user attitudes. As these latter factors have not, to date, received the attention they warrant in the academic literature, a follow-up, qualitative study was initiated to explicitly review their importance.

The paper is organized into several sections. The following section presents a summary of the relevant information systems literature before presenting and justifying three research objectives. The justification for, and implementation of, the multiple case-study research design and research methods are discussed in section three. The research results are presented in a series of tables and diagrams, which are discussed in the fourth section. Finally, the importance of this research for the NHS and other organizations is assessed in the concluding section.

CONTEXTUAL BACKGROUND AND RESEARCH OBJECTIVES

In the past twenty years much interest has been generated in the identification of factors critical to the successful outcome of systems development projects (For example: Yap et al., 1992; Sauer, 1993; Willcocks & Margetts, 1994; Keil, 1995; Whyte & Bytheway, 1996; Flowers, 1997; Li, 1997). The aim, therefore, of this section is to review the most common best practice factors highlighted in the literature, prior to reviewing the potentially important contributions of positive user attitudes and user ownership to the successful outcome of a systems development project. In so doing, the objectives of this research are established.

Best Practice in Systems Development Projects

A number of empirical and in-depth studies have been conducted which examine success factors in the development and implementation of information systems. These and other studies have helped to focus IT professionals' attention on the importance of factors such as: user involvement (Wong & Tate, 1994; Whyte & Bytheway, 1996); senior management commitment (Beath, 1991; Sauer, 1993); staff training (Miller & Doyle, 1987; Whyte & Bytheway, 1996); systems testing (Ennals, 1995; Flowers, 1997) and user support (Miller & Doyle, 1987; Govindarajulu & Reithel, 1998). There is, therefore, a well-documented body of 'best practice' knowledge that should guide the IT practitioner in the effective development and implementation of information systems. However, there exists a paradoxical situation in that far too many projects still fail, despite the availability of this body of knowledge, which should help to promote success. Why in so many instances should this be the case? It could perhaps be that the advice is either: blatantly disregarded; not universally appropriate; not well disseminated or not always possible to heed. Alternatively it might be that the adoption of existing best practice guidelines is not, by itself, sufficient to ensure the successful outcome of systems development projects.

The Importance of User Ownership

Van Alstyne et al. (1995) have stated that: *'ownership is critical to the success of information systems projects'* with the key reason for this being *'self-interest; owners have a greater vested interest in system's success than non-owners'* (p. 268). However, Clegg et al. (1997) suggest that in far too many projects it is the developers rather than the users and user managers who own the system, which may have undesirable consequences for the system's performance. Unfortunately, this apparently important concept has received relatively little explicit attention in the information systems' literature. Where ownership has been addressed in studies it has typically been in the context of increasing user acceptance (Robey & Farrow, 1982; Guimaraes & McKeen, 1993) or minimizing user resistance (Markus, 1983, Beynon-Davis, 1995). Based upon this review of the literature, and the results of the preliminary stages of this research, the following working definition for user ownership has been derived:

'The state in which members of the user community display through their behavior, an active responsibility for an information system'.

To clarify this definition, it is necessary to add the two following qualifiers. Firstly, it must be stressed that whilst it is highly desirable that user ownership should be exhibited by the whole user community, throughout all stages of the system's development and operation, this may not always be the case. Secondly, it should be noted that the users may not be able to claim exclusive ownership of the system, as ownership will be shared with members of the steering committee and the development team, especially in the system's developmental stages.

The Importance of Positive User Attitudes

In purely quantitative terms the importance of positive user attitudes has probably received more attention in the literature than user ownership. It is, for example, widely recognized that it is desirable to attain positive user attitudes as this may have a beneficial impact upon user behavior, ultimately influencing user acceptance of the system (Lucas, 1978 & 1981; Zmud, 1983; Ginzberg et al.,

1984; Joshi, 1990 & 1992). More specifically, Grantham & Vaske (1985) and Davis (1993) have suggested that positive user attitudes are an important predictor of system's usage. In the context of this research, the following working definition for positive user attitudes has been derived:

> '*The state in which members of the user community display positive opinions and beliefs towards the information system*'.

It should be noted that, as for user ownership, levels of positive user attitude may vary between different members of the user community and also between different phases of the system's development and operation. Finally, the working definition of positive user attitudes appears in many ways similar to constructs used in other studies, such as '*user satisfaction*' (DeLone & McLean, 1992), '*user information satisfaction*' (Bailey & Pearson, 1983; Srinivasan, 1985) or '*user reactions*' (Clegg et al., 1997). However, there is one important distinction; whilst user satisfaction, user information satisfaction and user reactions are typically formulated as responses to a recently implemented system, positive user attitudes is a state which can begin from the project's inception and continue throughout the system's working life.

Critique of the Literature and Establishment of Research Objectives

Unfortunately, despite the substantial body of knowledge with regard to best practice within systems development projects the incidence of systems failure and systems under-performance remains stubbornly high. This may in part be due to the following limitations with regard to existing literature.

1.   The 'best practice' literature, which is extensive, has limitations in terms of either depth or generalizibility. For example, survey studies, whilst providing the breadth of coverage, lack the capacity to effectively deal with the complexity of the system development process (Sauer, 1993). By contrast, case studies, whilst far better suited to handling the complexities of systems development, either relate to only one case or focus upon a number of unrelated cases; in both instances the generalizibility of findings is problematic.

2.   Whilst some studies have noted the importance of user ownership and positive user attitudes, little work has specifically targeted these factors to identify why they are significant and how they can be achieved. Furthermore, this research has typically been conducted in isolation from the research into best practice. For example, most studies of best practice factors (for example: Miller & Doyle, 1987; Whyte & Bytheway, 1996; Doherty et al., 1998) do not include user ownership and positive user attitudes. Consequently, it is difficult to judge the relative importance of these factors and their relationship with other best practice factors.

To overcome these weaknesses, a qualitative study was initiated, targeting the development and implementation of community information systems. This approach isolated a single organizational sector, Community Trusts, in which different instances of a standard application of IT were being applied and ensured that the following research objectives could be addressed:

1. Identification of the relationship between the ability of the project teams to encourage user ownership and the resultant level of success or failure of the operational information system;

2. Identification of the relationship between the ability of the project teams to encourage positive user attitudes and the resultant level of success or failure of the operational information system;

3. Identification of the relationships between user ownership, positive user attitudes, other best practice factors and the resultant level of success or failure of the operational information system.

It was envisaged that through the exploration of these issues new evidence could be provided with respect to the importance and role of user ownership and positive user attitudes in systems development projects. In addition, it would be possible to provide advice to IT practitioners on the importance of taking steps to foster user ownership and positive user attitudes. More specifically, the research should provide important insights into the successful development and implementation of information systems within the NHS in general, and Community Trusts in particular.

RESEARCH METHODOLOGY

Doherty et al. (1998) have noted that existing research on best practice has tended to focus on developing a critical set of factors affecting IT implementation success with less emphasis being placed on 'how' and 'why' these factors interact together to produce either success or failure. Gable (1994) and Pare and Elam (1997) advocate the greater use of case study research to explore and develop an increased understanding of these complex relationships. The aim of this section is to provide an overview of the methods by which a case study-based piece of research was initiated and executed to explore the objectives described at the end of the previous section.

Research Design

The initial stages of this research project comprised a detailed case study at a single Community Trust and a survey of all Community Care (NHS) Trusts in the UK. Whilst both of these studies provided important insights and facilitated the design of the research presented in this paper, both can be criticized from a

methodological perspective. For example, whilst it has been argued that *'case study research is particularly appropriate for the study of information systems development, implementation and use within organizations'* (Darke et al., 1998, p. 278), Galliers (1992) notes that case studies are usually restricted to a single event or organization and that it is difficult to collect similar data from a sufficient number of similar organizations making it difficult to generalize from case study research. Similarly, it can be argued that survey-based studies, whilst providing the breadth of coverage, lack the capacity to effectively deal with the complexity of the system development process (Sauer, 1993).

Multiple case studies however, allow the study of phenomena in more diverse settings and facilitate cross-case analysis and comparison. This multiple approach allows the researcher to confirm that findings are not being unduly influenced by confounding variables unique to individual research settings (Cavaye, 1996). In addition, multiple cases may also be used either to predict similar results (literal replication) or contrasting results for predictable reasons (theoretical replication) (Yin, 1994, p. 46). Based on the desire to explore and interpret the complex relationships between best practice, user ownership, positive user attitudes and success a multiple case study approach was undertaken.

Research Instrument Design

Past literature on best practice and organizational impact as well as the evidence from the initial case study research and the questionnaire survey were used to develop questions to be included in a semi-structured interview schedule. The choice of a semi-structured interview over a standardized interview was made because of the exploratory nature of the research and the fact that it would not have been possible to create a fully structured guide from current knowledge (Diamantopoulos & Souchon, 1996). The interview schedule had four sections: biographical/introductory; the adoption of best practice variables; the attainment of user ownership and positive user attitudes; and the determinants of success. The final section of the interview consisted of a short questionnaire that used a five point Likert scale to measure various aspects of the perceived system success. The success measures were adapted from the six generic measures developed by DeLone & McLean (1992) and addressed both user and management perspectives on various aspects of the system. Each interviewee was sent a letter outlining the aims of the research project and indicating the specific areas that would be explored through the interviews.

Targeting & Execution of the Interviews

In studying the responses to the questionnaire survey it became clear that one particular community information system (Comwise, designed by Systems Team)

was most common among respondents. It was therefore possible and desirable to concentrate on this sample as it removed the confounding factor of variations in system design from the analysis. However, in order for the results from the Comwise sample to be generalized to the rest of the respondents it was necessary to confirm that the Comwise sample was representative of all the respondents. Statistical means and variances were calculated for each question on the survey and compared for both the main group of respondents and the Comwise sample. No significant differences between the means or variances for each group were identified and consequently it was concluded that the Comwise sample was representative of the main group of respondents to the questionnaire. The Comwise sample group consisted of 18 Trusts and had a further advantage in that the performance of the system in different Trusts appeared to vary considerably as perceived by the respondents to the questionnaire survey. Therefore, a multiple case study approach would enable a range of Trusts to be studied that were using the same CIS but were producing contrasting results in terms of success.

On the basis of their perceived CIS performance a range of five Trusts were contacted and in each case the initial contact was through the respondent to the questionnaire, either the IM&T Manager or the Information Manager. An interview was conducted with each of these key informants at the end of which requests were made for additional members of the Trust to interview. It was considered particularly important that staff from areas outside the Information and IT Departments of the Trust be interviewed to record their perspective on the use of a CIS. The clinicians form the largest stakeholder group that use a CIS and one of the key measurements of the success of a CIS is the clinicians' satisfaction with the system. A criticism frequently levelled at quantitative IS research is that it tends to concentrate on documenting and studying the views of IS professionals who have a clear vested interest in the success of the system. Consequently the opportunity to interview and document other staff views towards the system was considered to be of great importance.

The key informants were asked to identify an administrator, a clinical manager and a clinical user who would be willing to participate in the study. As can be seen, from the breakdown of interviewees presented in table 1, it was not always possible, for practical reasons, to achieve the desired mix of informants, but sufficient numbers of informants participated from each Trust to ensure that the sample reflected a range of views.

In addition to participating in the interviews, the IM&T Managers were asked to provide, if possible, documentary evidence, such as published articles, internal reports or newsletters, which were used to help contextualize, explain and verify the interview responses. As can also be seen from the information presented in Table 1, such information was forthcoming in a number of cases. Each interview was

Table 1: Range of informants interviewed at each trust

Informant	Trust A*	Trust B	Trust C*	Trust D	Trust E
IM&T Manager	✓	✓	✓	✓✓	✓
Manager		✓	✓	✓	✓
Clinical Manager		✓	✓✓		✓
Clinical User	✓	✓	✓	✓	✓
Totals	2	4	5	4	4

conducted, in-situ, at the Trust and lasted approximately an hour. To ensure the validity of the interview process, the informants were asked to supply specific evidence and examples to support their assertions. In the vast majority of cases, the face to face interview was complemented by a follow-up phone call that was used to clarify issues and attain supplementary information. Both the initial interviews and the follow-up phone calls were tape recorded and later transcribed verbatim.

In terms of the characteristics of the Trusts visited, Table 2 shows that although there was some variation in the range of services they provided and premises they used, they also exhibited a number of common features. The Trusts all operated on

Table 2: Case study trust profiles

Trust Profile	Trust A	Trust B	Trust C	Trust D	Trust E
Service Provision	Community	Community	Community	Community	Community
		Acute	Acute	Acute	
	Mental Health	Mental Health	Mental Health	Mental Health	Mental Health
Number of Hospitals	3	7	4	5	5
Number of. Health Centres/Clinics	11	16	42	8	7
Staff Groups Using System	District Nurses* Health Visitors School Nurses PAMS	District Nurses* Health Visitors* School Nurses PAMS	District Nurses* Health Visitors* School Nurses PAMS	District Nurses* Health Visitors* School Nurses PAMS	District Nurses* Health Visitors* School Nurses PAMS
System Profile	**Trust A**	**Trust B**	**Trust C**	**Trust D**	**Trust E**
System Name	Comwise	Comwise	Comwise	Comwise	Comwise
Version	2.2	N/S	2.2+	N/S	2.2
Supplier	Systems Team Ltd	Systems Team Ltd	Systems Team Ltd	Systems Team Ltd	Systems Team Ltd
Level of Implementation	Fully Implemented	Fully Implemented	Partially Implemented	Fully Implemented	Fully Implemented
System Uses Portable Technology	Yes	Yes	Yes	Yes	No
Staff Using the System	Clinical and Clerical Staff	Clinical and Clerical Staff	Clinical and Clerical Staff	Clinical staff	Clinical and Clerical Staff

* Main staff groups using system   N/S - Not Supplied

a decentralized basis with a small number of hospitals and multiple health centres. Most importantly, the same core staff groups used the system within each Trust. Similarly, because all the Trusts are based within the community healthcare sector they are guided by common policy and priority goals identified by the Department of Health. Furthermore, table 2 also demonstrates that all the Trusts were using the same software package and supplier for their community information systems. Consequently, by targeting these five Trusts it was possible to minimize the effect of confounding factors such as healthcare sector, type of system and system design.

Data Analysis Strategy

The analysis follows the three concurrent activities identified by Miles & Huberman, (1994, p. 10) of data reduction, data display and conclusion drawing/ verification. This approach is necessary to ensure that the researcher does not become overloaded from unreduced data transcripts and their information processing abilities impaired (Faust, 1982). Data reduction was conducted on each interview transcript using mainly '*in-vivo*' codes, that is codes derived from phrases used repeatedly by informants (Strauss & Corbin, 1990). In-vivo codes (as opposed to codes determined prior to the analysis) are appropriate when the research is essentially exploratory and are more useful in identifying new variables than adopting constrained literature-based codes (Diamantopoulos & Souchon, 1996). In addition, marginal remarks were used during the coding period to add clarity and meaning to the transcripts as well as having the ability to help revise and improve the coding structure (Chesler, 1987).

From the codes it was possible to develop a series of within-case matrix displays for each Trust. The within-case analysis was primarily conducted using the following three displays:

1. **Time ordered displays:** The time ordered display was used to show the variations in each variable over time and the major events during the CIS project identified by respondents. This display is primarily descriptive although it does have the value of preserving the historical flow and permitting a good look at the chain of events (Miles & Huberman, 1994, p. 110);

2. **Conceptually ordered displays:** This display was used to study the variables in more depth and generate more explanatory power. A thematic conceptual matrix was developed for each case to study the manifestation of the variable, the facilitators and inhibitors directly related to that variable and any solutions that had been subsequently proposed or adopted (Miles & Huberman, 1994, p. 131);

3. **Effects matrix:** Finally an effects matrix was also constructed for each Trust. This display concentrates on the outcomes of each of the variables concerned and their effects on other variables and areas associated with the CIS project.

Each variable was analyzed for positive and negative effects on specific outcomes and whether they were considered by informants to be direct or indirect relationships (Miles & Huberman, 1994, p. 137).

Following the within-case analysis the displays were synthesized into a series of fewer cross-case displays. The cross-case analysis took the form of a composite thematic conceptual matrix (Miles & Huberman, 1994, p. 183) and a causal network display (Miles & Huberman, 1994, p. 222). The composite thematic conceptual matrix allowed us to study the similarities and differences between the facilitators and inhibitors for each variable. The causal network was developed from a series of linear sub-models that displayed the linkages between variables more clearly before they were synthesized into a single overall causal model. It is primarily the results of these cross-case displays that are presented in the following section of this paper.

RESEARCH RESULTS

The research findings are reported in this section by presenting evidence in the form of specific examples and comments gathered through the interview process. To make the discussion of these findings more meaningful they are related to the three specific research objectives identified in section 2.4.

The Relationship Between User Ownership and Success

To explore the relationship between user ownership and success, informants were specifically asked during the interviews whether user ownership was occurring within their Trust and whether achieving user ownership had been planned or was occurring as a reaction to the development and operation of the system. Furthermore, each interviewee was asked to assess the effect that achieving user ownership was having on the operation of the CIS.

From the results of the cross-case analysis it was clear that there was a mixed experience across the Trusts with respect to user ownership. In four out of the five Trusts (A, B, C & D) it was found that achieving user ownership had been planned. However, only informants in one Trust (A) said that user ownership was already occurring at high levels. As one clinical user noted: '*there is ownership because we use it to inform our clinical practice*' and '*I think it [user ownership] was a deliberate policy by IT and I think the new Head of Information will extend that even further than it is now*'.

Informants in Trust B provided contrasting views on the occurrence of user ownership indicating that user ownership was perceived to be occurring at high levels in some areas, but not others. For example, whilst the IM&T Manager (B) stated: '*this is something the Head of Information has been working towards and this process is now coming where we are saying this is your system, what do you want us to record? Whereas before they were told what to record'*, a manager (B) suggested: *'I don't think staff have ever had ownership of the system and I think that is an extremely important issue'*.

Informants in Trust C stated that user ownership was starting to occur, but only at moderate levels so far, with one manager (C) noting: *'we may be a little hard on ourselves but we still don't believe that we have got adequate user ownership'*. However, in the majority of the Trusts (A, B & C) high levels of user ownership were expected in the future, once greater access to information was provided (A & B) and the CIS was fully implemented (C). By contrast, informants in Trusts D and E indicated that there was little or no user ownership occurring. For example, in Trust D a clinical user noted *'it has certainly been useful but I wouldn't have thought of it as our system'*, whilst the IM&T Manager at Trust E reflected: *'I think users see it as part of the daily grind of filling in these Daily Diary Sheets and so on and that's it really'*. One manager at Trust E summarized the situation more bluntly: *'its just a necessary evil'*. However, it was only the informants from Trust E who stated that user ownership had not been planned and was unlikely to occur in the future.

However, despite the range of experiences in achieving user ownership, there was a clear consensus across informants in all the Trusts, of the importance of user ownership to the ultimate success of a CIS. In three of the five Trusts (A, B & C) user ownership was identified as having particular importance in avoiding failure with informants making the

- *'The Trust is very reliant on user ownership because it is a Community Trust and staff are very decentralized. If the staff, the clinicians on the ground, don't own the system, feel how essential it is, it would be a complete failure'* (clinical user, A);
- *'Achieving user ownership will be the deciding factor of whether they use the system or not'* (IM&T Manager, B);
- *'If they [clinical staff] don't get ownership they will rely on non-clinical people trying to tell them how to use it which won't work'* (IM&T Manager, C).

It was interesting to note that the importance of user ownership was also recognized in Trust E, with a clinical manager commenting that: *'the Trust needs to encourage user ownership',* even though all informants from the Trust recognized that they had not experienced user ownership.

More specific benefits from achieving user ownership were also identified by respondents. For example, the IM&T Manager (A) stated that: *'having user ownership has meant that users are in control of their information'* and a clinical user (A) noted that: *'ownership is about recognizing and seeing the potential to develop things that are going to be clinically useful. Without the ownership you wouldn't be getting the ideas being generated and pushing the development of it [CIS] which in turn is improving patient care'*. Similarly, the IM&T Manager (C) stated that: *'I think once they [clinicians] own it they will try and optimize its use and they will try and explore different ways in which the system can be used to improve the service'*.

The importance of attaining user ownership has also been highlighted by the experiences of those Trusts that failed to achieve it. As a manager from Trust B noted *'without ownership of the data they [clinicians] don't feel they are involved or they are controlling it then we are going to have problems with the quality'*. Similar views were expressed at both Trusts D and E. For example, the IM&T Manager (D) stated that: *'I think the main problem is the quality of the data. They are not interested in what is going in so the quality is poor. That then undermines the quality of the reports that are pulled off'*. Similarly, a clinical manager (E) noted: *'It's not worthwhile entering the data from their [clinicians] point of view, they can't access the data and not being able to get the answers that they want further increases the amount of cynicism associated with the system'*.

The relationships that have been identified above clearly provide strong evidence to suggest that there is a relationship between user ownership and success. Furthermore, it has been demonstrated that the relationship can have either a positive or negative effect on the overall perceived success of a CIS, depending on how well user ownership is addressed during the systems development project.

The Relationship Between Positive User Attitudes and Success

The cross-case analysis of user attitudes indicated that all Trusts planned to develop positive user attitudes during the development, implementation and use of their respective community information systems. Informants at Trusts A and C stated that user attitudes were positive towards the CIS and that this positive attitude was thought likely to continue in the future. More specifically, the following examples were cited as evidence of positive user attitudes: an increased demand for reports (IM&T Manager, A; clinical manager, C); efforts by users to improve data quality (IM&T Manager, A); and general positive comments about the CIS during staff meetings (clinical user, A; clinical manager, C). Furthermore, in Trust C it was envisaged that the planned increases in access to information would further develop and enhance the users' positive attitudes. As one clinical user (C) commented: *'we are going to get more out of the system for our [the clinical staff] benefit looking at what we do in terms of monitoring things on various diagnoses and incidents'*.

Informants at Trusts B and D gave mixed responses as to whether they perceived user attitudes to be positive; indicating that there was a variation in perceptions towards the CIS across these Trusts. However, the IM&T Manager (B) did expect user attitudes to be more positive in the future commenting that: *'once we get the printers out there and the users start using the system and they start asking for more information it is going to be a great deal easier to give users information'*. Only informants at Trust E stated that although attempts had been made to develop positive user attitudes, at the time of interviewing attitudes were not positive and they were unsure whether attitudes would improve in the future. It was perceived by informants in Trust E that clinicians only considered their interaction with the system to be a mandatory routine that provided no personal benefit. Specific comments included: *'it's just what they call a necessary evil because of Billing'* (manager, E); *'positive is not the right word. It is part of a thing that we have to do, so we do it'* (clinical user, E); and *'the users tend not to ask for information. A lot of them don't seem to be interested'* (IM&T Manager, E).

The quality and availability of the information output was perceived as being key to the attainment of positive user attitudes:

- *'The single most important factor is that we have access to the information'* (clinical user, A);
- *'I think in terms of report writing, people are now coming to me and saying, can I get this information? How is this done? That is the best news, that they are taking it seriously and thinking maybe I can do something with it.'* (clinical user, C);
- *'I think there is a lot of evidence of positive user attitudes in the way people have adapted to using the system. Where it [CIS] has been a success they [clinicians] are starting to get ideas for the development of the system and people are starting to look at the information in terms of what can be collected'* (clinical manager, C);
- *'If you could get meaningful information out, then I think it would fire them up and they would be interested'* (manager, E).

There was general agreement, from informants in all Trusts, that there is a significant relationship between user attitudes and success. For example, it was noted that once positive user attitudes had been attained, there were significant resultant benefits with respect to the quality of the data input. As one clinical user (A) noted: *'I think the biggest benefit is staff are motivated to record and reflect what we do accurately'*. This view was endorsed IM&T Manager (A) who noted: *'they are committed to doing it [record information] and they are committed to ensuring that their colleagues also do it [record information] and record accurately'*. These views were echoed by an IM&T Manager from

Trust B who noted: *'it has made the user more responsible for feeding in the data in on time and correctly'.*

Conversely, in Trust E where positive user attitudes were not identified, there have been severe problems with data quality. The IM&T Manager (E) stated that: *'generally the staff aren't very interested in the activity once they have done it'* and as a result, *'we discovered that anything that we tried to get from it [CIS] was corrupted by poor data quality and I think we went into a little bit of despondency then'.* The negative impact of failing to achieve positive user attitudes was also recognized in Trust D, with the IM&T Manager noting that staff: *'always blame the system for the errors, it's never their own errors that have caused the problems'.*

The above findings suggest that information and data quality may be inextricably linked to the attainment and retention of positive user attitudes. In three Trusts (A, B & C) where information quality and accessibility were perceived as being high, positive user attitudes have resulted. This in turn encouraged the users to be more attentive to the quality of their data input, which ultimately enhanced the effectiveness of the system. Conversely, in Trusts D and E, where there has been poor quality in terms of the information output then this has contributed to negative user attitudes, which ultimately undermined the perceived success of the CIS.

The Relationship Between Best Practice, User Ownership, Positive User Attitudes and Success

During the interviews the role of several best practice variables and their relationship with the overall perceived success of the CIS were also reviewed. The importance of these best practice variables to information system success has already been established in the literature (see section 2) and the responses from informants strongly supported the existing research. However, the actual occurrence of these best practice variables did vary between the different Trusts as shown in table 3. This table indicates that Trust A, whose informants were generally very positive about the impact of their system, were very successful in the adoption of best practice. By contrast, the findings for Trust E, whose informants were far less positive about the impact of their system, indicate that they were the least successful in the adoption of best practice. The remaining three Trusts were generally better than Trust E but behind Trust A, both in the adoption of best practice and in terms of the perceived success of their systems. These results suggest that those Trusts that adopt high levels of all the best practice variables are more likely to achieve higher levels of perceived success associated with their CIS.

In addition, informants were also asked to discuss the main treatment approaches that had been adopted in their Trusts to achieve user ownership and positive user attitudes. In terms of achieving user ownership a range of treatment

Table 3: Level of adoption of different best practice variables at each trust

Best Practice Variable	Trust A	Trust B	Trust C	Trust D	Trust E
Senior Management Commitment and Participation	+	+	+	-	-
Well Balanced Project Team	+	+	+		
User Involvement	+	-	+	-	-
Management of User Expectations	+	-	+	-	-
User Training	+	+	+	+	-
User Support	+	+	+	+	~
System Testing	+	+	+	+	+
Success Score	4	2.6	3.2	3.4	2.4

Note: + denotes high occurrence of variable, - denotes low occurrence of variable, ~ denotes moderate occurrence of variable. The overall measure of success is based on a 5-point Likert scale ranging from 1, CIS is very unsuccessful to 5, CIS is very successful.

approaches were identified, however, there was clearly a strong emphasis on the role of best practice variables as the foundations for these methods. For example, in Trust A it was highlighted that high levels of senior management commitment had led to the provision of resources, which facilitated the delivery of regular, relevant reports to clinical staff and ultimately encouraged ownership (clinical user). User involvement and user training were also cited as being facilitators for developing user ownership with a clinical user at Trust A stating that *'we are using the CIS to support our clinical issues and I think that is because of the involvement of clinicians right from the very start'* and *'I think people who went to the training sessions came out recognizing that they would have to implement something that was going to be valuable to them in their clinical practice so the focus and the message from the training was very much to do with ownership'*. Best practice variables were also identified as facilitating user ownership at Trusts B and C with senior management commitment resulting in the appointment of a systems champion (B). Senior managers were also seen as making a concerted effort to give out a positive message that the CIS was for clinical staff benefit (C). User involvement demonstrated that the CIS was for staff benefit and helped to allay the fears of users (C) and training helped to introduce the users to the concepts behind using the information that will be available from the CIS (C).

However, as well as being effective treatment approaches, the lack of certain best practice variables were also identified as being significant inhibitors to the development of user ownership. Low levels of senior management commitment and participation were identified as contributing to the problems of clinicians attaining access to information, ultimately resulting in low user ownership (D & E). Additionally, low levels of user involvement resulted in the CIS being seen as being imposed on clinicians rather than being focused upon clinical needs (E). Finally, where clinicians had not been involved in deciding what information was collected, so the clinicians have not perceived the information to have any value for them (D & E).

As well as affecting the development of user ownership, informants also indicated that user attitudes were also frequently influenced through the adoption of best practice variables. The importance of having a well-balanced project team in developing positive user attitudes was identified in Trusts A, B and C with informants stating that:

- *'I think the thing that has been most important is having somebody with a clinical background. I have a clinical background and I think the thing that has made the difference is that clinicians have faith in you because they think you understand what you are doing'* (IM&T Manager, A);
- *'I think they [clinicians] had more of an affinity with the Head of Information because of his clinical background. I think they felt he was one of their own and their needs would be understood and their requirements would be addressed'* (manager, B);
- *'The fact that we have got a Clinical Development Advisor in place is helping to develop the system as well which from a clinician's point of view is excellent'* (clinical user, C).

Similarly, good management of user expectations (A & C) and good quality user training with friendly staff, (A, C & D) were also cited as directly contributing to positive user attitudes.

It was also significant to note that as in the case of user ownership, not adopting certain best practice variables were also perceived to directly inhibit the development of positive user attitudes. A lack of senior management commitment to using information, low levels of training for clinicians and not realizing user expectations were all identified at Trust E as having a negative effect on user attitudes. Similar problems in terms of managing user expectations were also cited as causing negative user attitudes at Trusts B and D. In addition, low senior management commitment at Trust D resulted in low levels of resource provision for the CIS and frustration among clinical users, which was also cited as directly contributing to low user attitudes.

This evidence suggests that best practice variables have a dual role in systems development projects. Not only do they have a direct relationship with the perceived level of success associated with the CIS but they are also important facilitators for managing and developing user ownership and positive user attitudes, both of which are perceived to have a positive relationship with system success. An overview of the relationship between the adoption of best practice, the attainment of user ownership and positive attitudes and their resultant impact on system's success is presented in figure 1.

DISCUSSION OF FINDINGS

Having reviewed the role of user ownership and positive user attitudes in influencing the successful application of community information systems, it is important to contextualize these findings within the relevant literature and in so doing, establish their contribution. Furthermore, the implications of this study, both for healthcare practitioners and IT professionals also need to be reviewed, as do the study's potential limitations.

Whilst the importance of user ownership and positive user attitudes has previously been touched upon in the information systems literature (For example: Davis, 1993; Van Alstyne et al., 1995), their precise role and the mechanisms by which they are achieved has not previously been explicitly explored. Consequently, this research makes two significant contributions. Firstly, it confirms the importance of user ownership and positive user attitudes to the successful outcome of information systems projects through investigating a common organization and system type. Secondly, and more importantly, it presents evidence that both user ownership and positive user attitudes have to be explicitly planned and then facilitated through the adoption of best practice; in essence they play an important mediating role between the adoption of best practice and the ultimate achievement of system's success. Despite the relatively small sample on which these findings are based, they are given added credibility when interpreted in light of the behavioral sciences literature, especially that concerned with organizational change. For example, Pierce et al. (1991) argue that motivation and positive behavioral responses to change are the result of '*psychological ownership*' and Barbara Senior (1997) highlights the importance of creating positive employee attitudes, to reduce resistance to change initiatives. Furthermore, it is suggested that user ownership and positive user attitudes can be facilitated through employee participation (Bartkus, 1997), education and training (Kotter & Schlesinger, 1979) and senior management commitment (Clarke, 1994).

These findings are of particular importance as they have a number of significant implications for the practice of information systems development and project management from both a healthcare and also a more general information systems perspective. Starting with the policy implications for healthcare professionals, the most recent NHS Information Strategy (Burns, 1998) suggests that clinicians: '*must deliver the new [IT] agenda*', be part of a culture that is '*change focussed*'

Figure 1: Diagram showing the relationships perceived to exist between best practice variables, user attitudes, user ownership and their impact on the CIS project at different trusts

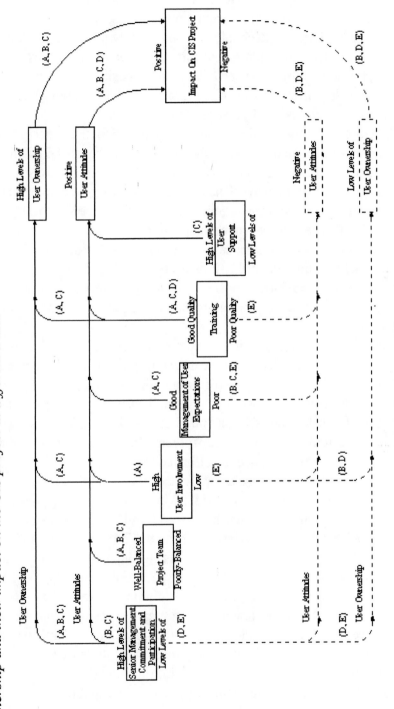

Note: Lines indicate where evidence of causality has been found at the trusts highlighted in brackets

and able to take advantage of new technology' and have access to *'fast reliable and accurate information about the individual patients in their care'*. The results of this research suggest that these policy objectives will only be achieved if levels of user ownership are improved and if individual users develop more positive attitudes towards information technology. Consequently, all future IM&T projects within the NHS must adopt coherent change management strategies explicitly focussed upon the attainment of user ownership and positive attitudes, facilitated through active user participation, senior management commitment, high quality training and education and well-balanced project teams.

When it comes to the implications of this research for the wider practice of information systems development, any generalizations may have to be qualified. The UK's National Health Service is an extraordinarily large and complex organization, which is still very labor-intensive. It has very strong traditions, cultures and sub-cultures running throughout and is generally perceived as being slow to change (Handy, 1993). Consequently, when embarking upon change programs, such as the introduction of new systems, managing the human resources and the behavioral issues is probably more important than in other contexts. Whilst, therefore, it is likely that attaining user ownership and positive user attitudes are generally important, especially in labor-intensive organizations, they may not be as important as they are within the NHS.

Research into the adoption of innovative technology, within the organizational context, is an ambitious undertaking and therefore contains a number of inherent limitations. In particular, the adoption of the in-depth case study format limited the number of organizations it was possible to target and hence reduces the generalizibility of the results. The selection of a small number of stakeholders at each Trust to participate in the study is also the source of potential bias. However, the variations in opinion recorded from the different informants and in particular, the negative comments provided by some clinicians, provided a strong indication that the results were not unduly biased, despite the IM&T Managers acting as gatekeepers to informants. Furthermore, although each Trust typically has large numbers of clinical users, it was only possible to interview one from each Trust. However, the clinical user interviewed always reflected the main user group within the Trust and the clinical managers provided a further clinical perspective on the development and use of the system in each case. Finally, a further limitation relates to the scope of the study and the fact that it was not practical to study every possible variable that may have influenced the successful outcome of systems development projects. Consequently, although the study provides many interesting and novel insights, the aforementioned limitations should be taken into account when interpreting the results. Such limitations also highlight the need for follow-up studies, employing different methods, targeting different populations and focussing upon different combinations of variables.

CONCLUDING REMARKS

This paper provides an in-depth study of how information systems are being developed and applied within Community Trusts; an important, yet largely neglected research domain. It explicitly explores the role of user ownership and positive user attitudes and in so doing provides important new insights into how they can be achieved through the well-focused application of user participation, senior management commitment and high quality training and education. In a rapidly changing and ever more challenging organizational environment, where information technology plays an increasingly important operational and strategic role, such insights into the effective practice of information systems development have become critical.

ENDNOTES

[1]   *All our Tomorrow's* Conference, Earls Court, London. 2nd July 1998.
[2]   This organization was used as there is an established research link with the Authors' institution.

REFERENCES

Audit Commission. (1997). *A Study of Information Management in Community Trusts*. London: Audit Commission for Local Authorities and the National Health Service in England and Wales.

Bailey, J.E., & Pearson, S. (1983). Development of a tool for measuring and analysing computer user satisfaction. *Management Science, 29(5),* 530-545.

Bartkus, B.R. (1997). Employee ownership as catalyst of organisational change. *Journal of Organisational Change Management, 10(4),* 331-344.

Beynon-Davis, P. (1995). Information systems 'failure': the case of the London Ambulance Service's Computer Aided Despatch Project. *European Journal of Information Systems, 4,* 171-184.

Burns, F. (1998). *Information for Health*. Leeds: NHS Executive.

Cavaye, A.L.M. (1996). Case study research: A multi-faceted research approach for IS. *Information Systems Journal, 6,* 227-242.

Cerullo, M.J. (1980). Information Systems Success Factors. *Journal of Systems Management, 31(12),* 10-19.

Chesler, M. (1987). Professionals' views of the "dangers" of self-help groups. *(CRSO Paper 345), Centre for Research on Social Organisation.* MI: Ann Arbor.

Clarke, L. (1994). *The Essence of Change.* Hemel Hempstead: Prentice-Hall.

Clegg, C., Axtell, C., Damadoran, L., Farbey, B., Hull, R., Lloyd-Jones, R., Nicholls, J. Sell, R., & Tomlinson, C. (1997). Information Technology: A study of performance and the role of human and organisational factors, *Ergonomics, 40(9),* 851-871.

Coombs, C.R., Doherty, N.F., & Loan-Clarke, J. (1998). The factors determining the success of a CIS: A case study. *Information Technology in Nursing, 10(3),* 9-15.

Coombs, C.R., Doherty, N.F., & Loan-Clarke, J. (1999). Factors affecting the level of success of community information systems. *Journal of Management in Medicine, 13(3),* 142-153.

Darke, P., Shanks, G., & Broadbent, M. (1998). Successfully completing case study research: Combining rigour, relevance and pragmatism. *Information Systems Journal, 8,* 273-289.

Davis, F.D. (1993). User acceptance of information technology: System characteristics, user perceptions and behavioural impacts. *International Journal of Man-Machine Studies, 38,* 475-487.

DeLone, W.H., & McLean, E.R. (1992). Information systems success: The quest for the dependent variable. *Information Systems Research, 3(1),* 60-95.

Diamantopoulos, A., & Souchon, A.L. (1996). Instrumental, conceptual and symbolic use of export information: An exploratory study of UK firms. *Advances in International Marketing, 8,* 117-144.

Doherty, N.F., King, M., & Marples, C.G. (1998). Factors affecting the success and failure of Hospital Information Support Systems. *Failure and Lessons Learned in Information Technology Management, 2,* 91-105.

Ennals, R. (1995). *Preventing Information Technology Disasters.* London.: Springer.

Faust, D. (1982). A needed component in prescriptions for science: Empirical knowledge of human cognitive limitations. *Knowledge: Creation, Diffusion, Utilisation, 3,* 555-570.

Flowers, S. (1997). Towards predicting information systems failure. In D. Avison, (Ed.), *Key Issues in Information Systems,* Maidenhead: McGraw-Hill, 215-228.

Gable, G.G. (1994). Integrating case study and survey research methods: An example in information systems. *European Journal of Information Systems, 3(2),* 112 - 126.

Galliers, R.D. (1992). Choosing information systems research approaches. In R.D. Galliers, (Ed.), *Information Systems Research*, London: Blackwell Scientific Publications, 144-162.

Ginzberg, M.J., Schultz, R., & Lucas, H.C. (1984). A structural model of implementation. In R.L. Schultz & M.J. Ginzberg (Eds.), *Applications of Management Science: Management Science Implementation.* Greenwich, CN: JAI Press.

Govindarajulu, C. & Reithel, B.J. (1998). Beyond the information centre: An instrument to measure end user computing support from multiple sources. *Information and Management, 33,* 241-250.

Grantham, C.E., & Vaske, J.J. (1985). Predicting the usage of an advanced communication technology. *Behaviour and Information Technology, 4(4),* 327-35.

Guimaraes, T., & McKeen, J.D. (1993). User Participation in Information System Development: Moderation in All Things. In D. Avison, J. E. Kendall, & J.I. DeGross, (Eds.), *Human, Organisational and Social Dimensions of Information Systems Development.* North Holland: Elsevier Science Publishers.

Handy, C.B. (1993). *Understanding Organisations.* 4th edn, London: Penguin.

Hochstrasser, B., & Griffiths, C. (1991). *Controlling IT Investment.* London: Chapman & Hall.

Joshi, K. (1990). An investigation of equity as a determinant of user information satisfaction. *Decision Sciences, 21(4),* 786-807.

Joshi, K. (1992). A causal path model of the overall user attitudes toward the MIS function - The case of user information satisfaction. *Information and Management, 22,* 77-88.

Kearney, A.T. (1990). *Barriers to the Successful Application of Information Technology.* London: DTI & CIMA.

Keen, J. (1994). *Information Management in Health Services.* Buckingham: The Open University Press.

Kotter, J.P., & Schlesinger, L.A. (1979). Choosing strategies for change. *Harvard Business Review, 57(2),* 106-114.

Li, E.Y. (1997). Perceived importance of information systems success factors: A meta analysis of group differences. *Information & Management, 32(1),* 15-28.

Lucas, H.C. (1978). Empirical evidence for a descriptive model of implementation. *MIS Quarterly, 2,* 27-41.

Lucas, H.C. (1981). *Implementation: The Key to Successful Information Systems.* New York: McGraw Hill Book Company.

Lyytinen, K., & Hirschheim, R. (1987). Information systems failures: A survey and classification of the empirical literature. *Oxford Surveys in Information Technology, 4,* 257-309.

Markus, M.L. (1983). Power, politics and MIS implementation. *Communications of the ACM, 26(6)* 430-444.

Miles, M.B., & Huberman, A.M. (1994). *Qualitative Data Analysis: An Expanded Sourcebook,* 2nd Edn., London: Sage Publications.

Miller, J., & Doyle, B. (1987). Measuring the effectiveness of computer-based information systems in the financial services sector. *MIS Quarterly, 11(1)* 107-124.

National Audit Office. (1991). *Managing Computer Projects in the National Health Service.* London: HMSO.

National Audit Office. (1996). *The NHS Executive: The Hospital Information Support Systems Initiative.* London: HMSO.

Pare, G., & Elam, J.J. (1997). Using case study research to build theories of it implementation. In A. S. Lee, J. Liebenau, and J. I. DeGross, (Eds.), *Information Systems and Qualitative Research, Proceedings of the IFIP TC8 WG 8.2 International Conference on Information Systems and Qualitative Research, 31 May-3 June 1997, Philadelphia, Pennsylvania, USA.* London: Chapman and Hall.

Pierce, J.L., Rubenfeld, S.A., Morgan, S. (1991). Employee ownership: A conceptual-model of process and effects. *Academy of Management Review, 16(1),* 121-144.

Rademacher, R.A. (1989). Critical factors for systems success. *Journal of Systems Management, 19(6)* 15-17.

Robey, D., & Farrow, D. (1982). User involvement in information system development: A conflict model and empirical test. *Management Science, 28(1),* 73-85.

Sauer, C. (1993). *Why Information Systems Fail: A Case Study Approach.* Henley: Alfred Waller.

Senior, B. (1997). *Organisational Change.* London: Pitman.

Srinivasan, A. (1985). Alternative measures of systems effectiveness: Associations and implications. *MIS Quarterly, 9(3),* 243-253.

Strauss, A.L., & Corbin, J. (1990). *Basics of Qualitative Research: Grounded Theory Procedures and Techniques.* Newbury Park, CA: Sage Publications.

Van Alstyne, M., Brynjolfsson, E., & Madnick, S. (1995). Why not one big database? Principles for data ownership. *Decision Support Systems, 15,* 267-284.

Whyte, G., & Bytheway, A. (1996). Factors affecting information systems' success. *International Journal of Service Industry Management, 7(1),* 74-93.

Willcocks L., & Margetts H. (1994). Risk assessment and information systems. *European Journal of Information Systems, 3(2),* 127-138.

Wong, E., & Tate, G. (1994). A study of user participation in information systems development. *Journal of Information Technology, 9,* 51-60.

Yap, C., Soh, C., & Raman, K. (1992). Information systems success factors in small business. *OMEGA, 20(5),* 597-609.

Yin, R.K. (1994). *Case Study Research: Design and Methods.* 2nd Edn, London: Sage Publications.

Zmud, R.W. (1983). *CBIS failure and success, Information Systems in Organisation.* Glenview, Illinois: Scott Foresman and Company.

Chapter 8

Introducing Computer-Based Telemedicine in Three Rural Missouri Counties

Kimberly D. Harris
Duquesne University, USA

Joseph F. Donaldson and James D. Campbell
University of Missouri–Columbia, USA

This study investigated predictors of utilization of the computer-based telemedicine in three rural Missouri counties. Participating health care agencies were given computers and access to an Internet-based workstation that provided e-mail and World Wide Web (WWW) services. Utilization data for e-mail messages sent and WWW pages accessed were collected through proxy servers. A survey was distributed to those employees who are enrolled in the Rural Telemedicine Evaluation Project (RTEP), which addressed perceptions of the Internet-based RTEP workstation. The results of the survey were analyzed to see how perceptions and demographic variables predicted actual utilization. The findings of the study revealed that for e-mail, behavioral intentions/attitude, age, organizational support, and time were the most significant predictors. For WWW, only the behavioral intentions/attitude subscale predicted utilization. The majority of respondents did not utilize the e-mail technology. Strategies need to be developed through training interventions and organizational policies to address non-utilization.

Previously Published in the *Journal of End User Computing, vol.13, no.4*, Copyright © 2001, Idea Group Publishing.

INTRODUCTION

Technology is perhaps one of the greatest tools under the control of mankind. It can be used for positive or negative purposes, and has proven a powerful force for change (Surry, 1997). In fact, some would argue that technology is a key governing force in society, and that technological change drives social change (Smith, 1996). The Internet is one technology that has contributed to societal change, and has provided opportunities to revolutionize health care. The Internet has afforded the medical community a mechanism to provide access to information in a timely manner. This is particularly important in today's society due to the continually expanding body of medical knowledge, and the changes in health care delivery that require practitioners to make more important and complex decisions in less time (Lundberg, 1998).

The Internet has the potential to improve the care provided to patients and to enhance biomedical research by connecting practitioners to the most up-to-date information available (Gallagher & McFarland, 1996). However, an important consideration in the diffusion of information technologies was put nicely by Enrico Coiera (1995) when he said, "Medical informatics is as much about computers as cardiology is about stethoscopes.... Any attempt to use information technology will fail dramatically when the motivation is the application of technology for its own sake rather than the solution of clinical problems" (Coiera, 1995).

Rural health communities face unique issues in providing care to their population. Not only has it been difficult to recruit health care professionals, but also to retain them. Isolation, lack of communication, difficult access to updated medical information, little contact with colleagues, and lack of continuing medical education opportunities have been identified as factors contributing to low retention rates and shortage of supply of rural health care providers, particularly physicians (Conte, et. al, 1992; Harned, 1993; Mackesy, 1993; Forti, et. al, 1995; Anderson, et. al, 1994; Rogers, 1995; Davis, 1989). As a consequence, rural health care suffers. One of the main goals of telemedicine technology is to make an impact on improving rural health care, including nursing care, administrative efficiency, and communication amongst and between all health care providers.

Research on the acceptability of telemedicine as a particular form of technology is limited. Thus, this study was informed by literature and research related to adoption of innovations, medical educational technology, and rural health care to explore factors associated with acceptance of telemedicine by rural health care providers. It does so by addressing issues of acceptability of a specific aspect of the University of Missouri's Telemedicine technologies by health care providers in three rural Missouri counties.

BACKGROUND OF THE TELEMEDICINE EVALUATION PROJECT

The University of Missouri-Columbia's Telemedicine Demonstration Project was developed in December of 1995 to address rural health care provider needs such as isolation, lack of communication, rapid access to updated medical information, contact with colleagues, and continuing medical education opportunities. The Missouri Telemedicine Network (MTN) includes two components: video conferencing and computer infrastructure. Funding for the project came, in part, from the National Library of Medicine (NLM), with the stipulation that the University would provide a thorough evaluation on the computer component. Thus, the evaluation portion of the Telemedicine program is referred to as the Rural Telemedicine Evaluation Project (RTEP). This study focused on the utilization of a portion of the computer component, known as the RTEP workstation, in three rural Missouri counties.

The RTEP workstation is an Internet program that is housed on a server on the Internet in three rural Missouri communities. Elements of the RTEP workstation include access to e-mail, the World Wide Web (WWW), community information, and an address book - all designed to address the unique challenges of rural health care, including access to electronic clinical records.

While on the surface the RTEP workstation appears to have the ability to address successfully some of the issues of rural health care identified earlier, the individuals who are enrolled in the demonstration project may not be willing to utilize the new technology in a way that will allow the RTEP workstation to address those issues. Examining the utilization of this technology gives insight into the various issues surrounding acceptance of this technology by the participants.

Theoretical Foundations

Diffusion of innovation research examines how various factors interact to facilitate or impede the adoption of a specific, new product or practice among members of a particular group. The four major factors that Rogers (Rogers, 1995) identified as influencing the diffusion process are the innovation itself, how information about the innovation is communicated, time, and the nature of the social system where the innovation is being implemented. From Rogers' original work in 1962, an onslaught of diffusion research has been conducted, resulting in various predictive models with the intent of utilizing the model to accelerate the adoption of the innovation. One such model is the Technology Acceptance Model (TAM).

Fred Davis (Davis, 1989) originally developed the TAM, under contract with IBM Canada, Ltd., in the mid-1980s for the purpose of evaluating the market potential for a variety of then-emerging PC-based applications in the area of multimedia, image processing, and pen-based computing. TAM was used to guide investments in the early development of these various technologies (Davis, 1995).

The TAM purports to provide a basis for tracing the impact of external factors on internal beliefs, attitudes, and behavioral intentions. The TAM suggests that behavioral intentions (BI) are jointly determined by the person's attitude (A) and perception of the technology's usefulness (U), with relative weights estimated by the regression: $BI = A + U$ (Davis, 1989).

In the TAM, the behavioral intention (BI) of the users to actually utilize the technology is determined by their attitude toward using. However, the attitude has first been influenced by two specific beliefs: the user's perception of how easy the technology is to use, or 'perceived ease of use' (EOU) and the perception of how useful the technology will actually be in the user's job, or 'perceived usefulness' (U). In other words, EOU has a direct effect on U, and together, they affect the A. Then, the A determines the user's BI, which results in their actual utilization (Davis, 1989; Davis, 1989; and Davis, 1996).

Research Questions

Research Question 1: Is utilization of the e-mail and WWW portion of the RTEP workstation, as measured by the automated tracking of use on the proxy servers, predicted by the perceptions, behavioral intentions, and attitudes represented in the TAM model?

Research Question 2: After adjusting for the TAM variables, are the demographic variables: age, gender, educational level, and occupation associated with the utilization of e-mail and the WWW, as measured by the automated tracking of use on the proxy servers?

Figure 1: The technology acceptance model

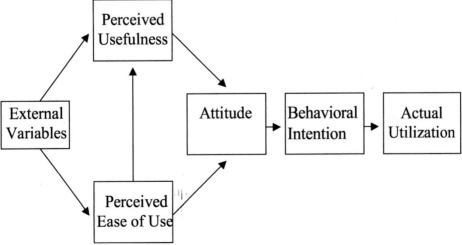

Research Question 3: After adjusting for the TAM variables and the demographic variables, do the five factors identified from previous interviews from the participants: time, access, apprehension, technological problems, and ownership, along with 'organizational support,' individually significantly predict utilization of the e-mail and world wide web portion of the RTEP workstation?

Research Question 3a: If it is found that a factor from Research Question 3 individually significantly predicts utilization, after adjusting for the TAM variables and the demographic variables, what is the relationship between that factor and the TAM variables?

Method

This study employed a survey method. This method was chosen because the study is examining perceptions of the participants regarding the technology. One way to find out what those perceptions are, and then to quantify them, is through the survey method (Babbie, 1990).

Subjects

The subjects in this study are employees of health care organizations who have volunteered to participate in a series of evaluation studies as part of the RTEP project. In order to receive access to the RTEP workstation, the participants completed an enrollment package, which included a consent form, which allowed data about their utilization of the RTEP to be collected and employed in a variety of evaluation studies. While all employees were allowed to participate, this study is limited to the physicians, nursing personnel (excluding certified nurses aids), and administrative personnel. There were a total of 276 potential participants. There were 69 participants from Cooper County, 107 from Linn County, and 100 from Macon County. The total population (not a sample) of physicians, nurses, and administrative personnel were delivered a survey.

Variables

The dependent variables were utilization of the World Wide Web (WWW) through the RTEP workstation, and e-mail communications sent through the RTEP. These were collected unobtrusively and automatically from the proxy servers located in each county. The independent variables that were based on the TAM included attitude, behavioral intentions, perceived ease of use, and perceived usefulness. Other independent variables included age, gender, educational level, occupation, and organizational support. The independent variables that were based on the preliminary results of a prior qualitative telemedicine evaluation study were time, access, technological problems, apprehension, and ownership.

Instrumentation

The survey instrument was intended to gather as much information as possible as to the reasons why, or why not, people utilize the RTEP workstation. The first section collected demographic and self-report data, the second section addressed the barriers that had previously been identified through interviews with participants in a prior telemedicine evaluation study, and the last section dealt with the variables from the TAM. A page was also included at the end for respondents to provide any additional comments. The instrument was pilot-tested for face validity, item clarity, directions, and readability.

Results

Three months of utilization data were collected; October, November, and December of 1998. These three months were chosen due to the targeted completion date in September 1998 of training for all participants on use of the RTEP workstation.

The overall response rate was 78%. Physicians had a 50% response rate, while administrative personnel (85%), nurse practitioners (100%), and nurses (79%) responded at a higher rate. The mean age of respondents was 42.49 years. The majority of the respondents were female (184, or 85.6%), only 30 (14%) were male respondents. This was expected, due to the distribution of gender in the population. This reflects the female domination of the nursing profession in these counties and elsewhere.

The Technology Acceptance Model

Davis (1989) reported that the instrument he developed from the TAM was shown to be reliable through psychometric testing. Adams, et. al (1992) found further support for this instrument through psychometric testing. These authors found it to be reliable, have construct validity, and composed of two distinct factors, U and EOU. Morris and Dillon (1997) used the four original factors in Davis' TAM, i.e., EOU, U, A, and BI, claiming, "TAM offers a valid means of predicting system acceptability, as measured by system use" (p. 64).

The results of this survey were subjected to factor analysis of the original four variables to test further its validity and address the first research question. An alpha factor analysis was completed on all of the TAM subscales (for both e-mail and WWW), with a cut off point of .35. After a Varimax rotation, four factors were identified: perceived usefulness (U), behavioral intentions/attitude (BI/A), perceived ease of use (EOU) for e-mail, and perceived ease of use for the WWW. Reliability tests were conducted on both the e-mail and WWW TAM subscales.

Davis (1989; 1993) originally designed the model, but Adams, et. al (1992), Szajna (1994), and Morris and Dillon (1997) have replicated it. To replicate it

Table 1: Linear regression of TAM for e-mail

TAM subscales	B	Standard Error of B	t	p	R^2	Result
EOU→U	.751	.050	14.98	.000**	.548	Supported
U→BI/A	.734	.047	15.63	.000**	.570	Supported
EOU→BI/A	.614	.056	10.96	.000**	.385	Supported
BI/A→usage	5.121	1.223	4.19	.000**	.080	Supported

Note. The p value for 'BI/A→usage' may not be strictly accurate due to the departures from normality in the dependent variable.

*$p < .05$.

**$p < .001$.

further, a series of linear regressions were computed on the three TAM e-mail subscales: EOU, U, and BI/A, in order to examine the relationships between the three subscales for e-mail utilization. Table 1 presents the linear regression statistics.

The e-mail TAM subscales worked together as purported by Davis (1989). Only 8% of the variance was accounted for in the linear regression when actual utilization was used. However, when the total self-report of e-mail utilization was used in this same regression, 13.5% of the variance is accounted for. This is similar to the R^2 that was reported in the previous studies that used self-reported utilization data.

The same procedure was conducted on the WWW TAM subscales [Table 2]. Again, these subscales worked together as purported by Davis (1989). The variance accounted for in the WWW TAM is higher (11%) than in the e-mail TAM when using actual utilization data in the regression. However, when the self-reported data were used in the regression, the R^2 decreased to .034, or 3.4% of the variance was accounted for by the behavioral intentions/attitude variable.

E-mail Utilization

E-mail utilization of the RTEP workstation, as measured by the proxy servers in each county, was not as high as expected, with 141 (66%) respondents never utilizing

Table 2: Linear regression on WWW TAM subscales

TAM subscales	B	Standard Error of B	t	p	R^2	Result
EOU→U	.650	.056	11.62	.000**	.422	Supported
U→BI/A	.808	.043	18.71	.000**	.655	Supported
EOU→BI/A	.643	.055	11.67	.000**	.417	Supported
BI/A →usage	233.989	47.082	4.97	.000**	.110	Supported

Note. The p value for 'BI/A →usage' may not be strictly accurate due to the departures from normality in the dependent variable.

*p < .05.

**p < .001.

it during the three-month period of analysis. Due to the magnitude of non-utilization, resulting in clear violations of normality, logistic regressions were computed rather than multiple regressions. The dependent variable of e-mail utilization was dichotomized, i.e., either respondents used it, or they did not (yes/no). A logistic regression was computed on the TAM variables alone, with behavioral intentions/attitude as the single predictor of e-mail utilization. When the demographic data were added into the logistic regression model to answer the second research question, age was also a significant predictor. The full logistic regression model was computed to address the third research question, including all independent variables, revealed the following significant predictors of e-mail utilization of the RTEP workstation: behavioral intentions/attitude, age, time, and organizational support.

WWW utilization

More respondents utilized the World Wide Web (WWW) component of the RTEP workstation, as measured by the proxy servers in each county, than the e-mail technology. Nevertheless, there were 75 (35%) respondents who never utilized the WWW during the designated time period of analysis. Again, due to the magnitude of non-utilization and violations of normality, logistic regressions were computed rather than multiple regressions. The dependent variable of WWW utilization was dichotomized (yes/no). A logistic regression was computed on the

Table 3: Full logistic regression on e-mail utilization

Variable	B	S.E.	Wald	df	Sig
BI/A	-2.0895	.5796	12.9980	1	.0003**
EOU	.1813	.3879	.2185	1	.6402
U	-.0507	.4408	.0132	1	.9084
Age	-.0511	.0230	4.9553	1	.0260*
Edu level			.8998	4	.9246
Edu(1)	.0721	1.4884	.0023	1	.9613
Edu(2)	.5638	1.2195	.2137	1	.6438
Edu(3)	.3501	1.1633	.0906	1	.7634
Edu(4)	.8078	1.1638	.4817	1	.4876
Occupation			4.2630	3	.2344
Occ(1)	2.6606	1.8328	2.1074	1	.1466
Occ(2)	.8679	1.8416	.2221	1	.6374
Occ(3)	-.0518	1.8679	.0008	1	.9779
Gender	-.1144	.7722	.0219	1	.8823
Time	-.5836	.2930	3.9691	1	.0463*
Apprehension	.2756	.2689	1.0504	1	.3054
Org Support	.5971	.3052	3.8277	1	.0504*
Ownership	.4153	.2613	2.5265	1	.1120
Access	-.1145	.3194	.1284	1	.7201
(Constant)	2.0560	2.4264	.7180	1	.3968

*p < .05
**p < .001

TAM variables alone to address the first research question, with behavioral intentions/attitude as the single predictor of WWW utilization. With regard to research questions 2 and 3, the only significant predictor of WWW utilization when all of the independent variables were included was the behavioral intentions/attitude variable from the TAM. The full logistic regression is presented in Table 4.

Research question 3a posited that if it was found that a factor from Research Question 3 individually significantly predicted utilization, after adjusting for the TAM and demographic variables, what was the relationship between that factor and the TAM variables? If the relationship was statistically significant, one would expect there to be a weak correlation between that factor and the variables in the TAM model. Conversely, if there was weak additional predictive power, then there may be a strong correlation between the weak factor and one of the TAM variables. A correlation matrix was performed on all the independent variables.

The variables, 'BI/A,' 'age,' and 'time' were the most significant predictors of the probability that a respondent would utilize the e-mail component of the RTEP workstation. 'BI/A' was the strongest predictor (.0003), followed by 'age' (p=.0269), then 'time' (p=.0494). 'Organizational support' was a weak predictor (p=.0504). 'Age' was a strong predictor in the logistic regression model for e-mail utilization; therefore, one would expect a weak correlation with the TAM variables. In fact, 'age' does not significantly correlate with two of the variables within the TAM, EOU and U. 'Age' is statistically significant at the p=.05 level with 'BI/A,' with a correlation coefficient of –.162 (p=.022), however, it is not meaningful in that it only accounts for 3% of the variance (R^2=.026).

'Organizational support' and 'time' were fairly weak predictors, therefore, stronger correlations would be expected with the 'BI/A' factor. In fact, there was a stronger correlation for 'organizational support,' with a correlation coefficient of .470 (p=.000), accounting for 22% of the variance (R^2=.22). 'Time' was not as meaningful a correlation as 'organizational support,' with a correlation coefficient of .299 (p=.000), accounting for only 9% of the variance (R^2=.089).

Limitations of the Study

The large amount of non-utilization was a limitation for the purpose of analysis. There were 141 (66%) respondents who did not utilize e-mail, and 75 (35%) respondents who did not utilize the WWW during the three-month time period of time for which utilization data were collected. As a result, it was important to use logistic regressions rather than linear or multiple regressions. A linear regression assumes a normal distribution, and the utilization data were so skewed due to non-utilization that logistic regressions were necessary in order to analyze the data appropriately. However, the very fact that there were so many 'non-users' was significant in and of itself.

Table 4: Full logistic regression on WWW utilization

Variable	B	S.E.	Wald	df	Sig
BI/A	-.8457	.3916	4.6650	1	.0308*
U	-.0516	.4035	.0164	1	.8982
EOU	.1055	.3388	.0969	1	.7556
Age	-.0291	.0209	1.9391	1	.1638
Gender	-.0221	.7654	.0008	1	.9770
Occupation			3.7516	3	.2896
Occ(1)	6.1190	20.845	.0862	1	.7691
Occ(2)	6.5388	20.867	.0982	1	.7540
Occ(3)	4.1908	20.890	.0402	1	.8410
Edu level			2.2704	4	.6862
Edu(1)	-.9146	1.7045	.2879	1	.5915
Edu(2)	-.8781	1.4492	.3671	1	.5446
Edu(3)	-.5366	1.3979	.1474	1	.7011
Edu(4)	.2356	1.4445	.0266	1	.8704
Time	-.5042	.2691	3.5119	1	.0609
Apprehension	-.0415	.2574	.0260	1	.8720
Org Support	.2981	.2765	1.1618	1	.2811
Ownership	.0370	.2517	.0217	1	.8830
Access	-.2744	.2844	.9310	1	.3346
(Constant)	-5.362	20.904	.0658	1	.7975

*p < .05

Another limitation to this study was the overwhelming number of female versus male respondents. This was expected due to the population from which the respondents came. The nursing population is female dominated in these three counties, as well as at the national level (Cervero, 1988).

The unequal group size of occupations was also a limitation. With only four nurse practitioners, it was difficult to make any conclusions with respect to utilization of the telemedicine technologies for that group.

Training was supposed to have been completed by the end of September 1998. However, there were a few respondents who claimed they had never received any kind of training on the technology. One respondent commented that she did not have a password yet. Another respondent simply said, 'not trained.' Eight respondents requested more training.

The utilization data were limited to the activity of the respondents through the RTEP workstation. The respondents may utilize e-mail and WWW technology through another Internet provider for health care purposes. Conclusions from this study can only be drawn with respect to the respondents and their utilization of the RTEP workstation.

DISCUSSION

The RTEP was designed to meet the physicians' needs, first and foremost. Each physician was given a computer for his or her office. Nurses and administrators may have to share a computer, but the physicians were given their own. This was done in order to address the 'access to updated information' need identified by rural physicians. Therefore, this study was particularly interested in the physicians' responses and utilization. While the physicians who responded to this study scored favorably on the TAM e-mail subscales with regard to 'perceived usefulness' (mean=4.60), 'perceived ease of use' (mean=4.73), and 'behavioral intentions/attitude' (mean=5.67), only one physician utilized the e-mail technology. This inconsistency in response versus utilization may be due to 'social desirability,' or unconsciously trying to give socially desirable answers (Streiner and Norman, 1995).

There are studies that indicate that physicians do not perceive the Internet as useful. Three out of the ten physicians did not utilize the WWW component of the RTEP workstation during the three month time period of analysis. Only two physicians had over a thousand hits, one physician had slightly over one hundred hits, and two physicians had over 50 hits. The remaining two physicians had only approximately 20 hits. According to Brown (1998), physicians in the United States have had a lukewarm relationship with the Internet. This relationship is due to physicians' lack of 'perceived usefulness' of the Internet. Most physicians need to be convinced that the Internet offers a 'critical mass' of high quality information for both them and their patients. Brown claimed that only 25% of online physicians surveyed in 1997 liked to use the Internet and commercial online services for patient education, and only 44% of online physicians liked to use the Internet and commercial online services for Continuing Medical Education (CME).

With respect to the other respondents in the study, some respondents may not perceive the technology 'useful' in their work, but use the technology for other purposes. In other words, non-utilization does not necessarily mean that the respondents do not accept the technology. Some respondents did not utilize the technology at work, but used the Internet from home. One respondent commented, "Most of this information does not relate to me and my job at CCMH. I have very little access to the computer & resulting e-mail & WWW. I do my thing on my own personal computer at home."

The second research question addressed whether or not the demographic data would add any predictive value to the TAM. 'Age' added predictive value to the TAM. When divided into age groups, respondents between the ages of 30 and 49 had the highest mean for both e-mail and WWW utilization. Respondents over the age of 60 had the lowest mean for e-mail utilization (1.23 messages sent) and respondents between the ages of 50 and 59 had the lowest mean for WWW utilization (315.20 hits). This is inconsistent with Miller's (1996) study where he found that younger and older users of the Internet focus on communicating, while middle-aged users focus more on seeking information, such as health and medical information. However, for this set of respondents, it is the middle-aged with the highest means for utilization of both e-mail and WWW. This difference in findings may be due to several reasons. First, this study was limited to health care professionals. Second, and perhaps more importantly, it was limited to those professionals working in a rural area. Miller's study was an overall study of those people already using the Internet.

Segars and Grover (Segers, 1993) suggested that the relationships within the TAM may be more complex than previously thought. These authors agreed, and developed additional factors that may have more to do with the fact that the technology was implemented specifically in health care settings in *rural* areas. Therefore, based on the previous qualitative telemedicine research mentioned earlier, the third research question addressed additional factors that may add predictive power to the existing TAM.

The additional factors considered in the third research question were the subscales, 'time,' 'apprehension,' 'access,' 'organizational support,' and 'owner-ship.' The two subscales that added additional predictive power in the logistic regression model were 'time' and 'organizational support.' According to Treister (1998), "physicians often fail to embrace a complex information system, may not see its relevance to their practices [perceived usefulness], and are characteristically reluctant to invest the time [italics added] and energy to be trained in its use" (p. 20).

Physicians had an overall mean for the subscale 'time' of 3.92, which means, that overall, they reported neutral feelings regarding having the time to learn and utilize the RTEP workstation. Only one physician had sent e-mail messages during the three-month time period of analysis, however, all but three physicians utilized the WWW technology. Further investigation into physician utilization of e-mail revealed that they received messages, but did not send messages (with the exception of one physician). If the physician is opening his or her e-mail and printing the message, it could be said that they are, in fact, utilizing the technology. If the physician is requiring someone else to check his or her e-mail account, it could be said that they are using the technology via a 'proxy' user. This is similar to findings from the 1997 American Interactive Healthcare Professional Survey, which revealed that 43% of the physicians surveyed used the Internet for professional purposes. However, 26% of those physicians had someone else go on line on their behalf (Brown, 1998), using the Internet via a 'proxy' user.

'Time' was mentioned by several of the respondents in the 'comments' section contained in the last page of the survey instrument. One respondent said, "I would like to use it, but I just don't have the time," and another said, "I don't use the RTEP workstation - I'm usually busy with patient care and as soon as I would start a light would ring and I'd have to stop. Need time with no interruptions." There was one respondent who returned a survey, but did not fill out the questionnaire. Instead, she just wrote "NO TIME" across Section B (which contained the additional subscales), and "NO TIME TO USE" across Section C (which contained the TAM and ownership subscales) of the survey instrument.

Administrators had the highest overall mean for the 'time' subscale (4.2712), however, they would not have to take time away from patient care to utilize the technology as the physicians and nurses would. 'Organizational support' was the other significant predictor when all of the variables were added to the entire logistic regression model. The overall means for each occupation for 'organizational support' was over 5, which means that the respondents reported agreement that their organization was supportive of their use of both e-mail and WWW components of the RTEP workstation. Yet, due to the magnitude of non-utilization, it is clear that respondents have not accepted the e-mail component of the RTEP workstation. One respondent, who had reported a 'strongly agree' on both organizational support questions on the survey, commented on the last page of the survey instrument, "I would prefer NOT to use RTEP's email, but [I] have been told that [it] is the only one I will have access to unless I didn't [sic] use [the] University."

Research question 3a addressed the relationships between the additional significant predictors of utilization, and the TAM variables. For the WWW, there were no additional predictors. Only 'behavioral intentions/attitude' predicted the probability that a respondent would utilize the WWW component of the RTEP workstation. However, for e-mail, the additional predictors were 'age,' 'time,' and 'organizational support.'

'Age' had statistically significant correlations with the 'BI/A' for the e-mail component of the RTEP workstation. However, this correlation was not particularly meaningful, producing an R^2 of .026, or 3% of the variance for e-mail utilization. Therefore, because 'age' was a strong predictor in the e-mail logistic regression model, and had weak correlations with the TAM variables, 'age' is a separate consideration that should be included in future studies. The TAM by itself could not predict e-mail utilization as well as could when 'age' was included in the logistic regression model, for this set of respondents.

The subscale, 'time' did not correlate with 'age,' however, it did correlate with every other subscale and all the other demographic variables. The TAM alone could not predict for e-mail utilization as well as when 'age' and 'time' were included in the e-mail logistic regression model for this set of respondents. Therefore the variable, 'time' needs to be included in future studies of acceptance of information technologies (Treister, 1998; Aydin & Forsythe, 1998).

The last additional predictor, 'organizational support,' did not correlate with 'age,' 'gender,' or 'occupation.' However, it did significantly correlate with 'educational level,' and with every other subscale in the model. 'Organizational support' was only significant when all of the other variables were in the logistic regression model. It appeared that 'organizational support' was necessary, but not sufficient in and of itself. The strongest correlations were with the TAM subscales, therefore the TAM appears to account for much of the 'organizational support' subscale.

Because 'organizational support' was a statistically significant predictor in the e-mail logistic regression model, it is important to consider the organizational structure of these organizations. Particularly, the role of the physician within the rural setting, due to their authority and leadership role within the organization. The physicians in this study clearly have not accepted the e-mail technology, and most are only moderately utilizing the WWW. This indicates a need for further studies to examine the effect of physician leadership and organizational support on the acceptance of information technologies.

Examining the role physicians should take within health care organizations, Heydt (1999) claimed that physicians should take the lead regarding changes within the health care system, including technological change. As a physician himself, Heydt noted that these are 'disconcerting' times for physicians because of all the changes, driven largely by constraints on financial resources. However, physicians must recognize the need to adapt, and should take more control over these changes. "We must then lead change and at the same time govern its pace" (p. 43). Implementers of telemedicine technologies must realize the leadership role physicians have in rural health care organizations and allow them to lead in the technological changes.

Additional Findings

There were additional findings from this study that deserve some discussion as well. Examination of self-report utilization versus actual utilization revealed that nearly 30% of the respondents who reported using their RTEP e-mail account actually had no activity during the three-month period of analysis. In addition, nearly 30% of the respondents reported having a higher utilization of their RTEP e-mail than their actual utilization revealed. Only 25% of the respondents accurately reported non-utilization of the RTEP workstation's WWW. There may be several reasons for the discrepancies. Respondents may base frequency estimations on a rate of behavioral episodes without actually recalling any incidences. Discrepancies may also be due to the respondents' memory error, which are viewed as the greatest detriment to accurate reporting (Blair & Burton, 1987). Respondents may also have answered the self-report question with a social desire bias (Streiner & Norman, 1995). Future studies are needed that examine actual utilization as opposed to self-report utilization.

CONCLUSIONS

Three main conclusions may be drawn from this investigation. First, there are distinct differences between the use of e-mail technologies and the WWW. One is for communication purposes, and the other is for information gathering purposes. More people were willing to use the WWW component of the RTEP workstation than the e-mail component.

The second conclusion that may be drawn is that if it is assumed that acceptance of the technology is measured by its utilization, then this technology has not been widely accepted. Over half of the respondents (66%) did not utilize e-mail at all during the three-month period, and 35% of the respondents did not utilize the WWW. However, utilization is not mandatory within these rural health organizations, and therefore adoption may take longer.

The last conclusion drawn from this study is that, while the TAM was able to predict the probability that a respondent would use the technology, there were other significant predictors regarding e-mail utilization: age, organizational support, and time. The issue of e-mail communication appears to be more complex for this set of respondents than the TAM provides. Although there were strong correlations between 'time' and 'organizational support' with the TAM variables, 'age' was a weak correlation with the TAM variables. Therefore, to obtain a comprehensive predictive model for the utilization of computer-based telemedicine, these other variables should be included. The TAM was sufficient in and of itself regarding the prediction of the probability that a respondent would utilize the WWW component of the RTEP workstation.

Implications for Future Research

More studies need to be conducted to refine this survey instrument so that it may be adapted to various rural health organizations in aiding the implementation process of new information technologies. Adaptations need to address issues of rural versus urban settings, and communication needs versus information seeking needs.

The 'nursing' and 'physician' occupations may need additional time scheduled for training sessions to deal with specific learning needs, as identified by the participants. A refined survey may then be re-administered to measure changes in perceptions of the technology, and then tested against current or future utilization. More research is needed that investigates the impact that e-mail is having on rural health care. Communication studies need to be conducted that examine how e-mail between nurses and physicians can be time and cost-effective. This type of research needs to be done in nursing homes and hospitals in particular, where communication needs to occur between professionals that are not in the same geographic location.

More research is also needed that investigates what kind of impact the WWW is having on patient education. Patient education was listed as the most important use of the RTEP workstation. How does this impact the patient's care? Do the patients go on to take better care of their condition? Does the education aid the communication between the patient and the physician? What about between the physician and the nurse?

There are still many questions to be addressed in researching the impact of Internet technologies on rural health care. This study looked at predictors of the utilization of the technology. Many of them were not. Respondents indicated that they did not perceive e-mail to be useful. Respondents who did not use the WWW indicated that they did not intend to use the WWW, nor did they have the time to use it. Future research should examine why utilization was so low.

Overall, further research needs to be conducted to investigate the impact of computer-based telemedicine technologies on the impact of physician isolation and retention, patient care, communication, and medical education. There have been little or no wide-ranging studies indicating whether physician access to Internet technologies has improved patient care (Southwick, 1997).

REFERENCES

Adams, D. A., Nelson, R. R., & Todd, P. A. (1992). Perceived usefulness, ease of use, and usage of information technology: A replication. *MIS Quarterly*, 227-247.

Anderson, E. A, Bergeron, D, & Crouse, B. J. (1994). Recruitment of family physicians in rural practice. *Minnesota Medicine, 77*, 29-32.

Aydin, C. E. & Forsythe, D. E. (1998). Implementing computers in ambulatory care: Implications of physician practice patterns for system design. *Proceedings of the 1998 AMIA Annual Fall Symposium*, Orlando, FL, 677-81.

Babbie, E. (1990). *Survey research methods* (2nd edition). Belmont, CA: Wadsworth Publishing Company.

Blair, E., & Burton, S. (1987). Cognitive processes used by survey respondents to answer behavioral frequency questions. *Journal of Consumer Research*, 14, 280-288.

Brown, M. S. Physicians on the Internet: ambivalence and resistance about to give way to acceptance. *MEDICINE ON THE NET*, January 1998.

Campbell, J.D., Harris, K.D., Hodge, R. (2001). Introducing telemedicine technology to rural physicians and settings. *Journal of Family Practice, 50* (5), 419-424.

Cervero, R. M. (1988). *Effective continuing education for professionals.* San Francisco, CA: Jossey-Bass.

Coiera, E. (1995). Medical informatics. *BMJ*,310, (6991), 1381-1387.

Conte, S. J., Imershein, A. W., & Magill, M. K. (1992). Rural community and physician perspectives on resource factors affecting physician retention. *The Journal of Rural Health*, 8 (3), 185-196.

Davis, F. D. (1989). Perceived usefulness, perceived ease of use, and user acceptance of information technology. *MIS Quarterly, 3*19-339.

Davis, F. D. (1993). User acceptance of information technology: system characteristics, user perceptions and behavioral impacts. *International Journal of Man-Machine Studies, 38*, 475-487.

Davis, F. D., Bagozzi, R. P., & Warshaw, P. (1989). User acceptance of computer technology: A comparison of two theoretical models. *Management Sciences, 35*(8), 982-1003.

Davis, F. D., & Venkatesh, V. (1995). Measuring user acceptance of emerging information technologies: An assessment of possible method biases. *Proceedings of the 28th Annual Hawaii International Conference on System Sciences, 729-736.*

Davis, F. D., & Venkatesh, V. (1996). A critical assessment of potential measurement biases in the technology acceptance model: three experiments. *International Journal of Human-Computer Studies*, 45, 19-45.

Forti, E. M., Martin, K. E., Jones, R. L., & Herman, J. M. (1995). Factors Influencing Retention of Rural Pennsylvania Family Physicians. *JABFP*, 8(6), 469-474.

Gallagher, K., & McFarland, M. A. (1996). The wired physician: Current clinical information on the Internet. Missouri Medicine, 93(7), 334-339.

Harned, M. A. (1993). The saga of rural health care. *The West Virginia Medical Journal,* 89 (55), 54-5.

Harris, K. D. & Campbell, J.D. (2000). Internet by proxy: How rural physicians use the Internet. *Social Science Computer Review*, 18 (4), 502-507.

Heydt, S. (1999). Helping physicians cope with change. *Physician Executive*, 25(2), 40-43.

High, W.A., Houston, M.S., Calobrisi, S. D., Drage, L.A., McEvoy, M.T. (2000). Assessment of the accuracy of low-cost store-and-forward teledermatology consultation. *Journal of the American Academy of Dermatology*, 42, 776-783.

Lundberg, G. D. (1998). Medical information on the Internet. *The Journal of the American Medical Association,* 280.

Mackesy, R. (1993). Physician satisfaction with rural hospitals. *Hospital & Health Services Administration*, 38 (3), 375-385.

Miller, T. E. (1996). Segmenting the Internet. *American Demographics*, 18(7), 48-51.

Morris, M. G. & Dillon, A. (1997). How user perceptions influence software use. *IEEE Software,* 58-65.

Rogers, E. M. (1995). *Diffusion of Innovations* (4th ed.). New York: The Free Press.

Segars, A. H., & Grover, V. (1993). Re-examining perceived ease of use and usefulness: A confirmatory factor analysis. *MIS Quarterly*, 517-525.

Smith, M. R. (1996). Technological determinism in American culture. In M. R. Smith and Leo Marx (Eds.), *Does technology drive history: The dilemma of technological determinism.* Cambridge, MASS: The MIT Press.

Southwick, K. Online services come out swinging – the prize? Physician loyalty. *MEDICINE ON THE NET*, October 1997.

Streiner, D. L., & Norman, G. R. (1995). *Health measurement scales: A practical guide to their development and use.* New York, NY: Oxford University Press.

Surry, D. (1997). Diffusion theory and instructional technology. Paper presented at the Annual Conference of the Association for Educational Communications and Technology (AECT), Albuquerque, New Mexico.

Szajna, B. (1994). Software evaluation and choice: Predictive validation of the technology acceptance instrument. *MIS Quarterly*, September, 319-324.

Treister, N. W. (1998). Physician acceptance of new medical information systems: The field of dreams. *Physician Executive*, 24 (3), 20-25.

Westberg, E.E. & Miller, R.A. (1999). The basis for using the Internet to support the information needs of primary care. *Journal of the American Medical Informatics Association*, 6 (1), 6-25.

Chapter 9

VDT Health Hazards: A Guide for End Users and Managers

Carol Clark
Middle Tennessee State University, USA

INTRODUCTION

Managers must strive for a healthy and productive working environment for end users. Eliminating or reducing lost work days and improving worker productivity in turn relates to the organization's profitability. VDT related health issues are important to end users, managers, and the organization as a whole.

End user computing is becoming commonplace in most businesses. In 1993 more than forty-five percent of the U.S. population used computers at work according to the U.S. Department of Labor (1997). The proliferation of end user computing creates a host of management issues. One such issue involves the potential health hazards associated with video display terminal (VDT) use. Both managers and end users must address this issue if a healthy and productive work environment is to exist.

Government bodies have been addressing the VDT ergonomics issue. Legislation has been created or is in the process of being created to protect VDT end users. VDT related ergonomics should be proactively approached by management.

In fact, some companies have ergonomics plans in place that specifically include the use of VDTs. One such company is Sun in Mountain View, California. Sun has reduced its average repetitive strain injury (RSI) related

Previously Published in the *Journal of End User Computing, vol.13, no.1*, Copyright © 2001, Idea Group Publishing.

disability claim from a range of $45,000 to $55,000 to an average of $3500. They address not only equipment issues but also behavioral changes like taking frequent breaks. (Garner, 1997) The good news is that many recommendations, such as this, are relatively simple to implement into any organization.

This article outlines major health issues (e.g., vision problems, musculoskeletal disorders, and radiation effects on pregnancy), as evidenced by the literature and medical research, associated with VDT use. It provides practical suggestions for both end users and managers to help eliminate or reduce the potential negative health effects of VDT use.

MAJOR VDT RELATED HEALTH ISSUES
Vision Problems

Vision problems related to VDT use have raised concerns for both end users and managers for some time. How extensive is the problem? "A survey of optometrists indicated that 10 million eye examinations are given annually in this country, primarily because of vision problems related to VDT use" (Anshel, 1997, p. 17). In addition, seventy-five to ninety percent of all VDT users have visual symptoms according to a number of investigators (Anshel, 1997).

The term computer vision syndrome (CVS) has emerged. CVS is defined by the American Optometric Association "as that 'complex of eye and vision problems related to near work which are experienced during or related to computer use'" (Anshel, 1997, p. 17).

The symptoms included in CVS are "eyestrain, headaches, blurred vision (distance, near, or both) dry and irritated eyes, slowed refocusing, neck ache, backache, sensitivity to light and double vision" (Anshel, 1997, p. 17). Most of these symptoms have been a cause for concern for some time. But the development of a specific ailment, i.e., CVS, has solidified the concern.

What causes CVS? A variety of factors include an individual's visual problems, poor workplace conditions, and incorrect work habits (Anshel, 1997). An individual's visual problems, like astigmatism, are clearly medical concerns beyond the present scope. However, workplace conditions and work habits are directly germane to VDT use in the office environment and are appropriate to this discussion.

The problem of glare produced by traditional office lighting on VDT screens is well known. This lighting is suited to white paper work and not computer screens. The point-of-view has changed for the user. Instead of looking down (on the desk surface), one looks directly ahead at the screen. (Bachner, 1997) This change in work environment must be addressed and modifications made to accommodate the end user.

One study addressed ocular surface area (OSA) as a contributing factor in vision distress. The subjects performed wordprocessing as a task for ten minutes. The front of the eye was video taped with a small TV camera. VDT work involves a high gaze angle which induces a large OSA. VDT users look at both the screen and the keyboard. The study looked at this screen and keyboard distance and the related OSA. (Sotoyama, Jonai, Saito, and Villanueva, 1996) "A large OSA induces eye irritation and eye fatigue because the eye surface is highly sensitive to various stimuli" (Sotoyama, et al, 1996, p. 877).

Another study addressed the relationship between visual discomfort (asthenopia) and the type of VDT work activities performed by over ten thousand VDT operators. The types of VDT work were data entry, data checking, dialogue, word processing, enquiry, and various services. The number of hours of application was also included. The findings indicated that the type of VDT work was not a significant factor in visual discomfort. The results suggested that the main factor is the amount of time spent at the VDT. (Rechichi, DeMoja, and Scullica, 1996) This further indicates that visual discomfort can be present among several groups of workers with different VDT related responsibilities. Managers will need to address the possibility of vision related ailments across various end user areas.

Musculoskeletal Disorders

Musculoskeletal discomfort and related problems are another concern for VDT end users. These problems include carpel tunnel syndrome that affects the hand and wrist.

Working with VDTs usually requires small frequent movements of the eyes, head, arms, and fingers while the worker sits still for some time. Muscle fatigue may result after maintaining a fixed posture for extended periods of time. Muscle pain and injury can result. Musculoskeletal disorders are caused or made worse by work related risk factors. These disorders include injuries to muscles, joints, tendons, or nerves. Pain and swelling, numbness and tingling, loss of strength, and reduced range of motion are early symptoms of musculoskeletal disorders. (U.S. Department of Labor, 1997)

A review of musculoskeletal problems in VDT work was done by Carter and Banister (1994). They conclude that "musculoskeletal discomfort associated with VDT work is attributable to static muscular loading of the system, biomechanical stress, and repetitive work" (Carter and Banister, 1994, p. 1644). However, they indicated that a conclusion cannot be made about whether the frequency of occurrence of musculoskeletal problems is higher for VDT workers than non VDT workers (Carter and Banister, 1994).

Carpal-tunnel syndrome is one of the top workplace injuries that results in lost work time (Quintanilla, 1997). The Bureau of Labor Statistics recorded almost

32,000 cases of carpal-tunnel syndrome in 1995 (Quintanilla, 1997). The National Council on Compensation Insurance reported in 1996 that "carpal tunnel syndrome cases are a growing cause of workers' compensation claims"(Gjertsen, 1997, p. 8). In addition, more work days are missed as a result of CTS than from other injuries (Gjertsen, 1997). Missed work days mean reduced productivity which is, of course, of major concern to managers.

Reaching across the desk to use a mouse, squeezing a mouse hard, and button-pressing for long periods can affect the musculoskeletal system. Mouse related disorders ranged from 0 in 1986 to 216 in 1993. This is a relatively small number but in terms of repetitive stress injuries (RSIs) from computer use it represented six and one-tenth percent. (Lord, 1997) The potential for more cases is great given the proliferation of use of mouse devices among VDT users today.

A report from the Office Ergonomics Research Committee in Manchester Center, Vermont, says that many factors contribute to RSIs. They include a lack of training on prevention of injuries, physical differences among people and medical histories as well as psychological stress that may lead to physical pain in some. (Gjertsen, 1997)

Of the annual $60 billion workers' compensation costs, RSIs are one third, according to Federal OSHA (Occupational Safety and Health Administration) (Rankin, 1997). The potential impact on end users in terms of health and productivity is immense. From an organizational perspective, employee morale and productivity are at stake, as well as profits.

The Bureau of Labor Statistics figures for repetitive motion injuries (RMIs) related to repetitive typing or keying, that resulted in missed work days, show a drop of six percent from 1995 to 1996. There has been a total drop of seventeen percent since 1993. Also, it is reported that repetitive typing or keying accounts for only six-tenths of a percent of the total reported cases of RMIs. P.J. Edington, Executive Director of the Center for Office Technology, notes that "clearly, most repetitive motion injuries are not occurring in the offices of America." (Center for Office Technology Page, 1998a) Even though there is a decline in RMIs, some people are still being affected. The issue must continue to be addressed by end users and managers.

An estimate by the U.S. Department of Labor is that about fifty percent of the U.S. workforce will have some kind of cumulative trauma disorder by the year 2000 (Garner, 1997). So, no matter what the cause this issue needs to be addressed. Musculoskeletal disorders should not be ignored by either end users or managers. It is evident that some of the potential factors can and should be addressed at work to help to prevent the occurrence of or reduce the negative health effects associated with VDT work.

Radiation Effects on Pregnancy

The issue of radiation effects on pregnancy has caused concern among VDT users. This has prompted much research in the area. A debate has existed as to whether the use of a VDT during pregnancy results in adverse health risks, such as increased spontaneous abortions.

In 1991, the New England Journal of Medicine published the results of one such study. The final study group consisted of directory assistance and general telephone operators. There were 730 subjects with 882 eligible (as defined by the study) pregnancies during the 1983-1986 time period. Some of the subjects had more than one pregnancy. There were also sixteen pregnancies with twins. The directory assistance operators used VDTs while the general telephone operators did not. This represented the primary difference between the two groups. The study concluded that VDT use (and the electromagnetic fields) was not related to an increased risk of spontaneous abortion. (Schnorr, et al., 1991)

A second part of the study focused on the association between VDT use and risk of reduced birth weight and preterm birth. The results of this study were that the risks of reduced birth weight and preterm birth did not increase with occupational VDT use. (Grajewski, et al., 1997)

The general results and conclusions by the authors of one study state that there is no increased risk of spontaneous abortion with VDTs. The study group consisted of 508 women who had a spontaneous abortion and 1148 women who gave birth to healthy infants from 1992-1995. However, in the area of VDT use for word-processing activity and spontaneous abortion, a borderline statistically significant risk was found (after considering other potential confounding effects). (Grasso, Parazzini, Chatenoud, Di Cintio, and Benzi, 1997)

ADDRESSING VDT HEALTH ISSUES: PROGRAMS AND LEGISLATION

Ergonomics Programs

Ergonomics programs can address the issue of musculoskeletal disorders. A report entitled "Worker Protection: Private Sector Ergonomics Programs Yield Positive Results" was produced by the U.S. General Accounting Office in 1997. (Fletcher, 1997). It looked at five private companies to identify key components that are critical to ergonomics programs. The core elements to protect workers are: "management commitment, employee involvement, identification of problem jobs, development of solutions for problem jobs, training and education for employees, and appropriate medical management" (Fletcher, 1997, p. 71). The report suggests allowing flexibility in designing a program that depends upon the worksite. This suggestion was aimed at the continuing efforts by OSHA to develop ergonomics standards. (Fletcher, 1997)

It is possible to reduce or eliminate potential health hazards of VDT use. Managers should initiate a new ergonomic program or revamp an old one with these suggestions in mind.

Current VDT Legislation

A current legislative action that addresses ergonomics issues was finalized in 1997 in the state of California. In July of 1993, the governor of California signed a law requiring the development of statewide ergonomics requirements by the end of 1994. This mandate resulted in the proposal of the Occupational Noise and Ergonomics Hazards rule. (Williams, 1997)

The rule exempts employers with less than 10 workers (Ceniceros, 1997). It applies to workers who use computers for more than 4 hours a day or 20 hours a week (Williams, 1997). The rule addresses six areas: chairs, workstations, workstation accessories, lighting, screens and work breaks (Williams, 1997).

The California ergonomic standard on repetitive motion injuries was passed in 1997 (Guarascio-Howard, 1997). While it is enforceable a series of legal challenges are currently aimed at the standard. Managers and end users will want to keep a close watch on the outcome of the legal process and the ultimate enforceability of the standard. The introduction of this ergonomics standard will potentially play a role in future standard development. Managers may want to take a voluntary approach to ergonomics to protect end users.

RECOMMENDATIONS FOR END USERS AND MANAGERS

Recommendations: Vision Problems

Care should be taken to reduce the glare on the screen. Monitors that tilt are the norm today. However, office lighting should be addressed and modified to fit the new office environment that goes beyond traditional white paper work and includes the use of computers.

Dennis Ankrum, a certified ergonomist, says that the previously suggested computer monitor distance of 20-26 inches is too close. He suggests the distances of 45 inches for looking straight ahead and 35 inches for looking downward (at an angle like reading a book). He also suggests increasing the typeface size instead of getting closer to the monitor. He suggests that the eye muscles are most relaxed at these distances. (Verespej, 1997)

In some cases, corrective lenses are needed to avoid eye strain and headaches associated with VDT work. Taking a rest break every hour or so can reduce eyestrain. Also employees can simply change their focus (for example, looking across the room) to give eye muscles a chance to relax. (U.S. Department of Labor, 1997)

Eye irritation and fatigue are induced by a large OSA (ocular surface area). Two recommendations are made. One, adjust the desk height to suit the user's height. Two, place the monitor closer to the keyboard. The latter suggestion reduces the OSA. (Sotoyama, et al., 1996)

Recommendations: Musculoskeletal

Chairs

Work equipment should accommodate the human body and not vice versa (Fisher, 1996; Kamienska-Zyla and Prync-Skotniczny, 1996). For example, the purchase of adjustable chairs is important because chairs are not one size fits all (Rundquist, 1997). Research in chair quality and adjustability is needed. This of course will require time and effort.

In addition, the purchase of ergonomically designed chairs can be costly. However, one company considers the purchase of a $500 chair to be a minimal expense when compared to a disability claim. This is especially true when the cost is amortized over five years. (Garner, 1997) If the results could lead to happier, healthier, and more productive employees, it would be time and money well spent.

The actual implementation of this process could be facilitated by an ergonomic task force made up of a cross-section of employees (Rundquist, 1997). This approach would incorporate various end user areas and perspectives perhaps resulting in a more thorough evaluation.

Keyboards

A recent trial against a keyboard manufacturer (Digital Equipment Corporation) found in favor of the defendant. A similar judgement has resulted in many other cases. It was determined that "keyboards do not cause musculoskeletal disorders." This is a part of a trend recognizing that injuries are not caused by keyboards. (Center for Office Technology Page, 1998b)

However, position and level of force while keyboarding may contribute to RSI (repetitive stress injuries) symptoms. These are factors that can be controlled by the end user. Users should maintain a straight natural posture. The wrist should not bend up or down or twist left or right. The keyboard level should be adjusted also. It should be positioned near or below the elbow level. (Figura, 1996)

Should ergonomic keyboards be purchased? A study by NIOSH (National Institute for Occupational Safety and Health) reported no difference among subjects using standard and ergonomic (split design) keyboards. The study took place over a two-day period. However, the report suggests further research over a longer period of time and with subjects who have symptoms of fatigue or discomfort. (Gjertsen, 1997; Swanson, Galinsky, Cole, Pan, and Sauter, 1997)

Other new keyboard designs include fully adjustable tent-shaped models and those with rearranged keys to reduce finger reaching. However, it is not known whether or not these new designs reduce RSIs. (Figura, 1996)

Mouse

Many end users use a mouse at the computer. Place the mouse so that the wrist floats, i.e., position the arm at a 90 degree angle. The mouse should be within easy reach of the user. Do not reach across the desk. The forearm may get stressed after long stretches of button pushing. One suggestion is to switch between a trackball and a touch pad to vary the movements required (Lord, 1997).

Recommendations: Radiation Effects on Pregnancy

Even though VDT emission levels are low, radiofrequency and extreme low-frequency electromagnetic fields are still being debated. The relationship between VDT use and pregnancy continues to be addressed. Some workplace designs are increasing the distance between the operator and the workstation and between workstations to reduce the potential electromagnetic field exposures to VDT users. (U.S. Department of Labor, 1997)

Recommendations: General

One prevalent theme among ergonomic recommendations is for users to take brief breaks and exercise (for example, stretch). Software is available to remind workers to take a break. Two such programs are ScreenPlay and PowerPause. They pop up on the screen at scheduled intervals. (Lord, 1997)

Software may either monitor the passage of a specified time period of computer use or count keystrokes before it prompts the user to take a break. Other programs go beyond this and provide stretching exercise instruction or feedback related to the level of effort intensity. More advanced software prepares images that indicate postural risk to body parts. This would help health and safety managers and ergonomists to assist users in preventive measures. (Guarascio-Howard, 1997)

Other recommendations, in addition to breaks, include stretching, exercising and improving posture (Garner, 1997). Tips for reducing the discomforts also include training and good workstation and job design (Carter & Banister, 1994).

Most of these are common sense approaches that are not costly. Workers should be encouraged to include these in their work habits.

Recommendations: Laptops

There are additional recommendations for laptop computer users. Try to lighten the load. Do not carry extra equipment (e.g., extra battery) unless necessary. Shift the load from one side of the body to the other. Use a padded shoulder strap. (LaBar, 1997; Center for Office Technology, 1997) When using the laptop at the office, a full size monitor and keyboard may provide more comfort to the user from both a visual and musculoskeletal perspective (Center for Office Technology, 1997).

The mobile end user should follow the general guidelines as well as the specific ones given when using a laptop. Managers should not assume that end users will be aware of these recommendations. Managers should explicitly address the issues with laptop users to minimize the potential risks.

CONCLUSIONS

End users should stay abreast of the ergonomic recommendations made regarding VDT use in the work environment. Many such recommendations were given here. However, continued research will provide ongoing information pertinent to this issue. In addition, end users should take an active role in the development and implementation of office ergonomic programs. This will make end users aware of the potential VDT related problems and will involve them in the development of solutions for the problems.

Managers should be proactive in addressing the end user health issues described. The report on good ergonomic programs provides a basis for developing an ergonomic program in any organization. Managers should include current and future VDT ergonomic recommendations in their organization's ergonomic plan. Many of the current recommendations are not complex and can be easily incorporated. Other recommendations may require more time and effort on the part of both managers and end users.

REFERENCES

Anshel, Jeffrey. (1997). Computer Vision Syndrome: Causes and Cures. *Managing Office Technology*, (July), 42(7), 17-19.

Bachner, John Philip. (1997). Eliminate Those Glaring Errors. *Managing Office Technology*, (July), 15-16.

Carter, J.B. and Banister, E.W. (1994). Musculoskeletal Problems in VDT Work: A Review. *Ergonomics*, 37(10), 1623-1648.

Ceniceros, Roberto. (1997). California Oks New Standard on Ergonomics. *Business Insurance*, 31(24), (June), 1 and 33.

Center for Office Technology. (1997). *The Laptop User's Guide: Practical Recommendations for the Road Warrior*, Metaphase Publishing.

Center for Office Technology Page. (1998a). Office Place RMIs Decrease for Third Year in a Row Despite Increased Computer Usage. http://www.cot.org/blsmay.html.

Center for Office Technology Page. (1998b). Jury Again Finds No Link Between Keyboards and MSD Conditions. June 17. http://cot.org/digital.html.

Figura, Susannah Zak. (1996). Healthy Keyboarding: What You Should Know. *Managing Office Technology*, (July), 41(7), 27-28.

Fisher, Sandra Lotz. (1996). Are Your Employees Working Ergosmart? *Personnel Journal*, (December), 75(12), 91-92.

Fletcher, Meg. (1997). Core Components Crucial in Ergonomics Programs. *Business Insurance*, (September 15), 31(37), 71.

Garner, Rochelle. (1997). Painful Lessons. *Computerworld*, (January 20), 31(3), 89.

Gjertsen, Lee Ann. (1997). Study: Little Benefit From "Ergonomic" Keyboards. *National Underwriter Property & Casualty-Risk & Benefits Management*, (January 20), no. 3, 8.

Grajewski, Barbara, Schnorr, Teresa M., Reefhuis, Jennita, Roeleveld, Nel, Salvan, Alberto, Mueller, Charles A., Conover, David L., and Murray, William E. (1997). Work With Video Display Terminals and the Risk of Reduced Birthweight and Preterm Birth. *American Journal of Industrial Medicine*, 32, 681-688.

Grasso, P., Parazzini, F., Chatenoud, L., Di Cintio, E., and Benzi, G. (1997). Exposure to Video Display Terminals and Risk of Spontaneous Abortion. *American Journal of Industrial Medicine*, 32, 403-407.

Guarascio-Howard, Linda. (1997). Ergonomic Software Can Ease RMI Risk. *National Underwriter Property & Casualty-Risk & Benefits Management*, (October 6), 101(40), 12 and 24.

Kamienska-Zyla, M. and Prync-Skotniczny, K. (1996). Subjective Fatigue Symptoms Among Computer Systems Operators in Poland. *Applied Ergonomics*, (June), 27(3), 217-220.

LaBar, Gregg. (1997). Ergonomics for the Virtual Office. *Managing Office Technology*, (October), 22-24.

Lord, Mary. (1997). Is Your Mouse a Trap? *U.S. News & World Report*, (March 31), 122(12), 76 and 78.

Quintanilla, Carl. (1997). The Leading Workplace Injuries May Surprise You. *The Wall Street Journal*, (July 15), p A1(W) p A1 (E) col 5 (3 col in).

Rankin, Tom. (1997). Stop the Pain. *Cal-OSHA Reporter*, (March 10), 24(10).

Rechichi, Caterina, DeMoja, Carmelo A., and Scullica, Luigi. (1996). Psychology of Computer Use: XXXVI. Visual Discomfort and Different Types of Work at Videodisplay Terminals. *Perpetual and Motor Skills*, (June), 83(3), 935-938.

Rundquist, Kristina. (1997). Sitting Down on the Job: How to Do It Right. *Managing Office Technology*, (September), 42(9), 36-38.

Schnorr, Teresa M., Grajewski, Barbara A., Hornung, Richard W., Thun, Michael J., Egeland, Grace M., Murray, William E., Conover, David L., and Halperin, William E. (1991). Video Display Terminals and the Risk of Spontaneous Abortion. *New England Journal of Medicine*, 324, 727-733.

Sotoyama, Midori, Jonai, Hiroshi, Saito, Susumu, and Villanueva, Maria Beatriz G. (1996). Analysis of Ocular Surface Area for Comfortable VDT Workstation Layout. *Ergonomics*, 39(6), 877-884.

Swanson, Naomi G., Galinsky, Traci L., Cole, Libby L., Pan, Christopher S., and Sauter, Steven L. (1997). The Impact of Keyboard Design on Comfort and Productivity in a Text-Entry Task. *Applied Ergonomics*, (February), 28(1), 9-16.

U.S. Department of Labor, Occupational Safety and Health Administration (OSHA). (1997). *Working Safely With Video Display Terminals*, OSHA 3092.

Verespej, Michael A., (Ed.). (1997). New Monitor Advice. *Industry Week*, (May 5), 246(9), 18.

Williams, Paul. (1997). California Breaks 'Ergonomic Ground'. *Los Angeles Business Journal*, (October), 19(42), 36.

Chapter 10

The User Interface for a Computerized Patient Record System for Primary Health Care in a Third World Environment

P.J. Blignaut and T. McDonald
University of the Orange Free State, Republic of South Africa

The manual paper-based system for keeping track of patient history was replaced with a computerized system in a Primary Health Care clinic in a traditionally Black urban area. Several factors influenced the design of the user-interface. Aspects such as screen layout, data fields to be captured, mouse dependency, computer literacy of the users and adapting the system to the normal daily routine of users were considered. The study showed that special attention should be devoted to the design of the user interface for systems used primarily by third world users who do not want the computer to interfere or hinder them in their daily jobs.

Quite a few studies on the impact of computerization of nursing practice have been done in the past. Amongst these Marasovic et al. (1997) stated that "a clinical information system (CIS) is a point-of-care, patient-focused computer system that replaces all or some of the paper medical records" (p. 91). Adderley et al. (1997) constitutes that "computerization has allowed more time for personalized patient care and patient/staff interaction" (p. 45). They also

Previously Published in the *Journal of End User Computing, vol.11, no.2,* Copyright © 1999, Idea Group Publishing.

concluded that "it (computerization) has made information readily available for acquisition and analysis of data" (p. 45).

Given the unique circumstances of Primary Health Care (PHC) in the Republic of South Africa (RSA), however, the user interface for such a software system should be carefully designed. Special aspects that should be taken into account involves the level of computer literacy, cultural background and attitude towards computers of the potential users as well as the data set, the number of patients per nurse, et cetera.

The purpose of this article is, therefore, to highlight the lessons learnt with regard to the user interface when a study was done to determine the overall viability of computerizing a primary health care clinic in a third world environment.

METHODOLOGY

The study was done in a PHC clinic that is situated in the urban area of Mangaung, a third world residential area in the Free State province of the RSA. The clinic serves approximately 400 000 people from 12 squatter camps and 11 suburbs with permanent housing structures. The clinic is staffed by 18 people on a permanent basis of which 8 are professional nurses, 6 registered nurses and 4 administrative personnel.

Blignaut and McDonald (1997 (2)) showed that acquiring a ready-made product from a software vendor is not always feasible. After some discussion with the staff before this study commenced, it was evident that also in this case none of the currently available commercial systems could be used. Some of the reasons are listed below:

- The staff are totally computer-illiterate. It would not be feasible to train them to use a comprehensive system within a limited time.
- None of the commercial systems fulfill in their very specific needs. The professional nurses were quite adamant about not being limited by a system, especially one that did not closely resemble their current manual system.
- None of the commercial systems make provision for the specific distributed layout of the clinic chosen.
- It was important that the research be done with the minimum disturbance to the daily routine of the staff. Expecting them to adapt their routine to a given system would not be acceptable.
- In order to draw a comparison between the manual system and a computerized one, it is evident that the computerized system should, to a large extent, resemble the current manual system.

- The computer system must also be able to make a printout of the day's work so that the nurses can keep the manual system up to date.

In order to address these problems, a new system was developed from scratch with this specific environment and the current manual system in mind.

Every room in the clinic where patients were seen was equipped with a computer and connected to a central database by means of a local area network. New patients were entered into the database in the administrative office. The vital observations, i.e., blood pressure, weight and temperature, were taken by nurses in a so-called dressing room. Routine child immunizations were done by nursing students in the immunization room. The professional nurses attended to patients' complaints in their consultation rooms. All of these people updated the particular patient record on the computer after they have finished with a patient. The professional nurses could also prescribe medicine and a hard copy of the prescription was printed in the dispensary.

The front-end of the system was developed in Visual Basic 4.0 (Microsoft inc.), a development tool for graphical applications. The data was kept in an Access database (Microsoft inc.). Every computer had the front-end installed on it and had access to the database which was stored on the computer in the office.

Each one of the key role players had only one data-entry screen to cope with, branching directly from the opening screen.

Figure 1 depicts the screen that the administrative staff used. They registered new patients and allocated a unique patient number to each patient.

Figure 1: Screen for entering households and patients

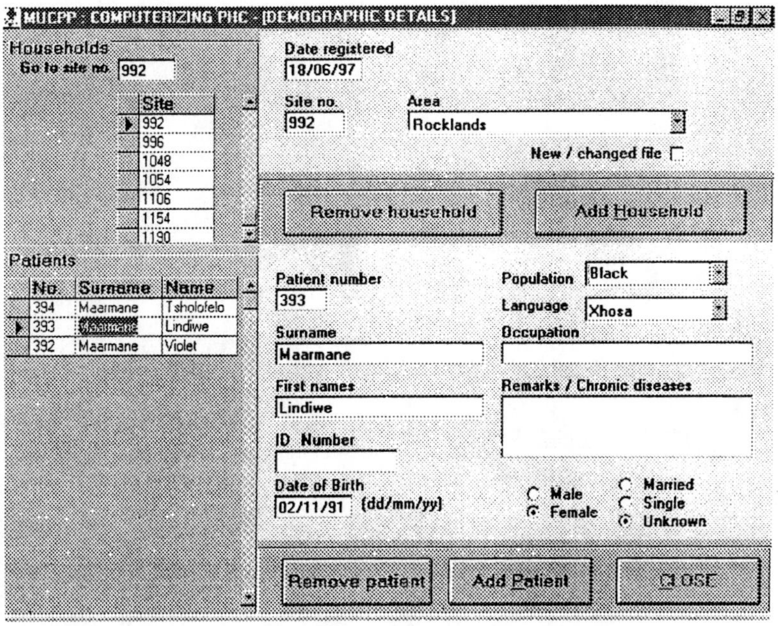

The records of existing patients were checked and updated if changes occurred. The unique patient number was given to the patient to carry with him while he moved around in the building.

This screen resembles the current manual system with regard to the specific data fields captured and the organization of patients into households. In the grid in the upper left-hand corner, a household can be selected according to site number and all residents on that site will then be listed in the grid underneath. A specific person can be selected in this grid and his/her personal details would then appear on the screen. Site numbers are listed numerically and residents alphabetically.

Vital observations

The nurses entered the unique patient number to find a patient's record in the database. Thereafter, they entered the vital observations (blood pressure, weight and temperature) on the screen showed in Figure 2.

Immunizations

Figure 3 shows the screen used by the nursing students to update the immunization records of children.

Figure 2 : Screen used to enter vital observations

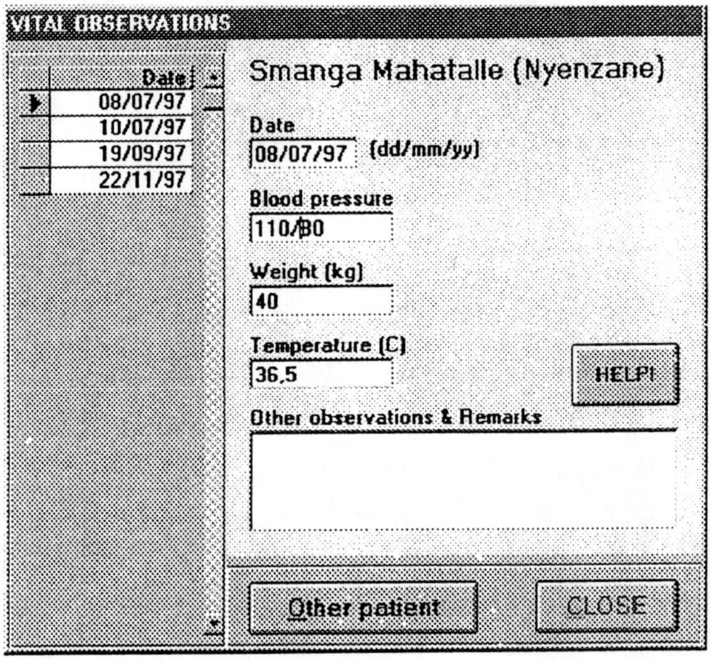

Figure 3 : Screen used to update immunization record of children

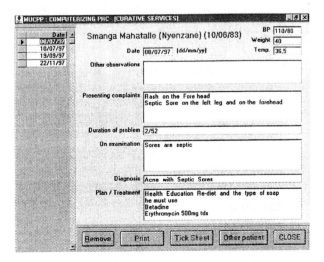

Entering clinical details

When the patient reported to the professional nurse, she also entered the unique patient number to find the patient's record in the database. The basic observations entered by the staff in the dressing-room immediately became visible on their screen. They then had the opportunity to type in other data into the text boxes as shown in Figure 4.

Figure 4 : Screen used by professional nurses

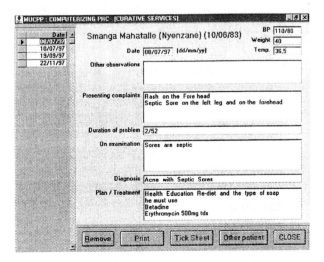

Capturing of statistics

The current manual system makes provision for a system of tick sheets on which statistical indicators are marked with a pencil. Periodically these tick sheets are submitted to the provincial health authority, who scans the tick sheets and processes the statistics.

An electronic on-screen tick sheet to capture statistics has already been proposed by Blignaut and Mc Donald (1997 (1)) and such a screen was originally included in this system. Because of the problems that the users experienced with handling the mouse as well as the duplication of work that it would involve, it was decided to omit it from this study and continue with the manual tick sheet.

FINDINGS AND CONCLUSIONS

Much has been said and written with regard to the nature of a computer-interface for electronic patient records. See Blignaut and McDonald (1997 (1)), Alonso et.al. (1997) and Plaisant et al. (1997) in this regard. For this study, however, some unique environmental limitations existed which made the development of the computer system a learning experience:

- The users had no previous experience of computers and were totally unaware of any of the advantages of using a computer.
- The clinic was typical of most clinics in a third-world environment.

Free text versus fixed fields

In the system that was developed for this study, the curatives-screen (Figure 4) was regarded as the most representative and the one most frequently used.

Initially it was thought that a screen with numerous fields in which the user either had to type a short word or sentence or select an item from a list, would be the best for the situation. Not only would it limit the amount of typing needed, but it would also facilitate the capturing and processing of statistical data. The users and specifically the professional nurses felt, however, that this was both confusing and limiting. They wanted the freedom to write anything they would like in their own words.

The system was thus implemented with only one large multi-line text box on the curatives-screen. After some days of practice, it was evident that the users were in any case entering data under fixed headings. The curatives-screen was thus changed again to accommodate these headings (fig. 4). The users were trained to move from one box to another by pressing 'Tab' on the keyboard. After some practice, the users could handle this screen.

Use of a graphical environment

After some exposure, it also became evident that using the mouse was a terrifying experience. The users experienced many problems using a point-and-click-method. It seemed as though the necessary hand-eye coordination skills were just lacking. Despite the fact that the buttons on all the screens are relatively large, the users had problems with clicking them with the mouse. The nurses in the dressing room, for instance, preferred the short-cut keys right through to the end of the study. The curatives-screen (Figure 4) had its buttons at the bottom of the screen and the professional nurses experienced some problems with the hidden task-bar of Windows 95. The task bar was therefore moved to the right-hand-side of their screens.

Both screens shown in Figures 3 and 4 originally had a text box in which the user had to type the unique patient number of the next patient. To shift the focus to this box, however, they had to click with the mouse pointer in it. Particularly the nurses in the dressing room experienced problems placing the mouse pointer accurately enough on top of the text box and then clicking it. Therefore, the text box was removed and a button was added to the screen. This button had a short-cut key connected to it and when activated, a message box appeared on the screen which had the focus by default. The users could now enter the unique patient number and press 'Enter' afterwards, a process which they found much easier.

On the entry screen, users had to select their name from a drop-down list and it proved to be both time-consuming and inaccurate. On the screen that the administrative staff used (figure 1), the area in which a household was living, as well as the population group and language, had to be selected with indexed drop-down lists. This meant that they could type the first letter of the entry and use the up and down arrows to locate the exact entry. It proved to be more time efficient.

Also on Figure 1, the administrative staff had to select the sex and marital status of each member of a household by means of option boxes. Originally they had problems doing this quickly, so it was decided to connect shortcut keys to these items. Later, however, they managed it, maybe because they had much more practice with the system. Henderson et al. (1995) also asserts that clerical staff experiences less problems with computerization than nurses themselves.

The nursing students had the least problems with the graphical environment of all the user groups. They could handle the mouse efficiently and had little trouble in understanding the overall functionality of their screen. It seemed thus that younger people who had previous experience with computers would adapt to a computerized environment easier. This conclusion has also been made by Simpson & Kenrick. (1997), McBride & Nagle (1996) and Marosovic et al. (1997).

Resemblance of current system

One of the basic principles of computerizing an environment is to simulate the original environment as closely as possible.

For this study, the current system was investigated with regard to the process followed and the data contents and format of the patients' files. Therefore, the computerized system was developed to have a separate screen to resemble each of the functional units in the process, i.e., the administrative office, the room for basic observations, immunizations and the consultation rooms of the professional nurses.

Furthermore, the professional nurses use narrative descriptions in free text during consultations and they were quite adamant about being able to do the same in the computer system. A screen with several single-line text fields, drop-down lists and option and check boxes would definitely not comply with their requirements.

Typing ability needed

The study showed that the biggest stumbling block in computerizing an environment like this is the lack of typing skills. The administrative staff could type and it took them less than 30 seconds to enter a new patient on the average. On the other hand, however, none of the nursing staff could type and they were remarkably slow to update a patient's record on the computer. However, they became more and more fluent with the typing as the study progressed. It is thus reasonable to assume that after sufficient exposure and training, this problem could be minimized.

RECOMMENDATIONS

During the study it became evident that, if clinics such as the one referred to in this study are computerized, the computer interface should be designed in such a way to accommodate the very specific needs of the users and comply to the environmetal limitations.

The recommendations following apply to clinics serving a third world community and staffed by African nurses with limited computer skills and typing abilities:

- The data entry-screens should not be overcrowded with text boxes, drop-down lists, option boxes and check boxes. Users preferred a limited number of free-format text boxes.

- The system should not be mouse dependent. It should be easy to move through the fields with the 'Tab' key. Short-cut keys for command buttons, option boxes and check boxes should be defined. Drop-down lists should be indexed so that an item can be selected by pressing the first letter thereof.
- The amount of typing expected from the user should be minimized. There should, therefore, be a well-considered trade-off between free format text boxes and mouse-dependent drop-down lists.
- The system should make provision for easy capture of statistical data without complicating the user-interface in doing so.
- The computer system should resemble the current manual system as closely as possible.
- The system should be easy to use with a rapidly increasing learning curve.
- Users should be well trained with regard to general computer-literacy and especially typing skills.
- The system should be reliable and robust enough to function in an environment of computer-illiterate users.

REFERENCES

Adderley, R.N., Hyde, C., Mauseth, P. (1997). The Computer Age Impacts Nurses. *Computers in Nursing.* 15(1), 43-46.

Alonso, D.L., Rose, A., Plaisant, C., Norman, K.L. (1997). *Viewing personal history records: A comparison of Tabular format and graphical presentation using LifeLines.* Technical report of the HCIL, University of Maryland.

Blignaut, P.J. & Mc Donald, T. (1997 (1)). A Computerised Implementation of a Minimum Set of Health Indicators. *Methods of Information in Medicine.* 36(2/97), 122-126.

Blignaut, P.J. & Mc Donald, T. (1997 (2)). To Buy or Develop: Software for Primary Health Care. *CHASA Journal of Comprehensive Health.* 8(1), 27-30.

Henderson, R.D., Deane, F.P., Ward, M. (1995). Occupational differences in computer related anxiety: Implications for the implementation of a computerised patient management information system. *Behaviour & Information Technology.* 14, 23-31.

Marasovic, C., Kenney, C., Elliott, D., Sindhusake, D. (1997). Attitudes of Australian Nurses Toward the Implementation of a Clinical Information System. *Computers in Nursing.* 15(2), 91-98.

McBride, S.H., Nagle, L.M. (1996). Attitudes Toward Computers: A Test of Construct Validity. *Computers in Nursing.* 14(3), 164-170.

Plaisant, C. & Rose, A. (1997). *Exploring LifeLines to Visualize Patient records.* Technical report of the HCIL, University of Maryland.

Simpson, G. & Kenrick, M. (1997). Nurses? Attitudes Toward Computerization in Clinical Practice in a British General Hospital. *Computers in Nursing.* 15(1), 37-42.

Chapter 11

The Knowledge Medium – A Conceptual Framework for the Design and Implementation of a Platform Supporting the Community of AIDS Researchers and Practitioners

Rolf Grütter and Katarina Stanoevska-Slabeva
University of St. Gallen, Switzerland

Walter Fierz
Institute for Clinical Microbiology and Immunology, Switzerland

INTRODUCTION

The health care industry is essentially knowledge-based. The quality and efficiency of work performed depends on the ability to both manage internally created knowledge, e. g., about healing practices and available expertise as well as to enrich and integrate it with relevant external knowledge created world-wide by pharmacy research teams, international health organizations, etc. Efficient management of knowledge in health care requires, therefore, concepts and solutions for cooperation and sharing of knowledge within and between communities (Greiner & Rose, 1997).

Communities must be supported by special "platforms" which consider both the common language and the community-specific communication and cooperation requirements. In this chapter, we will introduce the concept of the knowledge medium defined by Schmid and apply it as a conceptual framework to the design

Previously Published in *Challenges of Information Technology Management in the 21st Century* edited by Mehdi Khosrow-Pour, Copyright © 2000, Idea Group Publishing.

and implementation of a platform supporting the community of AIDS researchers and practitioners. Thereby, the Swiss HIV Cohort Study (SHCS) will be the core community and the starting point of our analysis.

SHCS is a multi-center clinical trial involving outpatient clinics of seven center hospitals (referred to as "Cohort Centers") and a Coordination and Data Center. SHCS was initiated in 1987 (1) to collect clinical, laboratory, and socio-economic data with the intention of analyzing the prevalence and progression of the HIV-infection in Switzerland, (2) to promote and facilitate clinical research, and (3) to improve the health care services provided to HIV-infected patients (Ledergerber, Von Overbeck, Egger, & Luthy, 1994). Currently, the technical infrastructure supporting the SHCS includes various legacy laboratory systems at the Cohort Centers and a relational database system at the Coordination and Data Center. This database system is the common repository of the Cohort Centers and provides the basis for statistical analysis and planning of clinical trials. All data (including the electronically available) are manually processed on a paper study form including various media breaks. As a result, the creation and dissemination of new knowledge based on study data is considerably delayed. In order to overcome this shortcoming, a Web-based platform has been designed and is currently being implemented based on the concept of the knowledge medium.

THE CONCEPT OF THE KNOWLEDGE MEDIUM
Definition and Components of the Knowledge Medium

Schmid defines a knowledge medium as a sphere for the exchange and generation of knowledge within a confined community of human and artificial agents (Schmid & Stanoevska, 1999). *Communities* are associations of agents which share a common language and world as well as values and interests and use media in order to communicate with each other by taking over (predefined) roles. Thereby, the (digital) media provide a metaphor for physical meeting spaces. *Online* or *net communities* use (interactive) electronic media, particularly the Internet, in order to communicate with each other (Lechner, Schmid, Schubert, Klose, & Miler, 1999). Supporting or initiating an online community means building the appropriate medium which meets the specific community requirements for communication and cooperation.

A knowledge medium is comprised of the following components (Grütter, Stanoevska, & Fierz, 2000; Lechner & Schmid, 1999; Lechner et al. 1999; Schmid & Stanoevska, 1999):

- a *logical space* defining the common syntax and semantics of the knowledge represented and exchanged by the medium;

- a *system of channels*, i.e. carriers, transporting explicit knowledge over space and time; and
- an *organizational structure* consisting of roles and protocols.

Language is the necessary prerequisite for the externalization and exchange of knowledge. The *logical space* of the knowledge medium provides the language, which is used in order to capture and code knowledge. It comprises the syntax and the semantics. The *syntax* defines the rules according to which correct sentences must be constructed and, in a broader sense, also the set of valid symbols and constructs. The *semantics* determines the meaning of the used language constructs, e. g., by reference to real-world objects or by operational semantics. The logical space provides a formal representation of a possible world. In computer mediated spaces, the language has to be interpretable by machines. This machine-interpretable representation provides the basis, e. g., for the automated classification, retrieval, and combination of explicit knowledge thereby allowing machines for mimicking human intelligence.

Channels are the carriers containing explicit knowledge which is exchanged between the communicating agents. A carrier includes a physical medium (sound waves in the case of human speech) and applies a language (syntax and semantics) for the logical representation of the contents. In the context of the knowledge medium, we particularly refer to those carriers resulting from the convergence of information and communication technology and traditional media. Interconnected channels provide a communication space which can be used by agents to exchange knowledge. Filled with content, channels turn to interactive, ubiquitous, and multi-medial information objects.

Communities of agents have an *organizational structure* which is defined by roles and protocols. *Roles* define the required capabilities, rights, and obligations of agents participating in the community. *Protocols* are a set of rules that govern the interaction of agents. The organizational structure can be represented in the logical space of the knowledge medium allowing for automated reasoning over roles and processes.

The above described components of the knowledge medium are related to each other and form a single entity of human and artificial agents generating and exchanging explicit knowledge within a common semantic space. Taken together, they furthermore represent a complete mapping of the real-world environment onto an artificial world based on information and communication technology. Agents of the community can enter the medium by taking over one of the roles defined in the organizational structure (Lechner et al., 1999).

Origin of the Knowledge Medium Concept

The term knowledge medium was introduced by Stefik (1988) as an information network with semi-automated services for the generation, distribution, and consumption of knowledge. According to Stefik, the goal of building a knowledge medium is to tie expert systems and communication media together into a greater whole. He pointed to some research questions which had to be answered as a necessary prerequisite for building knowledge media. First attempts to answer them were conducted at the Stanford University. The results of this effort are the Knowledge Query and Manipulation Language (KQML) and the concept of ontologies. *KQML* is a general purpose communication language enabling interoperability and the communication of software agents (Finin, Labrou & Mayfield, 1997). *Ontologies* are defined as controlled vocabularies providing the basic terminology necessary for representation of a domain of discourse (Gruber, 1999). Ontologies are considered the basic elements of knowledge media.

The concept of the knowledge medium defined by Schmid extends the Stefik and Stanford approach for building knowledge media in three directions: First, it not only considers expert systems, but generalizes knowledge sharing for all kinds of knowledge sources. Second, it explicitly includes the agents who create and use the knowledge medium by introducing the concept of community. Third, it explicitly considers not only agent communication processes but any kind of organizational structure and coordination processes applied by the community. Because of its more general approach, the concept of the knowledge medium of Schmid was chosen for our re-design project.

The basic steps for the implementation of a knowledge medium are 1) identification of the communities, their organizational structures and interrelationships; 2) design and implementation of the above mentioned components of the knowledge medium.

THE COMMUNITY OF AIDS RESEARCHERS AND PRACTITIONERS

The target community of our research project comprises the following components:
- The core community includes the participants in the SHCS;
- the extended community includes AIDS researchers and practitioners worldwide; and
- each of them interfaces further communities of individuals from various disciplines: clinicians, laboratory specialists, epidemiologists, social workers, computer scientists, and nurses.

Whereas the first two represent distributed "communities of practice" (McDermott, 1999), which have been constituted for a limited length of time and include agents that are distributed in space, the third reflects the well-known notion of the medical specialties.

Figure 1: The community of AIDS researchers and practitioners

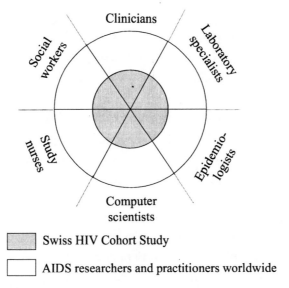

☐ (shaded) Swiss HIV Cohort Study

☐ AIDS researchers and practitioners worldwide

Put together, our target community can be depicted in Figure 1.

Figure 1 shows that any individual human agent participates at the same time in both a distributed community of practice and a medical specialty (for instance, he or she can be a clinician participating in SHCS). This is a result of his or her individual pattern of values and interests which is not fully matched by a single community. In addition, not only the various communities but also the individual agents must be considered as a single entity (for instance, an individual clinician provides health care services to *his or her* patients and is personally bound to discretion policies for information about them).

An example for an interaction scenario between the different communities is the dissemination of the results from a therapy study conducted by SHCS to clinicians leading to a change or modification of drug prescription in daily routine. Actually, the communication between SHCS and the clinicians takes place at regular face-to-face meetings of the "Working Group Clinics." Additionally, study results are published in scientific journals and, occasionally, individuals communicate on an informal bilateral basis. In Section 7, we will describe how the interaction scenario is expected to change by the leverage of the knowledge medium.

PLATFORM REQUIREMENTS

On this basis we would like to specify the following specific requirements for a platform supporting the community of AIDS researchers and practitioners:

• The platform must be scalable, it must provide different access levels to different kinds of data (patient information, anonymous study data, general statistical figures) for appropriate authorized communities/individuals;

- the platform must provide interfaces to communities of individuals from various specialties;
- it must be adaptable such as to include additional communities as time elapses.

In addition to these specific requirements, the general requirements for platforms supporting distributed communities of practice, such as those pertaining to their temporary nature and intended global scope must be considered.

EVALUATION OF THE KNOWLEDGE MEDIUM IN VIEW OF THE PLATFORM REQUIREMENTS

In order to check its applicability to the context of SHCS, the conceptual framework of the knowledge medium is evaluated in view of the platform requirements.

Scalability primarily affects the organizational structure of the knowledge medium in that different capabilities, rights, and obligations must be defined as parts of the various roles. Likewise, depending on the roles, the protocols for the communication within the knowledge medium may differ among the access levels. Additionally, the kind of explicit knowledge accessible to an agent may depend on his or her specific role within the community and on the state of a given process (e.g., health care delivery) (Nitsche, Holbein, Morger, & Teufel, 1998).

Interfaces to other communities require a mediation between different logical spaces thereby reducing the shared representation of the world when compared to the representations of each single community.

Adaptability reflects the dynamic aspect of the knowledge medium. Thus, the created and published knowledge may change the values and interests of loosely associated agents or groups of agents and, thus, attracts additional or newly established communities. As additional communities enter the knowledge medium, the language base is to be extended in order to provide a common denominator for communication. This extended language base integrates alternate representations of the world.

IMPLEMENTATION OF A KNOWLEDGE MEDIUM FOR SHCS

Based on the generic concept of the knowledge medium, first, the community supporting platform for SHCS was instantiated (resulting in the platform architecture) and is now implemented in a step-by-step approach. In the following, the architecture and the state of implementation will be described.

Figure 2: Platform architecture

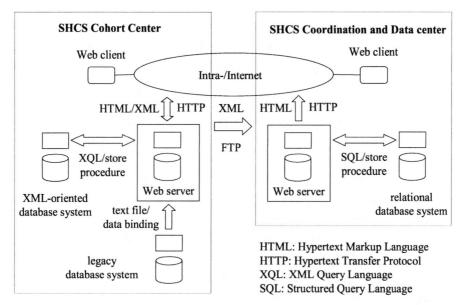

The Community Supporting Platform for SHCS

Figure 2 depicts the platform architecture of the knowledge medium for SHCS:

The scalability requirement is supported by the sum of different components. Access to individual patient information which is "personalized" for the treating clinician is provided by an XML-oriented database system at the Cohort Center. Anonymous study data can be accessed by authorized participants from a password-protected domain of the relational database system at the Coordination and Data Center. General statistical figures are publicly available from a Web server at the same location. In addition, the Web site hiv.ch (http://www.hiv.ch/) serves as a portal to third-party sites and provides a rich variety of explicit knowledge, not only to SHCS, but also to the global community of AIDS researchers and practitioners.

The interfaces requirement is not an explicit part of the current platform architecture. It has been neglected so far, as the participants in SHCS are limited in number and semantic clarifications can be made on an informal, bilateral basis. With a growing number of participants this "self-organization" may become inefficient and an architecture for a mediating logical space be required. However, the key concepts of the current language base are formally represented at the meta-level of the information objects in terms of the electronic study form, thereby providing the foundation for a computerized processing.

The adaptability requirement is supported by the use of an open, Web-based platform architecture and a non-proprietary, extensible technology, i.e., eXtensible Markup language (XML) (1998). Currently, the integration of an increasing number of private practitioners participating in SHCS, i.e., an additional community, with the knowledge medium is subject to a separate project.

Current State of Implementation

The current state of implementation includes a Web discussion forum supporting the communication among the project partners and a distributed prototype consisting of the following components:

- An electronic study form at one of the Cohort Centers. This is a client/server application for the automated input of laboratory data which are already electronically available and for the manual entry of additional data. At the front-end, it comprises a Web browser running a Java Virtual Machine (JVM) and supporting ActiveX. The back-end includes a Web server offering a dynamic HTML form. A Java applet implementing an XML parser is embedded in the form together with a text file containing JavaScript functions. These functions primarily enable the communication between the dynamic HTML form and the XML middle ware. Finally, the Web server provides an ActiveX control supporting data binding from text files generated from legacy (laboratory) database systems.
- An interface to the relational database system at the Coordination and Data Center. This interface comprises a lean version of the electronic study form application and uses proprietary "stored procedures" of the Oracle 7.x database system which are accessed by JavaScript.
- An Internet connection between the Cohort Center and the Coordination and Data Center. The XML files are transferred using File Transfer Protocol (FTP).

Currently, different XML-oriented database systems for the storage of individual patient information at the Cohort Centers are being evaluated.

Likewise, a Web site at the Coordination and Data Center for the provision of anonymous study data from password-protected domains and publicly available statistical figures is under construction.

DISCUSSION

As reported, the scalability and adaptability requirements specified in Section 4 have been implemented with the first version of the knowledge medium (or are currently, i.e., in October 1999, being implemented). The implementation of the interfaces requirement of the platform supporting the community of AIDS researchers and practitioners is outlined in the next section.

The general requirements for platforms supporting distributed communities, that are their temporary nature and intended global scope, are anticipated by the use of Web technology. As the Internet provides basic services up to layer 4 of the ISO/OSI model, application development is confined to the higher, application-related layers. This allows for short development cycles and, together with the often freely available Software Development Kits, favors the programming of customized applications instead of buying standard software products that provide an expensive functional overkill. Likewise, the intended global scope is realized along with the connection of the application to the Web as the spread of the latter literally is "World Wide." With the introduction of the Web discussion forum, those individuals of SHCS participating in the project have shifted from what we called a distributed community of practice to an online community as defined previously.

When returning to our interaction scenario of Section 3, the leverage of the knowledge medium can be described as follows: The application of the electronic study form is expected to improve the availability and accuracy of study data. Improving the availability of data, on the other hand, reduces the duration of clinical, e.g., therapy, studies, thereby speeding up the creation of new knowledge. Based on a re-designed technical infrastructure, this new knowledge can, in turn, be represented in the system and made available faster to the points of care. Currently, i.e., in October 1999, a test period of four weeks comparing the old paper-based and manual process with the new re-designed one is about to be terminated. Preliminary figures showing whether our assumptions are right will soon be available.

OUTLOOK: THE MEDIATING LOGICAL SPACE

As mentioned earlier, interfaces to medical specialties require a mediation between different logical spaces. As any given logical space provides a language representation of a possible world, mediation primarily implies translation between different languages. Although the languages of the communities interfacing with SHCS are not completely different, it applies in some cases that common concepts are expressed by different constructs and, contrary, the same constructs are used to represent different concepts. An example for the first are the constructs "CD4" cells used, for instance, by the laboratory specialists versus "helper cells" used by the clinicians, both indicating the same sub-population of the white blood cells (see Figure 3). Mediation between different classification schemes is an issue of high significance in the health care domain and dedicated research is carried out in order to deal with it (Straub, Mosimann, & Frei, 1999).

Generally, the translation between different conceptual schemas (which can be regarded as different language representations of possible worlds) can be achieved either by a direct mapping between them (Figure 3) or by a mapping

Figure 3: Direct mapping between schemas

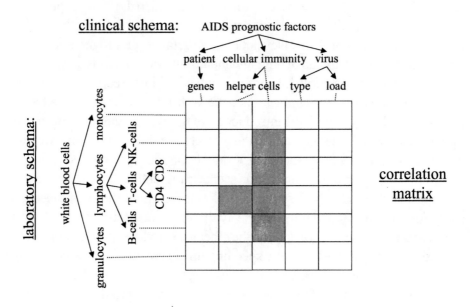

Figure 4: Mapping onto a mediating schema

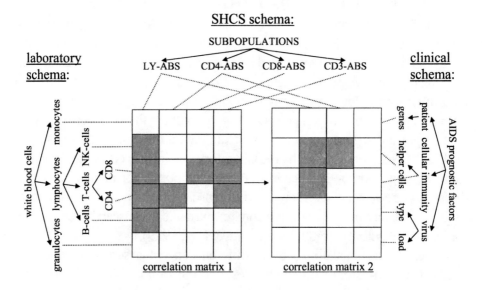

onto a mediating schema (Figure 4). Since the SHCS schema integrates selected concepts of all participating communities it can be regarded as a mediating schema.

The latter approach yields the advantage of the ability to mediate between more than two schemas. On the other hand, it can bring about a loss of information. For instance in Figure 4, the concepts of the clinical schema represented in the mediating SHCS schema (independent of how they are called in the respective "languages") are merely a subset of the first.

When related to the current implementation of the knowledge medium, both approaches are supported by the applied SGML/XML standardization framework:

- eXtensible Stylesheet Language (XSL) (1999), an application of XML, is a language for expressing presentation information. It consists of a language for transforming XML documents, and an XML vocabulary for specifying formatting semantics. Thus, XSL goes beyond merely specifying a syntax for defining style information. In a broader view, it is a transforming language that allows the conversion of documents complying with one schema into documents of another schema.
- A design principle of the first, pioneering SGML architecture (Newcomb, 1995) is a kind of meta-schema or template called architectural form (HyTime, 1997). Architectural forms are particularly useful for the creation of schemas that adhere to an industry-standard schema, but still use customized concepts. Since each schema can serve, in principle, as a meta-schema, architectural forms can be used to build up whole hierarchies of schemas. The property of such hierarchical schemas to inherit the constructs of the meta-schema from the level above makes architectures very similar to classes in object-oriented models. In fact, schemas can even inherit from multiple architectural forms.

If by means of mediation a semantic connection between various knowledge media can be established, the sum of the knowledge media form a knowledge media *net*. An example of a knowledge media net for the scientific community is described in Handschuh et al. (1998). Since the Web and, along with it, Web-based platforms evolve similar to a self-organizing system, the concept of the knowledge media net might be more realistic in the long term than the scenario of a single platform for AIDS researchers and practitioners at least as far as the *global* community is concerned (see Figure 1).

ACKNOWLEDGMENTS

The project presented in this chapter is generously supported by a grant from the Swiss HIV Cohort Study (SHCS).

END NOTE

The described SHCS Web prototype application has been further developed using XSLT and SVG technology and is in productive use since May 2001 (Fierz, Grütter & Eikemeier, 2001). The project in St. Gallen has had a catalyzing effect on all participating Cohort centers. Several are running their own project aimed at a Web-based integration and transmission of heterogeneous and distributed laboratory data using a common interchange format in terms of an XML schema. Particularly, the project at the Zurich Cohort center, which provides almost half of the data of SHCS, is completed, and there are ongoing projects in Geneva and Lausanne. Together with a business partner, a current effort strives to develop the application to a commercial product for clinical trials in general.

REFERENCES

Extensible Markup Language (XML) 1.0. W3C Recommendation 10-February-1998. Retrieved January 5, 2000 from the World Wide Web: http://www.w3.org/TR/1998/REC-xml-19980210

Extensible Stylesheet Language (XSL) Version 1.0. World Wide Web Consortium Working Draft 21-April-1999. Retrieved January 5, 2000 from the World Wide Web: http://www.w3.org/TR/1999/WD-xsl-19990421

Fierz, W., Grütter, R., & Eikemeier, C. (2001). Declarative programming with XSLT implemented on the example of a practical healthcare application. *Swiss Medical Informatics*, 47, pp. 21-27.

Finin, T., Labrou, Y. & Mayfield J. (1997). KQML as an agent communication language. In Jeff Bradshaw (ed.), *Software Agents*. Cambridge: MIT Press.

Greiner, C. & Rose, T. (1997, September). Knowledge Management in Global Health Research Planning. *Proceedings of the Workshop Knowledge-Based Systems for Knowledge Management in Enterprises, 21st Annual German Conference on AI '97*, Freiburg, Germany, retrieved September, 1999 from the World Wide Web: http://www.dfki.uni-kl.de/~aabecker/Freiburg/Final/Greiner/greiner.html.

Gruber, T. (1999). *What is an Ontology?* Retrieved January 5, 2000 from the World Wide Web: http://www-ksl.stanford.edu/kst/what-is-an-ontology.html

Grütter, R., Stanoevska-Slabeva, K., & Fierz, W. (2000). Enhancing Knowledge Management in a Multi-center Clinical Trial by a Web-based Knowledge Medium. In L. Eder (Ed.), *Managing Healthcare Information Systems with Web-Enabled Technologies*. Hershey PA: Idea Group Publishing, in press.

Handschuh, S., Lechner, U., Lincke, D.-M., Schmid, B. F., Schubert, P., Selz, D. & Stanoevska, K. (1998). The NetAcademy - A New Concept for Online

Publishing and Knowledge Management. In Margaria, T., Steffen, B., Rückert, R. & Posegga, J. (Eds.) *Services and Visualization – Towards a User-Friendly Design*, (pp. 29-43). Berlin/Heidelberg: Springer Verlag.

Lechner, U. & Schmid, B. F. (1999). Logic for Media – The Computational Media Metaphor. In Sprague, R.H. (Ed.), *Proceedings of the 32nd Hawaii International Conference on System Sciences (HICSS-32)*. Los Alamitos, California: IEEE Computer Society.

Lechner, U., Schmid, B. F., Schubert, P., Klose, M. & Miler, O. (1999). Ein Referenzmodell für Gemeinschaften und Medien – Case Study Amazon.com. Accepted for publication in the *Proceedings of the Workshop „Gemeinschaften in neuen Medien" GeNeMe'99*.

Ledergerber, B., Von Overbeck, J., Egger, M. & Luthy, R (1994). The Swiss HIV Cohort Study: rationale, organization and selected baseline characteristics. *Soz Praventivmed, 39*(6), 387-394.

McDermott, R. (1999). Learning Across Teams. *Knowledge Management Review, 8*(3), 32-36.

Newcomb, Steven, R. (1995). SGML ARCHITECTURES: Implications and Opportunities for Industry. Retrieved January 5, 2000 from the World Wide Web: http://www.oasis-open.org/cover/newcomb-sgmlarch.html.

Nitsche, U., Holbein, R., Morger, O., & Teufel, S. (1998). Realization of a Context-Dependent Access Control Mechanisms on a Commercial Platform. *Proc. IFIP/SEC '98*, Wien.

Schmid, B. F. & Stanoevska, K. (1999, June). Knowledge Media: An Innovative Concept and Technology for Knowledge Management in the Information Age. *Proceedings of the 12th Biennal International Telecommunications Society Conference - Beyond Convergence*. Stockholm, Sweden: IST'98.

Second edition of the HyTime standard (ISO/IEC 10744:1997), Annex A.3 Architectural Form Definition Requirements (AFDR). Retrieved January 5, 2000 from the World Wide Web: http://www.ornl.gov/sgml/wg8/docs/n1920/html/clause-A.3.html.

Stefik, M. J. (1988). The Next Knowledge Medium. In B. A. Huberman (Ed.), *The Ecology of Computation* (pp. 315-342). Amsterdam: Elsevier Science Publishers B.V.

Straub, H. R., Mosimann, H., & Frei, N. (1999). Begriffsarchitekturen der 1. und 2. Generation: hierarchische und multihierarchische Klassifikationen. *Schweiz Med Wochenschr 129*(Suppl 105/II), 27S.

Straub, H. R., Mosimann, H., & Frei, N. (1999) Begriffsarchitekturen der 3. und 4. Generation: multifokale und multipunktuelle Klassifikationen. *Schweiz Med Wochenschr 129*(Suppl 105/II), 27S.

Chapter 12

Mobile Computing at the Department of Defense

James A. Rodger
Indiana University of Pennsylvania, USA

Parag C. Pendharkar and Mehdi Khosrow-Pour
Pennsylvania State University, USA

This chapter is designed to relate the rationale used by the Department of Defense, to utilize Telemedicine, to meet increasing global crises, and for the U.S. military to find ways to more effectively manage manpower and time. A mobile Telemedicine package has been developed by the Department of Defense (DOD) to collect and transmit near-real-time, far-forward medical data and to assess how this improved capability enhances medical management of the battlespace. Telemedicine has been successful in resolving uncertain organizational and technological military deficiencies and in improving medical communications and information management. The deployable, mobile Teams are the centerpieces of this Telemedicine package. These teams have the capability of inserting essential networking and communications capabilities into austere theaters and establishing an immediate means for enhancing health protection, collaborative planning, situational awareness, and strategic decision-making.

INTRODUCTION

Telemedicine is an approach of providing care for patients that are geographically separated from a doctor. Telemedicine allows a doctor and a patient to interact with each other using computer networks. Telemedicine, when used in military, has a potential to heal patients in the war zone where doctors may not be

Previously Published in *Managing Information Technology in a Global Economy* edited by Mehdi Khosrow-Pour, Copyright © 2001, Idea Group Publishing.

readily available. The U.S. national strategy for military pre-eminence is based on technological superiority. Through new discoveries in advanced science and technology, the goal of the Department of Defense (DoD) under Joint Vision 2010 (JV 2010) is to develop the ability to directly and decisively influence events ashore and at sea—anytime, anywhere—to meet current and future challenges.

To successfully counter these challenges, the DoD must continue to move forward in its effort to incorporate telemedicine into its prime mission—to keep every service member healthy and on the job, anywhere in the world, to support combat operations, as well as humanitarian, peacekeeping, and disaster relief missions.

Telemedicine supports the DoD's goal by electronically bringing the specialist to the primary provider who directly cares for service members in austere, remote, and isolated environments (Floro, Nelson, and Garshnek, 1998). Telemedicine also creates an opportunity to provide rapid, accurate diagnosis and therapeutic recommendations (Garshnek and Burkle, 1998). The end result is that telemedicine helps to maintain the health of service personnel and their ability to quickly return to duty, minimizing logistically burdensome, inconvenient, and expensive transportation to distant specialty care (Bangert, Doktor, and Warren, 1998).

For telemedicine methods to be successful, however, their operational effectiveness, suitability, and importance to the warfighters' mission must continuously be tested, evaluated, and proven (Oliver, Sheng, Paul and Chih, 1999). In 1997, the U.S. Army, in partnership with the Navy and Air Force, was tasked to develop exercises to explore the integration of advanced technologies with existing systems and architectures to meet the requirements established under JV2010.

These technologies are all aligned with the Joint Vision 2010 concepts of Dominant Maneuver, Precision Engagement, Focused Logistics and Full Dimensional Protection. The technology initiatives utilize dedicated, small mobile teams, with a sophisticated IT infrastructure, to provide telemedicine capabilities wherever they are needed in the medical battlespace (Mann, 1997). This IT Infrastructure includes novel Medical Equipment Sets (MES) with digital capture devices such as digital cameras, digital scopes, digital blood and urine laboratories, physiological monitors, advanced digital radiography, and digital ultrasound (Perednia and Allen, 1995). Other, associated items of equipment include novel software, such as the Pacific Virtual Health Care System. This package offers electronic medical record archiving capability that enables automated, standardized teleconsultation by forward medics to higher echelon physicians (Rodger and Pendharkar, 2000).

This ACTD has charged itself with operating within the concept of Focused Logistics and Full Dimensional Protection. It is, therefore, pertinent to understand just how this ACTD can accomplish its missions/objectives and meet the operational concepts of JV2010. This operationalization is embodied in the following quote. "To protect the force, the Army will rely on a technically advanced, operationally simple network of multi-component intelligence sources capable of detecting and locating forces, active and passive obstacles, in-flight aircraft, ballistic and cruise missiles and their launch sites, chemical and biological agents, electronic jamming sources and a host of still-developing threats."

One technology that is mentioned in the document that applies to this ACTD is the use of "advanced soldier technologies." It is necessary for this ACTD to fit within this concept and provide the warfighter with information that identifies, early on, those countermeasures that can be used to defeat medical threats (Dardelet, 1998). It is also important to recognize other action that may be used to defeat enemy deployment of weapons of mass destruction (WMD), especially biological agent dispersal.

Focused Logistics makes only one mention of "telemedicine." "For the Army, Focused Logistics will be the fusion of logistics and information technologies, flexible and agile combat service support organizations, and new doctrinal support concepts to provide rapid crisis response to deliver precisely tailored logistics packages directly to each level of military operation." The document portrays medical support to Focused Logistics in the form of "internet triage" and "telemedicine" in order to enhance the survivability of the joint force (Zajtchuk, 1995).

Achieving 21st century medical support capability demands significant advances in the military's ability to provide force health care and medical protection and to deploy medical communications and information management in tactical operations (Institute of Medicine, 1996). The broad mission of Telemedicine in the military, is to assess advanced mobile applications that can potentially meet such demands (Paul, Pearson, and McDaniel, 1999).

US military has adapted a suite of software, databases, and architecture standards to provide deployable medical information management (Tanriverdi and Venkatraman, 1998). The Theater Medical Core Services (TMCS) is a database that stores data locally and is capable of sending encrypted e-mail to several redundant database servers via store-and-forward (Rasberry, 1998). The database servers aggregate information and store it in databases for distribution. Web servers supply data to medical personnel as customized encrypted reports.

The Medical Workstation (MeWS) is a network-based workstation equipped with portable medical devices, clinical support capabilities, medical information support, and a graphical user interface. The MeWS will support multi-patient monitoring, interface with the patient's clinical record, and provide access to a searchable database. It will also provide full Personal Information Carrier (PIC) read and write implementation. MeWS collect, store, and forward medical device data and images. By utilizing a Global Positioning System (GPS), MeWS have the capability to enter the patient's geographical location. The various software components of the MeWS help to facilitate clinical data entry, acquisition and retrieval. MeWS enable the generation of medical facility status reports, the monitoring of disease surveillance, the updating of supplies, and tracking of evacuation requirements.

The Field Medical Surveillance System (FMSS) is an expert system that systematically detects and monitors epidemiological trends and profiles patient populations. FMSS integrates patient information to the Global Infectious Disease and Epidemiology Network (GIDEON) knowledge base. Demographic and symptomatic information is used to arrive at a presumptive diagnosis or classify the patient using discriminate analysis. FMSS is also capable of providing incidence and prevalence trends for infectious diseases.

The Libretto is a commercial-off-the-shelf (COTS) hand held computer, manufactured by Toshiba. It has the capability to automate field medic PIC card software by reading service member's demographic information from the PIC into the software. It can also write GPS medical encounter information to the PIC and store the information as a pre-formatted message for transmission.

Tactical medical communications require updating of the existing IT infrastructure. The previously mentioned novel hardware, software, and interfaces were implemented in order to enable this change and facilitate the transmission of medical-unique information over the existing communications hardware and command, control, communication, computers, intelligence, surveillance, and reconnaissance (C4ISR) networks. However, telecommunications from the operational area of responsibility (AOR) to the medical sustaining base uses the existing Defense Information Systems Network (DISN).

The technologies described above have been assembled into an exportable capability that is specifically tailored to meet the medical Information Management (IM) and Information Technology (IT) needs of the unit it is supporting. This assemblage of technologies is referred to as the Capability Package. The capability package must work in concert with the unit's infrastructure, communications, tactical situation, and logistical constraints if the military is to realize its full potential in meeting today's global crises.

For such technologies to be successful, however, their operational effectiveness, suitability, and importance to the Telemedicine mission must continuously be tested, evaluated, and proven. To perform this task, the military established a Test and Evaluation Integrated Product Team (T&E-IPT) to evaluate candidate mobile models and architectures. These technologies are examined in a rigorous test and evaluation (T&E) environment with extensive user participation as a means of assessing their mobile applications. The T&E-IPT have leveraged and optimized existing communications technologies to transmit medical data. Database technologies for mobile technologies are utilized for epidemiological and trend analyses utilizing data mining of these data warehouses.

The initial concept of operations (CONOPS) was to employ a tailored Joint Task Force (JTF) to accomplish missions in controlled environment demonstrations. The first series of demonstrations, tested communication methodologies, functionality, and the field utility of collecting and sending patient data from the forward edge of the battlefield. As the information and results were obtained the CONOPS was expanded to use additional activities. These activities are as follows:

- The deployment of mobile technologies and agents, called Theater Telemedicine Teams (TTTs), to medical treatment facilities (MTFs) to establish and conduct telemedicine operations; coordinate with signal and Command, Control, Communications, Computers, and Intelligence (C4I) assets to establish and maintain tactical medical networks; receive, verify, and log Command information provided from lower echelons
- The use of advanced mobile information management models and technologies, such as software, databases, and architecture standards, that were adapted to provide deployable medical information management for advanced mobile applications
- Two radio frequency (RF) networking technologies that were enhanced for user interface design in a battlefield setting
- Modeling and simulation (M&S) capabilities provided through advanced mobile application software during training exercises.

All of these capabilities are being evaluated by the military. The goal of this approach is to first establish effective, interoperable mobile communications in the early stages of the exercises and to then implement more robust mobile database technology capabilities as the application matures. This chapter will provide the following details of this advanced mobile application.

- Types of mobile technologies that were identified and tested as potential candidates for enhancing Telemedicine capabilities
- Objectives of each mobile agents in the field
- Methods and applications of these mobile technologies
- Performance results of these mobile database technologies
- Recommendations, lessons learned, and feedback received from actual mobile users
- Overall findings and results of Telemedicine mobile field agents.

MEASUREMENT OF ISSUES AND FINDINGS

A series of measurements were conducted to test mobile communications methodologies and functionality. The field utility of collecting and transmitting near-real-time, far-forward medical data was examined and assessed as to how this improved capability enhanced medical management of the battlespace. This phase was also used to expand and improve the techniques for testing and evaluating the proposed mobile technologies and software enhancements.

The mobile technologies were operated by typical users who performed their intended mission tasks at the projected levels of workload within a realistic operational environment. Included were the use of dedicated, small, mobile teams with associated items of equipment to provide telemedicine capabilities when and where needed in the medical battlespace. These items included novel medical equipment sets (MES) with digital data capture devices, as well as novel software that enables automated, standardized teleconsultation by forward medics and corpsmen to rearward physicians with an electronic medical record archiving capability. A suite of software, medical databases, and architecture standards were adapted to provide deployable medical information management.

In addition, two radio frequency (RF) networking technologies were also tested and fielded. These included the Lucent Wireless WaveLAN II system, a commercial wireless networking capability that was enhanced for military applications, and the Joint Internet Controller (JINC), a tailored set of software and firmware that is geared toward providing lower bandwidth data networking capabilities to existing military field radio systems.

The medical play in several of the demonstrations was robust enough to provide a rich opportunity to observe how these mobile technologies provided support to the user in an operational setting. These results were then used as a baseline for follow-on demonstrations and exercises.

Both the WaveLAN and JINC demonstrated their primary intended functions of mobile tactical networking capacity. The WaveLAN system provided superior bandwidth and full wireless local area network (LAN) capabilities, and the JINC provided tactical networking over low bandwidth military radio systems.

Among the outcomes, it was found that mobile technologies could successfully replace wired LANs with wireless LANs and that mobile database technology software development and refinement should be continued.

The exercises demonstrated the following capabilities:
- Theater Medical Core Services (TMCS) system – a mobile database application used to provide medical reports
- Medical workstation (MeWS) – a mobile, functionally configured, network-based workstation designed to support the clinical and information support requirements of forward echelon providers ashore and afloat

- Toshiba Libretto end user terminal (EUT) – a lightweight, handheld computer capable of reading, storing, and transmitting the soldiers' demographic information in the field
- Desert Care II (DC II) Theater Clinical Encounter Application (TCEA) – a Web-based application that facilitates the user interface design, on the browser workstation, for mobile providers or medical technicians to record, view, and report patient encounter information in the field
- Personal information carrier (PIC) – a small, portable storage device containing demographic and medical information pertaining to the soldier who is wearing or carrying the device
- Theater Telemedicine Prototype Program (T2P2) – a Web-based delivery system of consultive care that gives healthcare providers from remote locations the ability to access the expertise of a regional facility for medical specialty consultations
- Theater Telemedicine Team (TTT) – a mobile team composed of a leader with a clinical background, a visual systems operator, and an information systems operator who provide telemedicine capability to select, deployed MTFs
- Aeromedical Evacuation (AE) Suitcase – a mobile system that provides critical voice and data communications to the AE mission of the U.S. Air Force (USAF) Air Mobility Command (AMC)

The tasks needed to achieve the objectives of the demonstration were carried out. These included the ability to collect and forward healthcare data in DC II and TMCS Lightweight Data Entry Tool (LDET), transmit it over existing communications [high frequency (HF) and International Maritime Satellite (INMARSAT)], extract it to a medical situational awareness system (TMCS), view those data in a Web environment on the TMCS server at Systems Center, San Diego (SSC SD), and conduct long-range clinical consultations. Although technical difficulties were experienced, the lessons learned from these exercises were evaluated, and solutions to these problems were incorporated into the next exercise. One good example of a lesson learned was the use of the wireless LAN to track patients within the MTF.

The exercises also indicated that essential data transport requirements of these mobile technologies can be met consistently, reliably, and cost effectively. Specific technologies were examined relative to each other for specific operational requirements of data throughout, transmission distance, time to setup, time to train, and actual costs to acquire, maintain and dispose. Among the significant achievements was the employment of the five-person mobile TTT, which successfully conducted clinical reachback capability.

Several parameters were not measured directly by the field exercise. These parameters can be determined through future exercises and battle laboratory testing and evaluation methods. For example, analysis still is not complete on the availability of mobile HF and very high frequency (VHF) radios, the overall reliability of the mobile laptops demonstrated, the software reliability of several of the communication modules, and the sustainability of several of the software database applications, hardware components, networks, and databases used in the exercise. As new data becomes available through future exercises and battle laboratory testing, a more complete picture of these advanced mobile applications of telemedicine will evolve.

Testing and evaluation of mobile Telemedicine applications have produced tangible evidence for the military utility of these technologies. Results from the field indicate that the essential data collection and dissemination requirements of these mobile technologies can be met consistently, reliably, and cost effectively.

The mobile models and architectures demonstrate the potential to enhance data collection and dissemination of information through the use of quality database software and robust, mobile communications infrastructure. Through its efforts, these mobile agents have developed a consistent pattern of progression. From an initial state of uncoordinated, service-unique solutions to the building of an overall mobile framework, this architectural solution is being developed and refined by several different technological concepts. These concepts have been and will continue to be assessed for operational and technical feasibility. The results from these operational and technical assessments will ultimately lead to the development and insertion of an emerging architecture, which will encompass these advanced mobile applications.

This first series of phases was conducted to test communications methodologies, functionality, and the field utility of collecting and transmitting near-real-time, far-forward medical data and to assess how this improved capability enhanced medical management of the battlespace. This phase was also used to expand and improve the techniques for testing and evaluating the proposed technologies and software enhancements specified in the exercises.

The technologies demonstrated were operated by typical users who performed their intended mission tasks at the projected levels of workload within a realistic operational environment. These technologies included the use of dedicated, small, mobile teams with associated items of equipment to provide telemedicine capabilities when and where needed in the medical battlespace. Associated items of equipment included novel MES with digital data capture devices (e.g., digital cameras/scopes, physiological monitors, and advanced digital radiography), as well as novel software (e.g., Theater Telemedicine Prototype Project) that enables automated, standardized teleconsultation by forward medics and corpsmen to rearward physicians with an electronic medical record archiving capability. A suite of software, medical databases, and architecture standards were adapted to provide deployable medical IM.

In addition, two RF networking technologies were also tested and fielded during the exercises. These included:
- Lucent Wireless WaveLAN II system
- JINC.

WIRELESS WAVELAN

The WaveLAN system was developed and maintained from commercial-off-the-shelf (COTS) wireless networking capabilities for the exercise. All JMO-T participation in this exercise was predicated on the work accomplished by the engineers to enhance the Lucent WaveLAN II system for military applications. In this regard, the WaveLAN represented an extension of a LAN via wireless means at data rates in excess of 2 million bits per second (Mbps).

JINC

The JINC system is a tailored set of software and firmware that is geared toward providing lower bandwidth (i.e., 2.4–64 kilobytes per second (Kbps)) data networking capabilities to existing military field radio systems. The basic concept behind JINC system development was to field a "programmable," mobile tactical networking system capable of exchanging digital data between ships, aircraft, combat vehicles, and individual soldiers in the field. The JINC system was enhanced from an existing COTS product to allow data connectivity between any two existing military radio systems without reliance on satellite communications (SATCOM). The intent behind this configuration was to avoid having the ACTD become involved in procuring and installing new generation radio systems.

The JINC is composed of three elements operating together – the host computer, Team Care Automation System (TCAS) software, and a Micro-INC data controller device.

TCAS

The TCAS software installed on the JINC computer host provided automated network connectivity for distributed facilities, remote users, and individual units all interconnected using existing military communications media. TCAS software is based on object-oriented technology to enhance data exchange at low bandwidths. Fundamentally, TCAS software operates in two basic modes. The first mode emulates any specified data package as an "object" in an object-oriented database structure. Using a common database distributed throughout the entire JINC network, the software takes the "objects" and compresses them using a proprietary compression scheme and then transmits the "object" across the RF network. At the receiving node, the object is decompressed and translated back into its original protocol stack prior to delivery; thus, hosts on either end of a JINC-supported RF network see the expected data format in the form it was transmitted. Using this object compression scheme, JINC is able to deliver near full use of available low bandwidth data links with very little administrative network overhead.

Micro-INC Data Controller

The Micro-INC (MINC) data controller provided the conversion from RS-232 serial data to a synchronous MIL-STD-1880-114 data stream. Each Micro-INC data controller can support up to two radio systems simultaneously. This data controller is normally located near the Single-Channel Ground and Airborne Radio System (SINCGARS) radio installation to reduce the length of the synchronous cable run. The controller requires no external or manual operation to function. All MINC functions are controlled by TCAS software.

Technologies Demonstrated

For this demonstration, a Mobile Medical Monitor (B) (M3B) computer system simulating a MeWS, was connected to a SINCGARS via the TCAS. A Libretto system running TCAS was connected to a second Libretto via the WaveLAN Personal Computer Memory Card International Association (PCMCIA) wireless networking devices. Abbreviated discharge summary documents in Microsoft Word format were prepared on the M3B based on input from the various sensors attached to the M3B. This message was transmitted as a file attachment to a TCAS freetext email from the M3B to the first Libretto via SINCGARS. The Libretto then ported the data, via preset forwarding rules, from the SINCGARS net over the WaveLAN net to the second Libretto using the socket interface.

The computer systems selected for the exercise consisted of Libretto 110CT-NT computers, which were similar to the 100CT Libretto EUTs. The principal difference was that JMO-T Librettos required the Windows NT 4.0 operating system to support the TMCS system. The Librettos used in the exercise generally used Windows 95/98. In addition to the basic computer system, each JMO-T EUT was provided with a Quatech four-port serial expander PCMCIA card, which allowed the connection of the PIC reader along with the Garmin 12XL Global Positioning System (GPS) device. The second PCMCIA slot on the Libretto was occupied by the WaveLAN II 803.11 PCMCIA wireless network card.

During this exercise, far-forward Hospital Corpsman (HM) transmitted medical information from four far-forward first responder sites to the medical command onboard the USS Coronado. Data was entered via the Libretto 110CT-NT, which was equipped with a PIC Reader and TMCS LDET software. Three stationary sites were located at Area 41 in Camp Pendleton, California, and one mobile platform, a High-Mobility, Multipurpose Wheeled Vehicle (HMMWV), traveled to Yuma, Arizona. Because no specific medical exercise took place during the ELB phase, each user was given a set of preprogrammed PICs to scan into the system. The data were then periodically transmitted.

Initially, the Joint Medical Semi-Automated Forces (JMedSAF) simulation was to be used in conjunction with the scenario played out on the ground to give the staff onboard the USS Coronado a more robust "picture" of the battlespace; however, early in the exercise, it became apparent that bandwidth was at a premium on the network. The demonstration manager, therefore, elected to "shut down" the JMedSAF feed to the USS Coronado to keep essential data feeds open to the Enhanced Combat Operations Center (ECOC). As a result, very little data generated from the simulation runs eventually made its way to the TMCS database. Furthermore, the scenario of the "real" battlespace was disconnected from the "virtual" battlespace.

RESULTS

JMO-T operations consisted of sending over 120 patient encounters via the TMCS LDET to the TMCS server located in the ECOC on the USS Coronado. Three nodes were operated by JMO-T personnel during ELB:
- HMMWV Mobile Node
- Area 41 Node
- Yuma Node.

Two basic WaveLAN modes of operation were used. The first (and most commonly used) was the "standard" mode, which allowed the EUTs to communicate with the rest of the WaveLAN network via a WavePoint router connection, which translated the packets for use by the rest of the network. Because the power output of the individual WaveLAN card was only 25 milliwatts, the JMO-T EUT had to be located within 1,000 feet of a WavePoint in order to access the network. In practice, this range was extended to as much as 2,000 feet at Area 41, but this was due primarily to a high antenna mast (about 40 feet) for the Area 41 WavePoint antenna.

The other method of operation was called the "ad hoc demo" mode, which was accessed by selecting an option on the WaveLAN card "properties" window. When activated, this allowed the EUTs to communicate with each other (i.e., for training) without the need for a WavePoint.

OPERATIONAL OBSERVATIONS BY SYSTEM NODE
HMMWV Mobile Node

The intent behind JMO-T operations from the HMMWV node was to demonstrate the ability to send medical data from a highly mobile platform. In practice, this actually involved JMO-T personnel going to the location where the HMMWV was parked and joining the net from that location. One corpsman from 1/5 Marines accompanied JMO-T engineering personnel to the HMMWV location at Green Beach. The corpsman transmitted nine patient records with transmission times as follows in Table 1.

Although additional periods of JMO-T participation were scheduled with the HMMWV node, revisions to the exercise schedule resulted in postponement and eventual cancellation of other HMMWV JMO-T operations because the HMMWV, was needed elsewhere in the exercise.

Area 41 Node

The majority of JMO-T operations occurred at the main exercise Area 41 operations center and relay node. Results of patient record transmissions are provided in Table 2 and 3.

Table 1: HMMWV Transmission Times

Patient Number	Transmission Time (min:sec)
1	1:45
2	2:30
3	17:00
4	1:00
5	0:20
6	1:10
7-9	0:25

Table 2: Area 41 Transmission Times

MSEL Event	Number of Patients Sent	Time to Send (min:sec)
401	8	19:40 (VTC was ongoing)
341	8	Various time (sent individually)
408	1	0:19 (about 500 ft from WavePoint in field)
	1	1:24 (about 1000 ft from WavePoint in field)
	1	1:13 (back in shelter)

Table 3: Area 41 Transmission Times (continued)

MSEL Event	Number of Patients Sent	Time to Send (min:sec)
	1	5:19
	1	0:55
	1	1:44 (sent by 1/5 Corpsmen)
	1	1:23 (sent by 1/5 Corpsmen)
	1	1:54 (sent by 1/5 Corpsmen)
359	5	2:30 (sent by 1/5 Corpsmen)
406	5	Various
412	4	7:03
368	7	Not sent (repeated time-out alerts). This was around 1200 and other videoconferencing events were ongoing. We made 5 attempts with no joy.

After the completion of the videoconference, JMO-T personnel and 1/5 Marines corpsmen experienced dramatically improved network performance. LDET transmission times for all patient encounters were in the 3-5-second range. In addition, the ECOC TMCS server was able to be viewed and browsed from the Libretto EUTs (something that had not been possible previously due to videoconferencing network delays). The corpsmen passed all required MSEL data and then resent) all previous MSEL data at the request of ELB authorities. The entire evolution was smooth and successful. In addition, all required imagery files, including four 2.35-megabyte (MB) images, were successfully transmitted. The 2.35-MB files took 2-3 minutes to transmit, and all were viewed on the ECOC TMCS server.

Yuma Node

JMO-T participation at Yuma demonstrated far-forward message reach-back capability. JMO-T was assigned to operate from a WavePoint assigned to a Naval Research Lab (NRL) mobile commercial SATCOM system mounted in a HMMWV. This SATCOM link provided a 2-Mbps relay directly back to Area 41 at Camp Pendleton. EUT operational modification only required an IP change.

As in Area 41, all JMO-T messaging was handled by a 1/5 Marines corpsman. The system was operated from the back of a vehicle within 200 feet of the NRL SATCOM HMMWV. Individual patient encounter messages were transmitted within 5-10 seconds. The ECOC TMCS server was able to be browsed to confirm delivery.

Five additional images, including two 1.35-MB images, were transmitted via File Transfer Protocol (FTP). Small files were transmitted in 10-20 seconds, and large files took 2:20 each. The only operational problem noted was a tendency for the Global Positioning System unit to stop sending position information when requested. This was traced to a loose cable on the Quatech serial port card; however, the cable was tightened, and the system returned to normal operation.

RESULTS

ELB technology provided a number of excellent options for medical communications. When the network was not overwhelmed by the demands of Videoconferencing, it provided an excellent method of collecting medical data-both TMCS textual data and images. During these times, Engineering Integrated Product Team (E-IPT) personnel working with data senders reported that TMCS data was sent in milliseconds, and the large files were transmitted in no more than 5 seconds. Data senders were able to use the handheld computers with ease. JMO-T participated in the longest leg of the exercise network by successfully sending TMCS and large data files from Yuma, Arizona.

The Libretto systems running Windows NT using 64 MB RAM performed satisfactorily; however, when the LDET, TCAS, Serial TCAS, and Medical Messaging Service (MMS) server were all running on one computer, the operation slowed significantly. One solution was to allow TCAS to speak TMCS (or Wave or any other medical software) in its native mode as a C++ object. Based on this experience, a more effective device for Echelon I use is a Windows CE computer, which weighs less than one pound, can easily fit into a Battle Dress Utilities (BDU) pocket, and provides resident software, a user friendly screen, and a long-life, inexpensive battery.

KB Prime (CG-1)

KB Prime (CG-1) consisted of an amphibious assault exercise with a robust medical activity imbedded inside the main training action. The deployed forces consisted of three Regimental landing force size units supported by appropriate Level III medical care both ashore and afloat. The medical force during the CG-1 phase included two BASs, two STPs, one SC, the USS Essex (LHD-2), which served as a Casualty Receiving Treatment Ship (CRTS), the USNS Mercy (AH-19) hospital ship, and a Fleet Hospital (FH). Plans were for roughly 500 total casualties in 5 days.

The medical play in KB Prime was robust enough to provide a rich opportunity to observe how the technologies provided support to the user in an operational setting. These results were then used as a baseline for follow-on exercises. Both the WaveLAN and JINC demonstrated their primary intended functions of mobile tactical networking capacity. The WaveLAN system provided superior bandwidth and full wireless LAN capabilities. The JINC provided tactical networking over low bandwidth military radio systems. The primary objectives and results are provided in Tables 4 and 5.

OPERATIONAL EFFECTIVENESS

The effectiveness of the systems used in the exercise was demonstrated by typical users, who operated them in a realistic operational environment. The Ca-

Table 4: Networking Objectives and Results for KB 99

Objective	Result
Achieve medical in-transit patient visibility through the use of the WaveLAN network	Achieved. When the WaveLAN network was in full operation, the delivery of LDET messages occurred in 3–5 seconds. Other ELB functions (i.e., VTC) significantly slowed network operations.
Achieve medical imagery file transfer using WaveLAN technology	Achieved. Multiple images were transferred using standard FTP programs.
Achieve medical in-transit patient visibility through the use of JINC network and tactical radio systems	Not achieved. While LDET messages were delivered between units on the network, LDET input did not reach the TMCS master server at Space and Warfare (SPAWAR). As a result, full patient in-transit visibility was not achieved.
Achieve MeWS medical messaging and file transfer capability through the use of JINC network and tactical radio systems	Achieved. Two test files were transferred between SC and USNS Mercy.

Table 5: Networking Objectives and Results for KB 99 (continued)

Objective	Result
Demonstrate internetting for units on different RFs	Partially achieved. Messages received over SINCGARS net were forwarded via HF net but required intervention for delivery. SINCGARS-to-WaveLAN automated delivery was accomplished during the UW exercise.

pability Package demonstrated the ability to collect both patient encounter and Annex Q-type information; however, it did not meet the threshold values established by the Performance Integrated Product Team (P-IPT) for transmitting that information to the theater medical command. The purpose of the exercise was to move patients through the evacuation system, and most decisions that needed to be made could be made without referring to the information stored on the TMCS server. In fact, most of the decisions did not require the type of information that was reported, and therefore, the staff instead used other data. As stated in the feedback questionnaires, the Marine Expeditionary Force (MEF) and Third Fleet Surgeons neither relied on the data provided by TMCS nor trusted its timeliness or reliability.

SUMMARY OF LESSONS LEARNED

The following were lessons learned from the exercise:

- To perform net-centric communications, it is necessary to have network management and good engineering support.
- All engineering initiatives during JMO-T assessments should be directed and coordinated by the E-IPT chairman based on requirements developed by the P-IPT using a Good Idea Cut-Off Date (GICOD).

- The Libretto configuration was too heavy and complex for the end users, and battery power was insufficient.
- A combination of PIC with chip and a simple bar code would read faster. A photo identification card would be helpful. These issues need to be coordinated with the Joint SMART Card and PIC offices.
- TMCS was not used by target JTF Surgeon Headquarters (HQ); its configuration and report makeup must be examined.
- Ship-to-ship communications of TMCS data works well with HF/SINCGARS.
- Land-based units had significant communications challenges because natural barriers (not in line of sight) shut down the ability to communicate outside of the unit.
- Estimated power requirements must be part of the articulated Technology Plan. Coordination with supported units must discuss power requirements.
- More detailed overall training packages and materials will be needed prior to future exercises. Training at the leadership level and documented training materials should be part of the deployed system.
- Baseline business processes must be assessed to identify change requirements of new technology.
- Liaison with participating units is required to ensure adequately trained users, informed leaders, and tested technology support.

RECOMMENDATIONS

Based on achievement of the stated objectives, the following recommendations are provided for continued wireless networking development:
- WaveLAN technology appears sufficiently mature to warrant use as a replacement for wired networking at field MTFs.
- A prototype network configuration to support an SC should be devised and prepared for testing.

The following recommendations are provided for continued TCAS software development:
- As demonstrated in the exercise, TCAS was based on a C++ Windows 95/98/NT executable program. Operational experience with the Libretto NT system at Echelon I showed the need for a smaller, lighter computing system to support this highly mobile group. The Windows CE operating environment appears most suited to this requirement. Port TCAS software into the CE environment is recommended.
- The greatest asset (and liability) of the TCAS/J software is its flexibility. Programming the various communications servers, forwarding rules, and message formats is similar to programming a full-featured network router. This implies

that a TCAS operator must be both computer literate and network knowledgeable. Simplification of the user interface, perhaps with more graphical network connection screens, appears necessary. In addition, the software should feature some type of "system lock" that will keep all settings under a password-controlled environment so that an inexperienced operator cannot change them by accident.

• Continued developmental work is needed to incorporate the full range of medical database-specific messages into TCAS. Message delivery in the exercise was achieved via a complicated process involving multiple serial port data exchange and encoding. This process can be streamlined by the provision of a medical system communications server to the TCAS software developers so that they can test their message servers directly.

CONCLUSIONS

Testing and evaluation of the JMO-T ACTD have produced tangible evidence for the military utility of telemedicine. Results from Demonstration I indicate that the essential data collection and dissemination requirements of JMO-T can be met consistently, reliably, and cost effectively.

The ACTD promises the potential to demonstrate technology-enhanced data collection and dissemination of information through the use of quality software and robust communications infrastructure. Through its efforts, the JMO-T ACTD has developed a consistent pattern of progression. From an initial state of uncoordinated, service-unique solutions to the building of an overall architectural framework, this architectural solution is being developed and refined by several different concepts. These concepts have been and will continue to be assessed for operational and technical feasibility throughout Demonstration II, which begins with Cobra Gold in April–May 2000 and FOAL Eagle in the Fall. The results from these operational and technical assessments will ultimately lead to the development and insertion of an emerging JMO-T architecture, which will encompass the "run" phase of the JMO-T ACTD.

REFERENCES

Bangert, D., Doktor, R., & Warren, J.(1998). Introducing Telemedicine as a Strategic Intent. *Proceedings of the 31ˢᵗ Hawaii International Conference on System Sciences* (HICSS-31), Maui, Hawaii.

Dardelet, B. (1998). Breaking the Wall: The Rise of Telemedicine as the New Collaborative Interface. *Proceedings of the 31ˢᵗ Hawaii International Conference on System Sciences* (HICSS-31), Maui, Hawaii.

Floro, F.C., Nelson, R., & Garshnek, V. (1998). An Overview of the AKAMAI Telemedicine Project: A Pacific Perspective. *Proceedings of the 31st Hawaii International Conference on System Sciences* (HICSS-31), Maui, Hawaii.

Garshnek, V., & Burkle, F.M. (1998). Telemedicine Applied to Disaster Medicine and Humanitarian Response: History and Future. HICSS. 10(6).

Institute of Medicine. (1996). *Telemedicine: A Guide to Assessing Telecommunications in Health Care.* National Academy Press: Washington, D.C.

Mann, S. (1997) Wearable Computing. *Computer.* 30(2), 25-32.

Oliver, R., Sheng, L., Paul, J.H., & Chih, P.W. (1999). Organizational Management of Telemedicine Technology: Conquering Time and Space Boundaries in Health Care Services. *IEEE Transactions on Engineering Management,* 46(3), 279-288.

Paul, D.L., Pearlson, K.E., & McDaniel, R.R. (1999). Assessing Technological Barrieres to Telemedicine: Technology-Management Implications. *IEEE Transactions on Engineering Management,* 46(3), 279-288.

Perednia, D.A., & Allen A.(1995). Telemedicine Technology and Clinical Applications. *Journal of the American Medical Association.* 273 (6), 383-388.

Rasberry, M.S. (1998). The Theater Telemedicine Prototype Project: Multimedia E-Mail in the Pacific. Proceedings of the 31st Hawaii International Conference on System Sciences (HICSS-31), Maui, Hawaii.

Rodger, J.A., & Pendharkar, P.C. (2000). Telemedicine and the Department of Defense. *Communications of the ACM,* 43(2).

Tanriverdi, H., & Venkatraman, N. (1998). Creation of Professional Networks: An Emergent Model Using Telemedicine as a Case. Proceedings of the 31st Hawaii International Conference on System Sciences (HICSS-31), Maui, Hawaii.

Zajtchuk, R.S. (1995). Battlefield Trauma Care. *Military Medicine.* 160, 1-7.

The views expressed in this paper are those of the authors and do not reflect the official policy or position of the Department of the Army, Department of the Navy, Department of Defense, or the U.S. Government.

Chapter 13

Physician Use of Web-Based Technology: Hype vs. Reality*

Linda Roberge
Syracuse University, USA

The Internet, particularly the World Wide Web, is redefining "how we do business" for the service and manufacturing sectors of our economy. In health care as in other industries, there is a growing pressure for physicians to create a "web presence" that will provide entrance into the realm of e-health service delivery. This research has surveyed 511 physician practice web sites to assess how the promise of the technology compares to the reality. We found that 94-95% of sites were using one or more site design elements, and providing educational content that would be attractive to potential patients. However, only 73% of the sites provided the professional credentials of the health care providers. Functionality that would yield cost reductions was much less common with only 39% of the sites using online forms to collect information. Automation for either scheduling or patient accounts was rare. Additionally, few sites had the infrastructure that would allow them to monitor site activity or provide secure transactions for their patients. Only 23% of the sites protected themselves against charges of providing medical consultations without seeing the patients by using a legal disclaimer. Clearly, this sample of web sites suggests that web technology is not yet being fully utilized by physician practices.

*This project was supported by a grant from the Robert H. Brethren Operations Management Institute at Syracuse University School of Management

INTRODUCTION

In the face of escalating health-related expenditures, physicians are seen as one of the keys to controlling service delivery costs. Competition among providers and alteration of financial incentives via managed care are two of the cost containment methods that are currently impacting physician practices. In other industries we have seen web-based technologies employed in a variety of ways that both enhance an organization's ability to compete and reduce the costs of doing business. This research addresses the question of whether physicians are responding to competitive forces by using web-based technologies in the same way that other industries have.

Recently, the American Medical Association conducted a survey of its members asking questions about how they related to the Internet. Of the physicians responding to the survey, 27% indicated that they have established web sites for their practices. While the current number of sites may be small, there is every indication that the numbers are growing as more physicians avail themselves and their practices of free and low-cost web development services offered by numerous commercial health sites. The existence of a web site, however, does not magically lower costs or improve competitive position. Other features such as those that enable more efficient dissemination of educational materials, collection and maintenance of billing information, and improvement in communication with patients are some of the features required before the strategic potential of the technology can be realized. Specifically, the goal of this project is to examine the extent to which the surveyed sites have incorporated technical and functional features that could enhance competitive position, improve client recruitment and service, and/or lower the cost of doing business.

LITERATURE REVIEW

Since 1997, medical literature, both professional journals and physician oriented lay publications, abound with articles detailing how web sites are being used to great advantage by some of the larger practices and health plans. (for example, see Gilbert, 1998; Hagland, 1998; Bloom and Iannacone, 1999; Coile and Howe, 1999; Kalb and Branscum, 1999; Reents, 1999; Anon(a), 2000; Chin(a), 2000; Chin(c), 2000; Tyson, 2000). Although several surveys have addressed how web technology is currently being used, most are directed toward large health plans rather than independent physician practices.(Cochrane, 1999; Anon(a), 2000) Typically, case descriptions are used to demonstrate how web sites are revolutionizing the delivery of health care services.

Among the health related uses of the internet described in the literature are email (Widman and Tong, 1997; Eysenbach and Diepgen, 1998; Eysenbach and

Diepgen, 1999; Mandl and Kohane, 1999; Furguson, 2000; Sands, 2000; Taylor, 2000), patient education (Richards, Coleman et al., 1998; Dawson, Gilbertson et al., 1999; Helwig, Lovelle et al., 1999; Grandinetti, 2000), and disease management (Anon, 1999; Cochrane, 1999; Peltz, Haskell et al., 1999). A few articles deal with competition and cost issues (Van Brunt, 1998; Herreria, 1999), while others discuss web site content (Impicciatore, Pandolfini et al., 1997; Winker, Flanagin et al., 2000). Together, these articles create a sense of urgency; physicians must either adopt use of the web for their practices or be left behind in the new health care environment.

While some reports give the distinct impression that physicians are responding to current pressures by flocking to the new technology as a means to control costs, attract new patients, and succeed in an ever increasing competitive environment (Kalb and Branscum, 1999; Anon(c), 2000; Chin(a), 2000; Chin(c), 2000), others lament the fact that few physicians are participating in the online revolution (Gilbert, 1998; Cochrane, 1999). Issues of physician adoption of web technology has been discussed briefly in a few articles (Peters and Sikorski, 1998; Anderson, 2000; Chin(b), 2000; Drezner, 2000), but there have been no formal studies of physicians' adoption patterns, and how they are related to pressures of competition and/or managed care.

THE STUDY

To begin to address the gap, this project used a variety of search engines to find physician web sites. These engines, including both crawlers and directories, employ different methods to compile their indexes, and different algorithms to rank sites. A multi-threaded engine, which sends parallel queries to multiple search engines, was also used. Search terms included quotes and the AND Boolean operator. For example, to locate web sites in New York we specified "M.D." AND "New York" using the engines. While there was no expectation that the search would be exhaustive, these techniques were able to unearth a wide variety of relevant sites. These sites were then studied to determine whether or not they contained features that would enable them to be used for strategic purposes.

While all sites located by the search engines have been included in the sample, 17 states were specifically targeted for inclusion in the study. These states provide a wide range of geographic regions, urban/rural areas, and managed care market penetration levels. Again, the selection was not meant to be all-inclusive, but rather to provide variation.

When appropriate sites were located, information about the practice, technical design, functionality, and intended audience were entered into a database and used to construct a picture of how existing sites are being used to respond to competitive pressures. By focusing on a limited number of features, we were able to minimize data collection while still providing an overview of the uses and complexity of the site. URLs, email addresses, and other contact information were collected for possible future use.

In particular, we were interested in gathering information about factors that would enable a web site to either enhance revenue generation or reduce costs for the practice. In terms of revenue enhancement, we looked at factors that might attract new patients to the web site itself, and from there to the practice as patients. For the web site, we looked for design elements that would make the site interesting, well organized, and easy to navigate (images, animation, frames, tables), as well as informative (patient educational material, FAQs, or hyperlinks). Features that could potentially lead a web surfer to become a patient were addresses and telephone numbers of the offices, directions and maps, the photographs of friendly office staff, and credentials of the professionals. Additionally, we looked at whether or not a site was intended to be used by other professionals as a referral generation source.

As an indicator of cost reduction, we looked at how the web site was used to provide services to existing patients such as on-line forms for gathering information, automated scheduling, on-line patient accounts, or other services. Patient educational materials and links were seen as both cost reduction and revenue enhancement features.

Because web sites can range from simple static pages to technically sophisticated marvels, we looked at the site's infrastructure for evidence of features that would support future revenue enhancement or cost reduction.   Data were gathered on cookies, counters, dynamic pages, applets or Java Script, use of key words, security, software used, and developer information.

FINDINGS

The search for physician web sites, which took place during July and August, 2000, yielded 551 sites in 40 states. Forty sites were deemed inappropriate and were eliminated resulting in a sample size of 511. The geographic distribution of the sample is depicted in Figure 1.

502 of the sites in our sample indicated specialties as listed in Table 1, with 9 sites not indicating a specialty. Three sub-specialties dominated the surgical group. Plastic or Cosmetic surgeons were the dominant sub-group with 87 sites, followed by Orthopedic surgeons with 29, and Ophthalmologists with 27. Six other sub-specialties accounted for the remaining 45 surgical web sites. The Internal Medicine web sites were not dominated by any particular sub-specialty but included Allergists, Oncologists, Cardiologists, Dermatologists, and Gastroenterologists, in addition to general Internal Medicine practices.

Figure 1: Geographic Distribution of Sample Web Sites

Table 1: Distribution of Specialties

Specialty Group	Number
Surgery	202
Internal Medicine	114
OB-GYN	63
Family Practice	44
Pediatrics	22
Anesthesiology	18
Psychiatry	14
Non-MD	11
Radiology	10
Pathology	4
Unknown	9

Revenue Generation

Web sites in the sample were generally attractive, well organized, and easy to navigate. Of the 511 sample sites, 486 or 95%, used one or more of the design elements with images and tables being used most frequently (90% and 86% respectively), and animation and frames being used least frequently (39% and 30% respectively). Among the specialties, 86% of the Pediatric sites used one or more design elements under study, with the other specialties that used one or more elements ranging from 90-100%.

94% of the sample (479 sites) also provided patient education content using either FAQs (23%), links to other sites (61%), or other materials (57%). Patient education content was more varied by specialty, however, than was the use of design elements. Only 82% of the pediatric sites used one or more of the methods of providing content, followed by Family Practice, OB-GYN, Psychiatry, and Surgery with 92-94% of sites, and Internal Medicine with 96% of sites. All of the

Anesthesiology, Pathology, Radiology, and the non-MDs (Chiropractic, Podiatry, etc.) sites provided educational content.

An important part of revenue generation is drawing patients from the web site into the practice as new patients, or enticing other professionals to make new referrals. The use of photographs, providing maps or directions, and Listing professional credentials could all be important devices in achieving this transition. While overall 95% of the sites studied (483) used one or more of these methods, only 46% provided maps, 49% provided directions, and 76% used photographs. Moreover, only 75% of the sites provided professional credentials, with 90% of surgical sites providing credentials, 82% non-MDs, 79% Psychiatry, 75% Pathology, 70% OB-GYN, 67% Anesthesiology, 66% Internal Medicine, 61% Family Practice, 59% Pediatrics, and 50% Radiology.

Cost Reduction

Although the sites studied had a high rate of patient educational content provision, other factors that might yield cost reductions were used infrequently. 39% of the sites used forms to collect various types of information, ranging from 50% of Family Practice, Radiology, and Pathology sites using forms to only 28% of Anesthesiology sites doing so. In contrast, only 12% (62) of the sites had any form of automated scheduling, with most relying on email to request an appointment, and none having what might be considered a truly automated system. Patient accounts with any sort of automation were truly rare (1% or 7 sites). Of the seven sites, however, two plastic surgery practices and one ophthalmology practice automated the process of securing loans for their patients for procedures not covered by insurance.

Infrastructure

In order to gauge a site's technical capacity for either revenue generation or cost reduction, we collected information on infrastructure. 51% of the sites listed a copyright or developer's name ranging from "Wally's Wonderful Websites" to various consultants with copyrighted names and incorporated organizations. No attempt was made to assess the quality of the developer's work, but one might fairly assume that not all developers are created equal.

42% of the web sites used key words or page descriptions to increase the likelihood of search engine retrieval. Again, the success of these tactics may vary greatly. Most engines have the ability to ignore spam, and at least one site employed the key words "Viagra Viagra Viagra Viagra Viagra Viagra ...".

Tracking web site activity can provide valuable information about the value of the site to the practice, but only 14% employed counters of any kind, and only one site used cookies. 20 sites (4% of the sample) had the capability to dynamically generate pages, while only 4 sites offered a secure section. Interestingly, none of the four secure sites appeared to have any type of patient account functionality.

Disclaimers

One interesting finding concerned the use of disclaimers. Despite the current debate about providing medical consultations without ever seeing the patient, only 23% of the sites surveyed employed any type of disclaimer stating that information on the site should not be considered advice. This was particularly surprising for specialties such as Internal Medicine (21%), Pediatrics (18%), and Surgery (16%) where these issues could potentially cause severe legal problems.

DISCUSSION

Faced with diminished compensation from managed care plans, physicians are increasingly seeking ways to reduce their own costs. Using practice web sites to provide educational materials for patients might provide one relatively simple cost reduction strategy. It is counter intuitive, then, that Pediatrics, a specialty with high demands for educational materials, would have a lower percentage (82%) of web sites providing educational content than do Anesthesiology, Pathology, or Radiology sites, which all provide the materials but generally have much lower demand. This is doubly puzzling because pediatric educational materials are readily available.

Other means of reducing costs such as using online forms to collect information from patients (39%), online appointment scheduling (12%), or online account servicing (1%) do not appear to be related to specialty. Because provision of these services is technically more complicated and thus more costly than provision of content, it is likely that more investment in the web sited would be required. Without a clear indication of return on investment, physicians may be reluctant to make the financial commitment.

In addition to pressure from managed care plans, competition among physicians in some specialties and in some markets is quite intense. Because surgery is one of the most competitive fields, it was no surprise to find surgical web sites (N = 202) outnumbering other specialties. Two surgical subspecialties that experience especially intense competition are cosmetic/plastic surgeons who accounted for close to half of all surgical web sites (44%) and ophthalmologists who accounted for 13%. This difference may be related to the number of procedures covered by insurance.

While some of the web site features that may enhance revenue generation are more common than those that reduce costs, the use of revenue enhancement features is not universal. Providing both maps and directions to office locations should offer a low cost service for new patients, and yet only 49% of the sites provided directions and only 46% provided maps. Although many more sites (75%) provided the professional credentials of their staff, this information is essential to both new patients and referring physicians; its lack on a quarter of the sample web sites is astonishing! Clearly, for the sites in the sample, web-based technology is not being fully utilized either to reduce the costs of doing business or to enhance revenue generation.

While this study provides a focused snapshot that helps to distinguish between the hype and the reality of how medical practices are currently using web sites to enhance competitive position and improve service delivery, the work has both strengths and weaknesses. Perhaps one of its greatest strengths is the variety of sites that have been included in the sample. An effort was made to include practices from a wide variety of geographic regions, urban/rural areas, and managed care markets. However, there is no assurance that the sample is representative and caution should be used in making any generalizations. Additionally, while we were able to collect information on numerous factors that **may** relate to revenue enhancement and cost reduction, there is not yet a sufficient body of research that can support the supposition that web-based technology, in fact, does either. Undoubtedly, physician adoption of web-based technology is a complex phenomenon with multiple drivers. Future research should include not only revenue/cost studies but also physician adoption behavior and investment decision making.

REFERENCES

Anon (1999). Internet-based system keeps diabetics, physicians in touch and patient care on track. *Data Strateg Benchmarks* 3(4): 59-60.

Anon(a) (2000). Health Systems on the E-Health Path, First Consulting Group. 2000. Available: http://www.fcg.com/.

Anon(b) (2000). Webmaster, MD. *American Medical News*. April 24, 2000.

Anderson, J. G. (2000). Computer-based ambulatory information systems: recent developments. *J Ambulatory Care Manage* 23(2): 53-63.

Bloom, B. S. and Iannacone, R. C. (1999). Internet availability of prescription pharmaceuticals to the public. *Ann Intern Med,* 131(11): 830-3.

Chin(a), T. (2000). More Doctors Catching Web Fever. *American Medical News*. January 17, 2000

Chin(b), T. (2000). NGI, Internet2: The information super duper highway. *American Medical News*. June 26, 2000.

Chin(c), T. (2000). On the clock with the wired doc. *American Medical News*. June 12, 2000.

Cochrane, J. D. (1999). Healthcare @ the speed of thought. *Integr Healthc Rep*: 1-14, 16-7.

Coile, R. C., Jr. and Howe, R. C. (1999). Health care E-commerce and the Internet: ten strategies for health care providers and health plans doing business on the Web. *Russ Coiles Health Trends* 11(9): 1, 3-8.

Dawson, R., J. Gilbertson, et al. (1999). Pathology imaging on the Web. Extending the role of the pathologist as educator to patients. *Clin Lab Med* 19(4): 849-66, vii.

Drezner, J. L. (2000). Understanding Adoption of New Technologies by Physicians, Medscape General Medicine, February 7, 2000, Medscape, Inc. Available http://www.medscape.com/Medscape/GeneralMedicine/journal/2000/v02.n01/mgm0207.drez/mgm0207.drez-01.html

Eysenbach, G. and Diepgen, T. L. (1998). Responses to unsolicited patient e-mail requests for medical advice on the World Wide Web. *JAMA,* 280(15): 1333-5.

Eysenbach, G. and Diepgen, T. L. (1999). Patients looking for information on the Internet and seeking teleadvice: motivation, expectations, and misconceptions as expressed in e-mails sent to physicians. *Arch Dermatol,* 135(2): 151-6.

Furguson, T. (2000). From Doc-Providers to Coach-Consultants: Type 1 Vs. Type 2 Provider-Patient Relationships, The Furguson Report Number 7 · May/June 2000 ,Tom Ferguson, M.D. Available http://www.fergusonreport.com/articles/tfr07-01.htm

Gilbert, J. A. (1998). Beyond billboards: building interactive Web sites. *Health Data Manag,* 6(12): 40-4.

Grandinetti, D. A. (2000). Doctors and the Web. Help your patients surf the Net safely. *Med Econ,* 77(5): 186-8, 194-6, 201.

Hagland, M. (1998). Glimpses of a Web-enabled future. *Health Manag Technol,* 19(4): 22-4, 26, 28-9.

Helwig, A. L., Lovelle, A. et al. (1999). An office-based Internet patient education system: a pilot study. *J Fam Pract,* 48(2): 123-7.

Herreria, J. (1999). America's Doctor Online provides easy access for consultations. *Profiles Healthc Mark,* 15(1): 31-2.

Impicciatore, P., Pandolfini, C. et al. (1997). Reliability of health information for the public on the World Wide Web: systematic survey of advice on managing fever in children at home. *BMJ,* 314(7098): 1875-9.

Kalb, C. and Branscum, D. (1999). Doctors go dot.com. *Newsweek,* 134(7): 65-6.

Mandl, K. D. and Kohane, I. S. (1999). Healthconnect: clinical grade patient-physician communication. *Proc AMIA Symp*: 849-53.

Peltz, J. E., Haskell, W. L. et al. (1999). A comprehensive and cost-effective preparticipation exam implemented on the World Wide Web. *Med Sci Sports Exerc*, 31(12): 1727-40.

Peters, R. and Sikorski, R. (1998). Building your own: a physician's guide to creating a Web site. *JAMA,* 280(15): 1365-6.

Reents, S. (1999). Impacts of the Internet on the Doctor-Patient Relationship: The Rise of the Internet Health Consumer, Cyber Dialog, Inc. Available http://www.cyberdialogue.com/pdfs/wp/wp-cch-1999-doctors.pdf

Richards, B., Coleman, A. W. et al. (1998). The Current and Future Role of the Internet in Patient Education. *International J of Medical Informatics*, 50(1-3): 279-285.

Sands, D. Z. (2000). Using E-mail in Clinical Care, The Informatics Review. March 1, 2000. Available http://www.informatics-review.com/thoughts/index.html

Taylor, K. (2000). The Clinical E-mail Explosion. *Physician Executive*, 26(1): 40-45.

Tyson, T. (2000). The Internet: Tomorrow's Portal to Non-traditional health care services. *J Ambulatory Care Management*, 23(2): 1-7.

Van Brunt, D. (1998). Internet-based patient information systems: what are they, why are they here, how will they be used, and will they work? *Manag Care Q*, 6(1): 16-22.

Widman, L. E. and Tong, D. A. (1997). Requests for medical advice from patients and families to health care providers who publish on the World Wide Web. *Arch Intern Med*, 157(2): 209-12.

Winker, M. A., Flanagin, A. et al. (2000). Guidelines for medical and health information sites on the internet: principles governing AMA web sites. American Medical Association. *JAMA*, 283(12): 1600-6.

Chapter 14

The Quality of Medical Information on the Internet: Some Current Evaluation Frameworks

Carmine Sellitto
Victoria University of Technology, Australia

This chapter provides an overview of some of the criteria that are currently being used to assess medical information found on the World Wide Web (WWW). Drawing from the evaluation frameworks discussed, a simple set of easy to apply criteria is proposed for evaluating on-line medical information. The criterion covers the categories of information accuracy, objectivity, privacy, currency and authority. A checklist for web page assessment and scoring is also proposed, providing an easy to use tool for medical professionals, health consumers and medical web editors.

INTRODUCTION

The Internet can be a valuable resource for people seeking health information. The quality of this information is critical as it could potentially affect health outcomes for many users. Because information on the Internet is subject to constant change, up-grade and alteration, it is difficult to assess for quality and accuracy.

The wide spread installation base of the Web allows patients and their families to easily engage in looking for health information. Such searches can be quite extensive with individuals exploring many sites and 'drilling down' through numerous pages in search of what they believe to be appropriate and relevant informa-

Previously Published in *Managing Information Technology in a Global Economy* edited by Mehdi Khosrow-Pour, Copyright © 2001, Idea Group Publishing.

tion. Some studies suggest that "Internet-Positive Patients" (defined as adults who access on-line health information) are on a par with the number of people who seek out information on sporting and entertainment subjects (Internet Medicine, 1999).

Traditionally, medical information publications have been required to meet a stringent review process before being printed. Such a process involves a peer group examination of submitted papers before they are published. This has assisted the health care profession by providing a form of publishing self-regulation and an important quality control mechanism. However, in the electronic age and with the proliferation of the World Wide Web (WWW), this review process can be circumvented allowing individuals to easily publish on-line. It has been suggested that some fifty percent of medical web information does not provide a list of citations or sources (Internet Health Care Coalition— FAQ, 2000). As the number of health sites on the WWW increase it is likely that the amount of medical misinformation will also increase.

The proliferation of on-line health information poses some potential problems for medical personnel, health-information consumers and web page editors:

- For the consumer, who may include patients, parents of a sick child or individuals who are endeavouring self-diagnosis, there is a risk of accessing health information that is either misleading, incorrect, dated or commercially biased toward the use of certain products.
- For the doctor there is the real possibility that patients will present in surgery armed with web literature that needs to be interpreted with respect to quality and legitimacy.
- Proliferation of on-line heath information has made the job of web page editors much more difficult. In organisations (teaching hospitals, clinics, university departments) that are involved with the dissemination of information, there is a need to have a well-documented guide to what is acceptable for on-line presentation. Web-editors, who are the information gatekeepers, need to be active in reviewing their site as well as understanding some of the 'medico-legal' issues of poorly 'labelled' information.

The following section investigates and discusses some of the information evaluation measures that can be applied to web information in general, and then examines some specific evaluation criteria with respect to medical information.

CURRENT EVALUATION FRAMEWORK AND ASSESSMENT CRITERIA

Not all web information is created equally and some web information is more valuable than others. Web information quality can be gauged by factors such as value, reliability, currency, content and source. The quality of on-line information is thus integral to web design. People are more likely to value good quality web information and this is one of the characteristics that appears to attract people back to a web site (Nielsen, 2000). Poor quality of information can be considered to be a reflection on web design.

The library community has historically evaluated information quality in the traditional print media using criteria such as content, purpose, scope, currency and cost (Gordon-Murnane, 1999). When it comes to evaluating web information, the library community has provided numerous suggestions for establishing criteria for determining on-line information quality. A "critical thinking" approach to web information evaluation has been suggested by Grassian, where sources of the information form the primary criteria for information validity (Grassian, 1997).

The Grassian list of assessment criteria includes:
- Content and Evaluation— Who does the site represent? Is the information based on research or scholarly undertakings? Are references available?
- Source and Date— Who are the authors and what expertise do they have? When was the web page produced, updated, revised and authorised?
- Structure— Is the structure and presentation style of the information consistent with the discipline that it represents?

Another methodology for evaluating on-line information is based on applying a series of questions to an informational web page (Alexander and Tate, 1999). Each affirmative response to a question posed about the information would suggest the information is of a high quality (high scores equate with high quality information). Alexander and Tate identify five criteria for evaluation and scoring of information quality:
- Authority— Can the author of the information be identified? Is there a telephone number or postal address stated? Is there a copyright or disclaimer?
- Accuracy— Can the information be corroborated in other sources? Are there referees listed for further investigation?
- Currency— Are there dates indicating when the web page was first created, updated and/or revised? Is the information current?
- Objectivity— Is the information provided as a public source (.gov or .org URL inclusion)? Is the information free of advertising? If advertising exists is it related to the information content?
- Coverage— Is the information complete? Is the information part of a larger piece of work?

Berkman provides a business perspective to on-line information evaluation. The assessment criteria he suggests addresses business requirements for using information to gain market advantage and strategic position. Berkman sets out a checklist for assessing the quality of business resources utilising interesting measures such as how searchable the information is, timeliness, how frequently up-dated and information storage (Berkman, 1998). The assumption is that such assessment is applied to sources after they have been found to be credible. Daven-port, on the other hand, identifies information and knowledge as being integral to an organisation and suggests some six categories for assessing information—ac-curacy, timeliness, accessibility, engagement, applicability and rarity (Davenport, 1997).

The chapter has thus far discussed various information evaluation criteria from a business and library perspective. There seem to be common categories of assessment that cover information currency, source, structure, authority and ob-jectivity. Some of the information quality characteristics relevant to health will now be discussed.

ON-LINE HEALTH INFORMATION

Silberg et al. suggests that a "framework for critical thinking" should be es-tablished so that a set of quality standards can be formulated and used to assess electronic medical documents on the Internet.

Silberg's core set of criteria recommends assessment of:
- Authorship— who are the contributors or authors?
- Attribution— are references clearly listed?
- Disclosure— web site ownership needs to be clearly stated. Sponsorship, ad-vertising, commercial involvement, underwriting must all be declared.
- Currency— when was the document posted?
  (Silberg et al., 1997)

Wyatt adds to the evaluation of web medical literature by discussing evalua-tion from a functionality perspective, suggesting important criteria such as:
- Determining the links to other quality pages.
- The effectiveness of multi-media that may be used to communicate information.
- How accessible the medical information may be via the commonly used web search engines (Wyatt, 1997).

In a revealing exercise, Impiccatore et al. compared on-line web information with the acceptable clinical management practice for treating fever in young chil-dren— a common problem that most parents encounter. They found only four web information sources (n = 41) compared favourably with the peer-reviewed published guidelines (Impiccatore et al., 1997). In a recent evaluation of 400 web pages for specific health information on the rare cancer condition of Ewing Sar-coma, Biermann and co-workers found that 6% of the pages were erroneous and could have undermined effective treatment. Therefore, Biermann et al suggest that a good starting point for evaluation of medical information is to categorise the source of the information as follows:

- Anecdotal or testimonial
- Alternative medicine therapy
- Medical case report
- General medical information
- Primary treatment

Within each caegory the authors then applied some of the previously outlined evaluation criteria that members of the library community use. Medical personnel then applied the typical peer review of the web information to determine compliance with the clinical literature (Biermann et al., 1999).

Pembleton and Goldblatt employ a simple checklist for medical information similar to Tate and Alexander's criteria. However, they include other important issues such as:

- Whether the institution that supports the author is reputable (branding)?
- Can references be easily verified and confirmed?
- Is the information associated with the sale of a specific product?
- What is the web site's source of revenue? (Pembleton and Goldblatt, 1998)

The Evidence for Best Medicine (EBM) groups utilise the web as a source for information gathering. EBM researchers have found that when assessing web medical information there is a lack of "scientific rigour and quality" with respect to the citations or sources of the information. EBM groups implement what they term a 'quality filter' when evaluating on-line information. EBM screens out inappropriate information by using the common criteria of currency, authority and attribution.

It is also interesting to note that much of the information is filtered out on the basis of the sources being identified as medical testimonials or opinion pieces (McKibbon et al, 1999).

Since 1997, the Internet Healthcare Coalition (IHC) has been openly working to provide some clear guide to the evaluation of on-line health information (Internet Health Coalition). There appear to be some similarities between the IHC and the World Wide Web Consortium (W3C). The W3C was established in the early 1990's and has been instrumental in providing an open forum for the Internet community, leading to the formulation of self-regulating standards in the areas of web accessibility (World Wide Web Consortium, 2000). IHC has widespread community support and, in an ambitious project, has formulated a set of eight guidelines that seek to evaluate web-based products, services and information. Some of the evaluation criteria suggested include:

- Candour: conflicts of interests must be stated, ranging from organisation, commercial or educational links.
- Honesty: there must be a differentiation between product promotion and editorial content and recommendations.

- Quality: encompasses numerous criteria including those that have been generally proposed by library community. The IHC introduces less tangible criteria when measuring information suggesting that it should be "understandable" and "easy-to -read."   (Internet Health Coalition, 2000)

Health portals address certain aspects of health sites which enhance the quality of medical information on-line. Numerous sites carry the Health on the Net Foundation Code of Conduct (HONcode) symbol. Health on the Net Foundation is a non profit organisation that has identified certain ethical criteria that health information sites should address in order to be seen as providing 'quality' medical information. Such criteria includes evaluation of on-line health information addressing issues such as confidentiality of data, site funding, advertising policy and author credentials. A simple and short on-line interactive questionnaire (Site Checker) is provided by Health on the Net Foundation that assists in the assessment of web sites for compliance to the principles highlighted by HONcode.

Since 1998, the British Medical Journal (BMJ) has published significant contributions on the quality of online medical information. One interesting article by Eysenbach and Diepgen (1998), propose that information be labelled by the content creators through metadata or tags, with a standard core vocabulary being developed. Other BMJ reports, suggest that a form of Cochrane "branding" of on-line information will go a long way to solving quality issues (Gary, 1998; Bonati et al., 1998).

The American Medical Association's recently issued web guidelines for AMA websites, addresses accessibility and quality issues by outlining precise requirements that allow conformance with amongst other things content, privacy, timeliness and sponsorship (Winkler et al., 2000).

Some of the most common evaluation criteria that have been proposed by various authors is summarised in the appendix.

PROPOSED CRITERIA FOR EVALUATING MEDICAL INFORMATION

Ultimately, the success of web sites will be judged by the user-community. As individuals continually return to a site, because of the valuable content they may find, so too does the site's reputation and status improve (Neilsen 2000). In the case of medical web sites, information content should be evaluated for quality and accuracy before any success criteria is applied.

Van Der Weyden indicates that initiatives to ensure a certain presentation format of Internet information should not be construed as a form of censorship (Van Der Weyen, 1998). Like the peer group review process, web information regulation should act as a quality assurance measure for the health consumer.

The proposed guidelines are an aid for medical information consumers, health personnel and web-editors. From the literature discussed, four reoccurring categories have been identified that address the basic and common tenets associated with evaluating aspects of health information. Each of the mentioned users communities can use these basics to build complexity into a quality evaluation framework that suits that community (e.g., doctors will have more stringent information measures than patients). The categories and measurement criteria are detailed in the matrix below.

EVALUATION MATRIX FOR INFORMATION QUALITY

How to Use the Matrix

When evaluating a web page a series of simple question(s) are posed for each category. An affirmative response to a question indicates that the page has met the particular evaluation criteria addressed by the question. If all questions are affirmative for a category, then the web page is deemed to have passed in that category.

Table 1: Evaluation Matrix

Evaluation Category	Assessment Questions	Result ✔ or ✗	Score (P/F)
Authority and Currency	Is the author's name present?		
	Is there a date of creation and/or date of last modification?		
	Is there an address or telephone number located on the web page (email only is insufficient)?		
	If an institution or organisation is identified, is it reputable?		
Accuracy	Are obvious references and/or sources to information content are provided?		
Objectivity	Is there a disclosure statement about ownership (About Us)?		
	Is the information content of the web page not associated with advertising or promotional material that may be present?		
Privacy	Is there a data confidentiality statement?		

How to Score

An information page must pass all the criteria in the four categories to achieve quality information status. This is an "all or nothing" assessment. The strict application of this assessment attempts to apply similar stringent rules that printed documents undergo before publication.

Some pages may fail in one or more categories. The matrix can thus be used as a tool by web editors to highlight areas that a web page may be inadequate—areas that can be addressed so as to meet information quality standards.

CONCLUSION

There are many methods using different criteria for the evaluation of information found on web sites. Methods range from widely based criteria to those that instigate a thorough and specific checklist. Several health information evaluation methods appear to be emerging, some robust and technical, others being more general and simplistic. This paper proposes criteria that will allow the assessment of information found on medical web pages on the basis of authority, currency, accuracy, objectivity and privacy. The guidelines can be considered to be a minimum set of evaluation measures which can be easily applied, assessed and scored by the health information consumer, medical practitioner and web editor. As the Internet evolves and becomes more sophisticated the delivery and presentation of medical information should also evolve. In the future, information evaluation protocols will need to change to deal with this increase in sophistication. Future information delivery via video and voice will no doubt need assessment rules similar to those that address quality issues related to print.

The proposed evaluation framework has been used to score several Australian public hospital web sites for information quality. Initial results suggest that much of the medical information that is found on these sites does not comply with the proposed evaluation criteria and would fail. It is hoped that this paper will stimulate discussion about the issues associated with assessing information online and lead researchers to investigate other simple models for validation of medical information.

REFERENCES

Alexander, J. and Tate, M. A. (1999). *Checklist for an Informational Web Page, Wolfgram Memorial Library Information Gateway*, Widener University [Online]. Available: http://www2.widener.edu/Wolfgram-Memorial-Library/inform.htm [last accessed January 2001].

Berkman, R. I. (1998). *Finding Business Research on the Internet: A guide to the Web's Most Valuable Resources*, New York: Find/SVP.

Biermann, S. J., Golladay, G., and Greenfield, M. L. (1999). Evaluation of Cancer Information on the Internet. *American Cancer Society*, Vol 86, 381-390.

Bonati, M., Impiccatore, P. and Pandolfini, C. (1998). Quality on the Internet. *British Medical Journal (BMJ)*, Vol. 317, 1501.

Davenport, T. (1997). *Information Ecology*, New York: Oxford University Press.

Eysehkack, G. and Diepgen, T.L. (1998). Toward Quality Management of Medical Information on the Interent: Evaluation, Labelling and Filtering of Information. *British Medical Journal (BMJ)*, Vol. 317, 1496-1500.

Gordon-Murnane, L. (1999). Evaluating Net Evaluators, *Searcher*, 7 (2), 57.

Grassian, E. (1997). *Thinking Critically About World Wide Web Resources*, UCLA College Library. [On-line] Available: http://www.library. ucla.edu/libraries/college/instruct/web/critical.htm [last accessed January 2001].

Gray Muir, J. A. (1998). Hallmarks for Quality Information, *British Medical Journal (BMJ)*, Vol. 317, 1500.

Health on the Net Foundation (2000). Site Checker [On-line] Available http://www.hon.ch/HONcode/HONcode_check.html [last accessed January 2001].

Health on the Net Foundation Code of Conduct (2000) (HONcode). [On-line] Available http://www.hon.ch/HONcode/Conduct.html [last accessed January 2001].

Impicciatore, P., Pandolfini, C., Casella, N., and Bonati, M. (1997). Reliability of Health Information on the World Wide Web: Systematic Survey of Advice on Managing Fever in Children at Home. *British Medical Journal, (BMJ)*, 314: 1875-1879.

Internet Health Care Coalition (2000). *FAQs Regarding the Code* [On-line] Available http://www.ihealthcoalition.org/ethics/code-faq.html [last accessed January 2001].

Internet Health Care Coalition (2000). *Tips for Health Consumers* [On-line] Available http://www.ihealthcoalition.org/content/tips.html [last accessed January 2001].

Internet Medicine: A Critical Approach (1999). *Internet-Positive Patients Driving You Crazy? Find out How to get Online and Cope.* July, 1 & 6.

Nielsen, J. (2000). *Designing Web Usability: The Practice of Simplicity*, Indianapolis: New Riders Publishing.

McKibbon, A. K., Richardson, S. W., and Walker-Dilks, C. (1999). *Finding Answers to Well-Built Questions, Evidence-Based Medicine*, 4(6), 164-167.

Pemberton, P. J. and Goldblatt, J. (1998). The Internet and the Changing Roles of Doctors, Patients and Families. *Medical Journal of Australia (MJA)*; Vol 169, 594-595.

Silberg, W. M., Lundberg, G. D., and Musacchio, R. A. (1997). Assessing, Controlling and assuring the Quality of medical Information on the Internet. *Journal of the American Medical Association (JAMA)*, 277, 1244-5.

Van Der Weyden, M. B. (1997). Medical Information and the World Wide Web. *Medical Journal of Australia, (MJA)*, 167, 571-572.

Winkler, M.A., Flanigen, A., Chi-Lum, B., White, J., Andrews, K., Kennett, R.L., DeAngelis, C.D. and Masacchio, R.A. (2000). Guideleines for Medical and Health Information Sites on the Interent: Principles Governing AMA Web Sites. *Journal of American Medical Association, (JAMA)*, 283, 1600-1606.

Wyatt, J. C.(1997). Commentary: Measuring Quality and Impact of the World Wide Web. *British Medical Journal, (BMJ),* 314, 1879-1881.

World Wide Web Consortium:W3C (2000). [On-line] Available: http://www.w3c.org/ [last accessed January 2001].

APPENDIX: SUMMARY OF CURRENT EVALUATION FRAMEWORK

Proposed	Criteria	Comment
Gordon and Murnane	• Value • Reliability • Currency • Content • Source	The library community has utilised such criteria for the evaluation of print sources. This evaluation framework appears to have been extended to assessing on-line information.
Grassian	• Content and Evaluation— Who does the site represent? Is the information based on research or scholarly undertakings? Are references available? • Source and Date— Who is the author and what expertise do they have? When was the web page produced, updated, revised and authorised? • Is the structure and presentation style of the information consistent with the discipline that it represents?	The 'critical thinking' approach to web information evaluation where information sources carry the most validity.
Alexander and Tate	• Authority— Can the author of the information be identified? Is there a telephone number or postal address stated? Is there copyright or disclaimer? • Accuracy— Can the information be corroborated in other sources? Are there referees listed for further investigation? • Currency— Are there dates indicating when the web page was first created, updated and/or revised? Is the information current? • Objectivity— Is the information provided as a public source (.gov or .org URL inclusion)? Is the information free of advertising? If advertising exists is it related to the information content? • Coverage— Is the information complete? Is the information part of a larger piece of work?	This approach applies a series of questions to assess information on a web page. The greater the number of affirmative responses equates with higher quality information.
Berkman and Davenport	• Accuracy, Timeliness, Accessibility, Engagement, Applicability and Rarity. • How searchable is the information? • How frequently is information updated? • Is the information stored?	Addresses information evaluation from a business perspective.
Silberg	• Authorship— who are the contributors or authors? • Attribution— are references clearly listed? • Disclosure— web site ownership needs to be clearly stated. Sponsorship, advertising, commercial involvement, underwriting must all be declared. • Currency— when was the document posted?	Proposes a 'framework for critical thinking' to establish criteria for medical information analysis.
Wyatt	• Determining the links to other quality	The evaluation of on-line medical

Chapter 15

Information System Failures in Healthcare Organizations: Case Study of a Root Cause Analysis

Pamela E. Paustian, Donna J. Slovensky, and Jacqueline W. Kennedy
University of Alabama at Birmingham, USA

Preparedness for response and continued operation of a health care facility following an information systems disaster must encompass two facets: continuation of patient care delivery and continuation of business processes. This chapter reports a root cause analysis following an information system failure that compromised the organization's ability to capture clinical documentation for a 33-hour period.

INTRODUCTION

Delivery of health care is an information-intensive process, and the technology associated with data capture and information management is a critical operational and strategic resource. Most HCOs prepare formalized plans, policies, and procedures for recovery of computerized information system (IS) functionality and the recovery of any lost data following an IS disaster. Unfortunately, many disaster recovery plans are inadequate to guide action when a disaster occurs for a number of reasons. Conducting a root cause analysis in the aftermath of an IS disaster can be an important first step in evaluating the adequacy of existing recovery plans.

Previously Published in *Managing Information Technology in a Global Economy* edited by Mehdi Khosrow-Pour, Copyright © 2001, Idea Group Publishing.

DEFINING DISASTER

In general usage, the term "disaster" describes an adverse event that occurs suddenly and unexpectedly. Terminology used to describe disasters within a specific context may incorporate several generic definitions to explain the contextual usage. Morris (1990) defined an automation-related disaster in a health care organization as "any situation that results in an automation support outage of sufficient duration to significantly disrupt hospital business and/or clinical services." This broad definition permits organization prerogative in designating the scope of information system disaster preparedness. This prerogative is not trivial as information systems in HCOs are both complex and dynamic. Information executives must make purposeful decisions about the time and financial resources expended to prepare and maintain disaster recovery plans – plans they hope never to implement. The degree of risk an organization accepts must be based on educated judgment about the likelihood given events will occur and the liability associated with failure to prepare for the eventuality.

INCENTIVES FOR IS DISASTER RECOVERY PLANNING

For hospitals, external disasters affecting the geographic market area served actually may increase the need to provide health care services. When the physical resources of the facility are compromised by environmental conditions, such as wind and water damage from a hurricane, delivery of care may become particularly challenging. Planning for and recovery from disasters, therefore, is mission-critical to HCOs. As HCOs are rapidly increasing their dependence on digital information capture and real-time data analysis to provide patient care, "protection of mission-critical information technology ... is gaining serious attention" (Bandyopadhyay & Schkade, 2000).

The delivery of health services is information intensive and information dependent – from both clinical and business management perspectives. Loss of all or a portion of IS functionality quickly compromises clinical and business processes, and information is recognized as a key strategic resource in health care organizations (Kelly, 2000). Loss of stored data and information can have far-reaching effects, potentially including patient injury, legal liability, and significant financial loss to the organization. In short, the health care industry has become dependent on information technology to conduct its business – delivery of clinical care. Anticipating and preparing for management of and recovery from information system disasters is as mission-critical for health care organizations as is preparing for continuation of patient care in the event a disaster occurs. Determining the underlying cause of IS failure is a pivotal factor in assessing the adequacy of recovery plans. Root cause analysis, which is directed specifically at finding the underlying cause, is an appropriate analytical model to employ. Thus, omitted or inadequate documentation in the disaster recovery plan can be improved.

EXTERNAL REGULATORY REQUIREMENTS

Several regulatory agents and some legislative acts compel health care organizations (HCOs) to have formalized disaster recovery plans. For example, hospitals seeking accreditation from the Joint Commission on Accreditation of Healthcare Organizations (JCAHO) must show evidence of compliance with published standards, which include disaster planning and protection of information resources. The Health Insurance Portability and Accountability Act (HIPPA) of 1996, potentially the most intrusive legislation affecting health care organizations in the past decade, incorporates many regulations specific to information resources.

INFORMATION SYSTEMS FAILURE

Information systems fail for many reasons, relatively few of which are attributable specifically to defects in system hardware or software. Although operational failures occur with some frequency, the length of downtime and operational impact usually are much less severe than failures due to disaster occurrences. Therefore, planning to avoid system damage or data loss and recovery in the event of damage or loss is focused on likely events of significant magnitude. It is important to prevent bad things from happening to good data, particularly when data loss or corruption can result in legal or financial liability.

Categorization of more than 5,000 computer outage incidents between 1982 and 1994 revealed that 47.1% of those outages resulted from events that would be classified as internal or external disasters. Another 27.7% were caused by power outages (Williamson, 1995). According to Robertson's (1997) findings, each online outage averaged 4 hours and cost companies an average of $329,000 in lost revenues and productivity, with 355 worker hours being lost for each hour of unscheduled downtime. Most HCOs are reluctant to report events resulting in negative impacts on patient care for liability reasons. Therefore, data quantifying the cost of information system outages relative to patient care are difficult to investigate.

CASE STUDY

This study was conducted as an investigation of a single case. A single case study is a desirable alternative to investigating multiple cases when the single case is critical, extreme or unique, or when it offers access to previously inaccessible scientific observation (Yin, 1994). The information available at the site was rich in detail not reported in current literature. A sampling strategy whereby the case site is selected because it is a "typical case" (Patton, 1990) was particularly appropriate for this investigation because extreme cases – those which were unsuccessful and those which offer solutions so unique they cannot be replicated – are of little use to instruct other managers or as a foundation to formulate testable hypotheses for future research. While each information outage is unique, the root cause analysis methodology can be applied in many situations (Spath, 1997).

DESCRIPTION OF THE INCIDENT

In August 2000, what should have been a standard, two-hour, information system upgrade in a Southeastern hospital turned into a 33-hour information disaster. The 300-bed hospital is the primary element of a multi-focus delivery system that provides technologically advanced health care in a competitive metropolitan market. Most clinical data are captured electronically at the point of service.

The enterprise-wide information system is configured as a sophisticated network of servers and PC workstations and terminals. Historically, the hospital employed a "best of breed" approach to applications development. Therefore, multiple vendors are represented among the clinical, administrative, and decision support systems. This type of IS structure requires collaborative relationships among vendors to develop interfaces between legacy systems and the emerging data repository. The primary vendor has been designated as responsible for communicating with other application and hardware vendors during system upgrades or new installs.

Events Leading to the IS Disaster

The primary vendor of the main information system was brought on-site to perform a minor hardware upgrade on a clinical documentation system. During the upgrade, the technicians determined that the hardware firmware would have to be updated to support the new hardware changes being made. After verifying that a good system backup existed for the server, the vendor identified the required firmware version and downloaded the patches to the system. From the time of this action, the chain reaction that followed was non-preventable. The restart of the system after the firmware update failed. The information system supporting clinical documentation for the entire hospital failed and was down.

Recovery Actions Taken

Procedures specified in the hospital's IS Disaster Recovery Plan were implemented. Hospital Information System (HIS) Department employees specified in the procedures manual were contacted to resolve the problem. HIS employees worked with the application and hardware vendors to evaluate the system status and to determine the extent of the recovery be required. The decision was made to attempt a quick recovery using the customized recovery tape created monthly.

Five hours after beginning this "quick" restoration, the system re-boot again failed. Further investigation by HIS personnel revealed that this version of recovery software had a known bug that sometimes created restoration tapes that were corrupted. Although aware the bug existed, the vendor had not installed the patch designed to fix the bug. The hospital had no knowledge that the bug existed. The vendor's failure to maintain the system properly prevented system recovery by restoring from a backup.

Ten hours from the occurrence of the disaster event, the HIS staff and supporting vendors determined that a complete system rebuild would be required. This would include operating system, database server installation, application interface installation, and data recovery from backup tape. The rebuild process required 23 clock hours to have the system up and functioning properly.

ROOT CAUSE ANALYIS

After recovery of the system failure, the IS manager initiated a formal analysis of the events that occurred and the responses taken to determine the root cause of the event and whether the root cause could be eliminated or minimized. A secondary goal was to determine whether existing procedures provided adequate guidance to investigate and manage the situation, and to identify any necessary revisions to the recovery plan documents.

Findings

The lack of adequate communication among the vendor groups supporting various elements of the organization's system was identified as the root cause. Instead of direct vendor-to-vendor communication, HIS employees (who had no knowledge of the bug) talked with the vendors separately and communicated information to the vendors. Without direct communication between the individuals most knowledgeable about the technical details of the system hardware and software, what was expected to be a simple two-hour hardware upgrade turned into a disaster.

The existing IS disaster recovery plan was implemented, but the plan did not contain a tested procedure specific to the type of disaster that occurred. Appropriate procedures and personnel notifications had been followed prior to the upgrade and approvals to proceed were given. The vendor that upgraded the system was familiar with the organization's current IS setup and anticipated no trouble with the "minor upgrade." The hospital could not have anticipated the failure would occur. Therefore, the existing plan and procedures for disaster recovery were determined to be adequate. One additional policy was incorporated into the plan to clarify the tape pull procedure.

SUMMARY

An information systems problem of the magnitude described in this case – 33 hours downtime – is commonly referred to as a disaster. The HIS department at this hospital not only responded to the systems problem and corrected it, they aggressively maximized the learning potential the event afforded by conducting a root cause analysis. In addition to identifying and correcting the communication problem between the vendors, several other important outcomes accrued from the post-event analysis. First, a previously existing bug in the information system was corrected. Second, the formal disaster recovery plan was improved by adding a policy regarding the tape pull procedure. Third, the hospital documented a successful test of the disaster recovery plan. Fourth, the manual clinical documentation procedures specified for use in the event of IS failure were tested and found to be adequate.

As organizations become more dependent on data communications networks and telecommunications, it is critical to be able to recover quickly from a disaster. The primary problem in this disaster was that inadequate communication occurred among the vendors involved in maintaining the information system. A professional audit, at least biennially, of all systems and vendors involved may be necessary to maintain the proper links of communication and to ensure the integrity of the disaster recovery plan.

Managers must attempt to avoid disasters by aggressively looking for weak areas within the recovery plan. Frequent testing and improvement of the recovery plan is more desirable than demonstrating a successful recovery in a disaster situation.   A plan can become outdated in as little time as one business quarter, because of internal changes. Organizations cannot "afford to place their plans on the back burner" (Kelly, 2000).

* References available from contact author.

Chapter 16

Intermediation Structures in Electronic Healthcare Portals

Jonathan Wareham & Richard Klein
Georgia State University, USA

Despite the fact that commercial intermediation accounts for over 15% of the US GDP (Spulber, 1996), it has commanded limited attention from the academic community. Moreover, popular discourse has heralded the Internet's ability to dis-intermediate supply chains and channels, directing attention away from intermediation. In contrast, this chapter focuses upon a sector of the economy that has witnessed a surge in electronic intermediation, namely, the healthcare industry. Founded on a survey of leading healthcare portals, this paper documents and analyzes four predominant patterns of functional intermediation in this new form of IT-enabled commercial institution. Based upon an historical analysis of healthcare portals, functional, generalizable patterns of intermediation are posited.

INTRODUCTION

The vast majority of literature dealing with electronic commerce has exalted its ability to dis-intermediate traditional sales channels (e.g., Benjamin and Wigand, 1995; Armstrong and Hagel, 1996). Indeed, arguments have been perpetuated that the Internet will bring us a frictionless and intermediary-free economy. However, great differences still exist between popular rhetoric and reality. Despite the growth of eCommerce, it remains a marginal proportion of the economy (US Dept. of Commerce, 1999, 2000), and few new e-business models have proven their long-term economic viability. And although the dis-intermediation on a broad

Previously Published in *Managing Information Technology in a Global Economy* edited by Mehdi Khosrow-Pour, Copyright © 2001, Idea Group Publishing.

scale is certainly viable and worthy of interest, less attention has been addressed toward the rival hypothesis, that electronic commerce enables the development of new intermediaries (e.g., see Bakos, 1998), despite the fact that commercial intermediation accounts for over 15% of the US GDP (Spubler, 1996).

Accordingly, this research focuses upon a sector of the economy that has witnessed a surge in electronic intermediation, namely, the healthcare industry. Electronic healthcare portals have emerged within the last 36 months as a phenomenon with the potential to fundamentally shift the dynamics of the healthcare market in North America.

For example, McKesson and Healtheon/WebMD have positioned themselves to provide the market participants with the ability to connect to doctors, medical institutions, consumers, and payers with comprehensive products to manage information, communications and transactions - all via the Internet, contending that the medium is the "platform common to everyone" (Egger, 1999). Moreover, the information needed by the various participants, i.e., doctors, hospitals, insurers, pharmacies, and patients, can easily and efficiently be moved via the Internet (Egger, 1999; Cole-Gomolski, 1999), saving various market participants what has been speculated to be unnecessary inefficiencies and unproductive overhead costs (Downend, 1999).

Intermediaries are often assumed to play two roles (Brousseau, 1999): a purely informational role, whereby intermediaries are perceived as entities that gather, sort and arrange information about both parties' plans in order to match them, or an economic matching role, where the assumption is made that the intermediaries do not have the capability to perfectly match producers' and consumers' plans. While unanimous definitions of commercial intermediaries are difficult to identify, Brousseau (1999) delineates the following typology in which intermediaries ensure adjustments in terms of availability, volume and quality, as well as securing transactions and liquidity: (1) information management, (2) logistics management, (3) transaction securitization, (4) insurance, and (5) liquidity.

PATTERNS OF INTERMEDIATION

Despite the fact that commercial intermediation constitutes over 15% of the US GDP (Spulber, 1996), the subject has not commanded a great deal of attention for mainstream managerial and economic theorists. Most contributions in this area are predominantly from finance (Lewis, 1995). However, there are several publications dedicated to the intermediation of goods and services (Hackett, 1992; Bentacourt and Gautschi, 1993; Michael, 1994; Spulber, 1996; Brousseau, 1999).

Intermediaries are often assumed to play two roles (Brousseau, 1999):

1. A purely informational role, whereby intermediaries are perceived as entities that gather, sort and arrange information about both parties' plans in order to match them, or

2. An economic matching role, where the assumption is made that the intermediaries do not have the capability to perfectly match producers' and consumers' plans.

In the first case, information matching is sufficient and the business model is often based upon the intermediary seizing a margin of the transaction amount. In the second case, the inability to perfectly match producers' and consumers' plans requires that the intermediary hold inventories and assume a risk-bearing partnership in the subsequent exchanges, thereby facilitating economic matching.

The popular press has assumed an extreme argument - that the provision of complete information will enable consumers and producers to match plans and deem intermediaries as superfluous third parties. Hence, the growth of the Internet has been viewed as determinant of, if not synonymous with, disintermediation. However, even if one assumes that the astronomical task of matching all transaction parties' optimization plans is tractable, additional coordination challenges may persist.

- First, information asymmetries constitute more than just asymmetries in the knowledge of plans. Agents in a decentralized economy know different things, ranging from skill sets to the Hayekian "knowledge of the particular circumstances of time and place" (Hayek, 1945, p. 524.). These asymmetries in knowledge enable the realization of economic rents. In addition, a great deal of consumption is not simply a function of endogenous needs assessment and explicit plans, but is largely dictated by exogenous factors, such as the weather. Governments, for example, stockpile food reserves for many reasons, including the acknowledgement that circumstances outside the control of the farmer can result in a bad crop yield and consequent food shortages.

- Second, even in the instance that all plans could be made available to all parties, there is no reason to assume that they would match. Production plans are often dictated by economies of scale. Production and logistic cycles take time, and are often much longer than the typical needs assessment and fulfillment cycles of consumers. Business models based upon the creation and fulfillment of wants in the present moment in a specific geographic location, augmented by the instantaneous or compulsive behavior of consumers, would have little validity without the assistance of intermediaries to coordinate needs within local markets.

- Finally, asymmetries in skill, experience, and specific knowledge of time and place, cause difficulties in as asessing the amount of return obtainable in any given exchange. This leads to the classic problems of moral hazard and adverse selection (Milgrom and Roberts, 1992) that are very often mitigated to some degree by the participation of a credible third party intermediary.

While this argument is not exhaustive, it does serve to suggest that intermediaries do more than merely coordinate information. Moreover, it implies that changes in the cost and character of information that we have witnessed in the last decade are not only reducing the aggregate level of intermediation, but are spawning new forms of intermediaries that fulfill very traditional processes of commercial intermediation with unique methods or in novel combinations. Hence, a review of the classical roles of commercial intermediation may aid the understanding of the new class of intermediary currently witnessed in the healthcare sector.

Classic Intermediary Roles

While unanimous definitions of commercial intermediaries are difficult to identify, Brousseau (1999) delineates the following typology in which intermediaries ensure adjustments in terms of availability, volume and quality, as well as securing transactions and liquidity:

- Information Management: aggregator and filter of information
- Logistics Management: performing the basal tasks of sorting, packaging, storing, stocking and transporting goods
- Transaction Securitization: controlling and guaranteeing the products are delivered and assuring payment to producers
- Insurance: purchasing production before consumer demands are expressed
- Liquidity: buying products from the producer before demand is manifested

Data Collection and Assessment

This study is based on a survey of existing medical healthcare portals from the Fall of 1999 through the Spring of 2000. As this study is exploratory, our definition of intermediary was broadened to include any type of Internet presence that aggregated the products or services of multiple organizations within the healthcare sector. Thus, individual medical supply companies with Internet sites that exclusively represent their own products and/or services were not included. A many-to-many relationship between suppliers and consumers was required to fulfill the definition of an intermediary. By some estimates, there are over 17,000 web sites with some form of medical content (Fox, 2000). Consequently, a sample of 22 organizations cannot be considered comprehensive. However, a thorough scanning of the media was made to identify the most significant members of the sector to form a representative sample.

Our preferred form of data collection was personal interviews with senior and middle management (Creswell, 1997; Mason, 1996; Miles and Humerman, 1994). The interviews were semi-structured and guided by the assumption that there were two types of companies entering this venue - either new startups/joint ventures that are seeking to build a completely new client base as a first mover, or existing companies in more traditional areas of pharmaceutical distribution or insurance claims processing that are seeking to expand into an Internet lead business by leveraging an existing client base. With the former organizations, we sought to illuminate the characteristics of the medical industry and the technological environment that motivated the move to a web-intermediated business model. Why did the management believe that such a proposition was feasible? What antecedents presented the opportunity of considerable gains in this sector (e.g., fragmentation, high search costs, etc.)?

With the latter group of organizations, we focused on the rationale behind their movement into an intermediary-based business model. How did they intend to leverage their existing business in this different media? Could they identify specific exogenous forces that motivated their expansion beyond their traditional venue?

Secondary data was employed including information collected from web sites, annual reports, newspaper articles, and third party analyses such as stock analysts and venture capital media. This historical data was used to supplement interviews as well as documenting the evolutionary path of the intermediary. In many instances, companies began their existence completing one form of intermediary function, and then proceeded through alliance or acquisition to fulfill other forms.

ANALYSIS

In an analysis of the types of services offered by the healthcare portals, a number of broad, generic functions were identified.

1. Consumer content aggregation
2. Professional content aggregation
3. Patient management
4. Records management
5. Practice management
6. Physician career management
7. Insurance claims processing
8. Supply chain management
9. Quasi-markets and vortals
10. Application service aggregation

For each company, we identified and catalogued their offering of services according to this typology. Secondly, we categorized each function against the classic intermediation roles described in preceding section. This analysis is pre-

Table 1: Identification of healthcare portals and generic functions

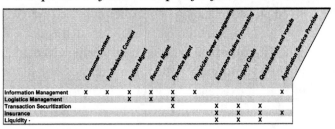

	Consumer Content	Professional Content	Patient Mgmt	Records Mgmt	Practice Mgmt	Physician Career Management	Insurance Claims Processing	Supply Chain	Quasi-markets and vortals	Application Service Provider
HBO & Co.	X	X	X	X	X			X		X
channelHealth	X	X	X		X		X			X
DrKoop.com Inc.	X	X	X		X					
WebMD Inc.	X	X		X	X		X	X		
Medscape Inc.& MedicaLogic	X	X		X	X					
Caredata.com	X	X					X			
Physicians On-Line	X	X					X			
Helios Health	X	X							X	
SeniorPlanet.com	X									
IDX Systems Corp.			X	X	X			X		X
Healthcare			X	X			X	X		
Abaton.com			X	X						
Mediconnect.com			X				X			
Health Claim			X		X		X			
Equarius			X		X					
dotcomments.com			X		X					
Digital Medical Systems			X							X
Kinetra					X		X	X		
Medical Resources Mgmt			X				X			X
Healtheon							X	X		X
McKesson								X		
Neoforma.com Inc.									X	

Table 2 Comparison of domain-specific functions with intermediation types

	Consumer Content	Professional Content	Patient Mgmt	Records Mgmt	Practice Mgmt	Physician Career Management	Insurance Claims Processing	Supply Chain	Quasi-markets and vortals	Application Service Provider
Information Management	X	X	X	X	X	X				X
Logistics Management		X	X	X						
Transaction Securitization					X		X	X	X	
Insurance							X	X	X	X
Liquidity ·							X	X	X	

sented in Table 1. Based upon this preliminary analysis of what services each company is offering and what type of intermediation role it constituted, the information was mapped on a two-dimensional grid according to intermediary role and historical entry path; that is, Internet pure-play or established industry function. The subsequent discussion elaborates this analysis, utilizing historical data concerning acquisitions and managerial decisions to identify four distinct paths of intermediation in the healthcare sector.

Four Patterns of Intermediation
Pattern 1- Internet-based Infomediaries - content aggregators

The emergence of Amazon.com (Bailey, 1998) as a household expression in the mid-90's brought attention to a new paradigm of business - that of virtual companies and infomediation. The prospects of stores with no physical inventory or infrastructure to speak of, combined with a blossoming venture capital market, quickly popularized the possibility of building virtual institutions and supra-normal market valuations through a savvy for aggregating and redistributing information and content for a profit. The first predominant pattern of healthcare portals identified does exactly this. As pure-play Internet infomediaries, they attempt to acquire, re-bundle and market content based upon the assumption that the Internet enables them to build communities of consumers and professionals who have previously only been able to obtain information from fragmented sources (Armstrong, 1996), if at all. Companies like Helios, DrKoop, Medscape, or WebMD in its early form, fit this profile.

Pattern 2 - Established professional services – light information logistics

One group of companies has expanded upon its traditional services such as practice management, patient management, and records management, via alliances to offer a quasi- market solution addressing the light information logistic functions of healthcare management. These companies have leveraged their existing base of customers and skill sets via the Internet to offer a broader portfolio of services by aggregating their own products and services with those of others. These companies include Abton, Digital Medical Systems, Equarius, and Mediconnect.

Pattern 3 - Established professional services – physical & transactional logistics

There is a significant group of existing professional service companies that have sound, non-Internet-dependent businesses in insurance claims processing, medical supply logistics, practice and facilities management, and software development and consulting of standard applications to large clinics and hospitals. These companies have seen an opportunity in leveraging their existing infrastructure and competencies with an Internet mediated distribution channel. For example, IDX, a vendor of large standard software packages for the administration of clinics and hospitals, has spun off their own portal called ChannelHealth. This portal will aggregate a variety of services, primarily their own portfolio of insurance claims processing and patient records management, with consumer content sourced from WebMD as well as other vendors. Another example is McKesson HBOC, which aims at leveraging McKesson's well-established position in pharmaceuticals with other vendors in a quasi-market, offering full supply chain management for larger medical organizations. Like the companies in Pattern 2, the overriding logic of these companies is to use the Internet to spin off an additional channel for an established and tested business model. Other instances of this trend can be seen in Medical Resource Management and Healthcare.com, companies that are attempting to cultivate portal- based channels to their own offerings within software, insurance claims processing, and human resource management with complementary offerings from partner vendors.

Pattern 4 – Internet-based infomediaries – maturing to information, physical and transactional logistics

One very marked pattern identified was the recent merger-driven expansion by WebMD. This company began as a content aggregator, sourcing consumer and professional content from respected sources. However, the company was quick to realize that, despite a highly institutionalized name acquired through massive expenditures in first mover branding, the position of content aggregator is very difficult to defend, due to the low relative costs of information acquisition and distribution. WebMD thereafter merged with Healtheon, a company focused upon insurance claims management, records management and patient management. It has since then moved into other areas of commercial intermediation such as information logistics functions of laboratory and radiology record transactions through its acquisition of Kinetra, breaking stories for the medical profession through its acquisition of MedCast (expanded content aggregation), as well as alliances with Neoforma, a portal which matches buyers and sellers of medical assets.

Discussion

The last example, Pattern 4, would seem to suggest that there may be some overwhelming logic in expanding out of the infomediary role into one of information and physical logistics, as well as transaction securitization. And indeed, the example of WebMD in many ways parallels the well-known plight of Amazon, which was forced to develop an infrastructure of physical inventories, despite original intentions to the contrary. Competition from established publishers such as Barnes and Nobel which could source products without distributor markups, forced Amazon to buy inventory in large quantities to realize volume discounts (Bailey, 1998; Brousseau, 1999), thus abandoning their highly praised model of infomediation with limited tangible ballast.

The decision to abandon a pure-play Internet strategy of subscription-based content aggregation with heavy branding may have proven to be wise, given the recent developments of DrKoop, one of WebMD's strongest competitors within content aggregation. DrKoop has made significant and costly attempts to institutionalize their brand through the use of the former Surgeon General's reputation for integrity and expensive marketing endeavors, including restrictive agreements with AOL and Walt Disney-Go.com that call for DrKoop to make huge payments in return for being the exclusive health content provider to the two companies' web properties (Yates, 2000). Yet, despite the arduous attempts at first mover branding and advantages, the position of infomediary in isolation has proven very difficult to maintain, such that the company is projected to run out of cash by August of 2000 (Yates 2000). This may be due to the fact that the market is too thin to support the current offering of medical content providers. But alternatively, it may be a function of the fact that it is very difficult to cultivate and defend the position of an economically prosperous infomediary.

These observations are consistent with Brousseau (1999) who argues that those intermediaries best-positioned to offer an information management function are those intermediaries currently facilitating logistics, transaction and liquidity management. While content aggregation can be viewed as provision of an asset in its own right, the general challenge faced by pure content providers is that the assets provided are often not requisite to the operations of the business. Thus, the most central platform to market supplementary content may in fact be the applications facilitating the revenue stream, such as the insurance claims processors. This pattern can be seen in Healtheon/WebMD and IDC/ChannelHealth, where functions of transaction securitization enable control of the "meat and potatoes" (Kanell, 2000) of their clients. Through management of the revenue stream, intermediaries can logically extend liquidity management through the purchasing of accounts receivables forward (Medical Resource Management). Moreover, logistics functions, central to the metabolism of the organization, also command a central role in the needs for intermediation. In this instance, companies like McKesson/HBOC, who control large networks of pharmaceutical and medical supply provision, also realize advantages in marketing complementary products of their own and associated companies.

Generalizations

The analysis presented above would suggest that the most viable path towards intermediation, be it electronic or otherwise, would be to facilitate transaction securitization (revenue stream management) and logistics management. Through command of these basic, yet vital, operations of a business, one could easily extend offerings into the arenas of market making, content provision and infomediation. The opposite strategy, however, may be very difficult to defend. While channel dis-intermediation does provide compelling logic of greater consumer welfare, a pure economic matching function of buyers and sellers is relatively inexpensive and, consequently, easy to emulate. In fact, returning to our analysis, we see that purely electronic intermediaries neglect the paramount functions of physical logistics, transaction securitization, liquidity, and inventory management, as buffers to uncertainty and bounded rationality. The ability of commercial intermediaries to hold inventories, re-bundle products, and subsidize portfolios of goods and services as dictated by the end user, enables a resolution of the problems generated by information asymmetries. Moreover, the requisite investments in relational assets by the transactional and logistics intermediary permits, in many instances, superior levels of information management due to the transactional knowledge which is a natural by-product of their given activity. Finally, the intermediaries inherent incentive to invest in a reputation for fairness and efficiency, as well as mutual trust among transacting partners, help mitigate problems of adverse selection and moral hazard.

Hence, those controlling the lifeblood of transactions and logistics will always reap the benefits of superior information of the transaction, as well as economies of scale nurtured through investments in infrastructure. As such, the very basic functionaries in the economy may be best-positioned to offer some form of infomediation in an e-business context. This advantage is derived from central placement in revenue and logistic management, as well as an ability to leverage transactional knowledge as a source of information-based rents.

CONCLUSION

This chapter has described and documented the emergence of a new form of intermediary in the medical sector, the healthcare portal. From a representative sample, generic functions of healthcare portals were identified and typed according to theoretical views on commercial intermediation. Based upon an historical analysis of managerial decision and acquisitions, four evolutionary patterns of commercial intermediation are identified within healthcare portals: (1) Internet-based Infomediaries-content aggregators, (2) Established professional services–light information logistics, (3) Established professional services–physical & transactional logistics, and (4) Internet-based infomediaries-maturing to information, physical and transactional logistics. From a perspective of generic intermediary roles, the potential of generalizing these patterns beyond the healthcare industry is explored.

REFERENCES

Armstrong, A. and Hagel, III, J. (1996). The Real Value of On-Line Communities, *Harvard Business Review*, 74(3), pp .134-141.

Bailey, J. P. (1998). Electronic Commerce, Prices and Consumer Issues for Three Products: Books, Compact Disks, and Software, DSTI/ICCP/Ie (98) 4, OECD, Paris.

Bakos, Y. (1998). The Emerging Role of Electronic Marketplaces on the Internet, *Communications of the ACM*, August, 41(8), pp. 35-42.

Benjamin, R. and Wigand, R. (1995). Electronic Markets and Virtual Value Chains on the Information Highway, *Sloan Management Review*, Winter, pp. 62-72.

Bentacourt, R.R. and Gautschi, D. A. (1993). The Outputs of Retail Activities: Concepts, Measurement, and Evidence, University of Maryland Department of Economics Working Paper Series 90-17, September, 39.

Brousseau, E. (1999). The Governance of Transaction by Commercial Intermediaries: An Analysis of the Re-engineering of Intermediation by Electronic Commerce, *Third Conference of the International Society for New Institutional Economics*, Washington D.C.

Cole-Gomolski, B. (1999). Extranet Services Target Health Care, *Computerworld*, 32(37), p.10.

Creswell, J. W. (1997). *Research Design: Qualitative and Quantitative Approaches*. Thousand Oaks, CA: Sage Publications, Inc.

Downend, P. (1999). Technology Energizes Health Insurance Distribution Process, *National Underwriter*, 103(16), pp. 35-36.

Duncan, M. and Garets, D. (1999). The 1999 State of the Healthcare IT: Business, Management and Strategy Drivers and Trends, *Gartner Group, Strategic Analysis Report*, R-09-3928, 28 September.

Egger, E. (1999). Fleet of Innovative New Firms Racing to Make Health Care Information Systems Obsolete, *Health Care Strategic Management*, 17(8), pp.16-17.

Fox Broadcasting Network (2000). Special Report on Internet and Healthcare, April 26.

Hackett, S.C. (1992). A Comparative Analysis of Merchant and Broker Intermediation, *Journal of Economic Behavior and Organization*, 18(3), August, pp. 299-315.

Hayek, F. A. (1945). The Use of Knowledge in Society, *American Economic Review,* 35(4) pp. 519-530.

Hempel, C.G. (1965). Aspects of Scientific Explanation. The Free Press, New York.

HIPAA. Tentative Schedule for Publication of HIPAA Administrative Simplification Regulations. Department of Health and Human Services. Available: http://ahima.org/infocenter/current/hipaa.html

Kanell, M. (2000). Healtheon/WebMD Competing with Established Software Firms, *Atlanta Journal Constitution*, 04-08-2000 G3.

King, Jr., R. T. (1999). McKesson Sets Deals to Expand Role on Internet, *Wall Street Journal*, B7, Nov.

Lewis, M.K. (1995). Financial Intermediaries. Elgar Reference Collection. International Library of Critical Writings in Economics, vol 43. Alsershot, U.K: Elgar.

Marceil, J.C. (1977). Implicit Dimensions of Ideography and Nomothesis: A Reformulation, *American Psychologist* 32(2), pp. 1045-1055.

Mason, J. (1996). *Qualitative Researching*. Thousand Oaks, CA: Sage Publications, Inc.

Mason, R.O., McKenney, J. L. and Copeland, D. G. (1997). Developing an Historical Tradition in MIS, *MIS Quarterly*, 21(3), pp.257-278.

Michael, S.C. (1994). Competition in Organizational Form: Mail Order versus Retail Stores, 1910-1940, *Journal of Economic Behavior and Organization* 23(3), May, pp. 269-286.

Miles, M. B. and Huberman, A. M. (1994). *Qualitative Data Analysis* (2nd ed.). Thousand Oaks, CA: Sage Publications, Inc.

Milgrom, P. and Roberts, J. (1992). *Economics, Organization & Management.* New Jersey: Prentice-Hall, International Editions.

Miller, A. (1999). McKesson HBOC Expands Internet Healthcare Holdings, *The Atlanta Journal Constitution*, Nov, 16E; 1.

Orlikowski, W. J. and Baroudi, J. J. (1991). Studying Information Technology in Organizations: Research Approaches and Assumptions, *Information Systems Research*, 2(1), pp. 1-28.

Raghupathi, W. (1997). Health Care Information Systems, *Communications of the ACM*, 40(8), pp. 80-82.

Spulber, D. F. (1996). Market Microstructure and Intermediation, *Journal of Economic Perspectives* 10(3), pp. 135-152.

U.S. Department of Commerce (1999). The Emerging Digital Economy II. Economics and Statistics Administration, Office of Policy Development, http://ecommerce.gov, June.

U.S. Department of Commerce (2000). Remarks by Secretary of Commerce William M. Daley, Press Conference On First E-Retail Sales, March 2. Washington, Office of Policy Development, http://ecommerce.gov, March 2, 2000.

Weber, D. O. (1999). Web Sites of Tomorrow: How the Internet will Transform Healthcare, *Health Forum Journal*, 42(3), pp. 40-45.

Yates, E. (2000). DrKoop on Life Support as AOL Takes 10% Equity Stake, The Street.com, April 25.

Chapter 17

CORBAMed and DHE: Middleware Service Approach in Healthcare Information Systems

Dongsong Zhang and Ralph Martinez
University of Arizona, USA

The healthcare organizational structure is often naturally distributed. In order to improve the quality of care, the adoption of standards to allow the effective and robust networking of the various centers for clinical, epidemiological, administrative information management purposes has been widely recognized as an urgent and strategic need in the healthcare community. This chapter analyzes the status and challenges that today's healthcare information systems have, and introduces two middleware service frameworks for information systems, namely CORBAMed and DHE, in detail. The middleware service can address heterogeneous problems and significantly assist interoperability and integrity of information systems by providing common services and a set of standard interfaces that enable different applications to interact with each other.

INTRODUCTION
Characteristics of Current Healthcare

Healthcare is experiencing rapid improvements due to its changing focus and tremendous achievements in computing and communication technology. Concurrently, the healthcare organizational structure is often naturally distributed, being geographically dispersed centers at different levels of complexity and scale. The various structures operating over the territory are heterogeneous in organizational,

Previously Published in *Managing Information Technology in a Global Economy* edited by Mehdi Khosrow-Pour, Copyright © 2001, Idea Group Publishing.

logistic, and clinical perspectives. Healthcare is driven to move quickly from single-provider, proprietary, mainframe systems toward multi-providers, scalable, component-based systems. Patients are provided with healthcare services by multiple institutions. The patient information is widely dispersed — a patient's record is held in medical records departments of multiple hospitals. Therefore, ubiquitous lifetime patient information needs to be obtained from many locations and be efficiently integrated. Electronic medical records are commonly used (Forslund, 1997). They can be easily maintained and distributed across a healthcare network.

Challenges of Developing Healthcare Information Systems

The distributed nature of healthcare determines the need of powerful tools to access patient medical records over a wide area and assemble various data from different sources. There is a strong desire to create and apply some common standards, which are assertions, not realizations of requirements, for the architecture of HIS. The adoption of them allows the effective and robust networking of the various centers for clinical, epidemiological, and administrative information management purposes. As a result, physicians will be able to maximize the utilization and sharing of resources to make the right judgment. However, it is far from trivial to make it a reality because of several challenges:

- Size/Scalability: Usually the size of the overall healthcare network is huge.
- Representationheterogeneity: Same patient information may be represented in disparate ways within different systems, which sets the barrier for data integration. There is no consensus on data formats.
- Platform and programming language heterogeneity: Individual healthcare information systems are often platform-dependent. They are usually developed using different programming languages on heterogeneous platforms, which causes incompatibility problems.
- Lack of computing interoperability: Hospitals use assorted devices, instruments and systems that collect and maintain patient information. It lacks of computing interoperability among them.
- Real-time capabilities: Gathering and integrating distributed patient information must be quick enough to be useful for diagnosis or treatment.
- Security: Today's healthcare providers are concerned with collecting relevant patient information from multiple resources. The security and limitations on data access and disclosure must be taken into consideration during patient information sharing. The security will be the key to the smooth flow and share of information among the providers in healthcare community.

Developing advanced healthcare information integration techniques and standards will address the above problems and greatly benefit the healthcare community. First, it helps assemble longitudinal medical records of a patient from multiple sources by specifying a set of information formats. Second, it promotes interoperability and enables the reliable sharing of medical information between healthcare organizations. Also, it supports remote synchronous and asynchronous healthcare consultation. Finally, it reduces the cost of healthcare information management. Therefore, there is a strong need for a distributed computing infrastructure accessible to a large variety of platforms, and a set of standard interfaces that links distributed data repositories together while maintaining integrity. The development of a fully-interoperable, component-based and open-standard framework for HIS will make healthcare organizations transcend the limitations and redundancies created by today's automated systems, and encapsulate the pieces of existing systems so that all of the system components could work together seamlessly. This chapter will introduce two middleware frameworks, CORBAMed and DHE that bridge the gap between different platforms and applications by providing standardized interfaces and services.

THE STATE OF HEALTHCARE INFORMATICS

The advent of HIS began in the 1960's. Originally, the were mainframe-based systems that primarily focused on supporting accounting and administrative functions in the hospitals. In the 1970's, department information systems, such as radiology information systems and pharmacy management systems, were developed to support administrative and information tracking functions at clinical departmentlevel.

Since the 1990's, healthcare informatics has begun to support the clinician and focus on the patient needs. It tries to incrementally construct a homogeneous and consistent set of information common to the whole organization that optimizes the cycle of healthcare activities. The healthcare community has increasingly recognized the urgent need for interoperable information systems. Obviously, centralized mainframe systems are not able to meet these requirements. Instead, distributed object technology seems ideal for this purpose because of the flexibility and simplification it provides.

There have been increasing efforts toward establishing patient data-interchange standards and designing distributed system architectures for healthcare, such as Health Level 7 (HL7), Digital Imaging and Communications in Medicine (DICOM), and Electronic Data Interchange for Administration, Commerce and Transport (EDIFACT), etc. These standards are widely used. However, most of them focus on health data exchange and only support part of patient information. These standards or protocols neither provide truly open systems that enable users to select best-of-breed applications, nor exchange data in a meaningful way. In order to achieve an open plug-and-play environment, industry-standard middleware architectures and interfaces should be well defined and adopted.

MIDDLEWARE SERVICE APPROACH IN HEALTHCARE INFORMATION SYSTEMS

Middleware

In order to develop enterprise-wide information systems, it is imperative to solve heterogeneity and distribution problems. To help solve these problems, vendors are offering distributed system services that have standard programming interfaces and protocols. These services are called "middleware services" because they sit in the middle of the platform layer and application layer.

Basically, middleware is a package of connectivity software that bridges the gap between application programs and heterogeneous hardware and operating system dependent platforms. It is extensively used in the heterogeneous, distributed environment through providing a functional set of Application Programming Interfaces (API) or a protocol to allow an application to get access to any popular platforms. A primary advantage of using object-oriented middleware is that any object can be inexpensively updated while the involved technologies remain intact and unchanged. The implementations of a middleware service must be able to run on multiple platforms. Otherwise, it is only a platform service. A middleware service has distributed nature: it can be accessed remotely or it can access other remote services and applications. Generally, the middleware services may include several components such as information management, computation, communications, control, system management and presentation management (Bernstein, 1996).

HIS architecture is dominated by the extensive use of object-oriented middleware functionalities. Today the most widely publicized middleware initiatives are the Open Software Foundation's Distributed Computing Environment (DCE), Microsoft's COM/DCOM, and Object Management Group (OMGTM)'s Common Object Request Broker Architecture (CORBAâ1). CORBA is a distributed object framework that intends to enable interoperability between objects in a heterogeneous, distributed environment. Its architecture separates the object interfaces from implementations, while a set of CORBA services facilitate the management of the distributed object infrastructure (Orfali & Harkey, 1998).

CORBAMedä2

What is CORBAMed? One of the leading efforts toward developing industry standards for healthcare information system is CORBAMed, which is the OMG's Domain Task Force on Healthcare. The mission of CORBAMed is to improve the quality of care and reduce cost by the use of CORBA technologies for interoperability, and to define standardized object-oriented interfaces between healthcare related services and functions (Forslund et al., 1999; OMG, 1997). Some important features of CORBAMed are described as follows:

- Opens the access to a larger range of software components.
- Provides a high degree of interoperability between disparate computer systems so that medical records can be integrated.
- Improves the quality of components and reduces the software cost by increasing the competition between healthcare providers.
- Is fully object-oriented.

The overall CORBAMed framework is presented in Figure 1 (ACL, 1998). It includes six major standard services that support HIS based on CORBA technologies. The first approved standard from CORBAMed was the Person Identification Service (PIDS). Its goal is to provide a standard method of locating person identifiers and their medical records across a distributed healthcare network. Lexical Query Service (LQS) that was secondly approved supports the use of multiple vocabularies in heterogeneous environment. The other four standards, namely Healthcare Data Interpretation Facility (HDIF), Clinical Observation Access Service (COAS), Healthcare Resource Access Control (HARC) and Clinical Image Access Service (CIAS), are either under assessment or to be submitted.

Person Identification Service (PIDS). Every person may have dozens of healthcare providers in their life. Each healthcare organization simply assigns a

Figure 1: CORBAMed Framework (ACL, 1998)

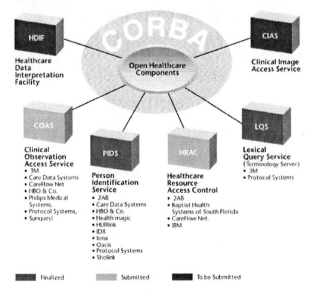

unique patient identifier within its local domain to a patient. These IDs are meaningless to other systems or organizations. In a distributed environment, a patient's medical information is dispersedly located at a number of organizations. Each part of the information belonging to that patient needs to be correctly identified and collected, which means a search has to be performed in each organization in order to identify the person and retrieve the related information. However, increased specialization of healthcare providers and continuous growth of organizations exacerbate the problems with managing patientIDs.

The building block of the CORBAMed PIDS model is the ID domain. The PIDS tries to manage patient IDs by supporting the assignment of IDs within a particular ID domain, correlating IDs among different domains, allowing both attended-interactive and message-driven unattended modes for searching and matching people, and supporting federation of PIDS services in a topology-independent manner. Although it provides the confidentiality and security mechanisms, PIDS itself is not required to enforce confidentiality. Its interfaces are delineated so that "request interceptors" can enforce any policy to protect personal information. In addition, PIDS enables plug-and-play interoperability by means of a "core" set of profile elements.

Lexicon Query Service (LQS). The LQS aims to provide "a set of common, read-only methods for accessing the content of medical terminologies". There are usually some typical uses of medical terminology systems. For example, using terminology services to assist information acquisition, translate coded information from one representation to another for information display, and help indexing and matching. It is a well-known fact that medical terminology systems can vary radically from a simple code-phrase pair list to a huge complicated scheme with heterogeneous representations. Therefore, it is critical to define a standard interface to any of the major medical coding schemes. The LQS specification proposes a reference model representing the common aspects of several different systems. Much of the functionality is optional, which can be implemented by a particular terminology system.

Healthcare Data Interpretation Facility (HDIF). It is difficult to interpret and integrate data coming from different information systems because of the diverse forms of data. Having standard interfaces for intelligent clinical data transformations will help easily incorporate intelligent systems into HIS to interpret data appropriately. Currently, the healthcare community lacks such a set of standard interfaces. HDIF targets to offer a general-purpose infrastructure in which a variety of intelligent transformations for clinical data will be embedded, as well as standard interfaces that can conduct intelligent healthcare data transformations when it is necessary. Some CORBA services, such as Security, Trader/Naming, and Events/Notification services, could be involved in this facility.

Clinical Observation Access Service (COAS). OAS is a set of interfaces and data structures related to how a server can supply clinical observations. A clinical observation refers to any information that has been captured about a single patient's medical/physical state and relevant context information. It consists of a significant portion of the information about any patient. Either medical instruments or healthcare professionals may derive this information during the examination of patients. COAS is designed as a "conduit" for medical information that offers opportunity to transfer well-defined data from standards such as HL7 and DICOM. It is desired to provide efficient ways to request and/or receive clinical observations and their associated context information, to be capable of filtering observations in terms of the observed subject, observation type and time frame, to define a query mechanism for observation retrieval, and to address the access policies that specify the range of context information associated with an observation. COAS is expected to determine a default set of observation types, which can be defined as either the format or structure of the observation, or the coding scheme being used in description of observed biological phenomenon. In order to deal with medical terms, a COAS server may specify the coding schemes or vocabularies used within an organization. COAS can make use of LQS to translate one code to another after it is received from a client. Some other mechanisms, such as publishing and subscribing to observations, will also be taken into consideration in COAS.

Healthcare Resource Access Control (HARC). The information of a patient that can be disclosed or shared by multiple healthcare organizations depends on several factors. For example, who is looking for that information, which legal rights or privilege the information-seekers have on that information, and what are the access policies of the organization that owns the information? In order to meet the requirements of the various groups involved in healthcare process, there is a need to support two groups of access control policies. One group is general policies related to the role of healthcare providers and the control of disclosure or access to patient confidential information. The other group is patient-specific access policies that are based on either the requirements of a particular patient, or the information being accessed or disclosed. CORBAMed HARC tries to define the mechanisms to support those complicated information access control in order to secure the resource. Obviously, the CORBA Security Service plays an important role in HARC.

Clinical Image Access Service (CIAS). Clinical images, such as X-rays and ultrasound images, are a subset of clinical observations and a critical part of patient medical record. CORBAMed CIAS, which will be a retrieve-only service, deals with mechanisms to access clinical images and related information. CIAS does not try to replace DICOM, which is the most prominent standard for image interchange in medicine. Instead, it intends to encapsulate portions of the DICOM standard as a service wrapper so that it could give a simplified view of DICOM information model that supplies images and limited meta-data to users in the formats compatible with well-known image standards. CIAS will provide automatic image scaling and windowing to meet the needs of non-diagnostic use of medical images by general clinicians or non-image specialists. It will offer the basic services for supporting electronic patient records transmission over low and moderate speed networks.

In summary, CORBAMed framework enables interoperability and integration among heterogeneous HIS by providing a set of standard services. In each service, standard interfaces are well defined and should be implemented by applications.

The Distributed Healthcare Environment (DHE) Middleware

Overall Architecture of HIS. The structure of individual healthcare centers is evolving toward the integration of a set of specialized departments with their own organizational, logistic and management requirements. Each department has its individual special activities and delivers specific medical services. Thus, the hospital information system can be modeled as a federation of autonomous applications that are optimized in functionality aspects and can mutually interact through protocols and interfaces (GESI, 1997). Currently, there are a number of available applications addressing the special needs of different departments. However, they are mutually incompatible with each other and can hardly be integrated to support the overall healthcare requirements due to the lack of standards. The strongest need is therefore to enable the interoperability among different applications. Although the applications might be developed by different vendors using disparate technologies, they can be "glued" together and behave like a whole towards the environment.

In order to be capable of behaving as a single system with respect to the overall organizational functioning, these applications rely on a set of common services and must fit into a consistent and comprehensive system architecture. This architecture can be decomposed into a set of components in terms of the objectives and interactions with the rest of the system so that changing one piece of the system will remain other parts unaffected. Considering these factors, CEN/TC251/PT010 (GESI, 1997) defines a conceptual architecture framework structured in three layers as follows:

- Application layer
- Middleware Layer
- Bitways Layer: to support physical connection, and meet network and distribution requirements

Correspondingly, the components of hospital information system are grouped into three layers:

- The basic technological layer is responsible for providing the interworking services in a distributed and heterogeneous environment.
- The layer of the common services implemented through Distributed Healthcare Environment (DHE layer) provides a set of common services and interfaces to the applications in order to ensure the appropriate interworking and synchronization of them. It supports applications from both the functional and the procedural point of views.
- The layer of application: the applications are designed and optimized to support specialized healthcare-related activities.

DHE middleware is a proprietary product of an Italian firm called Gestione Sistemi per l'Informatica SrL (GESI). The overall architecture of HIS containing DHE middleware is described in Figure 2. It consists of distributed databases, a set of application services, and interface modules in order to address various needs of the healthcare organization. It provides an open infrastructure that is capable of federating heterogeneous applications through a common set of healthcare-specific components.

The Applications. The applications are developed to support healthcare and medical activities, including clinical activities, and monitoring and optimization of the services provided. The classification of the application areas in the healthcare organization can be defined using a functional user-centered approach, which identifies individual users and activities that need to be carried out. Each basic application module of the system is responsible for one service/activity. This approach increases the flexibility and maintainability of the system. Generally, there are six functional application areas in healthcare center, namely patient management, medical care, nursing, medical support, ancillary services and organization and management.

Components of DHE Middleware. The DHE middleware comprises the basic functional infrastructure of healthcare centers. The fundamental role of DHE middleware in the HIS is to provide mechanisms to support different applications in accessing, sharing, manipulating and managing common data of the organization while maintaining the consistency and integrity of information. The DHE includes following components:

Figure 2. The overall layered architecture of healthcare information systems (with the DHE middleware) (GESI, 1997)

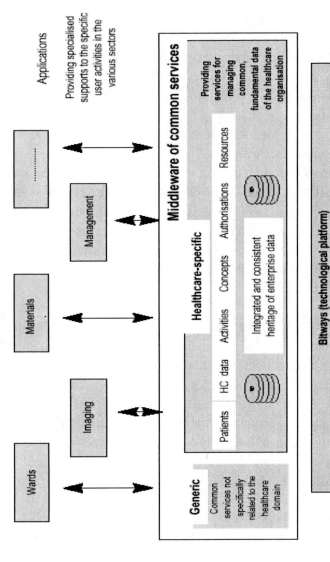
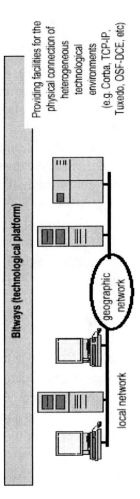

- An integrated but distributed database that contains the commoninformation. The DHE could manage five primary types of data: Activities and organizationdata describes the information related to the lifecycle of all organization activities. Resources data depicts the available resources within the healthcare center, such as personnel, instruments, beds, and drugs. Users and authorizations data contains information about the authorization of individual users of the system; Patients data handles personal, administrative and epidemiological data of the patients; Health data manages all available health data regarding patients, including clinical data.
- A set of servers that encapsulate the database and provide complete services to enable applications to enter, retrieve and manipulate the common data. Each server is self-consistent and is capable of concurrently interacting with multiple client applications.
- A set of configuration modules that allow the authorized users to configure the whole system through a GUI.
- A dictionary that assists developers and end-users to understand the overall functioning of the system.

The DHE Middleware Functional View. As explained, the DHE services can be directly used by applications to manage all information. To manipulate data, the DHE relies on the presence of a database management system. When the DHE server starts, it needs to select the port on which it will wait for the requests from clients. On the other side, client takes the similar procedure when it tries to contact with DHE server for the first time. The DHE server supports two types of connection modalities with the client. One is usual RPC interaction; the other is Internet-suitable interaction ? the socket is closed when a service is completed. The DHE provides APIs for both procedural (C, Visual Basic) and object-oriented (Java, CORBA, C++) programming languages so that Web applications can be developed easily with DHE.

Individual applications must interact with each other through DHE services and must refer to the data managed by DHE for consistent information. With respect to the use of DHE services by applications, there are two main approaches: DHE federation and DHE integration. DHE federation requires creation of interfaces between applications and DHE common services that represent components external to the application themselves. DHE integration implies the utilization of DHE services directly within the architecture of the applications to support activities.

The DHE allows the developers to adopt its own security mechanisms for establishing encrypted communications over the healthcare network. One of the most important issues in distributed healthcare is how to improve the quality of care while maintaining the patient privacy and confidentiality. In the DHE, several security features are implemented (Andany et al., 1999):

- Encryption/Decryption modules based on private and public keys can be activated on both client and server sides.
- Digital signature can be added when validating or entering health data.
- Certification of the user activities is provided for auditing to keep track of all interactions occurred that are signed and encrypted by the user.

Sitting between platform and application layers, the DHE middleware serves as a common glue to integrate loosely scattered applications into a highly effective network with interoperability.

CONCLUSION

The changing focus in the business of healthcare from hospital-centered to patient-centered has dramatically emphasized the urgent need of interoperability between heterogeneous healthcare information systems. Due to the high heterogeneity on hardware platforms, operating systems, programming languages, and data standards in HIS, there must be a consensus on common interface architecture to meet the interoperability challenges and improve the quality of care. Middleware service has been recognized as an ideal approach to connect different healthcare applications. Through the investigation of two prominent information system architectures adopting middleware service, CORBAMed and DHE, we believe that the middleware service approach can satisfy the various requirements of a distributed healthcare information system because of its reaching maturity and availability.

ENDNOTES

[1] CORBA is a trademark of Object Management Group, Inc. in the U.S. and other countries.
[2] CORBAMed is a trademark of Object Management Group, Inc. in the U.S. and other countries.

REFERENCES

ACL (Advanced Computing Laboratory, 1998). CORBA-based systems. http://www.acl.lanl.gov/telemed/Corba_Main.html.

Andany, J., Bjorkendal, C., Ferrara, F. M., Scherrer, J. and Spahni, S. (1999). Authorization and security aspects in the middleware-based healthcare information system. In *Proceedings of Medical Informatics Europe 99*, IOS Press, Amsterdam, pp.315-320.

Bernstein, P. A. (1996). Middleware: a model for distributed system services. Communication of the ACM, 39(2): 86 – 98.

Forslund, D. W. (1997). The Role of CORBA in Enabling Telemedicine (LA-UR-97-1010) Global Forum III: Telemedicine in Vienna, Virginia.

Forslund, D. W., George, J. E., Stabb, T. et al. (1999). Federated healthcare utilizing CORBAMed standards. Presented at RSNA Annual Conference, 11/29-12/3, Chicago, IL.

GESI (1997). The DHE Middleware Introduction (Version 1.1).http://www.gesi.it/gesi.htm.

OMG (1997). CORBAMed: Healthcare Domain Specifications. http://www.omg.org/corba/cmfull.html.

Orfali, R. & Harkey, D. (1998). *Client/Server Programming with JAVA and CORBA* (2nd ed.), New York: J.Wiley & Sons.

Chapter 18

Scanning and Image Processing System (SIPS) for Medication Ordering

Stephen L. Chan
Hong Kong Baptist University, Hong Kong

This chapter presents a physician order entry system in the ward (for medication prescriptions) by using scanning and image processing. Important design and operational requirements are presented. Then the scanning and imaging processing system (SIPS) is described. SIPS integrates different information technologies including scanning, bar code and other marks recognition, intelligent image capturing, server database access and retrieval, and network communication and printing. SIPS uses specially designed order forms for doctors to write orders that are then scanned into the computer that performs recognition and image processing. The resulting orders, including doctor's handwritten images and other order information, are transmitted to the destinations electronically. SIPS reduces human effort (and errors). We observe that SIPS is an innovative use of information technology to meet the needs of a hospital that requires paper-and-pen operations. SIPS can be extended to meet other operational needs as an alternate input method.

INTRODUCTION

This chapter presents a physician ordering entry system in the ward (for medication prescriptions) by using scanning and image processing. Important design and operational issues that need to be considered by developers of similar end-user computer systems are presented. Then the scanning and imaging

Previously Published in the *Journal of End User Computing, vol.13, no.3*, Copyright © 2001, Idea Group Publishing.

processing system (SIPS) is described. SIPS was developed for the Hong Kong Baptist Hospital (HKBH), Kowloon, Hong Kong, and has been in successful operation for over three years in the hospital.

The development of SIPS was based on end-user directed requirements. SIPS makes use of and integrates different information technologies, including scanning, bar code and other marks recognition, intelligent image capturing, server database access and retrieval, and network communication and printing. The use of SIPS led to the implementation of new operational procedures, resulting in improved quality healthcare delivery in the ward and increased productivity of the medical personnel.

The End-User Context

The end-user context of an end-user computer system is important. A recent study can be found in establishing the role of an end user per se in strategic information systems planning (Hackney, Kawalek & Dhillon, 1999). There are studies in establishing the importance of the end-user context in identifying requirements in end-user systems development (Gammack, 1999) and in measuring end-user computing success (Shayo, Guthrie, & Igbaria, 1999). As discussed in the study by Komito (1998) of the use of a system of electronic files to replace paper files, the end-user considerations were identified as the difficulties for the transition. Paper documents are perceived to be 'information rich', providing control of information for occupational status and position. As a result, there is a perceived need for the user to defend 'occupational boundaries,' thus discouraging the use of electronic information. Indeed, in our effort to computerize ward procedures, we found that the end-user context was very crucial in determining the available technical options. More specifically, in developing a medication ordering system in HKBH, we have the following real-life scenario.

It is a 700-bed private general hospital. The ordering of medication by the doctors is dominated by the practice of using the traditional paper-and-pen operations. For several reasons, it is considered not possible to replace this traditional way and to introduce a direct physician order entry (POE) method in which the doctors enter the medication orders directly into the computer. Firstly, there is a large number (1,000+) of visiting doctors. These doctors have very different backgrounds and their age range spans over 40 years. Furthermore, some of the doctors visit the Hospital only occasionally when their patients are admitted to the Hospital. Therefore, it is not practical to hold training classes for these doctors. Even if they are trained, they may not be able to remember how to use a POE system in their occasional visits. Secondly, the doctors are specialists in their own medical fields and many are not proficient in the use of the computer. For some individuals, even their typing skills are in doubt. (Typing skills were recognized as the biggest stumbling block in one hospital computerization effort by Blignaut and McDonald, 1999). Nevertheless, their aim is in the practice of their medical specialties and they would not see the need to learn to use the computer. Thirdly, many of the computer works are viewed as administrative and are considered to be the responsibilities of the Hospital. Some doctors would be resistant to spend time to learn and perform the tasks that are perceived as administrative and the responsibilities of the Hospital.

Furthermore, there are also pragmatic considerations. Doctors visit their patients in the Hospital outside the office hours of their clinics. They do not normally spend a lot of time at the Hospital and when they are at the Hospital, their main concern is with the patients. They would prefer to use their most proficient (and efficient) way to place their medication orders, which is the paper-and-pen method.

For such hospitals under such situational necessity and with such pragmatic considerations, it is therefore necessary to assume the paper-and-pen method as given. Nevertheless, such hospitals are to look for effective and efficient ways of handling the remaining business processes of filling doctors' medication orders.

Medication Ordering Overview

We break down the operational process of medication ordering into four sub-processes: Order Capturing, Order Sending, Order Receiving, and Order Processing. We summarize in Figure 1 our overview of several methods. Traditionally,

Figure 1: Methods of Order Entry Overview

Method	Order Capturing	Order Sending	Order Receiving	Order Processing
Traditional Manual	Paper and Pen Operations by Physicians	Manual Delivery by Hospital Staff	Manual Receipt by Pharmacy Staff	Medication Dispensing by Pharmacy Staff
Improved Manual	Paper and Pen Operations by Physicians	Delivery by Hospital Staff via Fax	Fax Printing at Pharmacy Fax Machine	Medication Dispensing by Pharmacy Staff
Direct Physician Order Entry	Computer Entry by Physicians into Database	Computer Processing of Database Information for Network Printing	Order Printing at Pharmacy Printer	Medication Dispensing by Pharmacy Staff with Database Information
Order Scanning and Imaging System	Paper and Pen Operations by Physicians	Computer Scanning of Orders at Ward into Database & Information Processed for Network Printing	Order Printing at Pharmacy Printer	Medication Dispensing by Pharmacy Staff with Database Information

our ordering method has been manual. Orders originate from physicians. These orders are captured by paper-and-pen operations performed by the physicians. Simply, they write down their orders on paper that may be specially designed forms and may be of multiple copies. A hospital staff member would then hand carry these paper orders to the Pharmacy, and the Pharmacy staff would receive the paper orders and dispense medication accordingly.

As facsimile machines are available, there are hospitals that use an "improved" manual method. With this method, the order capturing process continues to be manual, using paper and pen. However, the hospital staff sends the orders and the Pharmacy staff receives the orders by using the facsimile machine.

The computer-based Direct Physician Order Entry (POE) System has been put forth for over 20 years (Sittig and Stead, 1994). Based on the above breakdown of operational sub-processes, the direct POE System would require physicians to use the computers to enter their orders into the computer database. The order would then be transmitted via the network for the Pharmacy staff to receive the orders. One way is for the order to be printed at the Pharmacy printer, with relevant patient and order information. Sittig and Stead (1994) provide a good review of the state of the art, and reported on POE implementation cases and elaborate on the rationale for, the social barriers to, and the logistical challenges involved in, successful implementation of a direct POE system. System design issues were also raised. A recent evaluation of POE implementation in one hospital can be found in Lee et. al. (1996). We have developed a fourth method – the Scanning and Image Processing System (SIPS).

THE SCANNING AND IMAGE PROCESSING SYSTEM (SIPS) FOR MEDICATION ORDERING

The operation of SIPS makes use of specially designed medication order forms for doctors to write their orders. The forms are to be scanned by ward staff (clerks or nurses). The computer then performs recognition of barcode and marks. Handwritten orders in the scanned forms are captured as images. Orders are generated that include images as well as patient information (from the form as well as from the Hospital Information System (HIS) databases) and are transmitted to the Pharmacy printer via the network. Additionally, their order images are kept in the SIPS database for ready reference by means of unique order numbers generated by the system.

The system attempts to minimize the introduction of drastically new operational procedures. As far as the doctors are concerned, the operation of this system is very similar to the usual practice, i.e., they continue to provide handwritten orders. The system reduces human effort by eliminating the sending of the orders to the destination by hand. The system also has built-in features to detect and avoid possible scanning and processing errors.

SIPS was developed to tolerate faults for a smooth operation in the ward where staff are not normally highly proficient in handling the computer. For example, SIPS checks for the readiness of the scanner and printer. It detects and corrects skewing. This becomes even more important because of hardware aging and fatigue. The handwriting by the doctors may be too light and the images captured may not be legible. SIPS sets a high scanning intensity level so that such handwriting can be captured and legibility ensured. On the other hand, the barcode recognition requires SIPS to set a lower scanning intensity level. Finally, in order to avoid small dirty spots to be recognized as marks, SIPS allows a user-specified black value threshold for these marks.

SIPS Design and Operational Requirements

In developing an order entry system using scanning and imaging, we observe that there are design issues and operational requirements for the system in order that the system may serve as an effective supporting tool in real-life operations. The design and operational requirements (which reflect our lessons learned) for this system are as follows:

Paper-and-Pen Operations

There should be minimal impact on the physicians. In other words, it was considered a requirement that physicians should not have to be trained to use the system, nor should they be required to change their ways of doing things.

Automation

It was considered important that as much automation as possible should be used for efficient and accurate operations, as long as high reliability is maintained.

User Friendly

The system must be simple and easy to use. Supporting staff (nurses and ward clerks) have a varied degree of computer proficiency. Since this is a 24-hour operation, at times, the system has to be used at night when technical support is scarce. Thus, computer proficiency should not be required. Furthermore, there is always staff turnover. It is important that the system can be learned easily by new staff, with minimal on-the-job training.

Assured Quality

Quality must be assured. A goal was set such that it is 100% reliable. By this, we mean, when the system declares a job completed, it is completed totally correct. In other words, we need a high quality system that can detect errors and if possible, correct them. If the error cannot be corrected, the users should be notified and helpful information provided for the users to make the corrections. The information handled by the system must be accurate and complete. Our effort in reaching this goal was evolutionary. All anticipated errors were programmed with error capture, exception handling, and graceful degradation. Then, subsequent unforeseen errors were debugged and appropriate measures were built into the system. We then observed, after the first six months of operations, that we were able to account for all errors and failures. For example, due to scanner usage fatigue, at very rare occasions, the scanner returned a scanning success while failing to capture the image. The result was a successful scan but then the recipient was sent a blank order. To handle this, we added a test that would require the size of the scanned image to be larger than a certain minimum. If the size were to be below the minimum, while receiving a successful scan from the scanner, the program would declare a failure and would prompt the user to scan again. Furthermore, it seems obvious that recognition of hand-written orders would be disastrous and the error rate would be operationally unacceptable. One recent study reported 87%-93% accuracy in two handwriting recognizers of letters under specially constrained environment (MacKenzie and Chang, 1999). Even with such level of accuracy, errors would be disastrous in a hospital environment and any system with handwriting recognition would fail operationally.

Fault Tolerance
The system should have a high degree of fault tolerance. It should cater to as many exceptions as possible. Appropriate automated exceptions handling procedures should be built into the system and user intervention should be the last resort.

Contingency
A graceful degradation should be achieved in case of system failure. The contingency plan should aim for 'business as usual' backup procedures.

SIPS SYSTEM ARCHITECTURE
The overall system architecture of SIPS is shown in Figure 2. At each Nurse Station, there is a personal computer (PC), a scanner, and a printer installed. The scanner is used to scan medication order forms to be sent to the Pharmacy. The printer is used for local printing of scan reports. The computer (PC) communicates with the SIPS server and accesses data through a network. It also accesses the

Figure 2: System Architecture of SIPS

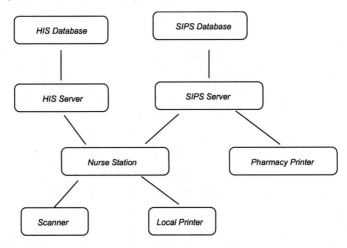

hospital's information system database via the Hospital Information System (HIS) server by calling SIPS/HIS interface routines.

The SIPS server stores and retrieves image data of patients (from the SIPS database) and redirects output images to remote Pharmacy printers for printing. These printers, physically located in the Pharmacy, are connected to the System via the Novell network. At the same time, order information is stored in Oracle tables in the SIPS database that is stored in the SIPS server hard disks.

The PC at the Nurse Station serves also as a client to the HIS server (run by the IBM RISC 6000 machine on AIX). In operating this system, data will have to be uploaded and downloaded between the HIS and SIPS databases. This is accomplished by various HIS/SIPS interface routines and procedures.

SIPS FUNCTIONAL FEATURES

The following functional features of SIPS are identified to be necessary system capabilities for an operational ordering system using scanning and image processing.

Recognition and Image Processing

SIPS performs bar-code recognition to determine the patient-owner of the form. There are specially designed marks to be detected for skew detection and for relative location identification. There are boxes to be recognized (to determine if they are marked) for specific actions such as if the order is an urgent order and/or a discharge order.

There are three image sections on the form. The first section contains patient information. This is always captured and included in the printed order at the

Pharmacy printer. The second section is for the doctor to write clinical/diagnostic information. For this section, a mark box is provided for the user to indicate whether this image section should be used in the printed order and saved for future use. Otherwise, the stored image should be used instead. Finally, the third section is for the doctor to write the medication order. Since the forms are used for multiple visits and orders, the relevant order image has to be identified by the user before each scan. A line-used column is available for the user to mark the portion of the page that is not relevant to the current scan, and the beginning and the ending of the relevant image. Based on these markings, SIPS would intelligently capture the image that is relevant to the current order.

Information Identification and Validation

The form owner (patient) is represented in the database by a unique number for the current admission. This admission number is bar code printed on the order form. After SIPS recognizes the value of the number, validation is required. The recognized admission number is used to search the hospital database. The admission number must represent an admission with a patient who is still not yet discharged. However, this is not sufficient because a slight error in recognizing the admission number may lead to a different but not yet discharged patient.

Another validation process was implemented. Two check digits are used for this validation. Each digit of the admission number is weighted by a prime number and the check digit is determined to be the remainder of the modulus for a certain value of the weighted sum. Since a juxtaposition of two digits with a slight change in their values may result into the same check digit, another set of prime numbers is used for a second check digit.

Fault Detection and Correction

Forms are either placed on the flatbed of the scanner or are fed into the scanner by an automatic document feeder. The primary fault is form skewing including translation and rotation. Skewing is detected and the degree of skewing determined in SIPS. Position and angle corrections are performed. But for large skewing which may induce significant errors, total rejection action is taken and the users are advised to rescan such forms.

Another possible fault may be due to hardware aging and failure. Various equipment fault detection and corrective actions are built into the system.

Database and Image Storage

SIPS is integrated with the hospital's Pharmacy system via a unique order number generated each time an order is successfully scanned. A record is created in the database so that subsequent query can be made to retrieve captured images that were stored in the database.

Security

The security for program access, database access, and network access is maintained.

SIPS MODULES

SIPS is composed of two modules: Ordering Module and Order System Maintenance Module. The Ordering Module provides all necessary facilities for the performance of necessary activities in sending requests of medications for the patients, from the wards to the Pharmacy. This module encompasses all the activities related to the ordering of medication. The basic process consists of the preparation of specially designed forms, the completion of these forms, the scanning of these forms, the printouts at the receiving end, and the managing activities of these orders subsequent to scanning. The Order System Maintenance Module provides needed facilities for maintaining SIPS.

COMMENTS

SIPS has been successfully implemented and has been in operation for over three years. Our key observations are summarised below.

Improved Operations

There are, on average, 500 scans per day, which are performed primarily in the morning. SIPS has been running very well and has improved operations. There is little change to the doctor's paper-and-pen method. Since each form can be marked in a matter of seconds and scanned in less than a minute, the orders can be sent quickly to the Pharmacy. At times, follow-up actions (if needed) such as the substitute of a drug in shortage can be initiated quickly. Furthermore, there is no need for making copies or sending the original order to the Pharmacy. SIPS has been operated mainly by ward clerks and thus, valued medical personnel (doctors and nurses) are freed from performing the ordering task. We observe that SIPS indeed has improved the operations with much reduced efforts and that the system has been in continued use without complaints or requests for an alternate procedure. As a matter of fact, it has been commented that the hospital cannot 'live without' SIPS.

System Integration of Information Technologies

SIPS is a system based on the integration of different information technologies including scanning, bar code and other marks recognition, intelligent image capturing, server database access and retrieval, and network communication and printing. Furthermore, we also have to integrate the printing and image processing of the Chinese characters used in the forms and the order images.

Business Process Reengineering (BPR)

The process of medication ordering was reengineered. We used the 'clean-slate' approach (Hammer & Champy, 1993) to develop SIPS. We first developed the operations and procedures for the system before defining the system specifications. The operations are concerned with *what* has to be performed. The procedures specify *how* the operations are to be accomplished. These have to be specified in detail in order that the system may work in live operations. Many details are defined in the system manuals (Chan, 1995).

As to the 'clean-slate' approach, we deviated from it in the implementation of the redesigned process. As discussed earlier, it was deemed necessary to assume the paper-and-pen method as given. On this basis, we looked for effective operations and efficient procedures for handling the business processes of filling doctors' medication orders with the aim of improvement in meeting patients' healthcare needs.

Referral Letters

There is an important complementary component to SIPS for it to work effectively in live operations in a hospital. Many patients to be admitted to the hospital carry with them a referral letter with medication and investigation orders for immediate action upon admission. In order that these medication orders can be ordered from the ward using SIPS, the medication orders in a referral letter must be 'transcribed' onto the order forms. Instead of 'transcribing' by hand, we have a system that scan and capture these referral letters as images and have them printed on the order section of the order form. Then, upon admission to the ward, SIPS can be used for placing these orders immediately. The basic features of this system are the capturing of a referral letter as image, and appropriately reducing the image size and then printing the image to fit into the order form.

Extension

SIPS has been designed to include scanning and image printing to various supporting units for a total of 15 different investigation order types such as operating theatre (for booking), laboratory, X-ray, ultra-sound, magnetic resonance imaging (MRI) orders, etc. There are additional designs such as a section for clinical and diagnosis information and the mark boxes for different destinations. Many more detailed operations and procedures have been specified.

CONCLUSION

In this chapter, we presented SIPS, a system that integrates different information technologies in a way to meet the needs of a particular end-user group. We presented different design and operational requirements of SIPS that could be considerations for the design and development of a similar system. The different functional features of SIPS presented should also be of relevance.

SIPS indeed meets the need of a particular type of end-user that requires paper-and-pen operations. With the improvement of computer competency of the medical profession, we foresee the need diminishing (perhaps slowly). But with the improvement of information technology, we conjecture the concept of "bringing the computer to the bed." There will no longer be a need to enter orders and placing orders separately. Physician orders will be directly entered into the computer and communicated immediately to the service organizations (such as the Pharmacy). In future, it may be pen computing, using a pen tablet or a palmtop computer. It may be voice input. These may all be running over a wireless network.

REFERENCES

Blignaut, P.J. & McDonald, T. (1999). The user interface for a computerized patient record system for primary health care in a third world environment. *Journal of End User Computing,* 11(2), 29-33.

Chan, S. L. (1995). *Computerized Image Processing System (CHIPS) - Ward Ordering Subsystem: System Manual, Operations Manual, Procedure Manual, Test Plan, Implementation Plan, and Contingency Plan - Version 2.*

Gammack, J.G. (1999). Constructive design environments: implementing end-user systems development. *Journal of End User Computing* 11(1), 15-23.

Hackney, R., Kawalek, J., & Dhillon, G. (1999). Strategic information systems planning: perspectives on the role of the "end-user" revisited. *Journal of End User Computing* 11(2), 3-12.

Hammer, M. & Champy, J. (1993). *Reengineering the Corporation - A Manifesto for Business Revolution,* Nicholas Brealey.

Komito, L. (1998). Paper "work" and electronic files: defending professional practice. *Journal of Information Technology* 13, 235-246.

Lee, F., Teich, J. M, Spurr, C. D, & Bates, D.W. (1996). Implementation of physician order entry: user satisfaction and self-reported usage patterns. *J Am Med Informatics Assoc.* 3, 42-55.

MacKenzie, I.S. & Chang, L. (1999). A performance comparison of two handwriting recognizers. *Interacting with Computers* 11, 283-297.

Shayo, C., Guthrie, R., & Igbaria, M. (1999). Exploring the measurement of end user computing success. *Journal of End User Computing* 11(1), 5-14.

Sittig, D.F. & Stead, W.W. (1994). Computer-based physician order entry: the state of the art. *J Am Med Informatics Assoc.* 1, 108-123.

Chapter 19

Organizational and Implementation Issues of Patient Data Management Systems in an Intensive Care Unit

Nathalie Mitev
The London School of Economics, United Kingdom

Sharon Kerkham
Salford University, United Kingdom

Since the National Health Service reforms were introduced, the NHS has moved towards a greater emphasis on accountability and efficiency of healthcare. These changes rely on the swift delivery of IT systems, implemented into the NHS because of the urgency to collect data to support these measures. This case study details the events surrounding the introduction of a patient data management system into an intensive care unit in a UK hospital. It shows that its implementation was complex and involved organisational issues related to the costing of healthcare, legal and purchasing requirements, systems integration, training and staff expertise, and relationships with suppliers. It is suggested that the NHS is providing an R&D environment which others are benefiting from. The NHS is supporting software development activities that are not recognised, and the true costs of this task are difficult to estimate. It is also argued that introducing PDMS crystallises many different expectations making them unmanageably complex. This could also be due to PDMS being a higher order innovation that attempts to integrate information systems products and services with the core business.

Previously Published in the *Journal of End User Computing, vol.13, no.3*, Copyright © 2001, Idea Group Publishing.

INTRODUCTION

The National Health Service (NHS) costs the UK approximately £38 billion a year (James, 1995) of which £220 million is spent on IT (Lock, 1996). New IT applications not only support administrative functions and medical diagnosis, but are increasingly used to support resource management and medical audit (Metnitz and Lenz, 1995; Sheaff and Peel, 1995). One such application is patient data management systems (PDMS) in intensive care units, where nurses' main task of planning and implementing patient care requires an awareness of a set of physiological parameters which provide an overview of the patient's general condition (Ireland et al, 1997). The collection of patient data is also a legal requirement of the NHS Executive. The implementation of these new technologies is not proving easy for the NHS. Healthcare professionals involved with IT projects often lack in experience of IT development. Risks are higher in clinical applications which require strong user involvement. These technologies are also being implemented into the NHS at a fast rate, because of the urgency to collect data to support accountability measures.

The NHS has changed quite dramatically over recent years, not least with the introduction of "competitive market forces" (Peel, 1996; Protti et al., 1996). The current healthcare reforms come from various government White Papers, moving the philosophy of the NHS towards emphasising business themes and client choice, and they rely on the 'swift' delivery of IT systems (Willcocks, 1991). All chief executives of health authorities and NHS Trusts are now 'accountable officers', responsible for the efficient use of resources, and are personally responsible for performance (Warden, 1996). Sotheran (1996) argues that using IT in the NHS entails new work structures and changes in activities performed, and that re-distribution of control and power will occur as a result. Bloomfield et al. (1992) found a diversity of interpretations by those involved, that the intended focus of the systems varied from management responsibility, medical speciality, doctor to patient group levels, and that views from one peer group could be imposed upon another. Lock (1996) advocates that "the impact of computer systems on patient care as well as on the business objectives of hospitals should be considered". The 'benefits realisation' approach (Treharne, 1995) is recommended to quantify and document benefits. Donaldson (1996) claims that this process can help justify the investments. However, it seems that the 'benefits realisation' methods are not being implemented or are failing for the following reasons (Treharne, 1995): an over emphasis on IT relative to other critical issues; a lack of focus; a shortage of skills; ineffective business/IT partnership; absence of benefit management process.

Generally, the rapid movement of information technologies into healthcare organisations has raised managerial concern regarding the capability of today's institutions to satisfactorily manage their introduction. Indeed, several healthcare institutions have consumed "huge amounts of money and frustrated countless people in wasted information systems implementation efforts" and there are "no easy answers as to why so many health informatics projects are not more successful" (Pare, Elam and Ward, 1997). In this light, the aim of this study is to provide a deeper understanding of how clinical information systems are being implemented, using a case study methodology.

OBJECTIVES AND METHODS

From a theoretical standpoint, it is suggested that adoption and diffusion of information systems (IS) depends on the type of IS innovation concerned. Swanson (1994) and McMaster et al. (1997) suggest there are three IS innovation types:
- Process innovations which are confined to the IS core.
- Application of IS products and services to support the administrative core of the business.
- Integration of IS products and services with core business technology.

PDMS are innovative computer systems, which attempt to integrate administrative functions and clinical decision-making. Introducing this third type of innovation tends to have far broader ramifications across the overall business domain. Our research objective is to illustrate the resulting complexity of the relationship between this type of technology and organisational change through the investigation of as many facets as possible of the implementation of a PDMS in an intensive care unit (ICU).

The case study explores these implementation issues and is based on an in-depth examination of the introduction of a PDMS in an ICU in order to offer insights to those who have responsibility for managing complex and risky information system implementation projects. Intensive fieldwork was carried out with members of a PDMS project in an intensive care unit (ICU) in a Northwest hospital, over a period of one year (July 1996 to July 1997). This corresponded to the introduction of a commercial PDMS and its early adaptation to this particular context, which was an interesting opportunity as PDMS were still rare in the UK in 1996. An online PDMS system was being introduced to help with the enormous amount of data that is produced from advanced monitoring equipment.

The case study approach was chosen because it allows the researcher to ask penetrating questions and capture the richness of organisational behaviour. A case study approach is also generally recommended in order to gain insight into emerging and previously unresearched topics and when it is difficult to control behavioural events or variables (Benbasat, Goldstein and Mead, 1987; Kaplan and Maxwell, 1994). This qualitative approach seemed particularly appropriate since incorporating computers into all aspects of daily ICU operations is a "formidable task" both technically and logistically, which requires "close cooperation between physicians, nurses, basic scientists, computer specialists, hospital administrators and equipment manufacturers" (Nenov, Read and Mock, 1994).

Given the research has a descriptive and exploratory focus, a combination of data collection techniques was utilised, as recommended by Marshall and Rossman (1989): observation of everyday practices, attendance at meetings and training sessions, informal participation and in-depth interviews with all members of the PDMS project (software suppliers, hospital information systems staff, medical physicists, nurses, medical consultants, hospital administrators). Of particular importance at the time were the legal, purchasing and administrative constraints specific to the NHS that were placed on the ICU. These were also researched using secondary internal sources to gain an understanding of the broader organisational set up and also because they affected how the software was purchased, modified and implemented. The commercial PDMS had to be dramatically modified to suit its users, and this transformation is currently still continuing.

This combination of such qualitative techniques has been used in other IS studies in healthcare (Kaplan and Maxwell, 1994); they enable the elicitation of organisational members' views and experiences in their own terms about sensitive matters and issues of their own choice, instead of collecting data that are simply a choice among preestablished response categories. Additionally, research of this kind is appropriate for unravelling the complexities of organisational change, for providing rich insights and generating an understanding of the reality of a particular situation, and can provide a good basis for discussion. On the other hand, relying on organisational members' qualitative interpretations and complex associations between events, facts and a range of organisational issues makes it more difficult to separate "data" from findings.

The evolution of information systems in healthcare and their introduction in intensive care is first briefly described. The case study events are then presented covering: the history of the project, the initial specifications, the choice of software, the hardware requirements and difficulties, the programming changes performed, the training carried out, the practical problems experienced, the continuing issue of software upgrades, user satisfaction, organisational practices and the role of suppliers. The main findings about implementation and organisational issues are identified as: time and cost constraints, underestimation of labour effort, the perception of IS implementation as a one off event, the power of suppliers, the lack of project management, the difficulties in managing expectations, the issues of IT expertise and internal conflicts. Discussion points centre on the vision of IS as a technical fix, the difficulty in transferring technical solutions to different contexts, the problem in estimating benefits, and the institutional barriers and politics. Finally, it is concluded that these implementation difficulties are symptomatic of a complex IS innovation which attempts to integrate technology to core business processes.

INFORMATION SYSTEMS IN HEALTHCARE

The introduction of PDMS in intensive care units is taking place in a broad context of using computers in the NHS. Hospital information support systems (HISS) are integrated systems supporting all the hospital operations. The activities and data relating to every patient (tests requested, results reported, etc.) are fed into the financial and information systems of the hospital, to enable hospitals to meet the requirements of the contracting environment (Thorp, 1995a). Guidelines were published as a result of studies of HISS implementation (Thorp, 1995b), which recommend, for instance, data interchange standards and the need for "benefits realisation."

The development of the electronic patient record (EPR) further supports clinicians in the recording of medical records (McKenna, 1996). The EPR describes the record of the periodic care provided by one institution. One aim of EPRs is to be developed into a "comprehensive" information system for the whole of a hospital and beyond. The UK EPR programme has five EPR and Integrated Clinical Workstation demonstrator sites (Peel et al., 1997; Urquhart and Currell, 1999). Implementing an EPR is a very complex operation and involves major organisational and technological changes (Atkinson and Peel, 1997). By holding all patient data electronically and interfacing with the various administrative and clinical systems, the aim is to extract information for all levels. For example, as part of its EPR project, the Wirral Hospital NHS Trust has implemented electronic prescribing, whereby patient data is assembled and the prescription can be issued and printed without the need to access manual records. Wirral Hospital has the largest computerised prescribing system in the UK and is developing a rule-based decision support system to trigger pharmacy interventions (Moore, 1995).

Decision support systems enhance medical diagnoses and there are broadly two types of support systems (Modell et al., 1995). Firstly, there are medical diagnostic DSS; these systems give alternative/supportive diagnostic information based on the input from the user and are implemented into specific areas of medicine. Broader systems are being developed to make use of EPRs (Miller, 1994; Pitty and Reeves, 1995). Secondly, there are databases that support the collection of clinical data, presenting and analysing the information for medical decision support (Wyatt, 1991). An example can be found in ICUs, where monitoring equipment collects data, which feed into a patient data management system.

Intensive care costs can account for up to 20% of a hospital's total expenditure (Metnitz and Lenz, 1995), and there is an increasing demand by management to cut these costs. Rapid development of monitoring devices has increased the data available from ICUs ten-fold. The aim of PDMS is to collect data from monitoring devices at the bedside of the patient, for medical and statistical management reporting. The ability to fully analyse this data has not previously been available, due to the large amounts of data that have to be processed and the slow arrival of outputs. There are only a few systems that have the ability to process PDMS data for quality management and cost accounting (Metnitz et al., 1996).

Nonetheless, "basic" PDMS are being introduced to help support these functions in the future. For instance, the University Clinics of Vienna have developed a system called ICDEV (Intensive Care Data Evaluation System), which is a scientific database tool for analysing complex intensive care data (Metnitz et al., 1995). It is built to interface with two commercially available PDMS, Care Vue 9000 (Hewlett Packard, Andover, USA) and PICIS Chart+ (PICIS, Paris, France). The ICDEV enables the PDMS to be used for cost accounting, quality control and auditing. ICDEV was first used at the Medical ICU of the Vienna General Hospital in June 1994 and its Neonatal ICU in December 1994 with Care Vue 9000, and in April 1995 with PICIS Chart+ at its Cardiothoracic ICU. Metnitz et al. (1995) report problems of integration with existing local networks and databases, which have required the expertise of engineers. Metnitz and Lenz (1995) have found that commercial PDMS can help optimise bed-occupancy and facilitate analysis for scientific and quality control.

On the other hand, they are expensive, require specialised maintenance, and they may not be faster than manual techniques. Metnitz and Lenz (1995) conclude that commercial PDMS still have some way to go before they are truly useful for both clinical and management analysis purposes. They state that those implementing PDMS must plan sufficiently before installation and implementation for reconfiguration, as most PDMS interfaces are presently not practical or reliable, and that cooperation between the system developer and purchaser is mandatory. Urschitz et al (1998) report on local adjustments and enhancements of Care Vue 9000 such as knowledge-based systems for calculating the parenteral nutrition of newborn infants or for managing mechanical ventilation in two neonatal ICUs. They state that PDMS have to be constantly adapted to the users' needs and to the changing clinical environment, and that there are yet unsolved problems of data evaluation and export.

In terms of implementation issues, Langenberg (1996) argues that PDMS require good organisation; specifications need to be defined before the process is started; a system should include data acquisition, database management and archiving of data; and coupling with a hospital information system and the possibility of data exchange is mandatory. However, Butler and Bender (1999) claim that the current economic climate makes the cost of ICU computer systems prohibitive for many institutions; that the literature describing ICU computer system benefits is often difficult to interpret; and that each implementation has many unique variables which make study comparison and replication potentially impossible. They suggest changes and issues can only be evaluated uniquely in each study unit or institution.

Pierpont and Thilgen (1995) measured the effects of computerised charting on nursing in intensive care; they found that the total time manipulating data (entering or reviewing data) post-installation was unchanged; that time spent in patients' rooms did not alter, although nurses had more time available for monitoring at the central station; and that computerised charting will not necessarily provide ICU nurses with a net excess of time for tasks unrelated to manipulating data.

CASE STUDY IN AN INTENSIVE CARE UNIT
History of the Project

The ICU at a UK Northwest hospital had long felt the need for a PDMS. The consultants first raised the idea for a computerised system that would collate and generate information from bedside monitors in the early 1980s. At the time the technology was not available. The "management team" for the ICU consists of medical consultants, a Directorate manager, representatives of the nursing staff, medical physicists and maintenance staff. The medical physicists build medical applications and equipment for the hospital. The management team determines organisational and purchasing issues for the ICU. In 1994, the management team realised that the ICU would have to update the existing patient monitoring system to function effectively. Investigations started and a request for purchasing a monitoring system and possibly a PDMS was given to the Regional Purchasing Office.

At the beginning of December 1994, the request for funds for capital equipment was agreed. The system, monitors and PDMS had to be on site by the end of the financial year (31 March, 1995). All purchasing for the NHS has to go out to European Open Tender before it is bought; this further reduced the time available to the management team to choose a system, leaving no more than six weeks for appraisal of possible systems.

PDMS Specifications

The management team developed the following criteria to which the system had to adhere: the hardware was to have a life span of 7-10 years; the PDMS was to be combined with the monitoring system; the cheapest system had to be chosen, unless the case was strong enough to convince the Regional Office otherwise; the PDMS could be adapted to "fit" around users; charts produced had to be the same as the existing paper charts. The paper charts used by the staff are an agreed standard within the unit, which has taken a very long time to develop.

Choice of Software

Due to the time constraints, the scale of evaluation had to be considerably reduced and investigations were limited to the UK. The only PDMS in working practice that the team was able to review was at Great Ormond Street Hospital in London. This PDMS did not fulfill all their criteria and was considered to be too difficult to use by the nursing staff representative. Once the purchase had been put out to European Open Tender, the ICU was then obliged to choose the cheapest system, which was the PICIS Marquette system, and also the team's preferred choice due to its adaptability, at a cost of approximately £600,000. The monitoring system was introduced in March 1995. However, the PDMS was not fully implemented due to problems with the reporting/charts facility and was still not fully implemented two years (summer 1997) after purchasing the system.

Hardware Laboratory Connections

The PDMS software program was to collate blood gas levels and observations directly from the monitoring equipment at the bedside of the patient. Some examples of measures are tracheal suction, heart rate, blood temperature, sedation score, peak pressure, ventilation mode, pain score, and pulmonary mean. However, data from laboratory results, ventilators, drug infusions and bedside observations which were intended to be available automatically through laboratory connections, were still entered manually during the period of the study.

Programming Changes

A systems manager from the medical physics department was appointed to adapt the system and has had to make considerable changes to it. PICIS Marquette have had to divulge information about the software that would not normally be given to the client. The systems manager has become an expert in the adaptation of this product and is consulted by the supplier for her expertise. There is no formal contractual agreement between the two parties. The relationship is very much based on trust. The systems supplier has reflected that, "*the software was never meant to be adapted as much as it has been*" (Interview, 1997). On the other hand, a medical consultant commented that "*the software was chosen because it could be adapted. The software would not have been used [as it was], even with training*" (Interview, 1996). The systems manager was originally employed to spend 1-2 days a week adapting the software. However, she worked full time for the period 1995-1997 and the following modifications were made: medical charts from the monitors and manual inputs have been reformulated to be the same as the written medical reports; new icons have been designed to ease user interaction; the drug list was extended; 10 screens have had to be altered to fit with nurses' practices, which has meant changing the original programming.

Training

Training for the monitoring equipment was relatively smooth since staff was already familiar with this technology. Generally within the unit, the nursing staff is not used to computers. The Directorate manager, who had considerable input into choosing the system, is not computer literate. Nursing staff received training from clinical trainers from PICIS Marquette for the monitoring equipment before the equipment was introduced. The PDMS software has been in constant development so the system manager has run the PDMS training, since she is adapting the system. A charge nurse was designated to work with the systems manager and to give user feedback about the modifications. Five nurses identified as "super" trainers are trained by the systems manager, and they then train the other staff.

Practical Equipment Problems

The ICU staff did not want the PCs that operate the PDMS to be on tables at the bedside. Firstly, this would violate health and safety regulations; secondly this would not be practical in an already busy and hectic environment. The PDMS that the team saw before selection were desk-based. A "cart" was designed to put the PCs in, which was at an extra cost to the ICU. The first cart to arrive was like a giant washing machine, which was too big and obscured the view of the patient. It is vital in an ICU environment for the nurses to always see the patients. Once the PCs were housed in the carts, it was then found that the monitors were overheating and blowing up. Fans were fitted to the carts to cool the monitors; however, dust particles were then being blown over the patient, carrying the obvious danger of germs being spread. Such practical problems have generally been sorted out on-site by the Directorate manager. However, because of the charting and reporting problems, a paper system was still running alongside the computer system for two years after the introduction of the system.

Continuing Software Upgrades

Partly based on their experiences at this hospital, PICIS Marquette then decided to improve reporting and were at the time producing an upgrade of the system to make it act as a database. New facilities were to include a drug prescription facility and laboratory connections. Moreover, the PDMS was to enable data collation for different statistical purposes (Therapeutic Intervention

Scoring System, Intensive Care National Audit & Research Care, Contract Minimum Data Set and Hospital Episode Statistics). All of these areas overlap and the NHS Executive was still in discussions to decide if such duplication of information is required (Interview Hospital Administrator, 1997).

Whereas in the first implementation *"time has been the big problem"* (Interview Medical Physicist, 1996), the systems manager envisaged the upgrade implementation being a smoother operation, as the first version was already partly in use and there would be an overlap period. A spare PC was to be used to make changes and test the new software before installing it for the nursing staff. A further difficulty was that upgraded software needs all the changes that were implemented into the original software. This will be the case for all future upgrades. The systems manager is expected to carry out this time consuming activity along with any maintenance that the system requires.

User Satisfaction

Overall, nursing staff felt that they adapted well to the new monitoring equipment, after a few teething problems. The management team expected the ICU to be totally "paperless" by June 1996; however, this did not happen. The Directorate manager felt that this caused the nursing staff to become disenchanted with the system. Major adaptations to the system caused considerable delays. The Directorate manager commented that, the implementation has *"taken longer than anticipated, probably because we incorporated more as we have gone along"* (Interview, 1996).

Matching Working Practices

Using the software as it stood would have meant totally changing the work procedures of the staff and this is not possible in a working ICU. The management team decided to change the software package not the working practices, and the software was chosen because it could be adapted. However, the Directorate manager reflected that at the time of purchase the medical consultants *"thought that the system was going to do exactly what they wanted. We didn't realise there would be so many problems"* (Interview 1996). PICIS Marquette trainers were able to convince the medical consultants of the adaptability of the system and the concerns of the systems manager were overlooked. The organisational hierarchy and the power of the medical consultants obviously played an important part in the decision making process (Knights and Murray, 1994).

Role of Suppliers

Throughout the interviews it became very apparent that the PDMS was still very much in the R&D stage. Little was known by the users about how much the software would have to be modified. The software was chosen because of its adaptability, but this was based upon the suppliers' views of their own product. Suppliers played a great part in the introduction of this system. However, without informed professionals within the NHS, the IT systems purchased may not meet internal organisational needs easily. In this situation, it is hardly surprising that: *"the most difficult aspect of the implementation has been to convince staff that the system will save time when it is fully implemented, but at the moment this is not the case"* (Interview Hospital Administrator, 1997).

ANALYSIS OF FINDINGS
Time and Cost Constraints

The PDMS had to be purchased quickly and to a strict budget, which is fairly typical in the NHS. For instance, the failed introduction of a computer-aided dispatching system at the London Ambulance Services also suffered from arbitrary time and cost constraints. Purchasers were obliged to take the lowest tender unless there were "good and sufficient reasons to the contrary" (Flowers, 1996). However, "tight time-scales and inaccurate, inflexible funding have often occurred (...) due to government and departmental political exigencies, policies and pressures. (...) these factors need to be counterbalanced, even if this slows up decision making and implementation, if effective systems are to be delivered" (Willcocks, 1991).

Underestimation of Labour Effort

Knowledge-based systems such as diagnostic tools are likely to require more, rather than less, labour (Drucker, 1996). However, this extra cost was not accounted for when the system was purchased. The lifetime of the system was assumed to be 7-10 years rather than 4-5 years, which is recognised as more appropriate (Sotheran, 1996). There is the danger of staff responsible for procurement failing to recognise that it is dealing with something it does not understand.

It was found that the systems manager has had to work on the project full time. With little training, she has been able to keep up to date with the documentation, to ensure that modifications are recorded. The commitment by those involved has resulted in the software being modified and developed at a relatively cheap cost. However, the institution has not benefited from the experiences and knowledge gained from this project. The project is not seen as a long-term project and, as a consequence, detailed information is not available and the true costs are very difficult to judge. Furthermore, the hospital cannot secure a method of benefiting from profits produced by the sales of software they have helped to develop.

Equipment (such as the modified cart) or software (such as better charting/reporting tools) produced by the Medical Physicists Department are not patented.

One Off Purchase vs Long Term Investment

Despite the existence of a set of guidelines governing the procurement of NHS computer systems, called POISE (Procurement of Information Systems Effectively), there was little evidence that these guidelines were employed at the ICU. POISE seems to be regarded by ICU staff as useful for large systems, such as HISS. Funding for the project did not reflect the fact that the PDMS was an infrastructure investment and required long-term investment (Willcocks and Fitzgerald, 1993). It is recommended that off-the-shelf systems be purchased by the NHS, with some later modification (Bates, 1995), thereby giving more power to suppliers.

When computers are used to support patient care in the NHS, budgets are often funded year to year. They are seen as one-off software projects with some modification. The extent of modification can be very ambiguous, as has been seen in the case study. The introduction of computers in areas other than administration is bringing with it new challenges for healthcare professionals. The medical consultants felt that the modifications they required could be achieved, based on the advice of the supplier. Internal staff can have a far better understanding of the application. Yet giving responsibility of IT applications in critical environments to non-specialists can bring an enormous amount of risk (Heathfield et al., 1997).

Power of Suppliers

Due to the problems encountered during implementation, PICIS Marquette has probably made a considerable loss. On the other hand, the supplier has been able to lock in the customer by providing monitoring equipment that is only compatible with its own PDMS. The vendor planned to use the system at the ICU as a launch pad for further sales, as it was their only reference site in the UK. It can be used to show other NHS clients how the system can be adapted. The systems manager has built a trust-based relationship with the supplier and she imparts her knowledge to the supplier, which was made available on the PICIS Marquette Website (PICIS, 1997). Adaptability is a strong selling point, especially since off-the-shelf systems with some modification are recommended for purchase at the NHS. PICIS Marquette supplies free copies of the upgraded software to the ICU (Interview Systems Manager, 1997), whilst it benefits from the development work being carried out at the NHS expense. At present this situation may suit the ICU. However, there are no formal contracts that could help resolve problems if relations deteriorate.

Moreover, the true cost of the system and its development is hidden, not only in terms of upgrade purchasing, but labour costs. The main developer of the system, the systems manager, is employed as a medical physicist and not at the ICU. So the cost of this labour has not been added to the system cost. Also, should PICIS Marquette decide that they would no longer supply free software, the ICU will have an extra cost that they will not have planned for. PICIS Marquette made the coding of areas of the software more accessible to the ICU, which will mask the true effort required for other modifications. As a result, other NHS departments could start to follow the same route, unaware of the hidden costs. The case study has shown that suppliers can bring useful expertise; but they are not entirely without their own interests. The suppliers need to gain command of the business they are applying their IT products to; and conversely, the purchasers must become more knowledgeable about their own IT requirements (Peel, 1994).

Project Management

The ICU project has not benefited from any project management methodology such as PRINCE, as recommended by the NHS. The systems manager had no training into methodologies or formal software development methods. This has meant that she has had to "*find her way around*" (Interview Systems Manager, 1997). This led to "a lack of appreciation of complexity of the project" (Flowers, 1996). Negotiating and constantly changing requirements have highlighted the difficulties in agreeing aims. Without experience and knowledge of project planning, it is generally acknowledged that difficulties will arise. The case study has shown that medical systems are still evolving. This continual enhancement requires management and resources, just as the project required at its birth.

Managing Expectations

Initially the users of the PDMS were very excited about the implementation, with medical consultants pushing for its installation (Interviews Medical Consultants and Nurses, 1996-97). However, over the implementation period enthusiasm dwindled (Interview Hospital Administrator, 1997). This has probably occurred due to expectations being raised too high by "unrealistic claims of immediate advantages and benefits" (Thorp, 1995a). User involvement has gone far beyond working with a requirements analysis team. The users have been actively involved with producing their own specifications even though they had no experience or training (Interview Nurse Manager, 1996).

IT Expertise and Internal Conflicts

The Medical Physicists department in which the systems manager works is not part of the IT department. The IT department deals with administrative hardware and software applications. The Medical Physicists department is responsible for clinical equipment and applications. Medical physicists are only responsible for the clinical software they are asked to deal with. Departments often have their own arrangements for clinical IT. This makes the dissemination of information particularly difficult (Interview Medical Physicist, 1997). The laboratory connections were not implemented due to internal conflicts between the Laboratory and the ICU as to their areas of responsibilities. The Laboratory may have felt that by giving information they may have become redundant or that the ICU and the Department of Medical Physics were treading on their territory. These fragmented relationships between departments reflect the complex mix of expertise required in medical informatics.

DISCUSSION

Technical Fix?

There is a "growing awareness amongst those involved in the development and implementation of clinical systems that social and organisational issues are at least of equal importance as technical issues in ensuring the success of a system" (Protti and Haskell, 1996). However, there is still a tendency to see technology as void of values (Bloomfield, 1995) and perhaps paradoxically, to expect it to solve clinical, financial, management and quality problems, but without realising the organisational and technical complexities, human resources implications and associated costs. As Atkinson (1992) claims, information is now perceived as the lifeblood of the NHS to "enable all operations, clinical, nursing, financial, estates, human resources." But Coleman et al. (1993) argue that the clinical computing system is complex and that as we press it further to work in the complete care context, it tends to become unmanageably so. Hagland (1998) also argues that automating intensive patient care areas requires a different level of IT product, design and development. Medical consultants' clinical expectations of the PDMS were high. As Hoffman (1997) has found, persuading U.S. doctors to use IT goes beyond monetary incentives. However, the technology could not deliver and this may be because it was intended to fulfill both medical and management requirements.

Transferring Technical Solutions to Different Contexts

An example of a problem arising from seeing technology as a neutral solution can be seen in the unforeseen large number of software modifications, which were due to the commercial package not fitting in with ICU nursing practices. An important factor was that the package used is European, and care planning embedded in the software reflects more hierarchical and prescription-oriented care planning practices, that differ from UK practices where responsibility is more equally spread across staff.

Benefits Difficult to Estimate

The drivers for change have been accountability, demands for high quality services and cost effectiveness, but introducing IT may not be as beneficial as expected. With respect to hospital information systems, Bloomfield (1995) comments that "it is not evident that the efficiency gains secured through IT will outweigh the costs of constructing and implementing the systems involved." Friesdorf et al. (1994) claim that the flexibility of PDMS is far from expectations and that maintenance requires continuous effort which cannot be afforded. East (1992) states that few conclusive studies prove that ICU systems have a favourable cost-to-benefit ratio.

Institutional Barriers and Politics

Because of the NHS internal market, NHS Trusts purchase their own off-the-shelf IT systems through tendering. They are therefore foregoing the economies of scale previously possible in a unified NHS. NHS Trusts may save money through the tendering process, and benefit from a freedom of choice (as long as it is the lowest tender), but overall at an extra cost. It is considered that indirect human and organisational costs can be up to four times as high as the technology and equipment costs; this savings seems small in comparison (Willcocks, 1991).

Implementation of IT will not automatically guarantee communication between departments, as witnessed by the failure to set up laboratory connections. The way technology is introduced and used is a political process, involving people with different occupational cultures (Knights and Murray, 1994), with values influencing its use.

CONCLUSION

Healthcare is now a service that can be bought and sold, and whose effectiveness and efficiency can be measured. IT provides the means of collating this information, not only for administrative functions but also within patient care and clinical decision making. It is being used for clinical diagnosis, along with online data collection from monitoring equipment. Research into the introduction of PDMS in an ICU shows that there is still some way to go before their usefulness can be realised, partly because the demands on the technology are complex and technology itself has yet to be fully assessed. Realistically, the project investigated in our case study is still at the development stage, even if it is not recognised.

It would appear that the introduction of IS in the NHS is still perceived as an innovation of the second type (Howcroft and Mitev, 2000), i.e., one which only supports administrative processes, as opposed to a third type which integrates IS to core business processes. This would explain: the one-off purchasing approach; the difficulties in sustaining enthusiasm and user involvement; the underestimation of continuing labour costs and the dependence on a particular individual; and generally the lack of awareness of complex organisational implications of such integration. For instance, software had to be extensively modified to adapt to complex working practices in the ICU, which led to undue reliance on suppliers. IT skills were poor and also needed to be complemented with medical physics and this was not supported organisationally.

Recommendations from the supplier about the possible adaptability to their product were considered to be the most informed even though the hospital systems manager eventually carried out many modifications. There has been a lack of understanding about the complexities surrounding development both by purchaser and supplier. The cost and times for the project were completely arbitrary, laid down by managers outside of the implementation. Whilst suppliers are having to put a great deal of work into getting these new technologies into NHS sites, in the long run the supplier will benefit most from the development that is carried out at the NHS's expense. Healthcare professionals are performing tasks outside of their experience, purely out of necessity to get the project implemented. They were unable to perform to the best of their abilities or understand the complex minefield they were embarking upon.

An understanding of PDMS as innovations of the third type would see them as long-term investments with important organisational ramifications. It may ensure that cost and time constraints are more realistic; that project management is better applied; that adequate labour resources are allocated; that collaboration between medical physics and IT skills is taken into account; that expectations are better managed; and that institutional barriers are removed. This mismatch in terms of perception needs to be addressed to avoid future difficulties.

It is also argued that introducing PDMS crystallises too many different expectations making them unmanageably complex, particularly in the current economic climate; that more generally technology is perceived as a blank screen on which many expectations are projected; and that it takes on the often-conflicting values of its promoters, developers and users.

REFERENCES

Atkinson, C.J. (1992). *The information function in health care organisations*, Health Services Management Unit, University of Manchester, Manchester.

Atkinson, C.J. and Peel, V. (1997). *Transforming a hospital through growing, not building, an Electronic Patient Record system*, Pre-publication paper, Health Services Management Unit, University of Manchester, Manchester.

Bates, J. (1995). Implementation planning, In *Information management in health care*, Series of Handbooks, Handbook D, Issue 3, Section D1.4, The Institute of Health Management, Longman Health Management, London.

Benbasat, I., Goldstein, D.K. and Mead, M. (1987). The case study research strategy in studies of information systems, *MIS Quarterly*, September, 369-386.

Bloomfield, B.P. (1995). Power, machines and social relations: Delegating to information technology in the National Health Service, *Organization*, 2(3/4), 489-518.

Bloomfied, B.P., Coombs, R., Cooper, D.J. and Rea, D. (1992). Machines and manoeuvres: Responsibility accounting and the construction of hospital information systems, *Accounting, Management and Information Technology*, 2(4), 197-219.

Butler, M.A. and Bender, A.D. (1999). Intensive care unit bedside documentation systems. Realizing cost savings and quality improvements, *Computing Nursing*, 17(1), 32-40.

Coleman, W.P., Siegel, J.H., Giovannini, I., Sanford, D.P. and De Gaetano, A. (1993). Computational logic: A method for formal analysis of the ICU knowledge base, *International Journal of Clinical Monitoring and Computing*, February, 10(1), 67-69.

Donaldson, L.J. (1996). From black bag to black box: Will computers improve the NHS? *British Medical Journal*, 312(7043), 1371-1372.

Drucker, P.F. (1996). The information executives truly need, *Harvard Business Review*, January-February, 54-62.

East, T.D. (1992). Computers in the ICU: panacea or plague? *Respiratory Care*, February, 37(2), 170-180.

Flowers, S. (1996). *Software failure: management failure*, John Wiley & Sons, London.

Friesdorf, W., Gross-Alltag, F., Konichezky, S., Schwilk, B., Fattroth, A. and Fett, P. (1994). Lessons learned while building an integrated ICU workstation, *International Journal of Clinical Monitoring and Computing*, May, 11(2), 89-97.

Hagland, M. (1998). Intensive care: the next level of IT, *Health Management Technology*, December, 19(13), 18-21, 23, 27.

Heathfield, H., Hudson, P., Kay, S., Klein, L., Mackey, L., Marley, T., Nicholson, L., Peel, V., Roberts, R., Williams, J. and Protti, D. (1997). *Research evaluation of ICWS demonstrators*, Report for NHSE IMG Integrated

Clinical Workstation Programme Board, January, Health Services Management Unit, University of Manchester, Manchester.

Hoffman, T. (1997). Techo-phobic MDs refuse to say 'Ah!' ER doctors wary of computerized records, *Computerworld*, Feb 24th, 31(8), 75-76.

Howcroft, D. and Mitev, N.N. (2000). An empirical study of Internet usage and difficulties among medical practice management in the UK, *Journal of Internet Research: electronic networking applications and policy*, 10(2), 170-181.

Ireland, R.H., James, H.V., Howes, M. and Wilson, A.J. (1997). Design of a summary screen for an ICU patient data management system, *Medical Biological Engineering Computing*, July, 35(4), 397-401.

James, B. (1995). 80% of all NHS treatments simply may not work, *Mail On Sunday Review*, 18th June.

Kaplan, B. and Maxwell, J.A. (1994). Qualitative research methods for evaluating computer information systems, In *Evaluating health care information systems: methods and applications*, edited by J.G. Anderson, C.E. Aydin and S.J. Jay, Sage, Thousand Oaks, California, 45-68.

Knights, D. and Murray, F. (1994). *Managers divided: organisation politics and information technology management*, John Wiley & Sons, London.

Langenberg, C.J. (1996). Implementation of an electronic patient data management system (PDMS) in an intensive care unit, *International Journal of Biomedical Computing*, July, 42(1-2), 97-101.

Lock, C. (1996). What value do computers provide to NHS hospitals? *British Medical Journal*, 312(7043), 1407-1410.

Marshall, C. and Rossman, G. (1989). *Designing qualitative research*, Sage Publications, Thousand Oaks, CA.

McKenna, P. (1996). Towards the paperless hospital: Implementing the electronic patient record at Edinburgh, *Conference on Current Perspectives in Healthcare Computing*, Harrogate, March 18th-20th, British Journal of Healthcare Computing Ltd.

McMaster, T., Mumford, E., Swanson, E.B., Warboys, B. and Wastell, D. (Eds.) (1997). *Facilitating technology transfer through partnership*, Chapman and Hall, London.

Metnitz, G.H., Hiesmayr, M., Popow, C. and Lenz, K. (1996). Patient data management systems in intensive care, *International Journal of Clinical Monitoring and Computing*, 13, 99-102.

Metnitz, G.H., Laback, P., Popow, C., Laback, O., Lenz, K., and Hiesmayr, M. (1995). Computer assisted analysis in intensive care: The ICDEV project development of a scientific database system for intensive care, *International Journal of Clinical Monitoring and Computing*, 12, 147-159.

Metnitz, G.H. and Lenz, K. (1995). Patient data management systems in intensive care: The situation in Europe, *Intensive Care Medicine*, 21(9), 703-715.

Miller, R.A. (1994). Medical diagnostic decision support systems: past, present and future, *Journal of the American Medical Informatics Association*, 1(1), 8-27.

Modell, M., Iliffe, S., Austin, A. and Leaning, M.S. (1995). From guidelines to decision support in the management of asthma, In *Health telematics for clinical guidelines and protocols*, edited by C. Gordon and J.P. Christensen, ISO Press, 105-113.

Moore, J. (1995). *Electronic prescribing: 'the perfect prescription'*, NHS Executive, NHS, London.

Nenov, V.I., Read, W. and Mock, D. (1994). Computer applications in the intensive care unit, *Neurosurgical Clinician North America*, October, 5(4), 811-827.

Pare, G., Elam, J.J. and Ward, C.G. (1997). Implementation of a patient charting system: Challenges encountered and tactics adopted in a burn center, *Journal of Medical Systems,* February, 21(1), 49-66.

Peel, V. (1994). Management-focused health informatics research and education at the University of Manchester, *Methods of Information in Medicine*, 33, 273-277.

Peel, V. (1996). Key health service reforms 1986-91, In *Information management in health care*, Series of Handbooks, Handbook A, Introductory Themes, Section A4.2, Health Informatics Specialist Group, The Institute of Health Management, Longman Health Management, London.

Peel, V., Heathfield, H., Hudson, P., Kay, S., Klein, L., Mackay, L., Marley, T. and Nicholson, L. (1997). *Considering an electronic patient record (EPR) and clinical work station (CWS) system: twenty critical questions for a hospital board*, Pre-publication paper, Health Services Management Unit, University of Manchester, Manchester.

PICIS Website (1997). Home page, http://www.picis.com.

Pierpont, G.L. and Thilgen, D. (1995). Effect of computerised charting on nursing activity in intensive care, *Critical Care Medicine*, June, 23(6), 1067-1073.

Pitty, D.L. and Reeves, P.I. (1995). Developing decision support systems: a change in emphasis, *Computer Methods and Programs in Biomedicine*, 48, 35-38.

Protti, D.J., Burns, H. and Peel, V. (1996). *Critical success factors to introducing a HIS and developing an Electronic Patient Record System: an interim case study of two different sites*, Unpublished discussion paper, Health Management Services Unit, University of Manchester, Manchester.

Protti, D.J. and Haskell, A.R. (1996). Managing information in hospitals: 60% social, 40% technical? In *Proceedings of IMIA Working Conference on Trends in Hospital Information Systems*, edited by C. Ehlers, A. Baker, J. Bryant and W. Hammond, North Holland Publishing, Amsterdam, 45-49.

Sheaff, R. and Peel, V. (1995). *Managing health service information systems: an introduction*, Open University Press, Buckingham.

Sotheran, M.K. (1996). Management in the 1990s: Major findings of the research and their relevance to the NHS, in *Information management in health care*, Series of Handbooks, Handbook B., Aspects of Informatics, Section B1.1.1., Health Informatics Specialist Groups (HISG), The Institute of Health Services Management, Longman Health Management, London.

Swanson, E.B. (1994). Information systems innovation among organizations, *Management Science*, 40(9), 1069-92.

Thorp, J. (1995a). Hospital Information Support Systems, In *Information management in health care*, Series of Handbooks, Handbook D, Issue 1, Section D4.1.1., The Institute of Health Services Management, Longman Heath Management, London.

Thorp, J. (1995b). The national HISS programme, In *Information management in health care*, Series of Handbooks, Handbook D., Issue 1, Section D4.1.2., The Institute of Health Services Management, Longman Heath Management, London.

Treharne, R. (1995). Approaches to benefits realization, In *Information management in health care*, Series of Handbooks, Handbook D., Issue 1, Section D1.3., The Institute of Health Services Management, Longman Heath Management, London.

Urquhart, C. and Currell, R. (1999). Directions for information systems research on the integrated electronic patient record, In *Information systems: the next generation*, Proceedings of the Fourth UK Academy of Information Systems Conference, University of York, 7-9 April 1999, 634-644.

Urschitz, M., Lorenz, S., Unterasinger, L., Metnitz, P., Preyer, K. and Popow, C. (1998). Three years experience with a patient data monitoring system at a neonatal intensive care unit, *Journal of Clinical Monitoring and Computing*, February, 14(2), 119-125.

Warden, J. (1996). New line of accountability for the NHS, *British Medical Journal*, 312(7042), 1320.

Willcocks, L. (1991). Information in public administration and services in the United Kingdom: toward a management era? *Information and the Public Sector*, 1, 189-211.

Willcocks, L. and Fitzgerald, G. (1993). Market as opportunity? Case studies in outsourcing information technology and services, *Journal of Strategic Information Systems*, September, 2(3), 223-242.

Wyatt, J. (1991). Computer-based knowledge systems, *The Lancet*, Dec 7th, 338, 1431-1436.

Chapter 20

Studying the Translations
of NHSnet

Edgar A. Whitley
London School of Economics and Political Science, UK

Athanasia Pouloudi
Brunel University, UK

This chapter explores the ways in which innovative information systems projects take on a life of their own. The chapter begins by reviewing some of the more traditional ways of making sense of this phenomenon: resistance to change, escalation and unintended results, before introducing the sociology of translation. This provides a theoretical framework for viewing the transformations that an information systems project undergoes. The framework is then applied to the case of the NHSnet project in the United Kingdom. Using the language of sociology of translation, we consider the underlying stakeholder relations in the case study and draw more general conclusions for the responsibilities of stakeholders involved in an information systems lifecycle.

INTRODUCTION

Few information systems projects follow a straightforward path from initial idea through to widely used working system. Instead, what typically occurs is that the nature of the innovation and the purpose of the project changes many times during the implementation process. Much information systems research attempts to try to explain what goes on over the life of the project. The purpose of this chapter

Previously Published in the *Journal of End User Computing, vol.13, no.3,* Copyright © 2001, Idea Group Publishing.

is to add one new element to the range of conceptual tools available to the information systems researcher trying to understand what happens to a particular innovation and to demonstrate how the insights from using this tool can add to our understanding of information systems implementation.

The chapter begins by reviewing some of the main ways in which the changes that an information systems project undergoes have been conceptualised. These include unintended effects; resistance to change and escalation. The chapter then introduces the notion of translation that has been used in the field of science studies and shows how it can be applied to the study of information systems, paying particular attention to the particular kinds of translations that an information systems project can undergo. The chapter then presents the case study, namely the introduction of a new shared network in the UK national health service (NHSnet). This project is seen as a series of translations and the paper explores some of the main translations and discusses their implications for relevant stakeholders. The chapter ends with a summary and discussion of the benefits of using this approach to analyse the "life" of information systems projects.

UNDERSTANDING THE LIFE OF A PROJECT

There are many different ways in which information systems researchers have tried to conceptualise the life of a project. One approach is to describe the events associated with a project and to talk about them in terms of anticipated, unanticipated and emergent changes. Another approach is to talk about the changes in terms of resistance to change and the mechanisms that can be used to counter the implementation of the system. A third approach is to consider the project as potentially escalating out of control.

Unanticipated Changes

Orlikowski (1996) describes an organisation introducing Lotus Notes as a groupware solution for a firm in the software industry. The firm, pseudonymously known as Zeta Corporation, is the developer of a range of powerful software products in the area of decision support and executive information. Their tools are based around the Omni fourth generation language and allow users considerable flexibility in how to analyse their data. As a consequence, many users have technical queries about how to make the products perform particular tasks. The groupware system was introduced into the product support area to enable the sharing of information about problems between the support team (Orlikowski, 1996, pp. 25–27).

The organisation had previously used a stand-alone system to store details about client problems. The existing system had limitations in terms of inconsistent usage, poor data quality and limited search capabilities. The intention behind the new system was to pool all the data in one, shared system. Thus advisors would be able to draw on the experiences of all previous interactions, rather than just their own. As an illustration of the success of this, the number of records of client problems in the database grew from 4,000 records to 35,000 in the two years from December 1992. As Orlikowski notes, however, the system was successful, in part, because of the particularly cooperative culture in the department. Thus, if the same technology had been introduced into an organisation with a less cooperative culture, it is unlikely that a similar success would have been noted.

In describing the changes that arose as a result of the system, Orlikowski differentiates between anticipated changes, opportunistic changes (which are not anticipated ahead of time, but are introduced purposefully as a result of an unexpected opportunity or event) and emergent changes which arise spontaneously out of local innovation. An example of an anticipated change arising from the system was the ability of managers to control the resources in the department more easily; by being able to monitor the number of calls they were able dynamically to change the allocation of work. An opportunistic change that arose from this was the decision to introduce the role of support partners who had specialist knowledge and who could support less experienced staff who handled the front line of calls. An unanticipated consequence was the way in which these front-line staff dealt with their new support partners. The organisation discovered that many junior specialists were reluctant to reassign calls to their support partners; often they felt that tackling difficult problems would help them to develop their own careers whereas on other occasions, the reluctance arose from a concern not to be seen to be dumping problems on their support partners.

Unfortunately, Orlikowski's analysis goes no further than differentiating between the three types of change. No explanation is given for why emergent changes arise, how they could be prepared for and how they can be controlled.

Resistance to Change

A second way of conceptualising the changes that a project undergoes is through the notion of resistance to change. This is perhaps best typified by the classic paper by Keen (1981) which outlines a variety of approaches which have been used to counter the implementation of a new information system. Amongst the counter-implementation games identified by Keen are *easy money*, *budget* and *territory* whereby a project is supported because it can be used to support some needed activity within the player's sphere of influence (p. 29). Another game is *tenacity* whereby a project is kept incomplete until one's particular terms are satisfied. *Odd man out* is used by players who give only partial support and withdraw when the project faces trouble (p. 29). Other games identified by Keen include *up for grabs* where a project with only lukewarm support is taken up by another player; *reputation* whereby a manager gets credit for being a bold innovator but leaves the project before the implementation stage and hence avoids any backlash arising from any problems that exist (pp. 29-30).

Thus, according to Keen, a project is under constant threat of counter-implementation and management must be prepared to take counter-counter implementation measures to ensure that the project succeeds. A similar argument is put forward by Markus (1983) who highlights the political aspects of any system implementation, seen from a perspective which emphasizes the effects of the interaction between the people and the systems.

Escalation

A third approach to understanding the phenomenon is through the notion of escalation. Keil (1995) defines escalation as a continued commitment in the face of negative information about prior resource allocations coupled with uncertainty surrounding the likelihood of goal attainment.

In order to study the factors that can lead to escalation, Keil describes the experiences that CompuSys (a pseudonym) had with a project called Config. Config was a rule based expert system that was designed to help the company's sales force produced error-free configurations prior to producing pricing estimates. Previously the company had made estimates based on incorrect configurations and had to bear the cost of any discrepancies itself. The organisation had had positive experience of another system (Verifier) which was used to produce correct system configurations and was therefore expecting that this project would be successful as well. The Config project was finally terminated 13 years after it was initiated. During this time, feedback about the project was predominantly negative. Eight years after the project was initiated, usage of the system had dropped to less than 2% of all transactions.

A number of explanations were given for the continued support of the project in the face of such negative assessments. Amongst the key arguments identified by Keil are the fact that the project was perceived to have a large net present value, that the project was regarded as an investment in research and development and that the problems appeared to be temporary setbacks rather than fundamental problems of concept.

Moreover, the organisation had a history of successful projects in this area, and the manager of the project was taking a high degree of responsibility for the success of the project. Indeed, Keil argues that the involvement of the strong project champion meant that the project was defended at times when it might legitimately have been cancelled.

Summary

Clearly there is overlap between each of these approaches; for example, what one sees as an unanticipated change could be viewed by another as an attempt at counter-implementation. This again could be seen by another as a project that is potentially escalating out of control. What all these approaches implicitly share, however, is a feeling that these occurrences are undesirable and avoidable. In contrast to this view, the next section presents an approach which takes it for granted that a project is likely to be changed over its life time and instead tries to understand the ways in which these changes come about. With this understanding it is possible to add a managerial agenda that can try to minimise these changes but the approach still accepts that even then, success is not guaranteed.

THE SOCIOLOGY OF TRANSLATION

The sociology of translation has its origins in social studies of science and the question of how statements come to become facts. Ignoring questions of ontology and epistemology (Searle, 1999; Sokal & Bricmont, 1998) a statement only becomes a fact when other people use it. A scientist may discover some phenomenon in nature but this will only become a fact when it is accepted as such by others (Latour, 1987). Clearly there are important questions about how others come to accept the statement as a fact which are not easily answered (for an appreciation of the complexities here, see Barnes *et al.* (1996); Collins and Pinch (1993); Biagioli (1999); Fuchs (1992)) but the social process whereby statements become transformed into facts is also important and has direct parallels with the way in which innovations come to be accepted within an organisation.

As Latour puts it: "(A) sentence may be made more of a fact or more of an artefact depending on how it is inserted into other sentences. *By itself a given sentence is neither a fact nor a fiction; it is made so by others, later on.* You make it more of a fact if you insert it as a closed, obvious, firm and packaged premise leading to some other less closed, less obvious, less firm and less united consequence" (1987 p. 25). Thus, the creation of facts is very much a collective process. If a statement is made that solves an on-going dilemma but no one reads it then it is as if it has never been made. "Fact construction is so much a collective process that an isolated person builds only dreams, claims and feelings, not facts" (1987, p. 41).

The issue, therefore, becomes one of making other people take up the statement and use it and there are direct parallels for the case of an innovation. An innovation only succeeds if other people can be convinced to make use of the new system. Unfortunately, there is *no* guarantee that the people will take up the fact or innovation nor that they will use it in the way intended. The innovators must therefore act at a distance (Miller, 1992) to achieve two potentially conflicting ends; they must enroll others so that they participate in the use of the innovation and they must control their behaviours in order to make their actions predictable and commensurate with the intentions of the innovator (Latour, 1987, p. 108).

The case of information systems innovations is made even more complex by the fact that the individuals who sponsor a new system are often very different from those who develop it, who are again different from those who will use the resulting system. The question of whose innovation it is, in these cases, is particularly complex. It is common to find project sponsors trying to convince the users of the benefits of a new system and then the developers trying to reconvince them of the benefits of the particular system they have ended up delivering.

For the innovator to be successful, therefore, two goals must be achieved, or more accurately, the observer must be able to see the actions of the innovator as matching these goals—it is always possible that this is not actually what the innovator intended. First the interests of the other actors must be translated into interests that match that of the innovator and then the other actors must be kept in line and under control.

The first activity, of translating interests, can be done in a number of ways, including the situation where the interests of the other actors already matches those of the innovator ("Here is a system that addresses the concerns you have"). Thus developers provide a system that is intended to address the concerns of a particular user group; experience has shown that such a straightforward solution is unlikely. Another situation arises where the innovator tries to persuade the other actors that they should want the solution proposed ("You should use this system"). The innovator may persuade the other actors that they have a problem and that the innovation provides a solution to that problem. This persuasion may require the users to redefine their identity. For example, the developers of video recorders had to persuade television viewers that they were not just people who missed a TV programme, but that this was an avoidable problem. If they chose to use a videorecorder, they could cease being people who missed their favourite programmes and instead be people who had the opportunity to organise their lives more flexibly as they could always record programmes when they were out.

Again, such situations are uncommon; a more likely scenario is where the other actors can be persuaded to adopt a new innovation that is almost like what they want ("It does most of what you want, so why not make use of it"). Thus they can take up the innovation if they only have to change their identity slightly rather than fundamentally. Another approach is to reshuffle the interests of the other actors, to make them more amenable to the innovation. This can be done by displacing the goals of the other actors: if they don't appear to have a problem then why not create a problem for them (for which you have the solution, of course), or by creating new goals for them and then becoming indispensable for the solution (Latour, 1987, pp. 108-121).

There are obvious parallels here with some of Keen's strategies of counter-implementation outlined above. For example, the easy money, budget and territory games are used by people who are trying to translate the interests of the original project to meet their own ends. Similarly, the up–for–grabs game translates a lukewarm project into the goals of the counter-implementer.

The Config case demonstrates how the various ways in which the project was translated over the life of the system. What began as a system which was designed to provide support for the sales force by enabling them to produce accurate quotations was, at various times, a project which existed because of its potentially huge financial potential, a project that represented a major investment in research and development and hence would provide the experience for future developments, and a project that was closely allied to the reputation of its manager. In each case, the project was translated from its initial intentions and adopted by new people for different reasons, changing the shape of the system substantially.

Having translated the goals of the actors to match those of the innovation, the next stage is to maintain the innovation on the path that it has set up. Here it is important to realise that the control over the innovation is only as strong as its weakest link. For example, a project may have been initialised and may have the support of a senior manager. If this manager leaves the position of support, then the control of the project may be weakened. The reverse situation occurred in the Config case, where the presence of the project champion kept the project going long beyond its feasibility.

The problems of maintaining control and remaining indispensable are also apparent in the case of the "unexpected changes" in the groupware project at Zeta corporation. The unanticipated (as opposed to emergent) changes arise when control cannot be maintained at a distance. Thus, the introduction of the system limited the control that the organisation could have on its front line help staff. They were able to control their jobs by separating out tasks to front line and support partners. They were unable, however, to control how these front line staff undertook their work. Zeta was unable to stop these people from translating their work into their own ends (i.e., they didn't transfer calls to their support partner in part because they didn't want to be seen to be ineffective operators as this would affect their career development plans). However, what they could do is revise their own behaviour (e.g., revise the reward schemes) in order to encourage (or coerce) operators to work as management envisaged. An interesting aspect of the Zeta case was the constant circle of translation, whereby the behaviour of one group had an impact on the behaviour and perceptions of the other.

VIEWING THE TRANSLATIONS IN AN INFORMATION SYSTEMS PROJECT

If we accept that information systems projects are likely to undergo a series of translations over the life of the project, we now have a useful technique for viewing the life of an information systems project and understanding what happens to it. The technique involves viewing the project over its life and identifying the various translations it undergoes. At each of these translations we are now able to determine the kind of translation that is undergone, the reasons for the translation and the effects of each translation.

This approach focuses on particular events and it may be necessary to investigate the context of each of the translations in more detail. This technique will now be used to describe the life of a project in the UK National Health Service (NHS) associated with networking the various actors into an integrated NHSnet.

Background to the NHSnet Case Study

The Information Management Group of the NHS Executive, the body responsible for the execution of health care policy in Britain (NHS Executive, 1997b), launched the NHS-wide networking project in 1993, as "an integrated approach to interorganisational communications within the NHS" (NHS Executive, 1994 p. 6). The objective of the project has been to enhance communication and information exchange between various healthcare providers and administrators. Therefore it has been intended as a response to a number of problems experienced in NHS communications. Such problems include inefficient purchasing, lack of integration, fragmented networks, limited future potential, aging private radio systems, and insufficient resources (NHS Executive, 1994).

The NHSnet is expected to support data communications that cover a variety of information flows across different levels. At a *national level*, it will support messaging between health authorities and the NHS Central Register; at a *regional level*, it will support access to centralised data processing (finance, payroll, etc.); at a *local level*, it will support links between primary care doctors (GPs) and hospitals (for the exchange of pathology test results, referral/discharge details, waiting list inquiries), as well as between GPs and health authorities (NHS Executive, 1994). More generally, the NHSnet infrastructure is expected to cover a variety of business areas, including patient-related service delivery, patient-related administration, commissioning and contracting, information services, management-related flows, supplies of NHS organisations (NHS Executive, 1995). Future links across these areas will rely less on paper and telephone communication and increasingly on EDI and electronic mail messaging.

Since 1996, wide area networking services for data and voice have been available and can be purchased; the NHSnet is available. Yet, despite the technological success of the project, and in particular its completion within schedule, its implementation has suffered from the lack of acceptance by the medical profession. Doctors remain sceptical of the security of this network. Their concerns have been overtly voiced, primarily through the British Medical Association (BMA), the national professional body of physicians in the United Kingdom, but also by their computer security consultants. These parties fear that patient data may be misused by both NHS members and external parties (Willcox, 1995; Pouloudi & Whitley, 2000; Pouloudi, 1998).

At the moment, although the network is used for administrative and purchasing purposes, its use falls well behind the initial NHS Executive plans which perceived the exchange of patient information as an important implementation objective.

Translations in NHSnet

The NHSnet presents an interesting case of an actor-network that has undergone a series of translations. These translations were noted by recording the viewpoints of the stakeholders of the network (Pouloudi, 1998), those who participate, influence or are affected by it, and are following the network over time, using it where possible to promote their interests, or the interests of the stakeholders that they claim to represent. These stakeholders were identified using the iterative method suggested in Pouloudi and Whitley (1997). The following paragraphs present the problems in the implementation of the system and break these down in a series of translations that the project has undergone.

Although the NHS Executive had piloted the project with doctors at an early stage, it was only after the network started being implemented and adopted at the local level that the doctors, through their representative body, the British Medical Association (BMA), reacted to the use of the network, arguing that it did not safeguard the privacy of medical information. Further concerns were raised when they were expected to have to pay for the service, even though the technological infrastructure was considered dated and unreliable. As a result of their concern, doctors have threatened not to participate in the electronic exchange of data unless they can be convinced that the privacy of patient data is safeguarded. Yet, the NHS Executive have argued that the proposed system is better than its predecessors, *ad hoc* manual and electronic exchange systems: data confidentiality was quoted as one of the shortcomings of the previous situation and one that the NHS-wide networking infrastructure would safeguard (NHS Executive, 1994).

The 1996 conference in Healthcare Computing (18-20 March 1996, Harrogate, UK) provided the opportunity for a direct confrontation of the two sides on the matter:

The measures we have put in place are to stop anybody who is unauthorised getting at data from, and via, the [NHS-wide networking] system, and one of the key parts of that system is a strong authentication challenge (Ray Rogers, then Executive Director, NHS Information Management Group).

The conflict has since slightly receded since the NHS adopted the BMA's suggestion to encrypt data, published a report on data encryption (NHS Executive, 1996), and thus improved the chances of cooperation on data security with the BMA (Creasey, 1996). Given the advantages of electronic exchange of healthcare data, there has been a general optimism that the NHSnet will be used and the debate will be resolved in a way that leaves both of the currently conflicting parties satisfied.

Underlying the confidentiality debate, the most visible conflict in the NHSnet case system's implementation, we can distinguish three interesting changes in the nature of the NHS-wide networking project as the various stakeholders understand or present the network from different perspectives in order to serve their interests.

Translation 1

First, the debate of the BMA and the Information Management Group on confidentiality has translated the network from *a technical system* (a network infrastructure to support information exchange in the NHS) into a system threatening the privacy of medical information, *an issue of confidentiality*. This issue has been at the heart of the debate because the doctors consider it as a key responsibility (and therefore part of the identity) of their profession. In response to this reaction, and in order to avoid the cost of another spectacular system failure in the NHS (cf. Beynon-Davies, 1995), the NHS Executive (and the government) have responded with a reconsideration of the security issue of the network. The "Zergo Report" (NHS Executive, 1996) proposed the use of encryption to safeguard the privacy of medical records. While the BMA debated which encryption algorithm would satisfy the NHS needs best, it is clear that as a result of this report, the NHS Executive has tried to translate the network, and the discussion about its adoption, back into a technical problem, that of encryption. Their suppliers have supported this view: "Firewall-to-firewall encryption could potentially act as an enhancement to NHSnet security and go some way to placating the BMA" (McCafferty, 1996). In order to face the challenge, the BMA has formed alliances with privacy activists (e.g., Privacy International) and academics on one hand, in order to raise the profile of the debate. On the other hand, they have created an alliance with security consultants, in order to challenge the technical features of the network as well (Pouloudi & Whitley, 2000). Following the debate, the NHS Executive has now made explicit its view of the NHSnet as a "secure national network" (NHS Executive, 1998a), effectively redefining the network.

Translation 2

The alliance between the BMA and security consultants resulted in the security consultant to the BMA at the time, Ross Anderson, becoming the spokesperson of the BMA on the NHSnet implementation:

> We have to take a long hard look at the IM&T strategy and rewrite it so that it is centred on clinical concerns rather than administrative concerns; so that it is oriented towards patients rather than administrators and optimised for the delivery of healthcare rather than as a means of enforcing bureaucratic power and control from the centre (Dr Ross Anderson, Security Advisor, BMA)

The debate about the capability of NHSnet to safeguard confidentiality has been most intense when Ross Anderson was acting as security consultant to the BMA and Ray Rogers was Executive Director of the NHS Information Management Group. Both people considered the NHSnet as a key system: one that endangers the privacy of medical data or one that is part of a vision to modernise the NHS. To a certain extent, the debate was perceived as a personalised issue, perhaps as both people took ownership of the debate and saw the progress of the network as their 'mission'. Some statements reflected an almost personal rivalry (e.g., *British Journal of Healthcare Computing & information Management,* vol. 13, no. 3, 1996, p. 6). This was noted by those involved ("I regret that discussions between the Department [of Health] and the BMA have been conducted in such a public and fraught environment" (Rogers, 1996)) and by those reporting on the conflict ("that debate was not at all times marked by reason and moderation" (Fairey, 1998)).

Ray Rogers has since been replaced by Ann Harding in the Director's post of the Information Management Group. Subsequently the Group was also dissolved and a new NHS Information Authority established to provide effective guidance in the implementation of the NHS strategy (NHS Executive, 1998b). Ross Anderson, while still a privacy advocate, is no longer acting formally as a security consultant or spokesperson for the BMA. Interestingly, as neither of these previous protagonists of the confidentiality/security debate holds the same position at the moment, the nature of the debate on the NHSnet has changed again and became less intense.

Translation 3

At the same time the Information Management Group was disbanded, the NHS put forward a requirement for all computerised general practices to connect to the NHSnet by the end of December 1999. The NHSnet is now formally described as "the best medium for the transfer of clinical information" (NHS Executive, 1998b). It is not clear, however, whether the compulsory link of GPs to the network will be equivalent to using the network as envisaged by either the doctor community or the NHS Executive. In any case, the network has undergone another translation. Rather than being a system that doctors *will want to use* as originally intended, because it speeds up the delivery of healthcare, facilitates communication with their peers, or is more secure than the systems used previously, it is a network that *they are required to use and pay for*:

Why are we still being pressurised to join a network with such poor performance and functionality, run by people without any wish to deliver what "the users" want? (GP).

This is a translation that is common to information systems implementation, and often underlying resistance to change phenomena. In interorganisational systems in particular where the asymmetry of power between sponsor and adopters is often prominent (Cavaye, 1995), the importance of end-user requirements tend to become undermined by the sponsor's policy and priorities.

Translations in the Broader Context

Our discussion so far has looked at the network and those events that were directly related to its progress. However, these translations should be considered in light of a broader set of changes in the context, which can contribute to our understanding of the NHSnet translations. Because of the importance, the public and political character of the NHS and as a result of the government setting its strategic direction, changes in the political scene or legislation in the UK have a direct impact on the translations of the NHS.

The following list gives an indication of the political scene in a series of additional events and publications with direct impact on NHSnet:

May 1997 Labour government elected "In my contract with the people of Britain I promised that we would rebuild the NHS" (foreword by the Prime Minister in (Department of Health, 1997))

December 1997 • "The new NHS" "replaces internal market with integrated care" (Department of Health, 1997)

• "Report on the review of patient-identifiable information" (Caldicott Committee Report)
This report has been the result of the "increasing concern about the ways in which patient information is used in the NHS in England and Wales and the need to ensure that confidentiality is not undermined" (NHS Executive, 1997a)

• White paper on Freedom of Information Act "to legislate for freedom of information, bringing about more open Government"

September 1998 Information for Health (NHS Executive, 1998b) "the Information Management Group will   be disbanded and replaced with an NHS Information Authority to provide a lead for   the new partnership development and to ensure effective guidance is given for successful delivery of the strategy"
Deadline for computerised GPs to link to NHSnet: by the end of 1999

November 1998 New Data Protection Act Will enhance the protection afforded to patients

It is therefore evident that, as the NHSnet underwent a series of translations, so did the NHS, prompting, in turn, further changes for the network. Also, the membership of the UK in the European Union and the need to comply with legislation on data protection has implications for the translation of the confidentiality debate, especially for the attention given to particular issues and the way in which these are 'translated' in the NHSnet case. It is worth noting that the impact of each change cannot be considered in isolation. Each piece of legislation also undergoes a series of translations as a consequence of the diverse interests that stakeholders – at a European and national level – serve, or wish to be seen to serve.

FOUR MOMENTS OF TRANSLATION

The previous section illustrated some of the translations characterising the NHSnet. These are translations in its technology (Translation 1), in the personal roles of stakeholders (Translation 2), in mode of adoption for the system (Translation 3) as well as in the broader context. Although we have separated them out for the purposes of our analysis, these translations are closely intertwined, not least because stakeholders respond to the views and changes introduced and supported by others thus introducing new changes. The sociology of translation literature presents and explains the changes through 'four moments of translation' (Callon, 1986; Introna, 1997). It is worth noting that these 'moments' are witnessed, but cannot be neatly separated in the NHSnet case. This is because each stakeholder of the network and each related technology or piece of legislation that has an impact on the network goes through similar 'moments' at different points in time. The following paragraphs illustrate how these four moments have been witnessed in the NHSnet case implementation with supporting statements from various stakeholders.

Problematisation: an actor defines an 'obligatory passage point' (an actor network linked by discourses presenting the solution of a problem in terms of resources owned by the agent that proposes it (Callon, 1986; Latour, 1987)). In the NHSnet case, for example, the response of the NHS to confidentiality concerns with the publication of the Zergo report meant that encryption algorithms became at that point the obligatory way to discuss the confidentiality issue:

For the first time the NHS has a strong, total security package. How much more does the Department [of Health] have to do before the BMA acknowledges what a large step forward this package is, and supports what we have put in place? What else is there to do? (Ray Rogers, Executive Director of the Information Management Group at the time).

In the broader sense of this translation moment, we can consider the use of the NHSnet as the primary system for discussing information exchange in the NHS.

Intéressement: actors try to impede alliances that may challenge the legitimacy of the obligatory passage point (or, in the contrary form alliances to support it). In the NHSnet case, this has been evident in the rhetoric used by the NHS Executive to establish the credibility of the network:

The NHSnet is more secure than all the other networks that are out there and will continue to be used until we manage to replace them (Ray Rogers).

This perception was reinforced with the publication of the Zergo report, where, as we noted previously, the debate was translated to focus on the issue of which encryption algorithm would be appropriate for the needs of the NHS and the rights of the patients. Similarly, the formation of the Caldicott Committee obliged the BMA and its allied stakeholders to become less polemic to governmental proposals:

The Caldicott Committee failed to lay down hard and fast rules for patient confidentiality, but because it produced a list of 'good intentions' it certainly made it harder for BMA and other concerned organisations like DIN to continue to breathe fire and brimstone about matters. In this the commission probably served its purpose well. (Chairman of the Doctor's Independent Network).

Enrollment: bargaining and concession – alliances are consolidated. In the NHSnet, some of the stakeholders did not engage in the debate but formed instead an alliance with those stakeholders standing for their interests:

Each local medical committee decides whether it supports the BMA's position and, so far, each committee has universally supported the BMA's position on this to the point that there was no dissent and that's because confidentiality is so closely linked to the general practitioners' hearts really. (Secretary to a group of local medical committees).

Mobilisation: defining the legitimacy of a spokesperson. As the debate about the confidentiality of patient data has been almost monopolised by the NHS Information Management Group and the BMA, it is not surprising that some of the 'by-standing' stakeholders' perceptions about this debate reflected the acceptance (as in the view of the local medical committees above) or reservation about the role, real motivation and legitimacy of the protagonists:

The BMA are on one hand rendering a public service: making sure that patient confidentiality is maintained. But, on the other hand, something else may come out; the BMA will seek some pay-off for sharing information. Let's not forget that the BMA is essentially a trade union, representing the interests of doctors, but cannot be accused of doing so openly because they also have professional concerns for the patients (member of the NHS Central Communications Management Group).

Other stakeholders voice their concern from the absence of another appropriate—in their view—spokesperson:

There was one representative of a patient association at the meeting and I was appalled because they said the NHSnet was a good thing. We have a problem with these people. It is inconceivable that the BMA moved in this debate faster and made suggestions before the patients' associations even made a press release. This will come down as the major anomaly in history (Director General of Privacy International).

Following from this analysis which highlights better the tensions between stakeholder groups that underlie the translations of the network presented in the previous section, we would argue that all stakeholder perceptions become important to our understanding of translations. Indeed, they are useful in illustrating changes in alliances, attitudes, expectations for the future. At the same time the translations have implications for the role and relationships of stakeholders as well. In the NHSnet case in particular, the translations have a direct impact on professionals and patients as they have to react to the changes and reconsider their relations with other participants in the healthcare delivery process.

IMPLICATIONS BEYOND THE NHSNET

This exploration of the stakeholders in the NHSnet project, their views on the network, and the ways in which they acted to translate the project to better match their own needs, allows us to raise some general issues from the paper. These are applicable to other healthcare applications, such as the GPNet in the UK, as well as other large information systems implementations.

In particular, the translations we have discussed signify for stakeholders a need to consider their role in the actor-network so that they can best promote their interests and safeguard their rights and do this in a way that doesn't shortcut *due process* (McMaster, Vidgen, & Wastell, 1998). The other side of the coin of course is that they also need to respect the rights of other stakeholders. Thus, treating others as legitimate stakeholders can be considered as part of being a responsible stakeholder. This view, in the information systems and management literature, is often limited to predefined notions of stakeholder roles (e.g., "a manager should make decisions that serve the organisation" or "an information systems developer should develop systems that are functional and useful to the user/customer"). Blyth (1998) defines responsibility as "a legal or moral obligation for bringing about, or maintaining, a certain state of affairs" (p. 259). Thus, responsibilities may be formal and institutionalised or informal and related to a stakeholder's set of values. Responsibilities can be prescribed, 'felt', taken up to avoid cost or punishment or they may be enabled by certain factors. Blyth, for example, notes that a responsibility also implies elements of accountability, liability, trustworthiness and blame (p. 259). However, the extent to which stakeholders are conscious or able to carry out these responsibilities may also be influenced by their interest, power or perceived legitimacy. The NHSnet case supports these different motivations for taking up a responsibility. Furthermore these motivations are interpreted differently depending on particular stakeholder perspectives.

Going a step further, stakeholders could interpret their stakeholder entity as an obligation to defend their values and interests, either directly or through some representative stakeholder. Direct involvement could signify participation in debates or meetings where their interests and values are discussed. In case of indirect participation, stakeholders have an obligation to contribute to any formal procedures for representation and criticise the representative bodies if they fail to represent the appropriate interests and values or if they fail to represent them appropriately (Pouloudi & Whitley, 2000). Thus, *the rights of stakeholders* (e.g., the right to participate, to be fairly represented, to be considered as a legitimate interested party) *can also be regarded as carrying an obligation for stakeholders to defend and honour these rights.*

This obligation of stakeholders will often need to be recognised by the stakeholder groups themselves rather than be expected or imposed by other stakeholders. This is a consequence of the problems relating to the asymmetry of information or other resources, access, power or perceived legitimacy and the diverse interests and values of stakeholders. If the responsibility of particular stakeholders to participate or otherwise act when their interests or values are at stake is institutionalised, less informed or less powerful stakeholders could find an inability to carry out their duties as stakeholders to be interpreted as a legitimate reason for other stakeholders to override their rights. Therefore there would be a danger of under-representation of some stakeholder interests.

Consequently, stakeholder responsibilities often need to be internalised by the stakeholder group. In practice this is common amongst certain professional bodies that consider themselves as a stakeholder group with a predominantly common set of values and interests. Healthcare professionals are a good example of such a stakeholder group as their fundamental professional responsibilities have remained essentially similar (hence the use of the Hippocratic Oath to this date). Stakeholder responsibilities may be more difficult to define for groups that have been formed more recently and whose representative bodies lack a well defined or a well understood identity by other stakeholder's identity. Clearly stakeholders who lack a group identity altogether, such as the patients rely more on their individual sense of moral responsibility and their perception of rights and responsibilities as a guide to their behaviour and their expectation from other stakeholders.

CONCLUSIONS

The NHSnet case shows that information technology has become part of the day-to-day practice of many healthcare professionals. Thus, they need to be aware of the capabilities and limitations of this technology, in particular to the extent that this may affect their professional responsibilities. Clinicians are not technical experts, and it wouldn't be fair to expect them to be. However, they need to be aware that the use of information systems is likely to have implications not only in their work processes but also in their relations with other stakeholders. If unable to evaluate these, healthcare professionals need to be aware of stakeholders or mechanisms that will help them address technological issues. Recent research reports the case of an NHS hospital trust which has not been able to learn from previous information technology failures in the healthcare area and has repeated common mistakes (Mitev & Kerkham, 1998). They were also unaware of the facilitating role that parties such as the Information Management Group (IMG) of the NHS Executive could play in their systems procurement and development. In cases however where prospective systems users in the NHS are familiar with the facilitator mechanisms that stem from the IMG's role as the information technology experts within the NHS, the perceived legitimacy of such stakeholders will also come into play. For example, the NHSnet case has damaged the IMG image as they were seen not to take on board important values of other stakeholders and arguably contributed to the dissolution of the group. Certainly, the legitimacy question is complicated by other organisational and political concerns that affect stakeholder relations in healthcare.

For network systems' developers and sponsors, the responsibilities are perhaps more complicated than those of the intended end users. Indeed, unless they succeed in convincing other stakeholders that they have taken their concerns on board, they undermine on one hand the way in which other stakeholders perceive their role and their professionalism and on the other hand the chance of successful adoption and growth of the systems they deliver. The role of interorganisational systems developers can be related to a certain extent to the previous discussion on the problems of stakeholder representation. Developers, being knowledgeable about technology need to understand the perspectives, interests and values of the users and other stakeholders because, ultimately, they will need to inscribe these to the system they build. Certainly, there is an important set of informal norms that cannot be transcribed in an information system. Also, a system "grows" (cf Atkinson & Peel, 1998) and undergoes a series of translations when it is used, as stakeholders start using it in "unexpected" ways or use the system as a mechanism to defend or establish values and procedures. It is therefore a major challenge for developers to provide systems that are not perceived to conflict with the interests and values of stakeholders and to 'sell' those that do. In an interorganisational context the reconciliation of diverse interests can become the developer's responsibility. The use of the sociology of translation to analyse previous experience can improve our understanding of information systems change and the subtleties of stakeholder relations and representation. The use of stakeholder analysis can facilitate developers in understanding the scope and difficulties of the task and act according to the distinct context requirements.

More generally, information systems professionals face increasingly complex dilemmas as systems tend to privilege the perspective of particular stakeholders. The information systems literature distinguished between three key stakeholder groups: managers, users and developers. As systems increasingly become interorganisational and are used in domains where stakeholder relationships are political and changeable rather than commercial or predictable, information systems developers need to be more sensitive to the multiple stakeholders, the complicated, evolving and context-dependent nature of their understanding of systems use and the implications that systems use will have for this broad spectrum of stakeholders.

This chapter has explored the different stages that an innovative project may undergo. Various approaches for understanding this process have been explored, although each provides limited assistance for generalisable understanding.

After reviewing notions of unexpected change, resistance and escalation, the paper presented the sociology of translation as a mechanism for understanding the various stages in an information systems innovation. This approach, drawing from a sociological understanding of the development of scientific facts, was then used to illustrate the various translations that the NHSnet project undertook in the United Kingdom. The language of the sociology of translation allowed us to see how the basis of the whole project was fundamentally transformed on a number of occasions and saw how these were related to the wider context of the system's development.

The NHSnet, at the moment, continues to be an expectation failure (Lyytinen & Hirschheim, 1987) from both the NHS Executive and the BMA perspectives. Indeed, issues like that of confidentiality and privacy of medical information have not been resolved. However, as a result of the various translations, including changes in spokespersons, in priorities and obligatory passage points, confidentiality no longer appears to be at the heart of the NHSnet implementation problems. At the same time, as many technological issues remain unresolved, including the architecture and storage of the electronic health record, but also organisational and political the responsibilities of stakeholders (e.g., 'Caldicott Committee Guardians' are to be appointed to all NHS organisations to monitor safeguarding confidential patient information), the network will continue to undergo 'translations'. In this paper we explained how these translations are the result of the actions of numerous stakeholders, and importantly, that these stakeholders have a right and an obligation to promote and protect individual rights, such as the privacy of medical information.

More generally, our approach to the lifecycle of information systems as actor networks undergoing a series of translations has proved to be an interesting way to study information systems implementation. By considering different stakeholder perspectives rather than restricting our analysis to actor involvement, we had an opportunity to consider technical, organisational and political issues shaping an interorganisational system. Our case study is another indication that interorganisational systems are political systems. Politics, as often manifested in stakeholder relations but also in the way in which various stakeholders attempt to 'translate' the system to serve their interests, are unavoidable and an integral part of an information system.

In practice, our approach is valuable to the stakeholders immersed in the situation, in this case healthcare professionals in particular, because it challenges them to make sense for themselves of translations, how these may be triggered by other stakeholder interests or capabilities. From a theoretical perspective, this approach also enables more general discussions about the rights and responsibilities of stakeholders, thus contributing to the normative aspect of stakeholder theory (Donaldson & Preston, 1995), which has been neglected in the information systems literature (Pouloudi, 1999).

REFERENCES

Atkinson, C., & Peel, V. (1998). Transforming a Hospital by Growing not Building an Electronic Patient Record. *Methods of information in medicine, 37*, 285-93.

Barnes, B., Bloor, D., & Henry, J. (1996). *Scientific knowledge: A sociological analysis*. London: Athlone.

Beynon-Davies, P. (1995). Information systems "failure": the case of the London Ambulance Service's Computer Aided Despatch project. *European Journal of Information Systems, 4*, 171-184.

Biagioli, M. (Ed.). (1999). *The science studies reader*. London: Routledge.

Blyth, A. J. C. (1998). Identifying requirements for the management of medical information technology. *International Journal of Technology Management, Special Issue on Management of Technology in Health Care, 15*(3/4/5), 256-269.

Callon, M. (1986). Some elements of a sociology of translation: domestication of the scallops and the fishermen of St Brieuc Bay. In J. Law (Ed.), *Power, Action and Belief: A New Sociology of Knowledge?* (pp. 196-233). London: Routledge & Kegan Paul.

Cavaye, A. L. M. (1995). The Sponsor-Adopter Gap -Differences Between Promoters and Potential Users of Information Systems that Link Organizations. *International Journal of Information Management, 15*(2), 85-96.

Collins, H. M., & Pinch, T. (1993). *The golem: What everyone should know about science.* Cambridge: Cambridge University Press.

Creasey, D. (1996). BMA says data security problems can be solved. *British Journal of Healthcare Computing and Information Management, 13*(4), 6.

Department of Health. (1997). *The New NHS: modern, dependable* (Cm 3807): The Stationary Office.

Donaldson, T., & Preston, L. E. (1995). The stakeholder theory of the corporation: concepts, evidence, and implications. *Academy of Management Review, 20*(1), 65-91.

Fairey, M. (1998). Editorial: "... is paved with good intentions". *British Journal of Healthcare Computing and Information Management, 15*(7), 3.

Fuchs, S. (1992). *The professional quest for truth: a social theory of science and knowledge.* Albany: State University of New York Press.

Introna, L. D. (1997). *Management, Information and Power.* Basingstoke: Macmillan.

Keen, P. G. (1981). Information systems and organizational change. *Communications of the ACM, 24*(1), 24-33.

Keil, M. (1995). Pulling the plug: Software project management and the problem of project escalation. *MIS Quarterly, 19*(4), 421-447.

Latour, B. (1987). *Science in action: How to follow scientists and engineers through society.* Cambridge, MA: Harvard University Press.

Lyytinen, K., & Hirschheim, R. (1987). Information Systems Failures - a Survey and Classification of the Empirical Literature, *Oxford Surveys in Information Technology* (Vol. 4, pp. 257-309). Oxford: Oxford University Press.

Markus, M. L. (1983). Power, politics and MIS implementation. *Communications of the ACM, 26*(6), 430-444.

McCafferty, C. (1996). Securing the NHSnet. *British Journal of Healthcare Computing and Information Management, 13*(8), 24-26.

McMaster, T., Vidgen, R., & Wastell, D. (1998). Networks of association and due process in IS development. In T. J. Larsen, L. Levine, & J. I. DeGross (Eds.), *Information systems: Current issues and future changes* (pp. 341-358). Laxenburg: Austria.

Miller, P. (1992). Accounting and objectivity: The invention of calculating selves and calculable spaces. *Annals of scholarship, 9*(1/2), 61-86.

Mitev, N., & Kerkham, S. (1998, 4-6 June 1998). Less haste more speed: organisational and implementation issues of patient data management systems in an intensive care unit. Paper presented at the *Proceedings of the 6th European Conference on Information Systems, Aix en Provence, France.*

NHS Executive. (1994). *A strategy for NHS-wide networking* (E5155): Information Management Group.

NHS Executive. (1995). *NHS-wide networking: application requirements specification* (H8003): Information Management Group.

NHS Executive. (1996). *The use of encryption and related services with the NHSnet: A report for the NHS Executive by Zergo Limited* (E5254): Information Management Group.

NHS Executive. (1997a). *The Caldicott Committee: Report on the review of patient-identifiable information* : http://www1c.btwebworld.com/imt4nhs/general/caldico/caldico1.htm.

NHS Executive. (1997b). *This is the IMG: A guide to the Information Management Group of the NHS Executive* (B2216): Information Management Group.

NHS Executive. (1998a). *IMG: Programmes and Projects Summaries* (B2232): Information Management Group.

NHS Executive. (1998b). *Information for Health - Executive Summary* (A1104): Department of Health.

Orlikowski, W. (1996). Evolving with notes: Organizational change around groupware technology. In C. U. Ciborra (Ed.), *Groupware & teamwork: Invisible aid or technical hindrance* (pp. 23-59). Chichester: Wiley.

Pouloudi, A. (1998). Stakeholder Analysis in UK Health Interorganizational Systems: The Case of NHSnet. In K. Andersen (Ed.), *EDI and Data Networking in the Public Sector: Governmental Action, Diffusion, and Impacts* (pp. 83-107). Boston: Kluwer.

Pouloudi, A. (1999, January 5-8). *Aspects of the stakeholder concept and their implications for information systems development.* Paper presented at the HICSS-32, Wailea, Maui, Hawaii.

Pouloudi, A., & Whitley, E. A. (1997). Stakeholder identification in inter-organizational systems: Gaining insights for drug use management systems. *European journal of information systems, 6*(1), 1-14.

Pouloudi, A., & Whitley, E. A. (2000). Representing human and non-human stakeholders: On speaking with authority. In R. Baskerville, J. Stage, & J. I. D. Gross (Eds.), *Organizational and social perspectives on information technology* (pp. 340-354). Boston: Kluwer.

Rogers, R. (1996). An NHS infrastructure - the long trek. *British Journal of Healthcare Computing and Information Management, 13*(7), 18-21.

Searle, J. (1999). *Mind, language and society: Philosophy in the real world.* London: Weidenfeld & Nicholson.

Sokal, A., & Bricmont, J. (1998). *Intellectual impostures: Postmodern philosophers' abuse of science.* London: Profile.

Willcox, D. (1995, 19 October). Health scare. *Computing,* 28-29.

About the Editor

Adi Armoni, Ph.D. is the Associate Dean and Head of Computer and Information Systems Department at the College of Management School of Business Administration. He was awarded a Ph.D. degree in Information Systems from the School of Business Administration at Tel-Aviv University. His research subject deals with medical diagnosis from the artificial intelligence point of view. He also has a B.Sc. in Industrial and Management Engineering

Dr. Armoni has published many articles in scientific journals and delivered lectures at international meetings and conferences. Major fields of interest, both research and practice, are information systems policy, health care information systems, E-commerce and decision support systems. Dr. Armoni is a senior consultant for the World Bank, and delivered many projects in Eastern Europe and South America. He serves as a senior consultant for many of the leading financial institutes, insurance companies, high-tech firms and health organizations in Israel, in the field of Computerized Information Systems Management.

Index